D1447327

Gloomy Terrors and Hidden Fires

The Mystery of John Colter and Yellowstone

Ronald M. Anglin and Larry E. Morris

ROWMAN & LITTLEFIELD
Lanham • Boulder • New York • London

Published by Rowman & Littlefield
A wholly owned subsidiary of The Rowman & Littlefield Publishing Group, Inc.
4501 Forbes Boulevard, Suite 200, Lanham, Maryland 20706
www.rowman.com

Unit A, Whitacre Mews, 26-34 Stannery Street, London SE11 4AB, United Kingdom

British Library Cataloguing in Publication Information Available

Library of Congress Cataloging-in-Publication Data

Library of Congress Cataloging-in-Publication Data Available
ISBN 978-1-4422-2600-5 (cloth : alk. paper) — ISBN 978-1-4422-2601-2 (electronic)

♾TM The paper used in this publication meets the minimum requirements of American
National Standard for Information Sciences Permanence of Paper for Printed Library
Materials, ANSI/NISO Z39.48-1992.

Printed in the United States of America

Contents

Acknowledgments

Sitting back now, almost eighteen years after I started this journey into the life of one man, I wonder where all the time went. It was in late December 1996, while sitting in a log cabin at Harriman State Park on Henry's Fork of the Snake River in Idaho, I first learned of John Colter. At the time, I was the Trumpeter Swan coordinator for the tri-state area, of Idaho, Utah, and Wyoming for the U.S. Fish and Wildlife Service. Unable to work one night because of a blizzard, I started reading Charles E. Brooks's book *The Henry's Fork*. Not far into the book, I came across the section on John Colter. Little did I know how that one section would change my life.

Someone once told me that searching for John Colter was like eating an apple. When you bite into the apple, you know you will eventually find the core, but not so with Colter. His tale is the opening chapter of the history of the American West. But unlike the men who would follow him, he left few tracks. As you begin your investigation, you say to yourself, it's a very straight forward story, it should be easy to find the answers to this man's life, but you soon find that no matter how hard you search you are no closer to the core of this man than when you began your quest. It is not a historical or biographical journey you are on, because he left few written records. And it's not exclusively a cartographical problem, though one finds that's part of the story. Probing into his life only brings more questions, with few answers.

Very soon into my journey of discovery, I became fascinated with the number of professional as well as amateur historians and genealogists who had devoted years into studying this man's life. Names such as J. William Barrett, J. Neilson Barry, Merrill D. Beal, Hiram Chittenden, Eva Emery Dye, Ruth Colter-Frick, William J. Ghent, Ralph Gregory, Aubrey L. Haines, LeRoy R. Hafen, Donald Holms, Burton Harris, Merrill J. Mattes, E. B. Trail, Stallo Vinton, John G. White, and Shirley Winkelhoch, to name but a few. This army of Colter researchers had committed hundreds if not thousands of man-years of time in the pursuit of his life. And now, I with the eternal optimism of a true believer and newcomer had started my own investigation. It wasn't long before I to, was convinced, if I could only find that one document or fact, it would unlock all of the secrets of his life. So I chased the stories of this man, chased him across the ridges of the Alleghenies, down the Ohio River, and up the Big Muddy (Missouri) River to Three Forks, Montana, and beyond, searching for that one clue that would unlock his history.

No one can make a search of early American history by oneself—it is only through the combined help of many that a journey can be made. I would first like to acknowledge my brother John, who lives in Washington, Franklin County Missouri, about eight miles from where John Colter settled and died on May 7, 1812. John introduced me to his long time friend, Larry Melton. Larry in turn arranged a dinner wherein I was introduced to Ruth Colter-Frick, a direct descendant of John Colter, who published *Courageous Colter and Companions*. Over the next few years up until the time of her death she was always gracious to me, and in fact let me copy a number of her files. She told me many times that she was sure that E. B. Trail knew more about where Colter was buried than he would ever let on.

What my association with Ruth, really accomplished was to open doors with the locals. Even though my brother had lived in the town of Washington for thirty years, he was still considered a newcomer, whereas Ruth's family reached back to the beginning of the state. Through her I became acquainted with Ralph Gregory, a self-educated local historian who knew and wrote about the area he deeply loved in a way that took you back to an earlier age. He also was deeply interested in John Colter and Daniel Boone and had spent years researching their lives in Franklin and Warren Counties. Ralph opened his files to me and let me copy anything I felt would be useful. Through Ralph I met Ken Kamper another self-educated historian who is now considered the foremost Daniel Boone historian. Ken also was a Colter researcher, but after seeing what I was doing he gave me copies of all of his files. As the three of us talked over time it became clear that we had each reached the same conclusions, independently and at different times, on where Colter had lived and died in Franklin County.

Another person who opened the local history to me was Washington Historical Society Museum Director Marc Houseman. Marc is one of those unique individual who makes everyone feel comfortable in his presence. If you ask him a question and he does not know the answer, he will tell you so, but will also find the answer or someone who knows, and get right back to you. Without a doubt, he was a big help on my journey

Kurt Humphrey is another one of those local historians in Franklin County that some would pass over, thinking he was only interested in family genealogy. True, Kurt's primary interest is his family, but his family is deeply connected with the Colter story. In fact, his ancestor was John Sullins. And the farm that he grew up on has been in his family since John Sullins first settled on it in the early 1800s. It is also the location where Bradbury met John Colter on March 18, 1811. I met Kurt on his family farm, and over the years he has gone out of his way to explain local history in and around the New Port area of the county.

I don't recall when or how I first became acquainted with a lady I now call a dear friend. Her name is Shirley Winkelhoch, a cousin of Ruth's, and another direct descendant of Colter. Shirley and Ruth were different in age, Ruth being the older—who started researching Colter first, I don't know. But over the years these two traveled all over the eastern and mid-western United States, searching out libraries and courthouses trying to find a clues on where John Colter came from. Shirley told me of their work together and of placing the monument to her "John," as she likes to say. "I never did believe that's where his grave is, Ruth wanted so hard to believe he was buried there, and I just went along with her," she said. Over the next few years, Shirley and I made a number of visits to places in and around Franklin County, Missouri. Without her help I would have never gotten as far as I did. She was always giving me that push in another direction.

In 1999, I learned of another researcher, Don Holms, a retired outdoor writer for the *Oregonian* newspaper; he was then living in Port Townsend, Washington. He was nearly blind, and in his eighties. When he started his journey, I don't know, but it was sometime in the 1960s and for the next thirty years, he never stopped. He started three books on Colter but could never finish them. Don gave me his files on Colter, and the start of his three books, and told me at the time: "Maybe you can complete what I was never able to do." But Don was like Barry, Ghent, White, Trails, and Barrett to name a few, and I put myself in this same group. It's hard to write anything because you keep thinking if I just dig a little deeper, and a little harder I will find that golden nugget on John Colter that will make it all worthwhile.

But you never do.

Another set of files I was given was the work of Frank Dickson, a direct descendant of Joseph Dickson whom Lewis and Clark wrote about on August 15, 1806, and who Colter traveled back up river with. Frank was not a fan of John Colter, but he did research him for upwards of forty years. He was killed in an automobile accident in 1976. His files were given to a long-time friend and fellow researcher Lillian Burnett. Mrs. Burnett worked on Frank's files and other related Lewis and Clark material up until the time of her own death in 1996. For years afterward, these files were placed in a storage locker, all but forgotten until I was able to locate John "Burnie" Gillespie, her grandson, who gave me her and Frank's files in 2011.

Yet another set of files were given to me by the daughter of Charles Galloway Clarke (no relation to William Clark of the Lewis and Clark Expedition), Mary Hiestand, in 2012. Mr. Clarke had started work on the men of the Lewis and Clark Expedition in the late 1930s, and continued up until the time of his death in 1983. He published a number of articles on his research and a book entitled *The Men of the Lewis and Clark Expedition*. Mrs. Hiestand was kind enough to allow be to go through her father's material and copy anything I felt I could use.

I would also like to personally acknowledge Bob Richard of Cody, Wyoming, who for over two years traveled with me in and around the Cody, Yellowstone area, imparting his knowledge of how, where, and why he believed Colter traveled in 1806/07. The editing of this work would have been infinitely harder for Larry and me without the assistance of my long-time friend Tom Strekal and his wife, Liz. Tom and I at one time worked on a manuscript on Colter, but we just could not make it flow. But he always said he thought it was a great project and would assist anyway he could to see it completed.

Finally, there are no libraries or archive that can be successfully probed without the help and intimate knowledge of the staff at these places. While Larry and I cannot acknowledge the over sixty or seventy libraries and universities we have used over the years on an individual basis, we sincerely appreciate the help given. With that said, I would like to single out five individuals: David Williams, for his 2½-year search of the Draper Collection for any items related to John Colter, at the University of Wisconsin, in Madison; Lynn Colter David and others for their three different searches of the records of the Kentucky Gateway Museum Center (formerly the Maysville Library) for information on John Colter, the Lewis and Clark Expedition, and William D. Hixon; Sara Daley for her search of the Eve Emery Dye Collection at the Oregon Historical Society; and Dorris Keeven Franke for her search of the St. Charles Historical Society archives for information related to Mrs. Edna McElhiney Olson and the history of the Fee Fee Baptist Church.

Last but not least, I'd like to thank my best friend of forty years, my wife, Kathleen, who never seems to get to upset with my many journeys.
—**Ron Anglin**

As I have researched the Lewis and Clark Expedition and the fur trade over the last fifteen years, it has been a great privilege to meet fellow researchers, especially those involved with the Lewis and Clark Trail Heritage Foundation (with headquarters in Great Falls, Montana) and the Museum of the Mountain Man, in Pinedale, Wyoming. I'd particularly like to thank the following people for their scholarship and their friendship: John Allen, Jay Buckley, Tim Coulter, Doug Erickson, William Foley, Clint Gilchrist, John

Guice, Jim Hardee, Adrian Heidenreich, Jim Holmberg, Ella Mae Howard, Lanny Jones, Mark Kelly, Barb Kubik, Clay Landry, Ron Laycock, Donna Masterson, Joe Mussulman, Don Peterson, and Stephanie Ambrose Tubbs.

Thanks to Brian Cannon and his associates at the Charles Redd Center for Western Studies, Brigham Young University. The Redd Center funded part of the research for this book.

As Ron indicated, we did research at scores of libraries and archives. I especially appreciate the invaluable assistance offered at the Missouri History Museum, St. Louis; the State Historical Society of Missouri, Columbia; the Filson Historical Society, Louisville; the Wisconsin Historical Society, Madison; the Oregon Historical Society, Portland; and the Family History Library, Salt Lake City.

Finally, thanks to Jon Sisk, Ben Verdi, Karen Ackermann, and the other editors at Rowman & Littlefield.

—Larry Morris

Chapter One

"Off He Started with the Speed of the Wind"

Colter's Run

In 1808, sometime after the first week of July but before the coming of a Rocky Mountain winter, John Colter and John Potts departed Fort Raymond at the mouth of the Bighorn River and plunged into the heart of Blackfoot country to trap beaver. They made their way to Three Forks, where the Madison, Gallatin, and Jefferson rivers converge to form the Missouri. These Lewis and Clark veterans had first seen Three Forks in July of 1805, an area that opened suddenly to "extensive and beatifull plains and meadows which appear to be surrounded in every direction with distant and lofty mountians." Far more memorable than the scenery, however, was the "emence number of Beaver," with "maney thousand" of them inhabiting "the river & Creeks near the 3 forks."[1]

Colter and Potts knew the risk, especially Colter, who had been wounded only weeks earlier fighting with the Crow and Salish against a horde of Blackfoot warriors. But thousands of beaver meant thousands of dollars, and the two men could earn more in a season of trapping than in several years' of labor in St. Louis or Louisville. Potts was so anxious to make his fortune that he had signed one promissory note after another, likely to buy a rifle, beaver traps, awls, blue beads, knives, flint and steel, blankets, needles and thread, fish hooks, powder and lead, an axe, a kettle, a tomahawk, a good supply of tobacco, and any number of other odds and ends, running up a debt to the tune of several hundred dollars for the privilege of risking his life in Blackfoot territory. (There is no record of Colter incurring similar debts.)[2]

1

Two years earlier and a hundred miles to the north, Sergeant John Ordway had recorded an unforgettable Expedition moment when "Colter & Potts went at running the canoes down the rapids to the white perogue." Those times were gone now, gone forever, and for Colter and Potts it was all business. Bypassing the Madison and Gallatin, they traveled to the river they knew best—the Jefferson, the river Lewis and Clark had followed westward until it was nothing but a trickling stream at the edge of the Continental Divide. Clark had described the "perfectly transparent" Jefferson as a haven of peace, with a riverbed of "smooth pebble and gravel" and "luxuriant" grass lining the banks, but for Colter and Potts it was now a place of peril: they set their traps at night, checked them in the early morning, and stayed concealed during the day. They saw no signs of Indians—nor had Lewis and Clark in 1805—but the Indians had likely seen them.[3]

Still, the differences between the Expedition and this excursion were striking: Lewis and Clark came with twenty-nine well-armed men, enough to give a hostile Indian nation pause before doing anything rash; Colter and Potts came by themselves. Lewis and Clark moved quickly through the area, hardly giving an enemy time to plan an attack; Colter and Potts had obviously settled in, showing no qualms about treating Blackfoot land as if it were theirs. Lewis and Clark traveled from the mouth of the Yellowstone River (in present North Dakota) to Lolo Pass (in present Idaho) without battling the Blackfoot nation; Colter had already fought on the side of Blackfoot foes.

But two simple facts of arithmetic overshadowed all other realities: thousands of beaver meant thousands of dollars, and Colter and Potts had earned $178.33 and 1/3 and $166.66 and 2/3, respectively, for their thirty-three months of service with Lewis and Clark.[4]

How long they trapped without seeing Indians is not clear, but early one morning they were checking their traps along the misty Jefferson when they heard "a great noise resembling the trampling of animals." Pulling his paddle back inside his dugout canoe, Colter warned Potts, traveling alongside in his own canoe, that they had to retreat immediately because Indians were nearby. Potts "insisted that the noise was caused by buffaloes" and called Colter a coward. Both men strained to see what had caused the noise, but the steep, high banks on each side of the river blocked their view. A moment later "their doubts were removed, by a party of Indians making their appearance on both sides of the creek, to the amount of five or six hundred, who beckoned them to come ashore."[5]

The two men dropped their traps into the river; then Colter obeyed the Blackfoot command and went ashore; he was promptly disarmed and stripped of all his clothing, including his moccasins. Colter urged Potts to come ashore as well, but Potts refused, saying he might as well be killed at once rather than being robbed and stripped as Colter had been.

Not waiting any longer, an Indian fired at Potts, hitting him in the hip. He tumbled into the canoe but quickly reappeared. "Colter, I am wounded," he cried. Colter urged him again to surrender, but Potts refused. Instead, he "levelled his rifle at an Indian and shot him dead on the spot." At this, Potts was "instantly pierced with arrows so numerous, that, to use the language of Colter, '*he was made a riddle of.*'"[6]

The Indians now rushed into the stream, pulled Potts's body onto the bank, and "with their hatchets and knives, cut and hacked it all to pieces, and limb from limb." The relatives of the slain Indian were "furious with rage and struggled, with tomahawk in hand, to reach Colter, while others held them back. He was every moment expecting the death blow or the fatal shot that should lay him beside his companion."[7]

Colter knew that nothing could be worse than slow death at the hands of the Blackfoot. A quick end was the best he could hope for—bullets were far better than the tomahawk. Suddenly a few chiefs gathered in council, and Colter knew his fate was being determined, though he could not understand the language. Then one of the chiefs turned to Colter, motioned toward the prairie, and said in the Crow tongue, "Go, go away."[8]

Colter hesitated, sure they would fire the second he was clear of the crowd. Then he began to walk, and an old man motioned for him to go faster. The old man was soon gesturing impatiently and wildly urging the captive on. Still Colter walked, perhaps thinking that any faster pace would compel the Indians to instantly give chase. After walking eighty or one hundred yards, Colter looked back to see the younger Indians casting off their blankets and leggings.

Now Colter understood what was happening: "He was to run a race, of which the prize was to be his own life and scalp. Off he started with the speed of the wind. The war-whoop and yell immediately arose behind him; and looking back, he saw a large company of young warriors, with spears, in rapid pursuit."[9]

Colter ran with all the speed he could muster. With the Madison River five miles away, he bounded over sagebrush, cactus, and rocks, glancing back to see the young warriors spread out behind him and thinking for the first time that he might have a chance. Then blood began gushing from his nose, and his legs were suddenly heavy, but he galloped on. When the river came in sight, he turned to see a solitary pursuer far ahead of the others, only twenty yards behind. Colter called out in the Crow language, hoping his pursuer would spare him, but the young Blackfoot either ignored or didn't understand him.

Determined to avoid the expected blow, Colter stopped , turned around, and raised his arms. "Surprised by the suddenness of the action, and perhaps at the bloody appearance of Colter," the Indian stumbled as he attempted to throw his spear: it stuck in the ground and broke in his hand. "Colter instantly snatched up the pointed part, with which he pinned [the Indian] to the earth, and then continued his flight."[10]

Colter charged toward the river, feeling, he later said, as if he had not run a mile. He knew exactly when the others had reached the body of their comrade because they let out a ghastly whoop. He ran on, through the cover of a cottonwood grove and a copse of willows before plunging into the cold water. Half-swimming and half-running, he "saw close beside him a beaver house, standing like a coal-pit about ten feet above the surface of the water, which was here of about the same depth." He immediately took advantage of this "refuge from his ferocious enemies," diving into the water and coming up inside the beaver house, where he found a dry and comfortable resting place on the upper floor or story of this singular structure. The Indians soon came up, and in their search for him they stood upon the roof of his house of refuge, which he expected every moment to hear them breaking open." They searched his side of the river, then crossed to search the other side, returning again about two hours later, with Colter anxiously awaiting what would happen next. "In this asylum Colter kept fast till night. The cries of his terrible enemies had gradually died away, and all was still around him, when he ventured out of his hiding place."[11]

He traveled all night, first going east to the Gallatin River and then ascending it to the south, with the mountains and rivers making it impossible for a man with his scouting instincts to get lost. Rather than going east across Bozeman Pass (the route William Clark had taken in 1806) he took an out-of-the-way route back to Fort Raymond in order to get out of Blackfoot country as fast as possible. Soon he reached the Gallatin Range, hastening toward a mountain pass after swimming the rapid river. Fearing that the Indians might be guarding the pass ahead of him—the only outlet from the valley—he "ascended the almost perpendicular mountain before him, the tops and sides of which a great ways down, were covered with perpetual snow. He clambered up this fearful ascent about four miles below the gap, holding on by the rocks, shrubs and branches of trees, and by morning had reached the top." He stayed concealed the entire day, descending only after darkness came.[12]

By dawn he was off the mountain. Now three days and forty or fifty miles from the Jefferson River, Colter hobbled on, his feet a rash of blisters and embedded cactus thorns. He may have stripped some bark from a sapling to soothe the pain. For most of the previous four years, Colter had hunted at will, feasting on buffalo, deer, elk, beaver, and sometimes bear (although there had been all kinds of other meat, including horse, dog, salmon, and trout). Now, surrounded by game tantalizingly out of reach, he turned his spear to a plowshare and dug roots. He had seen and heard a lot about roots both during and after the expedition: Lemhi Shoshone women gathered "agreeably flavored" roots that could be eaten "either green or in [their] dried state without the preparation of boiling;"[13] Salish women had given him camas roots turned sweet by baking; and Sheep Eater women had baked bitterroots (well named in Lewis's opinion). Over the course of the Expedition, Colter had also found and eaten currants, gooseberries, chokecherries, buffalo berries, and serviceberries, which Lewis described as "for the most part larger more luscious" than those in the east.[14]

All of this experience served Colter well as he crossed to the Yellowstone River and ascended it to the south, crossing into present Wyoming and Yellowstone Park, with the memory of Sacagawea gathering "wild Lickerish, & the white apple" proving crucial. "White apple," or breadroot, formed "a considerable article of food with the Indians of the Missouri, who for this purpose prepare them in several ways," Lewis had written. "They are esteemed good at all seasons of the year, but are best from the middle of July to the latter end of Autumn"—perfect for Colter—"when they are sought and gathered by the provident part of the natives for their winter store." Although he may have earlier agreed with Lewis that breadroot was "tastless insippid food," Colter probably felt quite differently now. Best of all, breadroot could be eaten raw. John Bradbury said that Colter subsisted largely on this root, which he called by its scientific name, *Psoralea esculenta*.[15]

Still, Colter was a man accustomed to eating meat every day. The sudden switch to berries and roots was bound to bring with it stomach cramps and diarrhea, followed by fatigue, weakness, body ache, and body sores. But Colter pushed on and on, growing more gaunt and more exhausted and probably covering less and less ground each day. At the confluence of the Yellowstone and Lamar rivers, he descended the Lamar to the northeast, now on the edge of Blackfoot country and drawing closer and closer to Crow allies. He crossed Dead Indian Pass and then followed Clark's Fork of the Yellowstone into present Montana. Soon Pryor Creek took him to the Yellowstone, which he now followed downstream; he found Clark's "great quantities of the Purple, yellow & black currents ripe . . . of an excellent flavour," but he also found rocks everywhere: "The river here is about 200 yards wide rapid as usial and the water gliding over corse and round Stones of various sizes. . . . The bottoms of the River are narrow. The hills are . . . generally rocky and composed of rocks of the same texture of a dark Colour of Grit well Calculated for grindstones &c. The high bottoms is composed of gravel and Stone like those in the Channel of the river."[16] Swinging wide of the river didn't help because there were no grassy meadows but more boulders, crags, stones, and pebbles, grinding and bruising feet already tender and sore.

Colter had been traveling for nine or ten days when Pompys Tower finally came into view, where William Clark had carved his name into the stone face of a cliff. Colter may have expected–and certainly hoped–to see fellow trappers but apparently saw none. He covered the final twenty-five miles still alone.

"He travelled day and night, stopping only for necessary repose, and eating roots and the bark of trees, for eleven days. He reached the Fort, nearly exhausted by hunger, fatigue and excitement." His only weapon was the spearhead, which he brought to the fort as a trophy. "His beard was long, his face and whole body were thin and emaciated by hunger, and his limbs and feet swollen and sore. The company at the Fort did not recognize him in this dismal plight until he had made himself known."[17]

Colter thus joined the ranks of renowned frontiersman who made daring escapes from Indians, a fraternity that includes the likes of Daniel Boone, Simon Kenton, and Samuel Brady. Colter is distinctly different from the other mythmakers of the era, however, because they all left documents behind that allow access to the men themselves. Colter, by contrast, left nothing, not a single letter, diary, or reminiscence, so that second- or third-hand accounts of his adventures are all we have. Not only that, but since Colter made his most notable sojourns alone, we have no witnesses to corroborate those hearsay narratives. The inevitable upshot is that the line separating Colter the man from Colter the legend grows hazy and indistinct, so that much "known" about him is not certain at all. For that very reason, however, his story is endlessly fascinating.

Chapter Two

"One of the Survivors, of the Name of Coulter"

Searching for Colter's Roots

In the spring of 1809, the physician William H. Thomas and an aspiring trapper named Thomas James started up the Missouri River with a host of other men tasked by Governor Meriwether Lewis with escorting the Mandan chief Sheheke and his family back to their North Dakota home. "On the 17th of May," wrote Thomas, surgeon to the party, "we set out from St. Louis with 10 barges and 160 men, well equipped, amongst whom were a few Delawares and Shawnese employed for hunting."[1] Over the next four months, Thomas and James both kept journals as the group toiled up the meandering Missouri River, fighting a strong current, irksome sandbars, half-submerged trees that could rip a keelboat open, rain, wind, hail, and endless waves of mosquitoes. Finally, late in September, they reached the Mandan and Hidatsa villages near the confluence of the Knife and Missouri Rivers.

After Sheheke's safe return, his escorts traveled ten or twelve miles north and built a trading post they called Fort Mandan (not to be confused with Lewis and Clark's Fort Mandan, which was south of the Mandan and Hidatsa villages). "Information was received here," continued Thomas, "that the Blackfoot Indians, who reside at the foot of the mountains, were hostile." Thomas told of meeting one of the survivors of Blackfoot hostilities, a man by "the name of Coulter, who had accompanied Lewis and Clark."[2] When his 225-word narrative of that survivor's remarkable escape from Blackfoot warriors was published in a St. Louis newspaper late in 1809,[3] John Colter was well down the road to becoming the only member of Lewis and Clark's

team (including the captains themselves) to be better known for his adventures following the Expedition than during it. As Stephen Ambrose has so
aptly written, when Lewis and Clark and their men "set off downstream [on
August 17, 1806], Colter turned back upstream, back to the wilderness, back
to the mountains, on his way into the history books as America's first mountain man and the discoverer of Yellowstone National Park."[4]

No doubt thinking his description of the Lewis and Clark veteran a minor
sidelight in a much longer account, the esteemed doctor had unknowingly
become the first in a long line of professional and amateur historians to tell
Colter's story—or at least part of the story. In May of 1810, when Colter
finally returned to St. Louis after a six-year sojourn in the wilderness, the
naturalist John Bradbury was there to greet him, producing a fascinating
narrative of "Colter's Run" that expanded considerably on Dr. Thomas's
effort. Published in 1817, five years after Colter's death, Bradbury's version
was put to good use by Washington Irving, an internationally best-selling
author who borrowed freely from Bradbury and included a detailed and
compelling version of Colter's escape in *Astoria*, the 1836 book that effec-
tively launched the Colter legend.[5] Over the next century and three-quarters,
an amazing number of people from all walks of life took up the pursuit of
Colter, chasing him more relentlessly than American Indians had ever done,
digging through census schedules, birth and marriage registers, probate in-
ventories, financial ledgers, tax rosters, muster rolls, town directories, and
any other record imaginable for a clue to his elusive identity. They demanded
to know where he had come from, why Lewis and Clark had selected him,
and how he had developed the traits that kept him alive in "the gloomy and
savage wilderness." But what this multitude of researchers discovered about
John Colter's life prior to the Lewis and Clark Expedition can be neatly
summed up in a single word: nothing.

Colter's advent on the historical scene—like a dust devil appearing out of
nowhere, whirling across the desert on a hot summer day—has made him one
of the West's most mysterious figures. Even the so-called first record of
Colter is not what it appears to be. Students of the Expedition naturally
assume that Colter was first mentioned on the day he enlisted—October 15,
1803—but if either Lewis or Clark made a record on that day, it has never
been found. The so-called enlistment record was actually created by Clark in
March of 1807, five months after the company returned to St. Louis. In his
roster of Expedition members, Clark listed "15 Oct. 1803 to 10 Oct. 1806" as
Colter's period of service (a generous calculation since Colter had actually
ended his enlistment with the Corps on August 17, 1806).

"Snow in the morning," Clark wrote on December 30, 1803. "I move into
my hut, Cloudy morning. Colter Kill a Deer & a turkey, Drewer & Sergt.
Odway set out for Kohokia."[6] This is the first known record of John Colter,
and in the two centuries since that snowy December morning in Illinois, a

multitude of reporters, teachers, history buffs, history scholars, librarians, archivists, amateur and professional genealogists, biographers, novelists, and screenwriters taken with Colter's story have put forth their theories. Among the most influential was a fascinating individual born four decades after Colter's death.

Eva Emery Dye (1855–1947) was a prominent proponent of women's suffrage, as well as a "civic leader, historian, traveler, researcher, orator, and wife." Originally from Illinois, Dye and her husband settled in Oregon in the early 1890s, and she soon began writing what might be called idealized history. In her most important book, *The Conquest: The True Story of Lewis and Clark*, published in 1902, Dye sets a sort of theatrical stage, with the players enacting powerful scenes that may or may not be factual. According to Katrine Barber, Dye "romanticized the historic West, turning it into a poetic epic of expanding civilization," her legacy "still embodied in the national 'memory' of the Lewis and Clark Expedition."[7] Dye's treatment of Sacagawea was particularly influential. Ascribing both physical features and heroic deeds to Charbonneau's wife that are not documented in Lewis and Clark's journals (or anywhere else), she propelled Sacagawea into international fame and made her a powerful symbol of women's suffrage.

A prodigious researcher, Dye contacted the descendants of several members of the Lewis and Clark Expedition, sometimes turning up new information. For example, the details of George Shannon's birth had been in doubt, but when Shannon's son William Russell Shannon received a letter from Dye requesting information on his father, he provided both the year (1785) and the state (Pennsylvania) of Shannon's birth. And although there is no evidence that Dye ever corresponded with any of Colter's descendants, she made three claims about Colter that have had a lasting impact: 1) he was from Virginia; 2) his family resettled at Maysville, Kentucky, where he grew to manhood; and 3) prior to the Expedition he served as a ranger with the great frontiersman Simon Kenton, who was closely linked with the Maysville area. Dye was apparently the first historian to make these claims, and although she supplied no documentation to back up any of the three assertions, they took root and were widely accepted throughout the twentieth century. A key element in this fascinating series of events apparently developed in the course of Dye's correspondence with the great historian Reuben Gold Thwaites.

Born near Boston, Thwaites (1853–1913) was a prolific compiler and editor of historical documents. His family relocated to Madison, Wisconsin, when he was a teenager, and as a young man he began frequenting the State Historical Society of Wisconsin, where Lyman C. Draper, the first secretary of the society, had amassed a huge collection of Western Americana. When Draper retired in 1886, he named Thwaites as his successor. Over the next two decades, Thwaites edited *The Jesuit Relations* (seventy-three volumes),

Early Western Travels (thirty-two volumes), and *Original Journals of Lewis and Clark* (seven volumes). The historian Frederick Jackson Turner described Thwaites as "short in stature, but with a compelling personality, his cheery, winning spirit shining out behind his twinkling eyes, always ready with a joke or story that impressed a point upon his hearers; alert, decisive, receptive, helpful, a man of honor and of character."[8]

By 1903, when Thwaites was working on his monumental edition of Lewis and Clark's journals (the first history of the Expedition to reprint the journals themselves), he and Dye had struck up a correspondence, and Dye had raised the issue of the family histories of the Expedition members. "I am not going into genealogical details relative to the members of the party," he explained, "not considering that a proper field in connection with the original journals. Nevertheless, any little stray bits of information which nobody else has touched upon, I am glad to work with."[9] Although Dye's letters to Thwaites have been lost, there is little doubt that she supplied a "stray bit of information" on Colter. As Dye wrote to another correspondent, she had concluded that Colter's family was "from Virginia and [later] settled at Maysville [Kentucky]."[10] Thwaites knew such details had not been "touched upon" before and wasted no time announcing them. The fourth volume of his *Early Western Travels* series, published in 1904, was *Travels in the Interior of America*, in which John Bradbury offered his rendition of Colter's run. Thwaites included his own footnote stating that Colter "was of Virginian birth, but afterwards lived at Maysville, Kentucky, where he joined the Lewis and Clark expedition in the fall of 1803."[11] Thwaites himself was apparently the first to claim that Colter enlisted with Lewis and Clark at Maysville, a reasonable assumption given Dye's other conjectures about Maysville.

Dye cited no sources to support her theory about Colter's birthplace, nor do her papers offer any clues as to whether someone else suggested it, but the theory was not unreasonable. After all, by Colter's day it was not uncommon for prominent Kentuckians, including William and George Rogers Clark and Simon Kenton, to have been born in Virginia. Nor was it likely to have escaped Dye's notice that Meriwether Lewis and one of the best-known American mountain men, Jim Bridger, were both Virginia natives. So, given Dye's modus operandi of liberally *reimagining* the past, she may have simply assumed or hoped that Colter was from Virginia and speculated accordingly. Regardless, Dye and Thwaites had such standing among historians that the declaration regarding Colter's birthplace was accepted without question and taken for granted by such respected scholars as Walter B. Douglas and William J. Ghent (in the early twentieth century), Burton Harris (in midcentury), and Gary Moulton (late in the century).

Two Colter researchers, Ghent and Stallo Vinton, grew so interested in the man that they both began writing biographies of him in the early 1920s. Ghent read an abstract of his work at the California Academy of Social

Sciences in Los Angeles in 1923, and it was well received. He submitted his manuscript to the Arthur H. Clark Company, a prominent publisher of Western history. Unfortunately for Ghent, however, Vinton published his book, *John Colter: Discoverer of Yellowstone Park*, with Edward Eberstadt in 1926, and Arthur H. Clark declined on Ghent's work, which for the last seventy years has languished unpublished in the archives of the Bancroft Library. (Colter scholars who have read both books generally agree that Ghent's is the superior biography.)

Ghent and Vinton both searched for Colter relatives and eventually contacted Janet Logan, a supposed descendant of one of Colter's uncles, and published new "facts" supplied by Logan.[12] Colter was, they concluded, the great-grandson of Micajah Coalter and the grandson of Michael Coalter. And while both biographers claimed Colter's mother was Ellen Shields Coalter, Vinton identified John Coalter Sr. as his father while Ghent said it was Joseph Coalter. Ghent added that Colter was born "in or near Staunton, Virginia, . . . probably sometime in 1775" (although Vinton wisely cautioned that it had not been "positively established that [Colter] was born in Virginia").[13] Logan's contributions, along with those of Dye and Thwaites, soon became firmly entrenched in Colter lore, as shown by the following examples.

In an important article published in 1944, Charles G. Clarke wrote that Colter was born in Virginia and "joined the expedition at Maysville, Kentucky . . . had been a ranger with Kenton." Eight years later, in his biography of Colter, Burton Harris referenced Vinton's research and Colter "family belief" that Colter was born near Staunton, Virginia, at Stuart's Draft between 1770 and 1775 and that Michael and Micajah Coalter were his grandfather and great-grandfather, respectively. By 1970, Clarke had transformed his article into the first book published about Lewis and Clark's men. He informed his readers that Colter was born about 1774, near Staunton and that he was the *grandson* of Micajah Coalter and the son of Joseph and Ellen Shields Colter. In 1986, Gary Moulton, Thwaites' successor as editor of Lewis and Clark's journals, wrote that Colter had been born around 1775 in Virginia.[14]

In 1989, the Virginia Department of Natural Resources erected a plaque in the Stuart's Draft area that reads as follows:

JOHN COLTER

John Colter, born in Stuart's Draft about 1775, was a member of the northwest expedition led by Meriwether Lewis and William Clark (1804–1806). During his subsequent, solitary explorations of the west, Colter traversed the area now comprising Yellowstone National Park and discovered several passes through the Rocky Mountains suitable for wagon trains. His escape from the Blackfeet Indians following a footrace for his life has become a legend of the West. Colter died in Missouri in 1813.

All of this offers a prime example of how a seemingly solid historical structure can be assembled on a house of cards. During the second half of the twentieth century, three descendants of John Colter—Ruth Colter-Frick, Shirley Winkelhoch, and Donna Masterson, all expert genealogists—began finding problems with the "party line" about Colter. In her 1997 book *Courageous Colter and Companions*, Colter-Frick made it clear that the John Coulter born to Joseph and Ellen Shields Coulter was still alive in 1815, while the John Colter of the Lewis and Clark Expedition died in 1812.[15] None of these three devoted researchers found any evidence that Colter had actually been born in Virginia. Janet Logan had no doubt been sincere, but she was mistaken—there was no evidence linking Colter to her Coalter/Coulter line.

But what about the "official" roadside marker identifying Stuart's Draft as John Colter's birthplace? The best that can be said is that the fine residents of Stuart's Draft are in good company. The citizens of Maysville, Kentucky, and Driggs, Idaho, also claim a proud connection to John Colter, with roadside plaques providing details of that connection, but careful research has failed to support either of those claims.

The obvious question is this: Do we know *anything* about Colter's origins?

The answer is yes. We still don't know his birthplace or his parents' names, but, as chapter 3 shows, William Clark and Meriwether Lewis offered a good deal of information about Colter's background and the skills he mastered as a youth.

Chapter Three

"In Quest of the Country of Kentucke"

John Colter and the Legacy of Daniel Boone

Although no evidence has been found linking Colter with Limestone (later called Maysville), Kentucky, William Clark made it clear that Colter was indeed one of "the nine young men from Kentucky," a phrase made famous by Nicholas Biddle, who interviewed Clark extensively and compiled the first history of the Expedition. As Biddle wrote, "The party consisted of [the two officers]; nine young men from Kentucky; 14 soldiers of the United States Army, who had volunteered their services; two French watermen [Cruzatte, Labiche]; an interpreter and hunter [Drewyer]; and a black servant [York] belonging to Captain Clark."[1]

Although a native of Virginia, Clark himself could have easily been called a "young man from Kentucky." In 1784, when young Billy was fourteen years old, his well-to-do family had come down the Ohio River on a flatboat loaded with slaves, livestock, and "anywhere from 20 to 70 tons of goods," settling near Louisville, Kentucky, at an estate they called Mulberry Hill. What one historian said of Clark no doubt applied to the nine young men—William Bratton, Colter, Joseph and Reubin Field, Charles Floyd, George Gibson, Nathaniel Pryor, George Shannon, and John Shields—as well: "In Kentucky he was able to master the skills that were essential to wilderness living, and for the first time he encountered native people in the flesh."[2]

Clark informed Meriwether Lewis that he had found the nine young men in "this part of the Countrey," meaning the Louisville region. As William E. Foley has written, "No one was better qualified to screen the applicants. Clark's frontier military experience, his familiarity with life in the woods, his standing in the Louisville community and extensive connections there, and his practiced eye in taking the measure of a man equipped him perfectly to make wise choices."[3] Indeed, Clark's "extensive connections" in the region make it quite likely that he already knew the nine young men or knew a friend who recommended them. Wherever they had been born, the nine of them—who, with the addition of George Drouillard were the best hunters and scouts among Lewis and Clark's men—had clearly lived in Kentucky long enough to master frontiersman skills and earn good reputations.[4]

The significance of Colter being an experienced Kentucky woodsman can hardly be overstated. It reveals a wealth of information about the man. And it comes as no surprise that when Thomas James offered a description of Colter, he compared him to the most renowned Ketuckian of all, Daniel Boone, writing that Colter's "character was that of a true American backwoodsman. He was about thirty-five years of age, five feet ten inches in height, and wore an open, ingenuous, and pleasing countenance of the Daniel Boone stamp. Nature had formed him, like Boone, for hardy endurance of fatigue, privations, and perils."[5]

The comparison to Daniel Boone seems inevitable. Born in Pennsylvania in 1734, Boone had been one of the early explorers of Kentucky in the late 1760s, had forged a trail through the Cumberland Gap, and had seen his own share of perils among the Indians. In 1776, three years after his oldest son, James, had been tortured and killed by Indians—who pulled out James's fingernails and toenails before tomahawking him to death—Boone and a small group of men ambushed an Indian war party and made a daring rescue of his daughter Jemima and two other teenage girls. Two years after that, Boone himself was captured and taken prisoner by the Shawnees. After running the gauntlet (a line of Indian warriors flailing at the victim with sticks or clubs) and surviving, Boone had been adopted in the tribe. He later escaped and made a famous 160-mile "run" back to Boonesborough to warn the settlers of a Shawnee attack.

Boone, George Rogers Clark (one of William Clark's older brothers), and Simon Kenton (who had risked his own life to save Boone's during a 1777 battle)[6] were comrades and brothers in arms, who, during the 1770s and early 1780s considered themselves to be fighting on the "western front" of the American Revolution. This is deeply ironic, however, for as Landon Jones notes, "There were now two wars of independence taking place. One was the struggle of the American colonies to achieve independence from the British empire. The other was the struggle of the Indian tribes of North America to preserve their independence in the face of the steady march of the Europeans into their homelands."[7]

For men like Clark, Boone, Kenton, and Colter, the Kentucky wilderness—with its rich natural resources, its ample supply of game, its transcendent beauty, and its more-than-adequate "elbow room"—had taken on a mythical quality. Little wonder that a family friend wrote to Jonathan Clark (another of William's older brothers) that "People are Running Mad for Kentucky hereabouts."[8] But several Indian nations, including the Cherokee, Chickasaw, Wyandotte, Yuchi, and the Iroquois Confederacy (comprising the Mohawk, Oneida, Onondaga, Cayuga, Seneca, and Tuscarora tribes)—but most particularly the Shawnee—viewed the land called *Kanta-ke* by the Iroquois as valuable hunting territory, and they understandably resented the invaders.

Throughout the 1700s, Great Britain, France, and Spain had jockeyed for control of North America, never questioning the assumption that Europeans somehow had the right to exercise power over land already inhabited from coast to coast by hundreds of native nations. But while all three European powers had both commercial and religious motivations for settling North America, the British in particular had a passion for colonizing, and thousands of common English folk poured into North America with vague but powerful notions of establishing their God-given rights and their independence by finding and working their own piece of land. They pushed westward, gathering momentum like a tidal wave.

The power struggle among the Europeans made for incredibly complex relations with the Indians, who, of course, had power struggles of their own. Britain, France, and Spain fought bitterly with some tribes and befriended others. Land was bought and sold, treaties were made (often illegally) and broken. Indians were sometimes seen as totally foreign savages and sometimes as friends and relatives. James Kenney, taken prisoner by the Shawnee, could hardly believe it when an Indian woman "boiled some water in a small copper kettle, with which she made some tea in a tea-pot, using cups and saucers of yellow-ware."[9] Despite these complexities, however, two realities remained constant: The British colonizers continued to push west, and the white men continued to presume they had ultimate authority over the natives.

The balance of power shifted forever with the French and Indian War in North America (1754–1763)—where young George Washington cut his military teeth—and its European counterpart, the Seven Years War (1757–1763), which was in many ways the first world war and involved Prussia, Great Britain, and Portugal on one side and Austria, France, the Russian Empire, Sweden, and Spain on the other. When the Treaty of Paris brought an end to the conflict, France ceded Canada to Great Britain and Louisiana to Spain. (Spain ceded Louisiana back to France in 1800, and France sold it to the United States in 1803.)

Reacting to a number of problems, including conflicts with Indians resulting from westward expansion, the British issued the Proclamation of 1763, which prohibited settlers from crossing west of a line that ran roughly along the Appalachian Mountains. This would have preserved the western sections of Pennsylvania and West Virginia, all of Ohio, and virtually all of Tennessee and Kentucky, as well as other areas. As one British official put it, the American interior was to be kept "as open and Wild as possible for the Purposes of Hunting."[10] The proclamation was intended only as a temporary measure, however, and even at that, it was largely ignored. The surge of settlers heaved west, and between 1765 and 1768 an estimated thirty thousand colonizers crossed the Appalachians.[11]

This land west of the Appalachians—often called the Trans-Allegheny Frontier—was a vast area roughly the size of Western Europe. As David Hackett Fischer has written:

> It extended 800 miles south, from Pennsylvania to Georgia, and several hundred miles west from the Piedmont plateaus to the banks of the Mississippi. It was the borderlands between the colonial east and the western frontier. The terrain consisted of corrugated ridges and valleys, rising from the coastal plain to the crest of the Appalachians, which then fell away into the western rivers.[12]

From the rivers, the natural highways for the early travelers, the ground gently sloped from the pebbled shore fringed with willows, giving way to cottonwoods, linden, and red maple. Elms, sycamores, beech, and yellow poplar were found in the moist bottomlands. Here too were seen the flowering buckeye and the fragrant spicewood, the sassafras, and on the upland slopes and drier sites were the oaks, hickories, sugar maple, and the stately chestnut, a tree all but unknown today except in song or verse. This ocean of trees was a dark and frightening place to traverse, never to be entered alone or without an experienced guide. A person unaccustomed to the forest would get the panicky feeling that hidden eyes were watching with threatening intent. And they were.

In his monumental work *Albion's Seed: Four British Folkways in America* (1989), Fischer discusses four migrations from Britain that shaped America. According to Fischer, the group that settled the Trans-Allegheny Frontier migrated from the "Borderlands" of Britain to the "Backcountry" of America. Called Ulster-Scots in Britain and Scotch-Irish (or Scots-Irish) in the United States, these new Americans were known by such names as Backwoodsmen, Frontiersmen, Long Hunters, and Long Knives. James Fenimore Cooper in *The Leatherstocking Tales* and Robert Montgomery Bird in *Nick of the Woods* immortalized these American originals. As Elizabeth Semancik has written,

> The people of [the Anglo-Scotch borders in Britain] sought comfort from such instability in strong family units called clans. They also found stability in their system of beliefs, which found answers in a perpetually questioning world, wrought with death and disaster, by turning to traditions and portents.

> When the people of this borderland immigrated to America, they carried their culture with them. They settled most often in America's backcountry, since it was geographically and politically parallel to the borders from whence they came. There arose, therefore, in the backcountry of America, a culture much like the one seen on the Anglo-Scottish borders.[13]

The so-called Scotch-Irish people did not begin to come to America in any numbers until after the beginning of the eighteenth century.

"Their pride was a source of irritation to their English neighbors, who could not understand what they had to feel proud about. It was said of one Scots-Irish man his looks spoke out that he would not fear the devil should he meet him face to face."[14] These were known as restless folk, independent, quick-tempered, defiant of authority, and proud of their self-reliance. The typical Scotch-Irishman had supposedly crossed the mountains with a rifle in one hand, a jug of whiskey in the other, and a Bible tucked in his armpit.

The surname Colter in its various forms—Coulter, Coalter, Colther and several other variations—is of ancient origin. It first appears in Scotland during the twelfth century and is the Scottish form of *Vrusk Kaldr*, a Viking name that arrived with the Norsk Vikings, who invaded Scotland and Ireland in the eleventh and twelfth centuries. In the mass migrations of Scotch-Irish families from Ulster in and before 1730, there were many Coulters and Coulter families. Although John Colter's personal genealogy still remains a mystery, his heritage—like that of Andrew Jackson and Ulysses S. Grant—was quite likely Scotch-Irish.[15]

British from the borderlands poured into western Pennsylvania in the late 1700s, and more than one historian has speculated that John Colter belonged to one of the Coulter families who settled that area. But, as with the Virginia hypothesis, no primary document has been found to make the case. One possible clue to Colter's Kentucky home is the old maxim that "Birds of a Feather Flock Together." When Colter finally settled down for good in 1810, he chose the settlement of St. John's, in what was then called Upper Louisiana (and is now the state of Missouri). St. John's settlement occupied both sides of St. John's Creek where it empties into the Missouri River, now within the city limits of Washington. (Daniel Boone and his extended family were nearby—they had settled across the Missouri at Femme Osage.) St John's boasted gunsmiths, a gunpowder manufacturing facility, and a horse-powered gristmill, all very important to these early settlers. Colter possibly chose to live here because St. John's and La Charette (directly across the river and not far from Femme Osage) were composed mainly of families who had emigrated from Kentucky and Tennessee, several of whom, he most likely knew from his youth. Among his neighbors were the Richardsons, Maupins, and Sappingtons, who had come from Madison County, Kentucky, near Fort Boonesborough, and the Sullens, who had come by way of Tennessee and Kentucky. Others included the Browns, Baileys, Heasleys, Green-streets, Sheltons, Millers, and Blizes (who became Colter's in-laws when his daughter, Evelina, married John Blize), all names likely to show up in both Kentucky and Missouri. Many of these families had apparently migrated west together. [16]

As Elizabeth Semancik has noted, "serial migration or stream migration . . . was common in the peopling of the backcountry. A few clan members opened a path for others, and were followed by a steady stream of kin." Explaining the notion of "clans" in the eighteenth-century American back-country, Semancik continued:

> The clans of the border were not precisely the same as those of the Scottish Highlands, and very different from the Victorian contrivances of our own time. They had no formal councils, tartans, sporrans, bonnets or septs. But they were clannish in the most fundamental sense: a group of related families who lived near to one another, were conscious of a common identity, carried the same surname, claimed descent from common ancestors and banded together when danger threatened. [17]

To all these pioneer families storming westward, the land draining into the Ohio River was a vast, trackless wilderness ready for the taking. However, it was anything but that. For thousands of years the Trans-Allegheny region had been inhabited by a variety of Indian nations. These Indian people had little use for the Europeans except for their trade goods. Moreover, the Indians and Europeans had radically different and incompatible mind-sets about the land. The Indians understood control of territory by force but not by ownership. How could anyone own the land? How could anyone set up borders and attempt to buy and sell sections of nature? And yet this was exactly what the Europeans were intent on doing. As the whites moved into Kentucky, both public officials and private entrepreneurs attempted to re-draw boundary lines, draw up new treaties, and purchase parcels of land from the Indians.

In 1775, a speculator by the name of Richard Henderson, known to the Indians as Carolina Dick, enlisted the help of Daniel Boone and others in attempting to illegally purchase hundreds of thousands of acres in present Tennessee and Kentucky from the Cherokee, even though the Cherokee claimed no right over the Kentucky land west of the Cumberland Mountains. Over the protests of a young chief named Dragging Canoe, the other chiefs agreed to the sale—although one witness described the items offered as "cheap goods, such as coarse woolens, trinkets, some firearms, and spiritous liquors." Dragging Canoe accurately warned that "new cessions would be applied for, and finally the country which the Cherokees and their forefathers had so long occupied would be called for; and a small remnant which may then exist of this nation, once so great and formidable, will be compelled to seek a retreat in some far distant wilderness." He further warned that "there was a dark cloud" over Kentucky.[18]

Dragging Canoe's "dark cloud," later liberally paraphrased as "dark and bloody ground," soon proved an accurate portent. Violence escalated, especially as Indians took the side of the British during the American Revolution, and atrocities on both sides became common. "Whole families are destroyed without regard to Age or Sex," settler John Floyd wrote to Thomas Jefferson. "Infants are torn from their Mothers Arms and their Brains dashed out against Trees. . . . Not a week Passes some weeks scarcely a day with out some of our distressed Inhabitants feeling the fatal effects of the infernal rage and fury of those Excreable Hellhounds."[19]

The colonists responded by waging a war of utter desolation. In the summer of 1780, George Rogers Clark, Boone, and others led a force of men that defeated the Shawnee in a fierce battle. The Americans repaid Indian atrocities in kind—one Indian woman was killed by a soldier's "ripping up her Belly & otherwise mangling her."[20] Boone wrote—in his edited "autobiography"—that Clark's army "finished with great success, took seventeen scalps, and burnt the town to ashes, with the loss of seventeen men."[21]

This strategy of starving the Indians continued unchecked. A little over a year later, again under Clark's command, Boone assisted in ravaging the countryside. "We continued our pursuit through five towns on the Miami rivers, Old Chelicothe, Pecaway, New Chelicothe, Will's Towns, and Chelicothe," he wrote, "burnt them all to ashes, entirely destroyed their corn, and other fruits, and every where spread a scene of desolation in the county."[22] Forced to rely almost exclusively on hunting to survive, the Indians virtually exterminated the eastern herds of buffalo that only a couple of decades earlier had seemed so endless.

By the time William Clark and Meriwether Lewis—and presumably the nine young men—became Indian fighters in the 1790s, many tribes had been pushed west, and conflicts had generally moved northwest, to the present states of Ohio, Indiana, and Illinois. But the strategy was much the same. In 1794, days after General Mad Anthony Wayne and his troops, including William Clark, defeated an Indian confederacy at the Battle of Fallen Timbers, often considered the final battle of the Northwest Indian Wars, Clark's report to his brother Jonathan was hauntingly familiar. He spoke of the army "cutting down and destroying hundreds of Acres of corn & Burning several large Towns besides small ones."[23] As Landon Jones succinctly summarizes, "George Rogers Clark's slash-and-burn tactics had finally been executed with a vengeance. Wayne's army was employing the same strategy the Virginians had bitterly denounced as barbaric when British Colonel Banastre Tarlton's dragoons swept through Albemarle County in 1781."[24]

When Meriwether Lewis wrote William Clark in June of 1803, inviting him to help command an expedition to explore "the interior of the continent of North America," he told Clark what kind of men he was looking for:

> When descending the Ohio it shall be my duty by enquiry to find out and engage some good hunters, stout, healthy, unmarried men, accustomed to the woods, and capable of bearing bodily fatigue in a pretty considerable degree: should any young men answering this description be found in your neighborhood I would thank you to give information of them on my arivall at the falls of the Ohio. [25]

A month later, Clark accepted Lewis's invitation, calling the enterprise one he had "long anticipated" and was "much pleased with." Echoing what Lewis had written, Clark reported that he had "temperally engaged some men for the enterprise of a discription calculated to work & go thro' those labours & fatigues which will be necessary." [26]

This brings us to the second key piece of information about Colter: He was capable of enduring the exhaustive labor, the hunger and thirst, the bitter cold, and every other hardship that were part of the mission. Ruth Colter-Frick has pointed out that while both of the captains and virtually all of the men were sick at one time or another, the journals make no mention of Colter ever being sick or injured. [27]

In a virtual catalog describing Colter's abilities, Clark added another when he reported that "the young men that I have engaged or rather promised to take on this expedition are . . . the best woodsmen & Hunters, of young men in this part of the Countrey." [28]

The Reverend Joseph Doddridge, who was born around the same time as Colter and grew to manhood about fifty miles south of Pittsburgh in what is now West Virginia had this to say about the values that would have been imprinted on John Colter during his formative years:

> Amusements are, in many instances, either imitations of the business of life, or at least, of some of its particular objects of pursuit; on the part of young men belonging to nations in a state of warfare, many amusements are regarded as preparations for the military character, which they are expected to sustain in future life. [29]

For Colter's generation, the most fundamental "imitation of the business of life" was marksmanship, and a key element of good marksmanship was good eyesight, so important that it easily made its way into the lore of the era. According to his descendants, Jesse Hughes, born about twenty years before Colter and said to be "one of the most active, daring and successful Indian hunters in the mountain region of Virginia," "had eyes like a panther and could see at night almost as well as [a panther]." [30] Aspiring frontiersmen hoped to be described similarly. In Colter's day, a youth growing up on the frontier was often taken out on a clear night to have his eyesight tested. One of the oldest of all eye tests is looking at the Pleiades. Poor eyes see a mere haze; excellent eyes see five stars. The boy would have been asked to count the stars—a good hunter or scout needed to see at least eight to ten, and some men have counted as many as thirteen. Colter likely passed such a test with flying colors.

Quoting Doddridge again, the frontier fort was "not only a place of defense, but the residence of a small number of families. . . . As the Indian mode of warfare was an indiscriminate slaughter of all ages and both sexes, [the fort] was as requisite to provide for the safety of the women and children as for that of the men."[31] A young man growing up during this very violent period was expected to help defend the fort and was often given a single-shot rifle or musket by the time he was ten. He then became a fort soldier and had his porthole assigned him. The weapon given him was in all likelihood taller than he was. It was an awkward burdensome treasure that would soon lighten into an extension of his right hand, finding its weight in the most perfect spot for a steady balance. Marksmanship was of paramount importance because lead and powder were precious on the frontier. He was taught to shoot offhand—from a standing position, steadying the weapon against his shoulder, and from a rest, such as the side of a tree, or to lay down placing some moss on a log to lay the rifle on. He learned to compensate for distances, by adding a little more powder to his load and raising his front sight and changing his site picture to one side of the target to allow for wind and movement, giving us the term "Kentucky Windage." For many more years, his weapon would never be too far from his reach, even while he slept.

What a single shot teaches one is patience, stalking, and the ability to hit what is aimed at with that first shot. What was said about William Clark as a Kentucky youth was likely true of Colter as well: "He was accurate enough a rifle shot to engage in the local sport of 'barking squirrels'—firing a bullet at a branch immediately below a perched squirrel, sending it flying."[32]

Clark became such an expert marksman that in the mid-1790s he was appointed to command General Anthony Wayne's elite Chosen Rifle company of sharpshooters. Wayne had been named commander of the newly formed "Legion of the United States," in March of 1792. Although Clark was initially quite skeptical of Wayne's methods, he eventually adopted them himself. Wayne instituted mandatory one-hour shooting practices each day and awarded a gill of whiskey to the best shot. Similarly, at Camp Dubois, Clark often sponsored shooting contests, offering a reward to the winner. As co-commander of the Corps of Discovery, Clark followed the philosophy Wayne had stated so well in a 1793 letter to Secretary of War Henry Knox: "I am also endeavoring to make the rifle men believe in that arm, the Infantry in heavy buck shots & bayonet, the Dragoons in the Sword, & the Legion in their United Prowess."[33]

First, the men had to truly master their arms—thus, the continual emphasis on target practice. Another important skill with a rifle, witnessed by many but mastered by few, was reloading a long rifle at a dead run. A rifle, its barrel interior configured with raised and spiraling lands, presents a more difficult task to normal reloading than does a smoothbore weapon. This is especially so after an initial discharge, due to the heavy residue of black powder. A young man spent weeks mastering this skill because one day his life would depend on that second shot. Wayne trained his men and equipped them with the right weapons, so that, "in Action . . . the eye of the soldier will therefore be constantly upon his Enemy, and he can pursue & load in full trot without danger of loosing any part of his powder."[34]

Colter, like Clark, learned that his understanding of weapons reflected his understanding of life and death. *"Always look to your gun, but never let your gun look at you"* is an old but wise saying, but some forgot the lesson. In the settling of the West, any number of men accidentally shot themselves.

Wayne's second objective was to convince the men of their "united prowess"—or *esprit de corps*. As one scholar has written, Wayne knew that this *esprit* came from proper training, from "loyalty to a popular commander," "from being well uniformed," and "from a feeling of belonging to a squad, a company, a battalion, a regiment, or an army."[35]

Following Wayne's lead, Clark chose his men carefully and found ways to build unity and enthusiasm. With the shooting contests, for instance, he often had his men compete against village sharpshooters. "Several of the Countrey people In Camp Shooting with the party," he wrote on May 6, 1804, "all git beet and Lose their money."[36]

The organization of the Corps of Discovery also reflected an emphasis on fair treatment and unity. Three squads were formed, each led by a sergeant, with each private assigned duties and privileges similar to others in his squad. Fighting and drunkenness were not winked at, but the punishment was not excessive. For example, in January of 1804, men who had gotten drunk, fought, and neglected their duty were ordered by Clark to build a hut for a woman who had promised to wash and sew for the group.[37]

Late in March, Colter and two others were court-martialed for disorderly conduct. Each begged forgiveness and promised to do better. No punishment was mentioned in the record; indeed, two days later all three were named to the permanent party. Colter's conduct apparently received special notice because he was assigned to deliver important letters only a month later, and less than two months after that, Colter himself served as a member of a court.[38] Colter was on his way to becoming a sort of right-hand man to Clark, just as Drouillard was to Lewis.

Clark's success in establishing *esprit de corps* was well reflected in a letter John Ordway wrote in May of 1804: "I am now on an expedition to the westward, with Capt. Lewis and Capt. Clark. . . . I am So happy as to be one of them pick'd Men."[39]

By 1796, Clark had "taken military expeditions up and down the Ohio and Wabash rivers, built a fort in the wilderness, fought in three Indian campaigns, and observed the making of a historic treaty. He had learned the fine points of dealing with Indians from the most experienced men in the country."[40]

All of this had a powerful and direct bearing on the kind of men Clark recruited for the expedition, and although we have no specific record of Colter before 1803, Clark's selecting him as one of the nine young men, as well as Colter's history during the expedition, make it quite clear that Colter had qualities extremely important to Clark.

During his three years with Lewis and Clark, Colter's skill with a rifle was evident from the start. As noted, Clark's first mention of him, on that snowy December day in 1803, was that he had killed a deer and a turkey. Joseph Whitehouse offered another example of Colter's marksmanship when he wrote:

> We left the Prairi at sun rise . . . towards evening, one of our men espied a Wolf laying a sleep on the shore, as we approached toward him, the noise of our Oars awoke him, he stood there to see what was coming, when Captain Lewis shot at him and struck him with a Ball, the Wolf then acted as if mad snapping continually at his hind parts. The Captain order'd one Colter to fire at him, which he did, and killed him.[41]

Colter had clearly learned marksmanship skills as a youth. Other accounts from Lewis and Clark's men show that he mastered other skills as well, much like Jesse Hughes, who "could hear the slightest noise made in the forest at a great distance and . . . was always disturbed by any noise he could not account for. He knew the ways of every bird and animal in the woods, and was familiar with the sounds and cries made by them. Any unusual cry or action of an animal or bird, or any note or sound of alarm made by either, caused him to stop and look about until he knew the cause." Not only that, but "he could go through the woods, walking or running without making any noise, unless the leaves were dry, and then he made very little noise."[42]

By the time Colter was in his teens he likely learned how to track men and animals. He needed to be able to look at a track and tell how old it was. To do this, he had learned to keep track of the weather and be an accurate judge of temperature and the effects of sun and wind on a trail. Colter was literate and he knew how to follow a compass, as well as how to navigate by the stars. Above all he had that sense—an instinct—for direction. Once his destination was fixed in his mind, he could go to it directly in the darkness as in daylight, on a calm, cloudy day or in bright sunshine with the wind blowing steadily from one quarter.

Hunting and shooting were closely linked to tracking, and Lewis and Clark depended on Colter's tracking skills throughout the Expedition. The first instance came in August of 1804, when George Shannon, the youngest member of the group, turned up missing. Shannon had been sent out on August 26, 1804, in pursuit of two horses that had strayed. He found the horses, but thinking the others were ahead of him, he panicked. Mounting one of the horses, he headed north along the river. Clark became alarmed at Shannon's absence and dispatched George Drouillard in pursuit, but he returned unsuccessful on the 27th. Next Clark sent John Shields and Joseph Field, but they returned on the next day, stating that Shannon was ahead of them and they could not catch up with him. After their return Clark became more anxious and wrote: "This man not being a first rate Hunter, [he referring to Shannon] we deturmined to Send one man in pursute of him with Some Provision." On the 29th he dispatched Colter, who for a time kept up a running pursuit. But Shannon was mounted and Colter on foot, with little possibility of catching up. Clark again wrote in his journal on the 3rd of September: "Saw Some Signs of the 2 men, who are a head, Colter has not over taken Shannon." On the 6th Colter finally gave up the chase, and rejoined the main group at the boat. He had in the meantime been busy with his rifle, as John Ordway wrote: "a cloudy morning . . . Colter Came to the Boat had not found Shannon nor the horses But had killed one Buffelow, one Elk 3 Deer one wolf 5 Turkies & one Goose—one Beaver also."[43] The greenhorn Shannon, by contrast, was virtually starving at that point.

Colter's hunting and scouting prowess is reminiscent of Boone, renowned as a great hunter by the time he was fifteen. He once boasted that he had killed 155 bears in a three-week period and that one morning he had "killed eleven by late breakfast time." (Boone and two sons-in-law later sold several dozen barrels of bear grease at a dollar per gallon.) Boone explored a good deal of Kentucky wilderness by himself, apparently never getting lost, sometimes camping in canebrakes and fleeing to those canebrakes—where it was virtually impossible to track a man—when at risk of Indian attack. "I was constantly exposed to danger, and death," he remembered. During his explorations, which spanned most of his long life, Boone seemed to have an innate and uncanny sense of where he was. Other colonizers said of him "that he never crossed a route he had once traversed without at once recognizing the place and knowing that he was crossing one of his former trails."[44]

Combat, as seen by Colter, and his contemporaries, was generally decided by the rifle. Unlike later in the West, the close-quarter arm of choice was the tomahawk or the knife, not the pistol. Throwing the tomahawk, which takes considerable practice, was another skill that Doddridge said boys of his time learned early. The knife was vastly more useful for nonlethal action but in

combination with the tomahawk or used by itself became a formidable weapon and gave rise to the term "Long Knives," the term Indians used to describe
men like Colter.[45] James Buchanan wrote of this type of warfare:

> If the mode of warfare of the Indians was ferocious, that of the enemy with
> whom we had to contend was equally so. Every man who has served in that
> country [Kentucky] can attest the fact, that the Kentuckians invariably carry
> the tomahawk and scalping knife into action, and are dexterous in using
> them.[46]

If a young man was deemed to have the necessary survival skills he
would often be teamed up with such men as Samuel Brady, Simon Kenton,
Andrew Poe, Tom Eddington, Sam Murphy, Daniel Boone, or maybe even
Lewis Wetzel. So it was not surprising that Eva Emery Dye had pegged one
of these legends—Kenton—as Colter's mentor. Kenton, a scout, frontiersman, pathfinder, solider, and friend of Revolutionary hero George Rogers
Clark (William Clark's older brother), had fought in the Kentucky and Ohio
Indian wars throughout much of the 1770s, 1780s, and 1790s and had made
more than one miraculous escape from hostile Indians. The trouble is, Dye
offered no documentation to support her claim, and a close search of the
Draper Collection—the papers most likely to offer details of a Kenton/Colter
association—has thus far yielded nothing. Nevertheless, Charles G. Clarke
wrote that Colter had "probably served as a Ranger with Kenton," and Meriwether Lewis's biographer, Richard Dillon, went farther than that, stating
that Colter "was a twenty-eight-year-old frontiersman who had been a Ranger with Simon Kenton. Blue-eyed like Lewis, he also resembled his commander in that he was a pleasant and ingenuous Virginian, quick in mind and
muscle, and as brave or braver than the captain from Ivy himself."[47]

Despite the lack of evidence linking Colter with Kenton, one thing is
clear: Colter fell into the same group of men as Kenton. Well represented by
James Fenimore Cooper's Natty Bumppo (Hawkeye), these men drew a distinction between killing and murdering Indians. Boone, for example, said
that while he had fought Indians for many years, he did not know positively
that he had ever killed one. As Boone's biographer, John Faragher, wrote:

> William Hancock, who saw a great deal of Boone at Chillicothe during the
> spring of 1778, was at a loss to understand [after their capture by Blackfish's
> band of Indians while they were making salt at Blue Licks in the Winter of
> 1778] "how Boone could be whistling and contented among the dirty Indians
> while he was so melancholy." This was all part of his plan, Boone later ex-
> plained to Filson, "always appearing as cheerful and satisfied as possible."
> Like the great hunter he was, Boone's greatest talent was his ability to blend in
> with his surroundings.[48]

Many other men, however, were Indian haters, intent on killing Indians in any possible circumstance. Bird repudiated the Natty Bumppo type of hero with his character Nathan Slaughter or Jibbenainosay (meaning an avenging devil), who was essentially an Indian hater. Captain Samuel Brady, Lewis Wetzel, and Jesse Hughes fell into this category and had a vendetta to kill all Indians they encountered for the killings that had occurred in their immediate families. Scott Barrows expressed this second type best when he wrote about Brady and Wetzel:

> When Brady's son John saw his first Indian scalp he said his father and Lewis Wetzel had gone across the Ohio with a boy named Alex Mitchell. They came across an Indian sitting in his camp, and "Mitchell being a young lad, they gave him the chance to shoot him. . . . When they came to the Fort my father had the scalp strung to his walking stick. . . . There was much rejoicing." Like a boy on his first deer hunt young Mitchell was initiated into male culture, in this case a culture that dehumanized and killed Indians.[49]

Cecil Hartley in his book *Life of Lewis Wetzel* wrote that Clark went out of his way to recruit Wetzel:

> General Clarke, the companion of Lewis in the celebrate tour across the Rocky Mountains, had heard much of Lewis Wetzel in Kentucky, and determined to secure his service in the perilous enterprise. A messenger was accordingly sent for him, but he was reluctant to go. However, he finally consented, and accompanied the party during the first three month's travel, but then declined going any further, and returned home.[50]

The ironic thing is, this story of Clark recruiting Wetzel is apocryphal. Clark had grown to manhood on the "Dark and Bloody Ground" and knew instinctively that Wetzel was not the kind of man he and Lewis wanted. Neither of the captains made any attempt to enlist Wetzel because they were not looking for Indian haters but for skilled frontiersmen, men who could defend themselves if necessary but who would first of all follow Thomas Jefferson's advice to "make a favorable impression" on the Sioux and all their neighbors.

From the first mention of Colter in the historical record—in 1803—to the last—in 1812—he proved that he was such a man.

Chapter Four

"Colter Came Running Along the Shore"

The Encounter with the Lakota Sioux

The forty-nine members of Lewis and Clark's Corps of Discovery woke to a fair and clear Sabbath morning on September 23, 1804, almost nineteen weeks after they had departed Camp Dubois and started up the Missouri River—and two years to the day before they would conclude the expedition.[1] Sometime during the day, John Colter mounted the last horse belonging to the corps and rode ahead to hunt, probably taking his Kentucky long rifle, a scalping knife, a bedroll, and a mosquito net—for the "musquiters [were] verry troublesom in the bottoms."[2]

By Clark's reckoning, they had traveled twelve hundred twenty-eight and a half miles; they were now about twenty miles southeast of the site of Pierre, South Dakota.[3] Clark noted that he saw great numbers of buffalo as he walked along the shore. "Gangs" of buffalo, as the men called them, were a common sight on the plains, but Clark also saw something else—a large prairie fire blazing in the distance, on the south side of the Missouri, "an Indian Signal," he noted, "of their haveing discovered us."[4]

The Indian nation making the discovery was the Lakota Sioux, "the iconic warrior horsemen of the Northern Plains," a tribe later remembered for Sitting Bull, Crazy Horse, and Red Cloud, for the Battle of Little Big Horn and the Wounded Knee Massacre.[5]

"On that nation we wish most particularly to make a friendly impression," Thomas Jefferson had advised Meriwether Lewis, "because of their immense power, and because we learn they are very desirous of being on the most friendly terms with us."[6]

The weather was pleasant, with a slight breeze from the southeast, and the Corps of Discovery made an impressive twenty miles, pushing, pulling, and rowing their 55-foot keelboat and two flat-bottomed pirogues (30-to-40-foot boats with six or seven men in each one) upstream on a stretch of river that was wide and straight but also shallow and pocked with sandbars. Around 6:00 p.m., the group made camp in a patch of woods, with the three sergeants—Ordway, Pryor, and Gass—assigning the privates and boatmen to handle such tasks as checking their weapons, pitching the tents, preparing a latrine, or "sink," gathering firewood, preparing the evening meal, and guarding the camp. In the midst of this bustle of activity, three Indian boys swam the seventy-or-so yards across the river to greet the corps. According to Clark, the boys announced that there were two groups of "a Band of Sieux called the *Tetons*" camped upstream, the first consisting of eighty lodges and the second of sixty. Next, they confirmed Clark's suspicions about the prairie fire by acknowledging they had set it themselves.[7]

Clark's casual mention that "those boys informed us" of such details tells only half the story, however, because no one in the corps spoke the boys' language. The actual communication probably involved a good number of false starts, as well as questioning expressions and hand gestures. One of the men, presumably Cruzatte (but possibly Labiche), spoke Omaha to the boys, a language in the Siouan family but hardly a familiar dialect. Drouillard likely tried sign language as the halting conversation continued.

"We gave those boys two twists of Tabacco to carry to their Chiefs & Warriors to Smoke, with derections to tell them that we wished to Speak to them tomorrow, at the mouth of the next river," wrote Clark, although the boys may have actually understood little of that.[8] Unfortunately, the French trapper Pierre Dorion Sr., who had been such a valuable interpreter in dealing with the Yankton Sioux a few weeks earlier—and who could have understood the boys—had remained with the Yankton nation so that he could accompany some of their chiefs to Washington.

Some of the men took the boys back across the river in a pirogue. Meanwhile, the ever-curious Meriwether Lewis—likely accompanied by his dog, Seaman—walked on the shore, perhaps paying particular attention to the plant life. Reubin Field, one of the best marksmen in the group, had been out hunting and returned with a single pronghorn, which the men called a goat. "Several wild Goats Seen in the Plains," Clark had written three weeks earlier. "They are wild & fleet."[9] But neither Clark nor Field could have realized how fleet they were, for the pronghorn, the sole surviving member of the ancient Antilocpridae animal family, is the fastest animal in the western hemisphere (only the cheetah is faster) and can run close to sixty miles per hour in twenty-foot bounds.[10]

The pronghorn was hardly enough to feed the entire group, so they may have also supped on soup, corn meal, and biscuits, as well as on the red currants and grapes plentiful in the area. The highlight of the evening came when each man received a four-ounce shot of whiskey, but Colter was not there to savor his ration. He camped alone on an island, perhaps feasting at his lonely fire on a freshly killed elk, sipping a little coffee, and enjoying a few dried apples. If so, his solitary meal that Sunday night was a fitting portent of his experience the next six years, when he would sometimes eat and camp alone for weeks on end, although usually in much harsher conditions.

Monday morning dawned clear and pleasant. "[We] passed a handsome prairie on [the north side]," wrote Ordway, "where we found large plumb orcheds covered with ripe plumbs." Early that afternoon, Colter hailed the boats from the island and informed Lewis that he had killed four elk. Lewis ordered the voyageurs manning one of the pirogues to stop, dress the meat, and load it on the boat. Moments later, "Colter came running along the Shore" and called out that the Indians had stolen his horse and bridle.[11]

As historian Royal B. Hassrick has noted, "The significance of the horse to Sioux society and culture cannot be overemphasized."[12] The Great Sioux Nation first acquired horses in the early 1700s, just a few decades after the nation had migrated to the Great Plains from Minnesota and Wisconsin. The Spanish had brought horses to the Americas in the sixteenth and seventeenth centuries, with large numbers of horses falling into the hands of the Pueblo Indians after their revolt against the Spanish in 1680. The Pueblos soon began trading the valuable animals to Plains Indians, and horses spread from New Mexico northward, reaching the Dakotas by way of Colorado and Nebraska. By the 1770s—perhaps ten or twenty years earlier—horses had radically transformed the culture of the Lakota, changing the way they lived (because they could now transport larger tepees), waged war, hunted, migrated from one place to another (allowing them to take sick or elderly people who previously may have been left behind), gauged social status, and carried on trade with outsiders.[13]

Not surprisingly, horses were also closely linked with firearms. Horses could be traded for guns, and guns empowered a tribe to obtain more horses, and on and on. "Tribes with the greatest access to horses and firearms could expand their territory and power at the expense of those tribes with fewer guns and horses."[14] Ironically, Europeans had supplied the firearms and animals that made a new, prosperous way of life possible for the Sioux, and within a few short decades, European culture and migration would also shatter that way of life. Guns and horses, of course, had a dramatic impact on the buffalo hunt, allowing a tribe to take more buffalo over a wider range. The buffalo, technically bison (*Tatanka* in Lakota), was a uniquely valuable animal, serving as the staff of life for Indian nations throughout the West. And while meat was vital (one animal could feed dozens of people), buffalo were also used for a multitude of other purposes. Traveling the southern plains in the 1770s, Athanase de Mezieres noted the bison's incredible value to the native nations:

> The brains they use so often to soften skins; the horns for spoons and drinking vessels; the shoulder bones to dig and clear off the land; the tendons for thread and for bow-strings; the hoof as glue for arrows; from the mane they make ropes and girths; from the wool, garters, belts, and various ornaments. The skin furnishes harness, lassos, shields, tents, shirts, leggins, shoes, and blankets for protection against the cold—truly valuable treasures, easily acquired, quietly possessed, and lightly missed, which liberally supply an infinite number of people, whom we consider poverty-stricken, with an excess of those necessities which perpetuate out struggles, anxieties, and discords. [15]

While Colter and his companions appreciated the grandeur of a buffalo herd, they saw the animals primarily as a source of food. The Lakota went a level deeper and viewed the buffalo with reverence, thankful that it would enter this world and sacrifice itself to give life to humans, an attitude was part of their larger belief in the Great Mystery or Great Spirit—*Wakan Tanka*—that imbued all of nature with sacredness. The sun, *Wi*, was chief of the benevolent gods that made up Wakan Tanka. "Patron of the four principal Sioux virtues—bravery, fortitude, generosity, and fidelity—[Wi's] power might be solicited through certain offerings and ceremonies. Chief among these was the Sun Dance, in which a dancer might communicate directly with Wi." [16]

Young men made solitary sojourns into the wilderness, fasting and praying and torturing themselves as they sought visions to guide their lives. After seeing his vision, which was interpreted through the help of a shaman, the youth could identify his guardian spirit, which might be embodied as an animal, plant, or inanimate object such as a stone. If the sacred object were an eagle, for example, the young man would honor eagles the rest of his life, never harming them and always carrying feathers, claws, totems, fetishes, or other representations of eagles to protect him. [17]

Thus initiated, a young Lakota man further proved his manhood by honing his riding and hunting skills and by obtaining a large number of horses, using some of them as a gift price for a bride. But getting horses was not easy. Wild horses roamed the prairie here and there, but they were hard to catch. Taking horses from enemy tribes was much more effective, so it was not surprising that the Lakota, as well as their foes, developed complex strategies for capturing enemy horses and herding them back to the safety of the village. In the mid-nineteenth century, the Lakota once captured more than one hundred ponies from the Shoshone in a single day, an event so memorable that the tribal record, or "winter count," identified that year as

"Big Horse Steal," with a corresponding pictograph representing the raid being painted on the deerskin that preserved the nation's history. [18]

The upshot of all this was, of course, that Lewis and Clark's party and the Lakota perceived Colter's missing horse in radically different terms. William Clark saw it as a simple case of horse theft, and when the explorers met five Lakota soon after the horse went missing, Clark "informed them we were friends, & wished to Continue So but were not afraid of any Indians, Some of their young men had taken the horse Sent by their Great father for their Chief and we would not Speek to them untill the horse was returned to us again." [19] (Ironically, in his demand of honesty from the Lakota, Clark was dishonest himself, for the horse had certainly not been sent by the great father—Thomas Jefferson—as a gift for a Lakota chief.)

From the Indian viewpoint, however, a captured horse was valuable capital, benefitting both the individual who took it and the tribe itself, realities that no doubt colored the thinking of Buffalo Medicine (*Tartongawaka*), one of the five Lakota Lewis and Clark met not long after the incident. With Cruzatte doing his best to interpret, the captains discovered Buffalo Medicine was a chief—they had a friendly conversation with him, shared their meal, and smoked with him. Buffalo Medicine said he knew nothing about the horse but would have it returned if it were found. After that, the horse was not mentioned again—nor was it ever found—but the effects of the accusation and the denial lingered, foreshadowing how the two cultures would fail to communicate during a crucial negotiation the next day.

Buffalo Medicine had arrived with two chiefs senior to him, Black Buffalo (*Untongasabaw,* also called Black Bull) and the Partisan (*Tortohonga*), and at least fifty or sixty warriors, who "came flocking in from boath Sides of the River." [20] The Lakota men kept their heads shaved, except for a small tuft on top, which they grew long. Men of high rank wore an eagle or hawk feather fastened to the top of their heads and decorated with porcupine quills. The warriors also wore loose buffalo robes adorned with quills and painted with symbols representing coups, breechcloths tied closely to the body, antelope-skin leggings ornamented by bits of enemy scalps, and buffalo-skin moccasins. (The standard attire for women was a buffalo robe, an elk-skin dress, knee-length leggings, and moccasins.) [21] Some warriors were armed with muskets but most with bows and arrows.

To reflect the seriousness of the occasion—and also as a show of force— Lewis and Clark and the two dozen or so soldiers with them paraded in their red-white-and-blue dress uniforms. The dark blue cutaway coats complemented by cuffs, lapels, and brass buttons must have been an impressive sight. Each man carried his rifle, and the two captains were also equipped with swords and espontoons—spear-like, six-foot-high weapons carried by infantry officers.

After the parade, Lewis and Clark raised a flag and set up an awning, and the council began. The meeting was crucial for both the Americans and the Lakota because, as James Ronda has noted, "In the intricate trade network of the Upper Missouri, the Teton Sioux played a dangerous and precarious game."[22] The Arikara, Mandan, and Hidatsa nations were all upriver from the Lakota, whose position on the river, as well as their military strength, gave them distinct strategic advantages in trading with other Indians and the North West Company, a powerful fur company headquartered in Canada. As long as they could control the river—or at least demand tolls from traders traveling the river—the Lakota could supply the food, guns, horses, furs, and other goods needed for their people.

Lewis and Clark had the very same interest: trade. Safe trading posts at key spots along the Missouri River meant a booming economy for merchants in St. Louis and beyond, but they also meant something much more important—the spread of American influence and power. Lewis and Clark naturally wanted to get the North West Company out of the picture and trade directly with the nations upriver (without using the Lakota as middlemen). But they couldn't do that without convincing the Lakota to guarantee safe passage for traders heading up and down the Missouri. With the stakes so high for both sides, it had to be disheartening for the captains and the chiefs to discover that even through an interpreter they could barely understand each other—if at all.

"We discover our interpeter do not Speak the language well," Clark wrote in typical understatement.[23] Still, things started well enough—probably because exchanging gifts of food and smoking together required little talking. Next, however, Lewis attempted to deliver a written speech, likely repeating much of what he had told the Oto nation a month and a half earlier: "*Children.* Know that . . . the great Chief of the Seventeen great Nations of America . . . , as powerfull as he is just, and as beneficient as he is wise, always entertaining a sincere and friendly disposition towards the red people of America, has commanded us his war chiefs to undertake this long journey, which we have so far accomplished with great labour & much expence, in order to council with yourselves and his other red-children on the troubled waters, to give you his good advice; to point out to you the road in which you must walk to obtain happiness."[24]

The interpreter, Pierre Cruzatte, born to a French father and Omaha mother, was a skillful boatman who had brightened the evenings with his fiddle playing. He did his best, rendering the speech into Omaha—along with any Sioux phrases he had learned in the last few weeks—but asking him to actually make Lewis's communique understandable to the Lakota was asking the impossible. He must have sensed the mounting frustration on both sides as the futility of the situation became evident.

"We oblige to Curtail [the speech] for want of a good interpeter," Clark wrote. And while the proud, independent Lakota were no doubt frustrated at not being able to understand the details of Lewis's harangue, they likely perceived his tone of civility mixed with condescension all too well—and they weren't used to being treated like children.[25]

Lewis and Clark attempted ease the tension with gifts—presenting "3 niew meddals & 1 american flag Some knives & other small articles" to the three chiefs and "a red coat & a cocked hat & feather" and some tobacco to Black Buffalo.[26] The captains next offered the chiefs a tour of the keelboat—anchored safely in the river—along with a shot of whiskey. But when the Partisan began to feign drunkenness and reel about the boat, Clark decided it was time to return the chiefs to shore in a pirogue, though they were reluctant to go. What Clark did not know was that the Partisan was possibly trying to somehow get the upper hand with Lewis and Clark because he and Black Buffalo were struggling for power within the tribe. (A year earlier, the Partisan had led a horse-sealing raid to the Ponca nation after Black Buffalo tried to establish peace with them. The Poncas had retaliated by stealing horses from the Lakota, shattering any hopes of peace and leaving the two chiefs understandably distrustful of each other.)[27]

When Clark and seven of his men reached the shore with the three chiefs, the rising tension ratcheted even higher, with three Lakota seizing the pirogue's cable and another grasping the mast. Clark's men readied their weapons, "with a full deturmination to defend me if possible," wrote Clark.[28] The Partisan demanded more gifts with such a violent tone that Clark drew his sword. Onboard the keelboat, Lewis "ordered every man to his arms. the large Swivel"—a cannon mounted on a pivot—"loaded immediately with 16 Musquet Ball in it," and "the 2 other Swivels"—blunderbusses, or scatterguns, also mounted on pivots—"loaded well with Buck Shot, Each of them manned."[29]

Clark was ready for a fight. A veteran of Indian wars in the Ohio country, he had seen his share of violence and had been commanding a convoy of seventy infantrymen and twenty mounted dragoons escorting seven hundred supply-laden packhorses when Indians ambushed the advance guard. Clark charged to the front and helped repulse the attackers.[30] "He is a youth of solid and promising parts, and as brave as Caesar," a family friend had written.[31] Now, Clark warned the Lakota that he and his men were warriors, not squaws, and that the great father could have the entire Lakota nation destroyed "as it were in a moment."[32]

"The chief Sayed he had warriors too," Ordway wrote,[33] and those warriors had already cocked their muskets or strung their bows and notched their arrows, pointing them "blank" at Clark and his men, meaning they were at "point blank" range.[34] No strangers to battle, the Lakota had killed seventy-five Omaha warriors only two weeks earlier—with about fifty Omaha women and children taken prisoner.[35] Lewis and Clark had superior firepower, but the Lakota had more men—and the archers also had the advantage of being able to shoot an arrow, draw another from a quiver, and shoot it much faster than a soldier could fire his weapon and reload by bringing the firelock down into priming position, opening the priming pan, shaking in powder, shutting the pan, turning the rifle into loading position, shaking powder into the barrel, inserting a square of linen and then the ball, tapping the powder, linen, and ball into place with the starter, pulling the ramrod completely out, turning it to the front, placing it in the barrel, pushing the ammunition down the muzzle, and withdrawing the ramrod. An Indian with a bow could shoot several arrows for every shot fired by a rifleman.

Both sides stood their ground, and no one fired a weapon. From the relative safety of the keelboat, Lewis and his men could have killed dozens of Indians. But it is just as certain that Clark and the men with him would have been killed in the first fusillade. Whatever the exact result, Stephen Ambrose perceptively notes that "had that cannon fired, there might have been no Lewis and Clark Expedition. The exploration of the Missouri River country and Oregon would have had to be done by others, at a later time. Meanwhile, the Sioux would have been implacable enemies of the Americans, and in possession of the biggest arsenal on the Great Plains."[36]

The man who stepped forward to prevent bloodshed was the same chief who had sued for peace with the Poncas a year earlier—Black Buffalo. While he and Clark were still exchanging threats, Black Buffalo diffused the conflict by taking the cable himself and having his men stand back. He eventually released the cable and counseled with several warriors. Clark ordered his men—except for two interpreters—back to the keelboat, and the pirogue "soon returned with about 12 of our deturmined men ready for any event."[37] Clark did not identify these men, but it's hard to believe that several of the nine young men from Kentucky were not among them, particularly Nathaniel Pryor, John Colter, George Gibson, George Shannon, and Joseph and Reubin Field, as well as George Drouillard.[38]

Clark next offered his hand, and although Black Buffalo refused to take it, he requested—rather than ordered—that the corps spend the night so the women and children could see the keelboat. Lewis and Clark agreed. Clearly taking control after the Partisan had tried to wrest it from him, Black Buffalo next asked if he and Buffalo Medicine and two warriors—but not the Partisan—could spend the night on the keelboat. The captains again agreed. This series of events repeated itself more than once the next few days. Genuine good will (Lewis and Clark feasted with the Lakota and watched a dance) was followed by insults and misunderstandings that resulted in cocked muskets, loaded cannons, and notched arrows but no bloodshed—to the credit of both the soldiers and the Indians. By the time the expedition departed Lakota country on October 1, both sides were still wary of each other. Not surprisingly, nothing close to a trade settlement had been reached.[39]

Although the Lakota had honored the captains by carrying them on buffalo robes into a council tepee, smoking the calumet pipe with them, and offering them buffalo and dog (a delicacy among the Sioux), neither Lewis nor Clark had anything good to say about the Lakota nation in the future. From Fort Mandan, in present North Dakota, Lewis wrote to Thomas Jefferson that Corporal Warfington's group, which was returning the keelboat—loaded to the brim with artifacts—to St. Louis, would certainly "be fired on by the Siouxs,"[40] but there is no indication that anything of the sort happened. (Indeed, Warfington made it safely to St. Louis with his cargo and crew and a number of Indian guests—and with a live prairie dog still in tow.)

Clark was considerably more harsh. "These are the vilest miscreants of the savage race," he wrote (also at Fort Mandan), "and must ever remain the pirates of the Missouri, until such measures are pursued, by our government, as will make them feel a dependence on its will for their supply of merchandise. Unless these people are reduced to order, by coercive measures, I am ready to pronounce that the citizens of the United States can never enjoy but partially the advantages which the Missouri presents."[41]

The nation dismissed so negatively by Lewis and Clark, however, seems to have given them the benefit of the doubt and remembered them with respect—something entirely lost on the captains. Iron Shell's count for this general time period named one winter "Good White Man Came," quite likely a reference to the Corps of Discovery because, as Hassrick notes, "The white man shook hands, brought gifts and food for all, and carried with him a document, but no one among the Sioux knew what he said, for there was no interpreter,"[42] certainly an apt and accurate description of part of Meriwether Lewis's interaction with the tribe. Likewise, American Horse remembered that "The Dakotas had a council with the whites on the Missouri River, below the Cheyenne Agency, near the mouth of Bad Creek," and Cloud Shield recorded, "Many people camped together and had many flags flying,"[43] two more descriptions that are quite appropriate.

In 1890, at a time when one would have hoped for harmony between the Europeans and the Indians, a fundamental misunderstanding concerning the Lakota "Ghost Dance" and a willingness to resort to "coercive measures" figured prominently in the death of Sitting Bull. That event triggered a flight by the Minneconjou Lakota leader Big Foot and a band of followers, who crossed the stark South Dakota badlands and headed to an Oglala council at the Pine Ridge Reservation. They were intercepted by soldiers of the Seventh Cavalry, who found a white flag flying from Big Foot's wagon and escorted him and his people to Wounded Knee Creek to await further orders. Five hundred well-armed soldiers surrounded 400 Indians, most of them women and children. In a conflict that began with Colter's missing horse, Lewis and

Clark had escaped disaster because no one on either side had fired a gun, but now, at Wounded Knee, a shot rang out.

"The firing was so fast and the smoke and dust so thick that I did not see much more until the fight was over," said one Indian. Another recalled that "firing followed then from all sides." As hand-to-hand combat broke out between some of the soldiers and Indians, most of the Lakota men, women, and children ran for cover, many seeking refuge in a dry ravine to the south. But even there the Hotchkiss shells rained down with brutal accuracy. "There went up from these dying people a medley of death songs that would make the hardest heart weep," remembered one Lakota survivor.[44] By the end of the day, more than 250 Lakota had been killed, including 150 women and children, possibly more.[45]

Robert Utley is probably correct in calling Wounded Knee "a regrettable, tragic accident of war that neither side intended."[46] But one must also account for what happened in the days, months, and years leading up to the massacre and how a white mindset of superiority, a failure to truly understand the Lakota, and a willingness to resort to violence all made the catastrophe possible if not inevitable. The United States displaced the Lakota repeatedly, employing legislation to renege on earlier treaties. Next, both malicious and well-meaning whites launched an all-out attack on Lakota culture. Traditional feasts, dances, marriage practices, religious ceremonies, and healing arts were all declared illegal. Indian children were taken from their families and "educated" at white institutions, which subjected the children to rigid schedules and harsh discipline, giving them new "white" names, forcing them to cut their hair (an essential aspect of Indian identity for both boys and girls), and prohibiting them from speaking their native language or taking part in any Indian ceremonies or traditions.

Tribal tradition suffered similar assaults. For centuries, groups of Indian families had bonded together into extended families called tribes, speaking the same language and believing that all the families of the tribe were related. White officials and Indian advocates alike, however, undercut tribal unity at every turn, the officials by restricting Indians to a single reservation and not allowing them to visit or live with fellow tribesmen on neighboring reservations, and advocates by urging the government to cease to recognize organized tribes.[47] Indian policy in the late nineteenth century basically came down to this: Indians were to be "civilized" whether they liked it or not. Certainly, some whites sincerely wanted to help the Indians, but they seemed incapable of questioning the deeply held presumption that Indian culture was inherently inferior to white culture and could morally be annihilated to achieve a higher good.

Four short years into the nineteenth century, Lewis and Clark had failed to understand the Lakota for want of an interpreter—and also for want of a desire to treat the Indians as equals. Sadly, this misunderstanding prefigured an entire century of false impressions, misreadings, distrust, and tragedy. On that pleasant day in September of 1804, when Colter looked up to see his horse gone, he could not have imagined what that missing horse would one day symbolize.

Chapter Five

"Colter Had Just Arrived with a Letter from Capt. Clark"

Perilous Rivers and Mountains

By the summer of 1805 it was apparent just how much the captains had grown to respect and trust Colter. On August 18, Lewis's thirty-first birthday, with Lewis and most of the Corps at the present site of Montana's Clark Canyon Reservoir (southwest of Dillon), Clark had taken Colter and ten others across the Continental Divide into Idaho on horseback to scout the Salmon River.[1] The captains had correctly concluded that the river flowed into the Columbia, and Clark wanted to see for himself if it were really as impassable as Sacagawea's brother Cameahwait had claimed. Clark and his men had axes and other tools to build dugout canoes if a water route proved feasible.[2]

Guided by a Shoshone the captains called Old Toby (his Indian name meant "Swooping Eagle"), Clark's group followed the Lemhi River north through a pleasant valley. By Friday, August 23, however, they found themselves in one of the most rugged wilderness regions in the United States. At the confluence of the Salmon and its north fork (near present North Fork, Idaho), Clark followed the main river west as it rushed down a narrow, rocky channel clearly not fit for canoes. Nor did a portage look possible. "We . . . proceed on with great dificuley," Clark wrote, "as the rocks were So Sharp [and] large and unsettled and the hill sides Steep that the horses could with the greatest risque and dificulty get on."[3]

Soon concluding that going further on horseback was impossible, the determined Clark decided to forge ahead on foot to examine if the river continued bad or was practicable. Instructing the majority of the men to stay and hunt or fish, Clark went ahead with Colter, Old Toby, and two other men, climbing over rocks and hiking along cliffs and through underbrush, at times following a faint wolf path, the chances of a river passage looking bleaker and bleaker. The men had seen no game; nor was there sufficient timber to build canoes. On top of that, the current was so strong that it was dangerous to cross the river, and yet it would be necessary "to Cross almost at every bend." Old Toby warned that perpendicular cliffs continued on both sides of the river "for a great distance and that the water runs with great violence from one rock to the other on each Side foaming & roreing thro rocks in every direction, So as to render the passage of any thing impossible."[4] Little wonder that this waterway would one day be called "the River of No Return."

Clark and Colter and the others trudged on for an amazing twelve miles, finally stopping at a creek, where they fished and "dined" on a few small salmon. Every step had confirmed Old Toby's prediction: The river was virtually "one continued rapid," with five severe rapids where canoe passage was "entirely impossible." Hardly done for the day, the band followed Old Toby another six miles along a well-beaten Indian path. With night falling, they ascended a "Spur of the Mountain," where they could see another twenty miles' worth of river flowing through the mountains, with snow-capped peaks straddling the horizon. Old Toby also pointed out a road to the north, which led to a large river where the Tushapass (Salish) nation dwelt. One hour after dark, the exhausted men finally lay down to rest.[5]

The next day, one bad omen followed another as Clark and Colter and their three companions made their way back to where the others were camped. Their food supply gone, they scrounged some berries for breakfast; then Clark slipped and crashed down on a rock, badly bruising his leg. "Every man appeared disheartened from the prospects of the river," he wrote after meeting the others, and not only was there nothing to eat, the choke cherries and berries the men had been consuming were making them sick, and the heavy dew and a passage through the river had left the bedding wet, all of this foreshadowing the crisis the Corps would face in the Bitterroot Mountains in less than a month.[6]

Clark had seen enough. "I wrote a letter to Capt Lewis informing him of the prospects before us," he recorded. Then he proposed two plans. The first was to "hire the present guide . . . and proceed on [north] by land to Some navagable part of the *Columbia* River," and the second was to send some of the men down the river while others carried provisions by horse and attempted to "come together occasionally on the river," a plan that Clark himself had already rejected.[7]

Clark had to get the letter delivered as soon as possible so Lewis could obtain horses from the Shoshone (called the Snake Indians by Lewis and Clark). The trouble was, Lewis was at that moment seventy miles to the southeast. Even with two sergeants present (Gass and Pryor), Clark called on Private Colter and "dispatched [him] on horseback with orders to loose no time reaching [Lewis]."[8]

The significance of this mission has hardly been lost on Colter researchers. In the early 1950s, Burton Harris suggested the duty "was actually a promotion for Colter, as it signified that he had advanced to that select group whose members the two captains considered competent to undertake difficult assignments on their own."[9] More than forty years later, Ruth Colter-Frick noted the importance of the assignment and also pointed out that in May of 1804, before the Corps started up the Missouri, Lewis had trusted Colter and Moses Reed to deliver an important letter to Clark.[10]

Colter set out alone, as he had so frequently on the Expedition, leaving late in the afternoon on Saturday, August 24. We don't know the details of his trip, but we know something of the conditions. Lewis wrote that the weather was "excessively cold," cold enough during the night to leave ice a quarter-inch thick on the vessels of water.[11] We also know that Clark's and Lewis's men were all going hungry because none of them had shot any deer or elk or pronghorn, even though some were spending most of their daylight hours hunting. Colter likely faced the same kind of hunger. He may have caught a few fish, like Clark, or eaten a little parched corn, like Lewis. Camping alone Saturday and Sunday nights and eating a scanty meal at his campfire, did he remember his hunting trip of a year earlier, right before meeting the Lakota Sioux, when he had killed four elk with relative ease?

Monday morning, Lewis and his party set out at dawn, stopping at a trickling stream that Lewis called the "extreme source of the Missouri," the river that had been their constant companion for fifteen months, the longest river in North America. They "halted for a few minutes, the men drank out of the water and consoled themselves with the idea of having at length arrived at this long wished for point."[12] Then they crossed the Continental Divide at scenic Lemhi Pass, where they could see "immense ranges of high mountains still to the West . . . with their tops partially covered with snow." Here they found "a handsome bold running Creek of cold Clear water, this stream a source of the great Columbia river."[13] They stopped to eat and graze their horses, "there being fine green grass on that part of the hillside." When they reached the Shoshone village about 6:00 in the evening, they "found Colter here who had just arrived with a letter from Capt. Clark."[14] Ordway wrote that Colter "had been with Capt. Clark a long distance down this River. he tells us that it is not navigable. no game and verry mountaineous."[15]

The two groups reunited within a few days and rode the horses provided by the Shoshone north into the Bitterroot Range. On Sunday, September 1, they set out at dawn and "proceeded on over high rugged hills," as Clark said.[16] It rained much of the afternoon, turning to hail at one point. "We descended a

Mountain nearly as Steep as the roof of a house," wrote Joseph Whitehouse. Camping in some old Indian lodges near the north fork of the Salmon, the men caught some salmon and also bought some from the Shoshone. One of the hunters killed a deer, a rare occurrence in recent weeks. It rained again during the night.[17]

The next morning was cloudy and wet. They got started about 7:00 A.M. "The way we had to go was verry bad," wrote Ordway, adding that they "passed through verry bad thickets where we were obliged to cut a road for our horses to pass through."[18] Clark wrote that the mountainside was so rocky and steep that the horses were in "danger of Slipping to Ther certain distruction."[19] Indeed, several of the horses fell and one or two gave out. Colter was likely one of the hunters who shot a few grouse but saw no game at all the entire day. The rain came again. "This is a verry lonesome place," recorded Ordway. "We call [it] dismal Swamp."[20]

Tuesday was another cloudy day. The explorers battled their way to the crest of the 7,000-foot Continental Divide and the Idaho/Montana border. Again, they cut a road through the thickets; again, several of the horses fell and rolled backward, with one horse nearly killed. "But little to eate," wrote Clark. "I killed 5 Pheasents & The [hunters] 4 with a little Corn afforded us a kind of Supper, at dusk it began to Snow & rain."[21] Ordway noted that some of the men wanted to kill a colt for food but decided to wait till the next day. "So we lay down wet hungry and cold," he concluded, "came with much fatigue 11 miles this day."[22]

The next day, September 4, the men woke to frost and snow and frozen moccasins and a meager breakfast of parched corn, but they did what they always did: they proceeded on. "The air on the mountains verry chilley and cold," wrote Ordway. "Our fingers aked with the cold." Luckily, they were able to eat at mid-day because one of the hunters had killed a deer. A second stroke of luck came toward evening, when the group arrived at a large encampment of friendly Indians. They hugged the men, smoked with them, and shared their food—serviceberries and chokecherries dried and pounded into small cakes. These were the Salish, mistakenly called Flatheads by Lewis and Clark.[23]

For centuries, the Salish proper and their close neighbors, the Pend d'Oreille, had dwelled in western Montana, particularly the region near Flathead Lake (south of Kalispell). They traded with the Okanagan and Spokane tribes to the west, but the powerful Blackfoot nation to the east was an enemy, particularly feared because their people had bartered for guns with traders from Hudson's Bay Company, obtaining firearms before the Salish did. Salish hunters made bows from the hard wood of the pacific yew tree and pursued buffalo on the east side of the Continental Divide and deer and elk closer to home, always taking care not to waste anything or to kill game wantonly.

Bitterroot plants and camas roots were also important sources of food. Early in the year, the people gathered to thank the Creator for the bitterroot and for life itself. The tribe used a variety of traps, tools, and hooks and lines for fishing, drying some of the catch to save for the winter—along with buffalo meat, roots, and berries. Pine nuts, elderberries, and red osier dogwood berries were all gathered, but serviceberries and chokecherries were most important. The Salish harvested chokecherries in late summer and early fall, pounding them with a stone mortar and pestle before forming them into the small cakes they had offered the Corps of Discovery.[24]

The meeting between the so-called Flathead nation and Lewis and Clark is vividly depicted in Salish oral tradition. Francois Saxa, the son of an Iroquois trapper and Salish mother, who was born about fifteen years after the captain's arrival, gave this account:

> The Flathead [Salish] Indians were camping . . . at the head of the Bitterroot valley, when one day the old chief, Three Eagles . . . left the camp to go scouting the country, fearing there might be some Indian enemies around with the intent to steal horses, as it was done very frequently. He saw at a distance Lewis and Clark's party, about twenty men, each man leading two pack horses, except two, who were riding ahead, who were Lewis and Clark. The old chief, seeing that these men wore no blankets, did not know what to think about them. It was the first time he had met men without blankets. What kind of beings could they be? The first thought was that they were a party of men who, traveling, had been robbed by some Indians of their blankets. He went back to his people and, reporting gave orders that all the horses should be driven in and watched, for fear the party he had seen might be on a stealing expedition. He then went back toward the party of strange beings, and, hiding himself in the timber, watched them.[25]

From the casual way the group traveled, Three Eagles concluded they were not hostile, even though one of them had apparently chosen to paint himself with black war paint. (This, of course, was York, William Clark's slave, but the Indians misunderstood because they had never seen an African American before.) When Lewis and Clark approached the Salish camp in a friendly way, there was universal shaking of hands. The Indians then presented the group with buffalo hides and robes. Both sides were delighted when they found that although neither liked the other's tobacco (a plant called Kinnickinnick in the case of the Salish), mixing the two worked fine. "All went on friendly," Salish tradition reports, "and after three days [Lewis and Clark's party] started off, directed to Lolo fork's trail by the Indians, as the best way to go to the Nez Perces' country."[26]

Clark's retelling echoed the Salish oral tradition. He noted that he traveled at the head of the group during the day and that the Indians "recvd us friendly, threw white robes over our Shoulders & Smoked in the pipes of peace, we Encamped with them & found them friendly." Clark added that he "was the first white man who ever wer on the waters of this river."[27] At the same time, the Salish explained that they had seen white traders on a river that was "6 days march" to the north. Remote contact with Europeans was also evident from the herd of four or five hundred "well looking horses" feeding in the valley.[28] The Salish had probably traded for the horses with the Shoshone, who had obtained them from the Commanche or Ute nations, with the trading genealogy going right back to the Spaniards. Tragically, another reality could also be traced to remote contact with whites: smallpox.

While archaeological evidence suggests that smallpox plagues may have struck the Salishan nation as early as the 1500s, originating with the conquistadors in Mexico and spreading from one native tribe to another, the disease definitely afflicted the Salish multiple times in the eighteenth and nineteenth centuries. In the quarter-century before Lewis and Clark, at least half and possibly two-thirds of the tribe perished from smallpox and other European diseases.[29] Smallpox, with its symptoms of high fever, severe headache, delirium, vomiting, diarrhea, and a rash that turned to pus-filled lesions, targeted children and young adults in particular and spread from one family member to another. In the years following Lewis and Clark, tribes all along the explorers' trail and beyond would suffer the same kind of heartbreak from smallpox.

"These natives have the Stranges language as any we have ever yet Seen," wrote Ordway. "They appear to us as though they had an Impediment in their Speech or brogue on their tongue. We think perhaps that they are the welch Indians."[30] While Ordway was mistaken about the Salish being the mythical Welsh Indians, a legend so prominent that Lewis and Clark took it seriously, his comments about the Salish language were quite perceptive. Salish is so unique that it forms its own group and cannot definitely be said to have descended from any other Indian language (nor can the exact relationships among the various Salish dialects be determined).[31] "Salish contains both unglottalized and glottalized versions of many sounds or letters. . . . These differences may sound subtle to an English speaker, but they make for complete differences in meaning in Salish words." As a result of this complexity, thirty-nine symbols are required for the Salish alphabet.[32]

Since the Shoshone were close and friendly neighbors of the Salish, the captains may have hoped that Sacagawea, a native Shoshone, would be able to communicate with these "Welsh" Indians. It quickly became evident, however that Shoshone and Salish were mutually unintelligible, so Colter and his companions witnessed a fascinating translation chain: the captains spoke English, which was translated into French by a French speaker in the Corps (probably Labiche); Toussaint Charbonneau then rendered the message in Hidatsa, and Sacagawea rendered it in her native language to a Shoshone boy living among the Salish, the final link in the chain, who offered the Salish interpretation. "With much difficulty," said Clark, "we informed them who we were, where we Came from, where bound and for what purpose &c. &c. and requsted to purchase & exchange a fiew horses with them."[33] The Salish possessed ellegant horses, and Clark purchased eleven that day and two more the next. The Salish women brought roots and berries for Lewis and Clark's party to eat. According to Salish oral tradition, the whites "didn't know that camas roots are good to eat."[34]

Two days after Lewis and Clark met the Salish, "all the Indians Set out on Ther way to meet the Snake Indians at the 3 forks of the Missouri."[35] The Salish were headed east, across the Continental Divide, to hunt buffalo with their Shoshone allies. The Corps proceeded on, following the Bitterroot River north for another three days until they reached a large creek flowing in from the west—they called it Travelers' Rest Creek (it is now known as Lolo Creek). Here they rested and prepared for their journey across the mountains to the west.

Tuesday, September 10, was fair and warm, wrote Ordway, and "all the best hunters turned out to hunt."[36] Colter followed Lolo Creek upstream and was hunting alone when he met three Salish warriors from a different village. "On first meeting him," Lewis wrote, "the Indians were allarmed and prepared for battle with the bows and arrows, but he soon relieved their fears by laying down his gun and advancing toward them."[37] Ordway explained that after the Indians signed to Colter to lay down his gun, he did so. "They then came to him [in] a friendly manner. He Signed to them to come with him and they took him on behind one of them and rode down to Camp."[38] Colter had clearly learned Indian sign language and Indian diplomacy, skills that would serve him well in the coming years. Burton Harris wrote that "Colter's impromptu diplomacy secured for the party a competent guide at a time when the scarcity of game and rapidly approaching winter made it imperative that they descend from the mountains."[39]

Lewis explained that the Indians were "mounted on very fine horses of which the Flatheads have great abundance; that is, each man in the nation possesses from 20 to a hundred head." Old Toby engaged the Salish in sign language and discovered that they were pursuing two thieves of the Shoshone nation who had stolen twenty-three horses from them. One of the Salish men informed Lewis and Clark that his relations "were numerous and resided in the plain below the mountains on the Columbia river, from when he said the water was good and capable of being navigated to the sea; that some of his relation were at the sea last fall and saw an old whiteman who . . . resided there by himself and who had given them some handkerchiefs such as he saw in our possession. He said it would require five sleeps wich is six days travel, to reach his relations."[40]

Two days later, the Corps headed west, back into the wilderness of present Idaho, the state that tested them to the limit. Patrick Gass, at first describing the mountains as "large" and "very steep," soon noted that they "made the travelling very fatiguing and uncomfortable," concluding that they were "the most terrible mountains I ever beheld."[41]

Chapter Six

"Colter Expressed a Desire to Join Some Trappers"

The Partnership with Dickson and Hancock

"The morning proved fair," Lewis wrote on Saturday, August 2, 1806, "and I determined to remain all day and dry the baggage and give the men an opportunity to dry and air their skins and furr. Had the powder parched meal and every article which wanted drying exposed to the sun. . . . We are all extreemly anxious to reach the entrance of the Yellowstone river where we expect to join Capt. Clark and party."[1]

The Corps of Discovery had made their way across the terrible Bitterroot Mountains; they had followed the Snake River to the Columbia and the Columbia to the Pacific. They had wintered at Fort Clatsop among friendly Indians, growing so tired of eating salmon that they began consuming dog. As one month faded into another, the expedition journalists took Colter's hunting and scouting duties for granted, making little special note of him.

Now, more than four months into the return journey, Lewis's group was following the Missouri River through northeastern Montana, near the present site of Fort Peck Reservoir. Clark's party, not seen for a month, was a hundred miles to the east, on the Yellowstone River, and had just crossed into North Dakota. In an effort to explore Montana, the corps had split into five groups, in hindsight taking unwise and unnecessary risks.[2] Luckily, they had all survived, although Lewis and three others had barely escaped from hostile Blackfoot Indians after killing two of them.[3]

On August 3, Colter and Collins took a canoe and set out early to hunt, apparently with the understanding that they would rejoin the party later that day. Lewis and the others passed the canoe later that morning, calling out for

47

Colter and Collins but hearing no reply. Shortly after that, Lewis overtook the Field brothers, who had killed twenty-five deer since leaving the previous day. The deerskins were particularly appreciated because they could be used for both clothing and shelter. (The men's clothes were now threadbare and their tents had disintegrated some time back.) Lewis also noted the delightful variety of wildlife: buffalo, "a great number of Elk, deer, wolves, some bear, beaver, geese a few ducks, the party coloured covus [black-billed magpie], one Callamet Eagle [golden eagle], a number of bald Eagles, red headed woodpeckers &c." It was a good travel day, and the group made an estimated seventy-three miles. Concluding his journal entry, Lewis noted that "Collins and Colter did not overtake us this evening."[4]

By Tuesday, August 5, Lewis was getting concerned about Colter and Collins. That morning he delayed, hoping the two would arrive. At noon, with no sign of them, Lewis decided the two hunters must be ahead of the group, thinking "they had passed us after dark the night of the 3rd." Finally on their way, Lewis's men traveled until late in the evening, when they camped on a high sandy beach. But their hope for a peaceful rest was thwarted by a furious thunderstorm. Lewis wrote that hail mixed with the rain, which "fell in a mere torrant and the wind blew so violently that it was with difficulty I could have the small canoes unloaded before they filled with water."[5] As if wind and hail and rain were not enough, "the Sand flew So that we could Scarsely See & cut our faces by the force of the wind," recorded Ordway.[6] Describing conditions that were all too common on the expedition, Lewis added that "our situation was open and exposed to the storm. In attending to the canoes I got wet to the skin and having no shelter on land I betook myself to the orning [awning?] of the perogue which I had, formed of Elkskin, here I obtained a few hours of broken rest; the wind and rain continued almost all night and the air became very cold."[7] Colter and Collins likely faced the same kind of night.

The corps had traveled this same stretch of river before, in May of 1805, and Lewis knew he was getting close to the Yellowstone, where he expected to meet Clark. Despite rain, strong winds, and "cold and extreemly unpleasant" air, the men pushed on. "The currant favoured our progress being more rapid than yesterday," Lewis wrote on Thursday, August 7, "the men played their oars faithfully and we went a good rate."[8] At 4:00 in the afternoon, after crossing into present North Dakota, they reached the Yellowstone River, which flowed in from the south.[9] Lewis was disappointed not to find Clark, but Clark's party had left notes. From these, Lewis learned that Clark had moved on because of the scarcity of game and the "troublesome" mosquitoes. Still thinking of Colter and Collins, Lewis wrote a message to them, "provided they were behind, ordering them to come on without loss of time; this note I wraped in leather and attatced onto the same pole which Capt. C.

had planted at the point; this being done I instantly reimbarked and decended the river in the hope of reaching Capt. C's camp before night."[10]

Lewis did not catch Clark that night. He did, however, pass someone's recent camp, with fresh tracks and a fire that was "blaizing and appeared to have been mended up afresh or within the course of an hour past." Lewis concluded that "Capt. C's camp could not be distant."[11] But Clark was actually farther ahead than Lewis thought. He had left the note for Lewis three days earlier. The most recent visitors to this camp had probably been Pryor, Hall, Shannon, and Windsor, who were trying to catch Clark themselves (and did so the next day).[12] Lewis had barely missed them.

Lewis tried again the next morning but still could not catch Clark. "I knew not what calculation to make with rispect to [Clark's] halting and therefore determined to proceed as tho' he was not before me and leave the rest to the chapter of accidents," wrote Lewis. "The men with me have not had leasure since we left the West side of the Rocky mountains to dress any skins or make themselves cloaths and most of them are therefore extreemly bare. . . . We found the Musquetoes extreemly troublesome."[13]

They next day, Saturday, August 8, the men continued dressing skins and making clothes—except for the Field brothers, whom Lewis sent out to hunt and look for Clark. "All hands employed makeing themselves comfortable," wrote Orday.[14] When Joseph and Reubin Field returned, they reported seeing no sign of either game or Clark's party. By the end of the day, Lewis's concern for the two missing men had taken a turn: "Colter and Collins have not yet overtaken us[.] I fear some missfortune has happened them for their previous fidelity and orderly deportment induces me to believe that they would not thus intentionally delay."[15] While confident that Colter and Collins could get by quite nicely under "normal" circumstances, Lewis was possibly worried that they had suffered a boating accident or had been attacked by Indians. Trying to help them was hardly possible because he had not seen them for six days and wasn't really sure whether they were upstream or downstream. He had to wait and hope.

Two days later, on Monday, August 11, after another miserable night of being pestered by mosquitoes, Lewis was out hunting elk with Cruzatte. As Lewis so vividly recorded:

> I was in the act of firing on the Elk a second time when a ball struck my left thye about an inch below my hip joint, missing the bone it passed through the left thye and cut the thickness of the bullet across the hinder part of the right thye; the stroke was very severe; I instantly supposed the Cruzattea had shot me in mistake for an Elk as I was dressed in brown leather and he cannot see well under this impression I called out to him damn you, you have shot me, and looked towards the place from whence the ball had come, seeing nothing I called Cruzatte several times as loud as I could but received no answer; I was now preswaded that it was an indian that had shot me as the report of the gun

did not appear to be more than 40 paces from me and Cruzatte appeared to be out of hearing of me; in this situation not knowing how many indians there might be concealed in the bushes I thought best to make good my retreat to the perogue, calling out as I ran for the first hundred paces as loud as I could to Cruzatte to retreat that there were indians hoping to allarm him in time to make his escape also; I still retained the charge in my gun which I was about to discharge at the moment the ball struck me. When I arrived in sight of the perogue I called the men to their arms to which they flew in an instant, I told them that I was wounded but I hoped not mortally, by an indian I believed and directed them to follow me that I would return & give them battle and releive Cruzatte if possible who I feared had fallen into their hands; the men followed me as they were bid and I returned about a hundred paces when my wounds became so painfull and my thye so stiff that I could scarcely get on; in short I was compelled to half and ordered the men to proceed and if they found themselves overpowered by numbers to retreat in order keeping up a fire. I now got back to the perogue as well as I could and prepared my self with a pistol my rifle and air-gun being determined as a retreat was impracticable to sell my life as deerly as possible. [16]

Lewis's concern for his men and his coolness under pressure reveal much about the man. As Lewis prepared for a fight, Gass and three others explored the area. They found no Indians, only Cruzatte, concluding that he had indeed shot Lewis, something Cruzatte himself acknowledged, although, by his account, he hadn't realized it at the time. (Lewis thought otherwise: "I do not believe that the fellow did it intentionally but after finding that he had shot me was anxious to conceal his knowledge of having done so.") On his return, Gass informed Lewis of his findings and then helped Lewis dress the wound, which they did by "introducing tents of patent lint into the ball holes." The wound bled considerably, but Lewis was happy to find that the bullet "had touched neither bone nor artery." [17] Had it done so, Lewis well might have been doomed. Even so, his wound was quite painful, and a high fever kept him awake most of the night. [18] There was still no sign of Colter or Collins.

Still determined to overtake Clark, the undaunted Lewis set off early the next morning in "good spirits," essentially ignoring a wound that was "stiff and sore." [19] "At 8 A. M.," Lewis wrote (still keeping his journal despite his discomfort), "the bowsman informed me that there was a canoe and a camp he believed of whitemen on the N. E. shore. I directed the perogue and canoes to come too at this place and found it to be the camp of two hunters from the Illinois by name of Joseph Dickson and Forrest Hancock." [20] Although none of the diarists mentioned it, the meeting with these two trappers was especially significant: These were the first Europeans the corps had seen in sixteen months (since April of 1805). Ordway noted that Dickson and Hancock "have gathered a great deal of peltry Since they have been out about 2 years and have carshed [cached] most of it in the ground[.] They tells us that they are determined to Stay up this river and go to the head where the beaver is pleanty and trap and hunt until they make a fortune before they return."[21] Lewis's report was not as optimistic—he wrote that Dickson and Hancock had been robbed by the Indians, that Dickson had been wounded by the Lakota Sioux, and that the two had "as yet caught but little beaver."[22]

Whether by serendipity or mere coincidence, Colter and Collins came downstream in their canoe at the very time Lewis and his men were talking with Dickson and Hancock. Absent for a week and a half, Colter and Collins—no doubt surprised to find Lewis wounded and doubly surprised to find Dickson and Hancock present—told Lewis they were fine and had not experienced any misfortune. Rather, after their first day of hunting, they had concluded that Lewis's party was still behind them. They had delayed for several days, waiting for Lewis, until finally deciding he was actually downstream. After that, they had apparently made good time. They had not lacked for food—Ordway noted that they had killed six buffalo, thirteen deer, five elk, and, perhaps most notably in the view of Dickson and Hancock, thirty-one beaver.[23]

Whether Colter talked with Dickson and Hancock at this point is unknown. Nor did any of the journal keepers indicate that Colter knew either or both of the men (as some historians have speculated). After Colter and Collins arrived, however, Dickson and Hancock had a change of heart. Although they had met Clark the previous day, Clark had made no mention of them wanting to join him. Instead, he reported that they were on their way to trap the Yellowstone River. After talking to them, he proceeded down river while Dickson and Hancock remained in their camp. Even in their initial discussion with Lewis, they gave every indication of continuing westward, for Lewis had given them detailed information on the Missouri River and locations where "beaver most abounded." He had also given them "a file and a couple of pounds of powder with some lead," articles "which they assured me they were in great want of."[24] Now, however, the two hunters decided to join Lewis and head back east. "Mr. Dixon concludes to go back to the Mandans in hopes to git a frenchman or Some body to go with him to the head of the river," wrote Ordway.[25]

Dickson and Hancock were thus present early that afternoon when Lewis finally caught up with Clark. "At meridian Capt Lewis hove in Sight," Clark wrote.[26] "And now, (thanks to God)," Gass aptly summed up, "we are all together again in good health, except Captain Lewis, and his wound is not serious."[27] Had any single day of the expedition been more memorable than this one?

Born in 1775 in Pennsylvania, Joseph Dickson had married in 1798, migrating first to Tennessee and then, in 1802, to Cahokia, Illinois, just south of St. Louis, on the opposite side of the Mississippi River. According to family tradition, Dickson traveled up the Missouri River late in 1802 and spent the winter felling trees for hire and trapping. By 1804, he had met Forrest Hancock, and the two of them formed a partnership. They agreed to ascend the Missouri River and trap together for two years. They left in August of 1804, three months after Lewis and Clark and almost three years before Manuel Lisa launched his first fur-trading expedition.[28]

Few men were born with a more fitting pedigree for exploring and trapping than Forrest Hancock.[29] Born in 1774 in Virginia, Forrest was the son of William Hancock (1739–1818), who was among the thirty men taken prisoner with Daniel Boone in January of 1778. Boone had led the men from Fort Boonesborough to a salt-making camp on the Licking River, and they were captured by Shawnee Indians and taken into the Ohio country, to a village on the Miami River the Americans called Chillicothe. (As John Mack Faragher points out, "Chillicothe was considerably larger and more impressive than any of the settlements Americans had planted in Kentucky.")[30] Convinced by Boone that he and his men would eventually lead the Shawnee back to Boonsborough and surrender the fort peacefully, the Shawnee did not harm the men—quite the opposite, some Shawnee adopted the Kentuckians into their families. Boone became the son of Chief Blackfish, and Hancock the son of "Captain" Will Emery (replacing a son of his who had died).[31]

After living among the Shawnee for four months, and becoming genuinely fond of his Shawnee family, Daniel Boone escaped, made his famous "run" back to Fort Boonesborough, and warned the residents of an impending attack. A month later, in July of 1779, after hearing a rumor that the British had supplied the Shawnee with artillery and guns "to batter down our fort," Hancock escaped and made a run of his own, one that would be echoed in Colter's harrowing adventure. Captain Will had discouraged escape by demanding Hancock's clothes each night and by sleeping near the cabin door, but one night when Captain Will returned home groggy with rum, Hancock slipped by his adopted father, managing to take three pints of corn—but not his clothes. He ran virtually nonstop, reaching the Ohio River on the second day. Plunging into the Ohio, he clung to a piece of driftwood and let the strong current carry him twenty miles or so downstream, where he landed on the Kentucky side but in territory he didn't recognize.

He strayed through the Kentucky wilderness for seven days, soon consuming the little corn he had left and finally collapsing of total exhaustion, "neaver to arise," he was convinced. When he awoke, he was astonished to see the name "Hancock" carved on a nearby tree and realized he and his father and brother had stalked game at this very spot less than a year earlier. He now had his bearings and struggled through the woods to the Kentucky River, which led to Boonsborough, only four miles distant.[32] After some settlers found Hancock near the river, Boone and others nursed him back to health and readied themselves for the assault on the fort. They successfully defended the fort from a ten-day siege—led by Boone's "father," Black-fish—in September of 1779.

Five-year-old Forrest Hancock had been present for both his father's return and the attack on the fort. His mother had reportedly kept a long iron panhandle as a weapon, sleeping with it during the siege.[33] Forrest continued the family association with Daniel Boone, marrying Boone's granddaughter Emily around 1795 and migrating from Kentucky to Missouri with Boone's party in 1799, with Boone leaving Kentucky, at least according to legend, "because he found a population of ten to the square mile, inconveniently crowded."[34] Boone and his followers stopped at a secluded spot along the Missouri River, soon called Boone's Settlement, and Forrest Hancock was possibly present when the Corps of Discovery came up the river in May of 1804.[35]

Peter Cartwright, a preacher who apparently met Joseph Dickson in 1824 or 1825 (but did not publish his account until 1857), wrote that after Dickson and Hancock ascended the Missouri for hundreds of miles and escaped "many dangerous ambuscades of the Indians, winter came on with great severity. They dug in the ground and buried their furs and skins at different points, to keep them from being stolen by the Indians. They then dug a deep hole on the sunny side of a hill, gathered their winter meat and fuel, and took up their winter quarters. The snows were very deep, the weather intensely cold; but they wintered in comparative safety till returning spring, which they hailed with transports of joy. They were robbed several times by the Indians, had several battles with them, and killed two or three of them."[36]

William Clark, by contrast, recorded his conversation with Dickson and Hancock the very day it took place. His notes supplied key information not mentioned by other expedition journalists. "The last winter they Spent with the Tetons in Company with a Mr. *Coartong* who brought up goods to trade," he wrote. "The tetons robed him of the greater part of the goods and wounded this Dixon in the leg with a hard wad. The Tetons gave Mr. *Coartong* Some fiew robes for the articles they took from him. Those men further informed me that they met the Boat and party we Sent down from Fort Mandan near the Kanzas river on board of which was a Chief of the Ricaras."[37]

In these brief lines, Clark made it clear that Dickson and Hancock had been near the Missouri/Kansas border (near the Kansas River) late in the spring of 1805 when Corporal Warfington's party came down the river from Fort Mandan[38] that they had spent the winter of 1805–1806 in South Dakota, near the Lakota Sioux and had experienced a conflict with that nation; and that they had worked with a man named Coartong. This was most likely a rather mysterious trader actually named Charles *Courtin*, who appears more than once in both the history of Lewis and Clark and the history of Dickson and Hancock. Courtin, a French Canadian who became an American, had labored in the fur trade in the Great Lakes region prior to 1806 and had occasionally traveled from the north to the upper Mississippi and upper Missouri.[39]

In September of 1804, just a few months into the expedition, Clark noted that when Shannon had been lost, he "lived on grapes waiting for Mr. [Clintens?] boat Supposeing we had went on,"[40] possibly a reference to Courtin. Lewis and Clark were just entering Lakota Sioux country at the time, where Courtin would meet Dickson and Hancock a year later. Courtin seems to have traded with the Poncas, the Lakota Sioux, and the Arikaras, moving back and forth from western Missouri to the northern section of South Dakota. Lewis and Clark would see him again, and so would Dickson and Hancock.

John Colter had met Dickson and Hancock on August 12, 1806. After a cold night—cold enough to keep the mosquitoes at bay—the party made eighty-six miles the next day. The day after that, they arrived at the Indian villages near the Knife River (near present Stanton, North Dakota), which Clark estimated was 1,606 miles from the Mississippi River. "About 9 A.M. we arived at our old neighbours the Grousevauntaus [Hidatsa] and Mandans," wrote Ordway. "We Saluted them by firing our Swivvel and blunderbusses a number of times[.] They answered us with a blunderbuss and Small arms and were verry glad to See us."[41]

No one left a record of any conversations between Colter and Dickson and Hancock, but they must have had a detailed and fascinating dialogue because on Sunday, August 17, Ordway wrote that "John Colter one of the party asks leave of our officers to go back with Mr. Dixon a trapping, which permission was granted him So our officers Settled with him and fitted him out with Powder lead and a great number of articles which compleated him for a trapping voiage of two years which they are determined to Stay untill they make a fortune."[42] Colter, who had shown a particular interest in trapping beaver during the expedition, was ready to try his hand as a professional.

Colter had not seen civilization for twenty-seven months, Dickson and Hancock for twenty-four; now the three of them were agreeing—apparently with relish—to spend a similar period of time in the wild. They knew that beaver were plentiful and that beaver pelts (called "plews" and usually weighing one to two pounds) could be sold for four or five dollars apiece in St. Louis. They also had the equipment and skill to trap beaver, and that was enough. Surprisingly, Dickson and Hancock were both married with young children, but that did not deter them. Even Colter, whose marital status is unknown, had a young son waiting for him.[43] Early that Sunday morning, with Colter's compatriots wishing him "every Suckcess,"[44] the three business partners climbed in a small canoe, stroked deep with their paddles, and headed upstream on the Missouri. Perhaps Lewis and Clark's men watched as the image of that canoe grew smaller and smaller until it was a dot on the horizon, then just a speck, then nothing at all. Perhaps, still staring upstream, they wondered if and when they would ever see Colter again. As it turned out, several of them would see him in less than a year—not in St. Louis but near present Omaha, Nebraska. William Clark, who never went west of Missouri after the expedition, would see Colter again in four years; Meriwether Lewis would never see him again.

Editing the journals just a few years after the expedition, Nicholas Biddle added this oft-quoted (and sometimes criticized) commentary on Colter's decision to join Dickson and Hancock:

> The example of this man shows how easily men may be weaned from the habits of civilized life to the ruder but scarcely less fascinating manners of the woods. This hunter has now been absent for many years from the frontiers, and might naturally be presumed to have some anxiety, or some curiosity at least, to return to his friends and his country; yet, just at the moment when he is approaching the frontiers, he is tempted by a hunting scheme to give up those delightful prospects, and go back without the least reluctance to the solitude of the woods. [45]

Although Colter was ostensibly traveling the same country he had just returned from, in some ways that country had changed radically and permanently, for he was no longer a soldier in the corps but a fur trapper and trader, now vulnerable to a multitude of new risks and entanglements. Under Lewis and Clark, for example, he had never had to flee or fight Indians—that would change quickly. And while the captains had fine-tuned their band into an effective and well-disciplined military contingent, some of Colter's future companions would prove undisciplined and even mutinous, making encounters with Indians that much more dangerous.

Then there were matters of law. "The trio [of Colter, Dickson, and Hancock] were the precursors of the fabled mountain men of our folklore," writes David Lavender. "(Colter, indeed, would soon create a large share of that lore.) They were also outlaws. The government trading licenses, which every white fur-gatherer was supposed to obtain before venturing onto Indian lands, gave permission to barter only. The privilege did not include the right to hunt or trap, pursuits prohibited by an act of 1802." [46]

Colter and Dickson and Hancock were presumably unaware of such legalities (although Lewis and Clark were probably well aware of them). Nor could they be expected to comprehend the complex economic and political realities surrounding trapping ventures to the upper Missouri. To the north were the British, still smarting from the Crown's defeat in the American Revolution two and a half decades earlier and doing everything possible to establish alliances with key Indian tribes and undermine American trading efforts. But the Canadians were hardly freelancers like Colter, Dickson, and

Hancock. They were employees of big companies. Founded in 1670, *Compangnie de la Baie d'Hudson*, Hudson's Bay Company, yielded enormous power, combining business and imperial motives in its quest for beaver pelts. The North West Company was a relative newcomer (founded in 1784) but was quick to spot talent and had hired the likes of Simon Fraser, Alexander Mackenzie, and David Thompson, offering stiff competition to Hudson's Bay.[47] On the American side, Manuel Lisa and John Jacob Astor would attempt to hold their own against the British mammoths, and the resulting battles would involve global shipping, international power struggles, complicated regulations and tariffs, trade with both Europe and China, and the rippling effect of the Napoleonic wars.

With so much pressure to produce more and more beaver plews, and with the western border of Canada and the United States still in dispute, the larger power struggles inevitably reverberated in North Dakota and Montana, where Colter would do virtually all of his trapping. Relations among Indian nations were just as complex as those among East and West, and incursions by both British and American trappers upset the balance of power. Some Indian nations welcomed trappers, hoping to obtain goods—especially guns—that could benefit their people and assist them in defending themselves against enemy tribes. Those unfriendly nations naturally considered anyone arming their enemies to be enemies themselves—and they responded by waging war. The prime example was the Blackfoot nation, who saw white traders not only as invaders but also as gun dealers who enabled such enemy tribes as the Flathead to the west and the Crow to the south to attack the Blackfoot people. The upshot was that an area rich in beaver was closed off by a "Blackfoot wall."[48] During that same period, conflicts between the Americans and the British, illustrated in part by fur-trading intrigue, continued to mount. Colter and his two associates thus led a surge of mountain men who unwittingly made up an important square in the checkerboard of intricate events leading to the War of 1812.

The fur trade was also a harbinger of the displacement of American Indians. The passion of Colter, Dickson, and Hancock to push west—and the conviction that they were entitled to go, even compelled to go—was a concrete and personal expression of a spirit that would later be abstracted as something called "Manifest Destiny." The European Americans would see it as their God-given duty and right to go west, continually west, but that drive would lead to tragedy for the Indians.[49]

While the Lewis and Clark Expedition abounds with first-person accounts, the opposite is true for the "Colter, Dickson, and Hancock Expedition." If any of them wrote a single word about their experiences together, it has not survived. What we know comes from secondhand sources of varying reliability, while some of what is thought to be known actually originates with rumor and speculation. Separating the wheat from the chaff is not always easy.

Virtually all historians have presumed, for instance, that the threesome headed up the Yellowstone River rather than the Missouri, but this cannot be proven. Sometimes the rationale is even used that Colter knew the Yellowstone from traveling it with Clark, but that, of course is mistaken, for Colter was with Ordway on the Missouri and never saw anything but the mouth of the Yellowstone during the expedition.[50] Still, the trio likely learned from Clark that the Yellowstone was "large and navigable with but fiew obstructions" and that its streams "furnish an abundance of beaver and Otter and possess considerable portions of small timber in their vallies,"[51] all valid reasons to stay to the left when they reached the confluence of the two waterways. Not only that, but Colter also knew—and had heard a firsthand account—of Lewis's troubles with the Blackfoot Indians in the north. He also presumably knew that the Crow Indians in the south were considered friendly, despite their "capture" of Pryor's horses. All of this makes the case for the Yellowstone reasonable if not certain.

According to Dickson's friend Cartwright, "the next fall [meaning the fall of 1806] his [Dickson's] partners fell out with him, bought a canoe of the Indians, left him alone, descended the river, dug up their furs, and returned home."[52] If accurate, this means that the threesome of Colter, Dickson, and Hancock were not together for long—probably two or three months at most. Colter and Hancock certainly did not return home, but they could have returned to the Hidatsa and Mandan villages and spent the winter of 1806–1807 there. Cartwright is the only one to mention the falling out, so we know no other details. (While Cartwright's version places no blame on Colter and Hancock, some subsequent—and purely speculative—retellings have treated them harshly for their supposed abandonment of Dickson.)

Cartwright goes on to vividly depict Dickson's solitary winter:

> Dixon fortunately secured most of the ammunition they had on hand. He again found a dreaded winter approaching. He resorted to the former winter's experiment, and dug his cave in the side of a steep hill, laid up his winter provisions, and took up his winter quarters all alone. In this perilous condition, his eyes became inflamed, and were very much affected from constant gazing on the almost perpetual snows around him, until, such was their diseased state, he could not see anything. Here he was utterly helpless and hopeless. He began to reflect on his dreadful condition, while he felt nothing but certain death, and realized himself to be great sinner and unprepared to die. For the first time in his life, almost, he kneeled down and asked God for mercy and deliverance from this awful condition. Then and there he promised God if he would spare and deliver him, he would from that solemn moment serve him faithfully the rest of his life. . . . All of a sudden there was a strong impression made on his mind that if he would take the inside bark of a certain tree that stood a few steps from the mouth of his earthly habitation, and beat it up, soft and fine,

soak it in water, and wash his eyes with it, he would soon recover his sight. . . .
When he awoke his eyes felt easy; the inflammation was evidently subsiding,
and in a short time his sight began to return, and soon was entirely restored. . . .
He fell on his knees to return thanks to God; a sweet and heavenly peace ran
all through his soul, and he then and there, all alone, shouted aloud the high
praises of God. [53]

Dickson family tradition, as well as Joseph Dickson's documented activities as a religious man, lend credibility to Cartwright's narrative. [54] It's also interesting that Dickson's frightening ordeal with snow blindness prefigured a similar episode (although lacking the religious overtones) that a group of trappers—including Colter and Hancock—would experience three years later, possibly in the same area of southern Montana.

These crucial facts remain, however: Cartwright's account is not only late and second hand, it offers no specific dates for the events it describes and no specific names (other than Dickson's) for the people it discusses. Moreover, neither Cartwright's narrative, nor any other, can definitively answer the question of what really happened between August of 1806–when Colter, Dickson, and Hancock were seen heading up the Missouri together—and June of 1807—when the three were seen going separately down the Missouri.

Still, the question cries out for some kind of answer.

William Clark drew up this list of expedition members in March of 1807. As shown, Colter was one of nine men who enlisted in 1803. Courtesy of the Beinecke Rare Book and Manuscript Library, Yale University

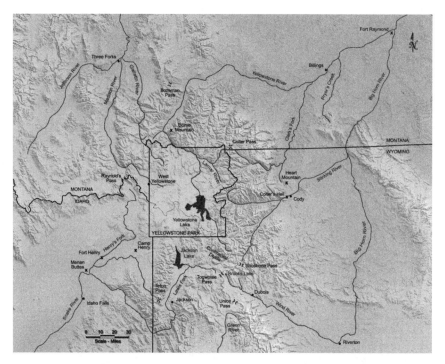

From the fall of 1806 to the spring of 1810, Colter spent the great majority of his time in this area, likely entering present Yellowstone National Park at least six times. Map by Clint Gilchrist

Merriweather Lewis. Lewis died in Tennessee of self-inflicted gunshots just a few weeks after Colter met Thomas James, Dr. Thomas, and others at Indian villages in present North Dakota. Meriwether Lewis by Charles Willson Peale, from life, 1807. Courtesy, Independence National Historical Park

William Clark. Clark and Colter stayed in touch after the expedition and saw each other less than three months before Colter's death. William Clark by Charles Willson Peale, from life, 1807-1808. Courtesy, Independence National Historical Park

William Clark's master map of 1810. The original was a little more than four feet wide and two feet high. Clark biographer Landon Jones called the map "a cartographic masterpiece, a remarkably accurate rendering of the inner continent of North America." Courtesy of the Beinecke Rare Book and Manuscript Library, Yale University

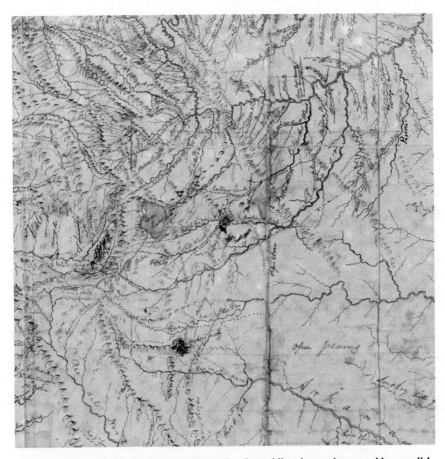

This section of Clark's 1810 map shows the dotted line (superimposed by a solid line added by the authors) that Clark identified as "Colters rout," a notation that has become the subject of intense debate among Colter scholars. Courtesy of the Beinecke Rare Book and Manuscript Library, Yale University

Thomas James wrote that Colter "ran with all the strength that nature, excited to the utmost, could give; fear and hope lent a supernatural vigor to his limbs and the rapidity of his flight astonished himself." Charles M. Russell (1864-1926), Colter's Race for Life, ca. 1922. Ink, opaque watercolor, and graphite on paper. Amon Carter Museum of American Art, Fort Worth, Texas

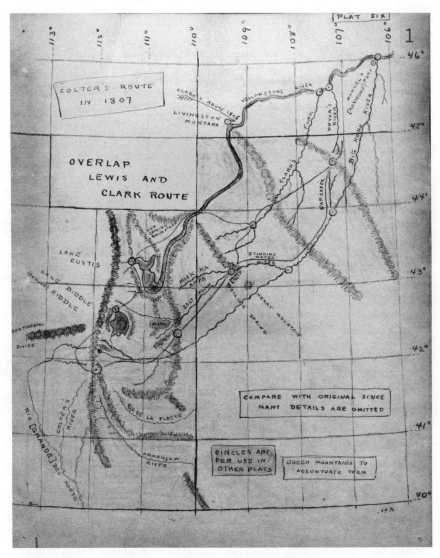

J. Neilson Barry's drawing of Colter's Route on the 1814 "Biddle map," circa 1943. Courtesy of the Library of Congress

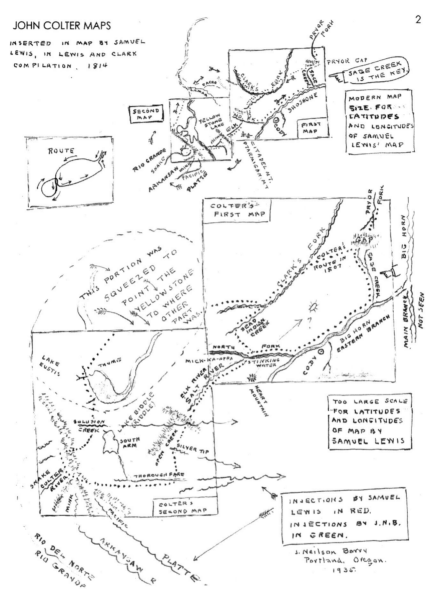

J. Neilson Barry's drawing of what he speculated were maps drawn by Colter and used by William Clark when producing his master map, circa 1935. Courtesy of Yellowstone National Park

Manuel Lisa. When Lisa and his men met Colter at the mouth of the Platte River in the summer of 1807, Lisa convinced Colter to head back up the Missouri with the trading party. Courtesy of the Missouri History Museum, St. Louis

Thomas James. James wrote of Colter: "He was about thirty-five years of age, five feet ten inches in height and wore an open, ingenious, and pleasing countenance of the Daniel Boone stamp." Courtesy of the Missouri History Museum, St. Louis

Construction site at Dundee, Missouri, 1926, where Colter's grave was supposedly destroyed, from Railway Age magazine, October 1, 1927. Courtesy of *Railway Age*

The construction site at Tunnel Hill as it appeared in the 1960s. Courtesy of the *Washington Missourian*

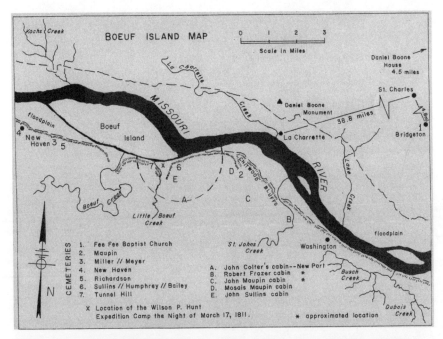

This map shows the path of the Missouri River around 1811, with possible locations for Colter's cabin and his burial site. Map drawn by Alex Dinatale, using information supplied by Ron Anglin

Col. Nathan Boone. Colter served under Nathan Boone, his friend and neighbor and son of Daniel Boone, in the War of 1812. Colonel Nathan Boone, 1781-1856. Research Division of the Oklahoma Historical Society

A Roll

Of the men who accompanied captains Lewis and Clarke on their late tour to the Pacific ocean, through the interior of the continent of North America, shewing their rank, with some remarks on their respective merits and services.

No.	NAMES.	RANK.	REMARKS.
1	John Ordnay,	Serjeant.	
2	Nathaniel Pryor,	ditto.	
3	Charles Floyd,	ditto.	Deceased the 20th of August, 1804; a young man of much merit. His father, who now resides in Kentucky, is a man much respected, though possessed of but moderate wealth. As the son has lost his life whilst on this service, I consider his father intitled to some gratuity, in consideration of his loss; and also, that the deceased being noticed in this way, will be a tribute but justly due to his merit.
4	Patrick Gass,	ditto.	Promoted to serjeant 20th of August, 1804, in the place of Charles Floyd, deceased; in which capacity he continued until discharged at St. Louis, November 10, 1806.
5	William Bratton,	Private.	
6	John Collins,	ditto.	
7	John Colter,	ditto.	
8	Pier Cruzatte,	ditto.	
9	Joseph Field,	ditto.	Two of the most active and enterprising young men who accompanied us. It was their peculiar fate to have been engaged in all the most dangerous and difficult scenes of the voyage, in which they uniformly acquitted themselves with much honor.
10	Reuben Field,	ditto.	
11	Robert Frazier,	ditto.	
12	Silas Goodrich,	ditto.	
13	George Gibson,	ditto.	
14	Thomas P. Howard,	ditto.	
15	Hugh Hall,	ditto.	
16	Francis Labuicke,	ditto.	He has received the pay only of a private, though besides the duties performed as such, he has rendered me very essential services as a French and English interpreter, and sometimes also as an Indian interpreter; therefore, I should think it only just that some small addition to his pay, as a private, should be added, though no such addition has at any time been promised by me.
17	Hugh M'Neal,	ditto.	
18	John Sheilds,	ditto.	Has received the pay only of a private. Nothing was more peculiarly useful to us in various situations, than the skill and ingenuity of this man as an artist, in repairing our guns, accoutrements, &c. And should it be thought proper to allow him something as an artificer, he has well deserved it.
19	George Shannon,	ditto.	
20	John Potts,	ditto.	
21	John Bapteist La Page,	ditto.	Entitled to no peculiar merit; was inlisted at Fort Mandan, on the 2d of November, 1804, in order to supply the deficiency in my permanent party, occasioned by the discharge of John Newman. He performed the tour to the Pacific ocean, and returned to St. Louis, where he was discharged, in common with others, on the 10th of November last. As he did not perform the labours incident to the summer of 1804, it would be proper to give him the gratuity only of two thirds as much as is given to others of his rank.
22	John B. Thompson,	ditto.	
23	William Werner,	ditto.	
24	Richard Windsor,	ditto.	
25	Peter Wiser,	ditto.	
26	Alexander Willard,	ditto.	
27	Joseph Whitehouse,	ditto.	
28	George Drulyard,	Interpreter.	A man of much merit; he has been peculiarly useful from his knowledge of the common language of gesticulation, and his uncommon skill as a hunter and woodsman; those several duties he performed in good faith, and with an ardor which deserves the highest commendation. It was his fate also to have encountered, on various occasions, with either captain Clarke or myself, all the most dangerous and trying scenes of the voyage, in which he uniformly acquitted himself with honor. He has served the complete term of the whole tour, and received only 25 dollars per month, and one ration per day, while I am informed that it is not unusual for individuals, in similar employments, to receive 30 dollars per month.
29	Touisant Charbono,	ditto.	A man of no peculiar merit; was useful as an interpreter only, in which capacity he discharged his duties with good faith from the moment of our departure from the Mandans, on the 7th of April, 1805, until our return to that place in August last, and received as a compensation 25 dollars per month, while in service.

GENERAL REMARK.

With respect to all those persons whose names are entered on this roll, I feel a peculiar pleasure in declaring, that the ample support which they gave me under every difficulty; the manly firmness which they evinced on every necessary occasion, and the patience and fortitude with which they submitted to and bore the fatigues and painful sufferings incident to my late tour to the Pacific ocean, intitles them to my warmest approbation and thanks; nor will I suppress the expression of a hope, that the recollection of services thus faithfully performed, will meet a just reward, in an ample remuneration on the part of our government.

MERIWETHER LEWIS, Capt.
1st U. S. regt. Infantry.

CITY OF WASHINGTON, January 15, 1807.

This list of the members of the Lewis and Clark Expedition, which was published in Washington, D.C., in 1807, is the first-known publication mentioning John Colter. Courtesy of the Beinecke Rare Book and Manuscript Library, Yale University

"Three Forks of the Missouri," A. E. Mathews, Pencil Sketches of Montana, 1868. Despite the danger, Colter returned to the prime trapping territory near Three Forks again and again. Courtesy of the Montana Historical Society, Helena

Chapter Seven

"Unruly Hands to Manage"

Up the Missouri with Lisa

On April 9, 1806, four months before Lewis and Clark's men met Dickson and Hancock, Secretary of War Henry Dearborn wrote to James Wilkinson (recently named governor of Upper Louisiana): "The Missouri and Mississippi Indian Chiefs, will leave this place [Washington] tomorrow for Pittsbugh, from whence they will descend the River & proceed on to St. Louis. Several have died; but what is more especially to be regretted is the death of the very respectable & amiable Ricara Chief, which happened on the 7th Instant."[1]

Lewis and Clark had met the Arikara chief, called *Ar-ke-tar-na-Shar* by Clark, in October of 1804 and had hired Joseph Gravelines to interpret for them. Gravelines was a French Canadian trader and interpreter who had lived for thirteen years among the Arikara, who dwelled along the Missouri River in the northern part of present South Dakota. In 1805, Gravelines had accompanied Arketarnashar to St. Louis and then Washington to meet Thomas Jefferson. Gravelines had apparently been Arketarnarshar's constant companion and had likely been with him when he died. Now he had been given the unenviable assignment of returning to the Arikara nation with gifts and also hand-delivering—and translating—a letter from Jefferson that informed the people of the death of their chief. "It gave me a great pleasure to see your beloved chief arrive here on a visit to his white brothers," Jefferson had written. "He found nothing but kindness & good will wherever he passed. On his return to this place he was taken sick; every thing we could do to help him was done; but it pleased the great Spirit to take him from among us. We buried him among our own deceased friends & relatives, we shed many tears over his grave, and we now mingle our afflictions with yours on the loss of this beloved chief. But death must happen to all men; and his time was come."[2]

Jefferson and Dearborn were clearly affected by the chief's death, and they were sincere in their expressions of sorrow, but the heavy burden had fallen on Gravelines alone, a longtime friend of the Arikara now thrown into an impossible situation, compelled to be the bearer of bad news and likely to be blamed for events he had been powerless to control. Still, he was determined to do the best he could. He would be escorted up the Missouri by a sergeant and four other soldiers and would return Arketarnarshar's medal, clothes, and other possessions to his favorite son. He would bring factory goods—Dearborn had authorized two or three hundred dollars' worth—to the chief's wives and children. He would also be furnished with "100 lbs. Of Powder and a corresponding quantity of Lead, to be distributed to the Chiefs of the Ricaras and Mandanes &c." Finally, Dearborn was sending "nine muskets for [Arketarnarshar's] sons, to be put into the hands of their uncles, for them as they become able to use them."[3] Gravelines thus headed west as Lewis and Clark—almost two thousand miles away—were on their way east.

Four months later—and four days after bidding Colter farewell—on August 21, 1806, Lewis and Clark met three trappers paddling up the Missouri. Two of them, Francois Rivet and a man by the name of Grenier, had wintered with the corps in 1804–1805. Rivet and Grenier had apparently seen Gravelines on the river because they informed the captains of Arketarnarshar's death. The two traders, however, had wisely said nothing about Arketarnarshar to the Arikara, and neither did Lewis and Clark when they met them later that day. (Lewis was still recovering from the wound he had suffered ten days earlier, and Clark took the lead in managing the men and in dealing with the Indians.) The corps fired guns as a salute, and the Arikara did the same as a large crowd gathered on the bank of the river. "They all appeared anxious to take us by the hand and much rejoiced to See us return," wrote Clark.[4]

Grey Eyes, a chief who had not been present for the council in 1804, took a prominent role this time, insisting that he would follow Clark's counsel not to wage war on his neighbors. He also said that several chiefs wanted to travel east and see their Great Father, "but wished to see the Chief who went down last Summer return first"; Grey Eyes then "expressed Some apprehension as to the Safty of that Chiefs in passing the Sieoux."[5] Clark, who had no official confirmation of Arketarnarshar's death—and who in any event had not been authorized to speak for Jefferson on the matter—had no choice but to remain silent. Nevertheless, all of this put more pressure on Gravelines, then on his way up the Missouri.

Three weeks later, Lewis and Clark arrived at the site of present St. Joseph, Missouri, and finally met Gravelines, the emissary to the Arikara, who confirmed the rumors of the chief's death. Gravelines was accompanied by Pierre Dorion Sr., and they were traveling with Robert McClellan, an

Army friend of Clark's in command of a large keelboat. "We examined the instructions of those interpreters," recorded Clark, "and found that Gravelin was ordered to the Ricaras with a Speach from the president of the U. States to that nation and some presents which had been given the Ricara Chief who had visited the U. States and unfortunately died at the City of Washington." No doubt to the captains' satisfaction, Gravelines had also been instructed to "make every enquirey after Capt Lewis and my self and the party."[6]

Two days later, with Colter, Dickson, and Hancock presumably now in eastern Montana and making slow but steady progress up the Yellowstone River, Lewis and Clark met the ubiquitous Charles Courtin. On Sunday, September 14, nine days before reaching St. Louis, as they followed the river along the current border of Missouri and Kansas (north of present Kansas City), the captains were worried about the Kaw (also called Kanza) Indians. "This being the part of the Missouri the Kanzas nation resort to at this Season of the year for the purpose of robbing the perogues passing up to other nations above, we have every reason to expect to meet with them." Lewis and Clark kept a close watch, determined that they would open fire on the Kaw "for the smallest insult." But they saw no trace of Indians, and, "at 2 P.M.," wrote Clark, "we met three large boats bound to the Yanktons [Yankon Sioux] and Mahars [Omaha] the property of Mr. Lacroy, Mr. Aiten & Mr. Coutau [Courtin] all from St. Louis, those young men received us with great friendship and pressed on us Some whiskey for our men, Bisquet, Pork and Onions, & part of their Stores, we continued near 2 hours with those boats, makeing every enquirey into the state of our friends and Country & c."[7] Although Clark had mentioned Courtin at least twice in previous journal entries, this was the first—and last—time Lewis and Clark actually met him. Nor did Clark give any indication that he connected this man with the one he had mentioned previously in his journals.

Courtin apparently made no mention of Arketarnarshar's death; he was probably not aware of it. But in a matter of months he would be impacted by it—and so would his former companions Dickson and Hancock.

Although Dearborn had hoped Gravelines would reach the Arikara homeland in the summer or autumn of 1806, that did not happen. Gravelines got too late of a start from St. Louis—understandable since he had still been in Washington in April. (The long wait no doubt exacerbated the already rising anxiety among the Arikara over Arketarnarshar's welfare.) Moreover, since Courtin, Lacroy, and Aiten were only days behind Gravelines, Dorion, and McClellan, as well as several other traders, it is quite possible that some of these parties temporarily joined together. They were all traveling late in the season, and several of them apparently spent the winter in Omaha country, heading north again as soon as the weather allowed.

In the spring of 1807, McClellan wrote a letter from the Omaha cantonment near Council Bluffs to Meriwether Lewis, informing him that "a Certain Mr. Corter [Courtin] a Kenedian who obtained Licinus to Traide with the Suoix & Poncas for the year 1806. Proceeds On a voige this spring up the Missouri Expecting to Reach the falls be fore he stops." McClellan added that he had no plans to go farther up the Missouri at that point and would soon be returning to St. Louis. What McClellan did not add was that his former passenger Gravelines was now traveling with Courtin.[8]

Courtin and his crew and Gravelines reached the Arikara villages on June 3, 1807; they were not warmly welcomed. In a letter intended for Governor Meriwether Lewis and his associates, Courtin informed "the Government of the United States of the evilness and bad disposition" of the Arikara Indians, who had stolen most of his goods not long after he and his men had unloaded the gifts intended for those same Indians. Other than a few items that Courtin managed to recover, "the whole was lost."[9] In a scene quite reminiscent of the winter he spent in Lakota Sioux country with Dickson and Hancock two and a half years earlier, Courtin had been robbed of a virtual boatload of valuable merchandise.

The letter also offered the first solid information about Dickson and Hancock since they had been seen paddling up the Missouri with Colter the previous August. "Ten days after [Courtin and Gravelines arrived at the Arikara villages]," wrote Courtin, "a Certain Hunter named Joseph Dickson . . . took his landing . . . directly this People went to the Canoe and Began by Plundering his meat & his Rifle then went to uncover his Peltries & furs and taken it away; Whilst Dickson was opposing himself to such a mischief, the Indian who had taken away the rifle fired at him and happily missed him, but wounded another Indian in the foot." Dickson apparently escaped unharmed.[10]

As for Hancock, Courtin wrote: "I cannot leave this Place, alledging the said Indians it is on account of their being at war with the Mandanes, but I have been informed that it was false, because the Mandanes have sent them a word on this Day by Forrest Handcock to come and Smock with them." This meant Hancock had arrived on June 22 (the day Courtin wrote the letter), nine days after his old partner Dickson.[11]

Courtin's letter offered a wealth of information but failed to fill in at least one piece of the puzzle: Where was Colter? Since Courtin had reached the Arikara villages on June 3, he had almost certainly been there when Colter came down the river from the Mandan, probably around June 12, two days ahead of Dickson. As far as is known, however, Courtin had never met Colter and had no particular reason to mention him (as he did with Dickson and Hancock). It is also possible that Courtin simply did not see Colter. Hoping to avoid a possible conflict with the Arikara, for example, Colter may have quietly passed the villages at night. What we do know is that sometime around June 28, Colter reached Omaha country. Henry Marie Brackenridge, who traveled up the Missouri with Lisa in 1811—and interviewed Colter on the way—gave this report: "At the river Platte, Lisa met one of Lewis and Clark's men, of the name of Coulter, who had been discharged at the Mandan villages, at his own request, that he might make a hunt before he returned. Coulter was persuaded [by Lisa] to return; his knowledge of the country and nations rendered him an acquisition."[12]

For the second time in less than a year, Colter had abandoned a return to European civilization for the lure of the trapping life. (Of course, the trapping life had charms of its own—striking vistas of rivers and streams and mountains and meadows; the thrill of seeing a mass of buffalo gallop the rolling prairie in one fluid motion; independence unheard of in the East, with freedom to hunt, hike, and sleep where one wished; and, at the Knife River villages, a second home offering good food, comfortable abodes, trading or bartering for needed supplies and conveniences, reunions with friends, fellowship around the campfire or in Indian lodges, and even marriage and family life if desired.)

Lisa may have sweetened his offer by not requiring Colter to sign a contract as the others had done, meaning that he would hunt and guide the party as they traveled up the river, but that he would not be bound to Lisa once they stopped and began trapping. He could then trap and trade without any obligation to Lisa.[13]

Lisa's other trappers, by contrast, had made a three-year commitment to engage

> in the capacity of Hunter, & fisherman of Beaver, to embark and follow a voyage from St. Louis, to the headwaters of the Missouri, . . . to assist the said Company or Society; in the transportation of baggage loading and unloading of the boats & all connected things . . . to Hunt, and trap the Beaver of the Missouri the best that he can, to gather together the meat of the furred animals, & peltries, & to remain with the said Company or Society, & to hunt in all the environs that he will find the most suitable on the waters of the missouri for the interest and advantage of the said Society . . . [and] to obey, to execute with promptness, & diligence all reasonable orders which can given by those in command of the expedition.[14]

Joseph Dickson apparently came down the river not long after Colter. He presumably met Lisa's group and talked to them. (Unfortunately, no record describing that meeting—or how Colter reacted—has survived.) If Dickson did meet them, Lisa, always looking for experienced hands, probably offered him a job. More than one historian has concluded that Dickson hired on with Lisa and headed back up the Missouri, but Dickson family tradition and Cartwright's narrative both indicate otherwise. "When he returned to St. Louis [after barely escaping harm at the hands of the Arikara]," wrote Cartwright, "he sold his furs for several thousand dollars, and returned to his family, after having been absent nearly three years. He then packed up, moved to Horse Creek, in Sangamon County [Illinois], took preaching into his cabin, joined the Methodist Episcopal Church, and continued a faithful member, leader, and steward for many years."[15]

As Courtin noted, Forrest Hancock was also traveling down the river and had reached the Arikara villages several days after Dickson. The record indicates that Hancock also accepted a job offer from Lisa and headed back west.[16]

When Lewis and Clark, thought by some to have perished in the wilderness, had arrived in St. Louis in September of 1806 and told of the wonders of the West, including streams abounding with beaver, Manuel Lisa was paying close attention. Partnering with Pierre Menard and William Morrison, prominent citizens of Kaskaskia, in the Illinois country, he planned a major trapping and trading expedition to the Rocky Mountains. The intent was to construct a series of forts along the Missouri and Yellowstone Rivers, offering the trappers in that area a home base and also providing a trading center for Indians. Lisa approached this venture with a focus and drive that seemed to characterize all his business dealings, soon outfitting two keelboats with $16,000 dollars' worth of supplies.[17]

Perhaps even more important, Lisa recruited several members of the Corps of Discovery for his own expedition. They not only had firsthand experience manning keelboats, navigating rivers, hunting buffalo, trapping beaver, traversing mountains, communicating with Indians—the list could go on and on—they were also accustomed to military discipline and knew how to follow orders. Lisa would have had a hard time finding more qualified men. Menard and Morrison, likely hearing of Lewis's profound confidence in George Drouillard, appointed him as their representative on the voyage. By the spring of 1807, five other Lewis and Clark Expedition veterans had signed on: Pierre Cruzatte, Jean-Baptiste Lepage, John Potts, Peter Weiser, and Richard Windsor.[18] (Colter brought the total to seven when he joined around the end of June.)

Colter and his fellow explorers had much to talk about. The latter had received a hero's welcome in St. Louis and had been rewarded with land warrants and double pay. Meriwether Lewis had paid a personal visit to Thomas Jefferson and had been appointed governor of the territory. William Clark was now U.S. Indian agent for all nations west of the Mississippi (except the Osage) and a brigadier general in the Louisiana militia. Alexander Willard and John Ordway had both married. Not a single expedition veteran had died. There was also less personal news: Aaron Burr had killed Alexander Hamilton in a duel (now three years in the past but still news to Colter); Jefferson had been re-elected president; Zebulon Pike had explored the upper Mississippi. For his part, Colter likely had fascinating details about his partnership and break-up with Dickson and Hancock; tales of trapping beaver and killing grizzlies on the Yellowstone (Lisa's ultimate destination); and possibly even news about Charbonneau, Sacagawea, and Pomp.

Among Colter's new companions were two unforgettable characters who would achieve singular reputations as mountain men—and who would both be killed by Indians: Edward Robinson and Edward Rose. Along with sharing a first name, they shard a Kentucky past. Edward Robinson, Washington Irving later wrote, "was a veteran backwoodsman, sixty-six years of age [in 1811]. He had been one of the first settlers of Kentucky, and engaged in many of the conflicts of the Indians on 'the Bloody Ground.' In one of these battles he had been scalped, and he still wore a handkerchief bound round his head to protect the part."[19] Robinson almost certainly would have known Daniel Boone and William Hancock and possibly William's son, Forrest. Hancock the younger and Robinson may have shared an unexpected and heartfelt reunion. Robinson and his two fast friends John Hoback and Jacob Reznor, who had also signed on with Lisa, would die at the hands of Shoshone in Idaho in 1814.

Rose was reportedly the son of a white father and an African American–Cherokee mother. Based on hearsay—and there was never any lack of rumor when it came to Rose—Washington Irving wrote that Rose was, "withal, a dogged, sullen, silent fellow, with a sinister aspect, and more of the savage than the civilized man in his appearance," that he "had formerly belonged to one of the gangs of pirates who infested the islands of the Mississippi, plundering boats as they went up and down the river." Joshua Pilcher, a St. Louis businessman who later entered the fur trade and succeeded William Clark as superintendent of Indian affairs, wrote in an 1823 letter that Rose was "a celebrated outlaw who left this country in chains some ten years ago."[20]

Rose was on his way to becoming one of the most notorious mountain men in the history of the fur trade. His friend, Captain Reuben Holmes, reported that Rose was born and raised near Louisville, Kentucky. "At the age of seventeen or eighteen years, he left Kentucky on a keel boat, and in the capacity of a boatman for New Orleans. After his arrival and during his stay at that place, he became celebrated for the eagerness with which he espoused the quarrels of his comrades, and particularly so as a true supporter of the dignity of 'Old Kentuck.'" Holmes further explained that the "most honorable mark" Rose bore was a prominent scar on his nose, "made by the meeting of the upper and lower jaws of a 'big' Chillicothean, about two thirds of an inch from the tip of his nose, and resulting in the total loss of the part thus separated."[21] The Indians would later call him *Nez Coupe*, or Cut Nose. Rose would be killed and scalped by Arikara Indians in Montana in 1832.

Just as he had three years earlier, Colter was struggling up the Missouri in a keelboat, in the heat of summer, with forty or fifty other men. Mosquitoes plagued him and his fellows, just as before, along with gnats, house flies, horse flies, "ear flies," and "brown flies." There was sunburn, heat exhaustion, the inevitable aches and pains and bouts of dysentery, windblown sand finding its way under fingernails and into eyes, ears, noses, shoes, and clothes. The sawyers and snags and troublesome sandbars seemed all too familiar, the wind halting all progress or even driving the boat back, the blinding lightening and deafening cracks of thunder in the dark of night, the rain and hail, the howl of the coyote and the rumble of buffalo herds. The labor consisted of the same monotonous tasks—pushing, pulling, or rowing a boat upstream, cleaning muskets, hunting, dressing meat, making camp, protecting the food from varmints and bugs (and overeager boatmen and traders), digging latrines, standing guard, and on and on. But in the midst of sameness, the *tone* of the voyage was entirely different. As Brackenridge perceptively wrote, "These trading expeditions are very different from journeys of discovery; the trader has unruly hands to manage, who think themselves perfectly at liberty when out of the reach of law."[22]

Nothing illustrated the striking dissimilarity between Lewis and Clark's expedition and Lisa's expedition more than what had happened to George Drouillard in May, at the mouth of the Osage River. A trapper by the name of Antoine Bissonnet had deserted, taking some supplies with him. Lisa was beside himself—he ordered Drouillard to find the deserter and bring him back "dead or alive." Drouillard went in search of Bissonnet, and sometime later the men heard a single gunshot. Then Drouillard returned with Bissonnet, the latter wounded in the back. Drouillard said he was sorry for what he had done, but Lisa was unrepentant, even to the point of harassing the wounded man and labeling him "a rascal who got what he deserved."[23] A few of the voyagers laid Bissonnet—who was repentant and not sure why he had deserted—in a canoe and started downstream for St. Charles, where he could get medical attention, but he died on the way.

The laws and customs of the time allowed for the deserter of a trapping expedition to be shot, on the logic that such disloyalty put the whole party in danger, particularly in Indian country. Indeed, when Drouillard was tried for murder in September of 1808, the jury—which included Lewis and Clark veteran George Shannon—acquitted him after deliberating for fifteen minutes. (Lisa had also been charged, but the prosecutor decided not to try him after seeing the result of Drouillard's trial.) Despite that, Drouillard deeply regretted his actions for the rest of his life. "You have without doubt learned of the misfortune which happened to me last spring on my way to the Upper Missouri," he wrote to his sister.

> I admit that this misfortune was very fatal to us but at the same time, I would have you observe without trying to excuse myself, that this has not been done through malice, hatred or any evil intent. Thoughtlessness on my part and lack

of reflection in this unhappy moment is the only cause of it, and moreover encouraged and urged by my partner, Manuel Lisa, who we ought to consider in this affair as guilty as myself for without him the thing would never have taken place. The recollection of this unhappy affair throws me very often in the most profound reflections, and certainly I think it has caused a great deal of grief to my family for which I am very sorry and very much mortified. That I have not lost the affection of my old friends proves that they did not believe me capable of an action so terrible through malice and bad intent.[24]

Lewis and Clark's records left no sign that Colter and Drouillard had been friends during the voyage to the Pacific—to the contrary, they had once argued. On May 6, 1808, as the corps was making its return journey across northern Idaho, Lewis "directed the horse which we had obtained for the purpose of eating to be led as it was yet unbroke, in performing this duty a quarrel ensued between Drewyer and Colter."[25] Neither of the captains said any more about the incident, but the "quarrel" hints at a sense of competition that existed between Colter and Douillard. They were both skilled and confident woodsmen, hunters, and scouts, and neither of them would have taken kindly to being given orders by the other.

When did Colter first hear of the sad Bissonnet affair? Did he find a new sympathy, if not friendship, for Drouillard? Did Drouillard's countenance betray his "profound reflections"? The record is silent on these questions. Still, Colter and Drouillard would spend a good deal of time together over the next thirty-three months, working more closely than they had during the expedition (when Drouillard was generally with Lewis and Colter with Ordway), and no conflict between them was ever mentioned. Laboring for Lisa, first and always a businessman, these two extraordinary mountaineers would make explorations much more significant than either had made during a voyage expressly founded for exploration. Among Lewis and Clark's men, only two, John Colter and George Drouillard, would contribute key elements to William Clark's magnificent 1810 "Map of Part of the Continent of North America," which would, as one modern scholar writes, "tremendously impact American images of the West and influence a new generation of maps of western North America."[26] It is possible—and it would seem quite fitting—that Colter and Drouillard maintained a truce of mutual respect during their final months together.

There was plenty of other trouble, however, and had been from the start, particularly with an engage by the name of Jean-Baptiste Bouche. On April 19, 1807, the day Lisa's men were to embark from St. Louis, Bouche was nowhere to be found. Lisa, who had apparently given Bouche an advance and did not want to lose his investment, had to swear out a warrant against him and have it served by a constable, who brought the reluctant employee to the boat. For the next fifteen months, Bouche would make a mockery of his agreement to "obey, to execute with promptness, & diligence all reasonable orders which can be given by those in command." As it turned out, Lisa would have done far better to write off his advance to Bouche and leave without him.

Lisa's complaints against Bouche, later listed in a deposition, were well catalogued: On July 12, Bouche was ordered but refused to cut twelve pieces of lumber to help repair a keelboat. Not only that, but he also threatened to provoke an Indian attack on the party. On July 23, when rations had been reduced to one-fourth of a pound of meat per man per day (probably not from lack of game but because Lisa was reluctant to send out his hunters in Lakota territory), Bouche began stealing and wasting pork from the kettles and "did this in order to make the expedition . . . fail and fall through. . . . To that by this usual conduct of the said Bouche, a Buck which weighed four hundred pounds lasted only one meal."[27]

On July 25, Benito Vasquez, second in command to Lisa, ordered Bouche to spread meat out to dry, but Bouche refused. Two days later, when Lisa was especially concerned about being "in the dangerous neighborhood of the Sioux nation of Indians," Bouche went hunting without permission and did not return for four days, causing the loss of favorable winds that could have hastened the party's upstream progress. Then, on two different nights, a keelboat was cut loose and pushed off from shore, mischief that Lisa attributed to Bouche. (Lisa saved the boat and cargo one night and Drouillard saved it the other night.[28] In the midst of all this, Lisa may have felt he was due a piece of good luck, and it came when he passed through Lakota country without even seeing any of that nation.

Colter had apparently passed through Arikara country without incident as he made his way down the river two months earlier. Now it was different. "Two or three hundred warriors were drawn up," wrote Brackenridge, "and on [Lisa's] approach, such as had fire arms discharged a volley before his boat, to indicate the place where he should land. He accordingly put to shore, but made it known, that no one of them was to enter his boat; while the chiefs appointed warriors to stand guard and keep off the crowd." Lisa's cocksureness, often ridiculed by his enemies, served him well in this tense moment (and continued to serve him well, for he never found himself in a battle with Indians). When an Indian rushed forward and slit open bags of corn being offered for trade by Arikara women, Lisa "instantly called his men to arms, pointed a couple of swivels which were fixed on his boats, and made every preparation for defence." The action was perfectly timed and the Arikara "dispersed in confusion" even though they considerably outnumbered Lisa's party. When the chiefs reappeared, they came with peace pipes, seeking friendship. "They came to him, and according to their custom, stroked him on the shoulders, begging him not to be displeased, declaring that the Indian who had offended him was considered a bad man."[29]

Lisa comes off triumphant in Brackenridge's account, but Brackenridge's sole informant was Lisa himself, a man hardly disposed to present himself in a negative light. The other source describing Lisa's meeting with the Arikara painted a different picture.

Shortly after Lisa had departed St. Louis late in April, William Clark had assigned Nathaniel Pryor, a sergeant on the expedition and now an army ensign, to muster a group of soldiers to escort a Mandan chief named Sheheke, his wife and son, and the interpreter René Jusseaume and his Indian wife and children up the Missouri to the Mandan villages. As they descended the river in 1806, Lewis and Clark had invited Sheheke to accompany them to St. Louis and later to Washington to meet Thomas Jefferson. Sheheke accepted the invitation, and Jusseaume, a French Canadian who had lived among the Mandan for several years, acted as his interpreter.

As Pryor was making final preparations for the voyage, fifteen Lakota leaders arrived in St. Louis. "They are Cheifs and warriors of considerable note and the representatives of several of the most numerous and vicious Bands of that nation," Clark wrote. Ignoring his previous resentment over his and Lewis's encounter with the Lakota in 1804 (precipitated when Colter's horse was stolen), Clark gave the Indians a good reception: "As the friendship of those people are important I have determined to send them back to their country in Safty with Medals and Flags (those sacred emblements of attachment) and such presents not exceeding 12 or 1500 $ as I think will be but calculated to please them and give their *bands* and exalted oppinion of the paterneal affections of the President to all the nativs who seek his protection &c."[30]

Learning of the positive visit of the Lakota, Sheheke requested to be sent up the river with them and their (and his) military escorts. This was a wise move because it strengthened the military contingent and also gave Sheheke opportunity to carry on a peaceful dialogue with the Lakota. Clark agreed and delayed Pryor, and when the party left in June of 1807 (about five weeks after Lisa), it consisted of more than one hundred individuals, including Ensign Pryor and his soldiers (escorting Sheheke) and interpreter Pierre Dorion Sr.; Lieutenant Joseph Kimble and his soldiers (escorting the Lakota); Auguste Pierre Chouteau and twenty or thirty traders and boatmen (bound for the Mandan and Hidatsa homeland); trader and interpreter Pierre Dorion Jr. and several of his men (who had brought the Lakota to St. Louis); and finally the Indians themselves, both Lakota and Mandan, including Sheheke and his family, as well as Jusseaume, and his family.[31]

Among Pryor's group were two other expedition veterans: George Gibson and George Shannon, two of Lewis and Clark's best hunters. Joseph Field, who outshone even Gibson and Shannon as a hunter, was possibly with Chouteau. One-third of Lewis and Clark's men were thus on the upper Missouri less than a year after returning. Not surprisingly, the Lakota reached their home safely, with Dorion Jr. staying in the area, and Pryor and Chouteau proceeded on without incident. (Unfortunately, Kimble's soldiers headed down the river after seeing the Lakota to their destination and were not with Pryor when he needed them most.) Hoping for the best, but well aware the Arikara had learned of Arketarnarshar's death since he had seen them last, Pryor reached the villages on the morning of September 9. "These people," he wrote to Clark, "as soon as we came opposite their village, fired several guns, the shot of which came very near us. The sub agent [Pierre Dorion Sr.], enquired in the Sieux Language 'What they meant.' They replied 'Put to shore, we will supply you with corn and oil.'"[32]

Pryor ordered the boats to shore, but in the next few minutes omens rapidly multiplied. First, Pryor learned the Arikara were at war with the Mandan, who had recently killed two of the former, the worst possible news for Sheheke, his wife, Yellow Corn, and their son, White Painted House. Next, six hundred and fifty warriors crowded onto the bank, all agitated and well armed. A captive Mandan woman then came on board and told Pryor, apparently through Sheheke's interpreter, Jusseaume, that Lisa had "passed up some time before: That he had given the Ricaras, through *compulsion* I conjecture, a number of guns and a considerable quantity of powder and ball."[33]

The Mandan woman's report convinced Pryor that Lisa, facing such hostility from the Arikara, had diverted

> the storms which threatened *his own boat*, by directing the attentions of the Ricaras to *ours*. He told them, as we learn from this woman, that two boats might be very soon expected; that we had the Mandane Chief on board; and that we were to remain, for the purposes of trade at their villages. On this, they pillaged him of about half of his goods, and suffered him to pass on, determining in their councils at the same time, to kill him on his return, and to lose no time in preparing to murder the Mandane and his Escort as soon as we should arrive.[34]

On hearing this, Pryor promptly ordered his men to prepare for action and secured Sheheke and his family in the cabin of the keelboat, hurriedly constructing a breastwork of trunks and boxes to further fortify the cabin. The Indians were also readying for a fight when Grey Eyes approached the keelboat. "I had no doubt of his wish to serve us; and as he was known to possess influence with his nation, I felt desirous of conciliating him. He presented me a letter from Courtney [Courtin], who had previously to the arrival of Lisa, been cruelly treated by these barbarians, and informed us that he alone had been friendly to that unfortunate Trader, who owed his safety and ultimate release to his friendly offices."[35]

Pryor had unwittingly picked up the trail of the shadowy Charles Courtin, who had apparently been saved by Grey Eyes and released before Lisa's arrival. (Unfortunately, the letter given to Pryor by Grey Eyes has been lost.) Courtin had gone north to the Mandan, and later to Three Forks and beyond, never to return to St. Louis. He was killed by Blackfoot Indians in present Montana in 1810.

Pryor did his best, negotiating, reminding the Arikara of their friendship with Lewis and Clark, presenting a medal to Grey Eyes, and stopping at the upper village to pay respects to the chiefs there, but he was only delaying the inevitable because too many of the Arikara were bent on war, especially with Sheheke onboard the keelboat. When the Indians finally fired their guns, Pryor was ready: "I had reserved my fire, and was so fortunate as to reach them, with a well directed volley of Swivels, Blunderbusses and small arms, before they sheltered themselves behind a young growth of Willows at the distance of about sixty yards."[36]

Pryor held off the Indians but knew he was too outnumbered to withstand a siege and ordered a retreat. Chouteau's boat, however, got stuck on a sandbar, and his men were forced to drag the boat into the current while the Indians fired on them at will. For a moment Pryor feared Chouteau's entire group would be lost, despite his best efforts to protect them, but they finally got the boat free, and Pryor and Chouteau headed downstream, navigating a narrow channel (between the main bank and an island), with Arikara shooting at them from both sides. The battle turned when one of the soldiers spotted a chief on the shore, took aim, and shot him. The wound was apparently fatal, and his warriors gathered around him and gave up the fight.

When they were sure the Arikara pursuit had ended, Pryor and Chouteau lashed their keelboats together and attended to the men who had fallen. Pryor had suffered no casualties, but two of his men were wounded, Gibson in the hip and arm and Shannon in the leg. Gibson apparently fully recovered, but Shannon endured the long trip back to Fort Bellefontaine only to have his leg amputated below the knee when he got there.[37]

Chouteau fared much worse, losing one man on the beach, one in a pirogue, and one onboard the keelboat. Another was mortally wounded and died nine days later. One of those killed may have been Joseph Field. It would have been characteristic of him to be in the thick of things. Was he one of those who dragged the boat back into the channel under a deluge of gunfire? Pryor did not list any of Chouteau's casualties by name (not unusual because he named neither Gibson nor Shannon in his rather official, impersonal report to Clark), but several bits of evidence point to Field being one of them. Although it is not certain that Field was with Chouteau, we know he was killed around this same time, the first member of the corps to die after the expedition. He was about twenty-seven years old. The expedition veteran to die last was eight or nine years Field's senior and would live for another sixty-three years.[38]

Because of his quarrel with Sheheke, Jusseaume ended up on Chouteau's boat rather than Pryor's when the fighting broke out. He was wounded badly in the thigh and shoulder—all this in the presence of his wife and sons—and was permanently disabled. Two and a half decades later, however, he was still working and living among the Mandan.[39] Several others were also wounded.

The battle with the Arikara must have been a terrifying ordeal for Sheheke's family, but Pryor was so determined to return Sheheke to his villages that he proposed going overland, using a seldom-used trail on the prairie. Pryor believed they could make the march in three days. "The chief declined this project," wrote Pryor, "alledging the impossibility of accomplishing it with his wounded Interpreter together with the additional incumbrance of their wives and children."[40] Knowing that they would not see their friends and loved ones for another year—at the very least—Sheheke and Yellow Corn and White Painted House headed back down the river.

Pryor believed that Lisa had been the cause of his troubles and expressed that to Clark; then he left the matter in Clark's hands. As far as we know, Clark never expressed an opinion on Lisa's culpability. In both his preliminary report to Dearborn, and later in a cover letter accompanying Pryor's account, Clark made no mention of Lisa's supposed involvement. Instead, he criticized British traders in the northwest, implying that they may have urged on the Arikara. Whatever Clark's private views, nothing ever came of Pryor's accusations.[41]

Even Jusseaume, who presumably interpreted for the captive Mandan woman and had good reason to blame someone, pointed to a different cause: "The Ricaras are jealous of the return of the Mandan chief, and wish to kill him," he wrote to Thomas Jefferson.[42]

Colter and his companions, of course, were unaware of Pryor and Chouteau's ordeal; they were having problems of their own, even at the Mandan and Hidatsa villages. Lisa went ashore while his boats continued up the river. "At the third village," wrote Brackenridge, "[Lisa's] presents were rejected, and the chief demanded some powder, which was refused: Lisa, knew that his life was in no danger while his death could not procure them his goods, and resisted their repeated solicitations in a bold and firm manner. . . . They were finally compelled to accept of such presents as he offered."[43]

The Indians of the upper Missouri had long exchanged and bartered goods with the British from Hudson's Bay and the North West Company, but the sudden influx of American traders from the south had thrown things out of balance. Clark had been more perceptive than he realized when he off-handedly wrote to Dearborn, "The great variety of interests concerned in the Indian trade of this country and the irregular method which they have carried it on, is calculated to give the Indians an unfavourable opinion of the American regulations." Clark also expressed fears that the British were about to bully the Americans right of the Indian trade. "I have been informed by several of the most respectable American, French and Canadian merchants of this place," he wrote, "that a company was formed last season at Michili-mackinac consisting of British and American merchants with the view of engrossing all the trade of this country. . . . This association appears to be calculated to injure this country very much, all the rich furs and pelteries with which this Teretory abounds will fall into the hands of British merchants who will take them imediately to Montreal, without leaveing one skin, or one cent of money more than be only sufficient to purchase a little corn to fee[d] their hands."[44]

As if on cue, the Assiniboine, a nation with close ties to Canadian traders, gave Lisa's party a hostile reception. According to Brackenridge,

> [Lisa] espied the Assineboin nation approaching, in a body of four or five thousand souls. These wandering people had learned from their [scouts], the approach of traders. The whole prairie, to use his expression, was *red with them*; some on horseback, others on foot, and all painted for war. His situation required the utmost boldness and intrepidity. He charged his swivels and made directly across to the savages, and when he had come within an hundred yards, the match was put, while there was at the same time, a general discharge of small arms. This was intended to strike them with terror; the effect was ludicrous, they fell back, tumbled over each other, and fled to the hills with precipitation. A few of the warriors and chiefs only remained. The pipe of peace was presented, and matters concluded amicably.[45]

Pushing on past Assiniboine country, Lisa and his men turned left at the confluence of the Missouri and Yellowstone and proceeded on, following the Yellowstone southwest, past the Powder and Tongue Rivers, likely being guided by Colter, Hancock, and Windsor.[46] In 1804, Lewis and Clark had traveled from May to October, making 1,600 miles (on the dot, by Clark's estimate) before they wintered at Fort Mandan. Lisa outdid even that, departing in April and continuing on until November, making more than 1,900 miles before he stopped.

Reaching the mouth of the Bighorn River in October or November of 1807, Lisa found a spot of plentiful timber and concluded this was the right place. He had good instincts: Three decades later, the explorer Nathaniel Wyeth said that the stretch of the Bighorn directly to the south offered some of the best trapping he had ever seen.[47]

Lisa determined to build a trading post and a fort, which he named after his son, Remon. This was quickly anglicized to "Fort Raymond." First the men started on the trading house, constructing two rooms and a loft, but Bouche was still balking. When Lisa ordered him to make wooden pins to cover the roof, Bouche refused. A few days later, Lisa had his hunters place a quantity of meat on scaffolds about a mile from camp. Lisa estimated the value of the meat at one thousand dollars. He instructed Bouche to "go and bring the said meat to the camp," but Bouche refused, "in consequence of which refusal on the part of the said Bouche the same was destroyed by the white bears and devoured by the wolves." Bouche was nothing if not consistent: when Lisa ordered him to bring in wood, he refused; when he was ordered to watch the coal kiln (apparently meaning a nearby surface deposit of coal available for fuel), he again refused.[48]

Colter would soon be free of Bouche, however. Brackenridge, whose brief narrative is the key source of information on Lisa's voyage, wrote that Lisa "shortly after despatched Coulter, the hunter before mentioned, to bring some of the Indian nations to trade. This man, with a pack of thirty pounds weight, his gun and some ammunition, went upwards of five hundred miles to the Crow nation; gave them information, and proceeded from thence to several other tribes."[49]

Brackenridge thus became the first writer to describe Colter's renowned odyssey into the wilderness, a description that would send generations of scholars, history buffs, and wayfarers alike on journeys of their own, checking maps, documents, and the landscape itself in seemingly endless attempts to track down the elusive Colter and see where his wanderings really took him.

Chapter Eight

"Lonely Wanderings"

The Riddle of Colter's Route

For the multitude of folks taken with the Colter legend over the two centuries since his death, two topics have overshadowed all others: Colter's Run and Colter's Route. The first, as discussed, was recorded by three men who heard the story directly from Colter; it has become the most famous Colter adventure. But not a single narrative was ever recorded about the second—the path Colter took in his solitary trek into the dark and gloomy wilderness—and the question of where he really went has become the chief Colter controversy.

Colter's Run made its way into Western lore only months after it happened; Colter's Route was largely ignored throughout the nineteenth century. It was finally carefully considered in the 1890s, however, and for the next one hundred years it was endlessly talked about, researched, investigated, discussed, and debated, with a host of Colter scholars and Colter buffs advancing their own theories about where he went, what he saw, and why—or if—his solitary trek was historically significant.

Early in the twenty-first century, advances in both technology and research shed refreshing light on Colter's Route, and a new version of *where* he traveled took hold. A close analysis of this proposed route also makes possible new explanations of *when* and *why* he traveled, discussed in detail below. But these new explanations are best understood in the context of what happened after Lisa and his men reached the mouth of the Bighorn River late in the fall of 1807.

Colter was not the only emissary sent out to the Indians by Lisa. Three other men were also selected—two veterans of the Lewis and Clark Expedition and one greenhorn. The greenhorn was Edward Rose. Whatever his character, Rose had a swagger about him that kept him in the limelight.

Captain Holmes wrote that by the time Lisa's group reached the Bighorn River, Rose "had given some proofs of his reckless bravery, and of a strong and vigorous constitution. His tact and facility in overcoming sudden difficulties and dangers, his untiring perseverance, and the faculty of 'turning his hand to every thing,' had not escaped the scrutiny of Mr. Lisa." Rose may have proved his nerve and his savvy when Lisa barely escaped skirmishes with the Arikara and Assiniboine, even though this was Rose's first contact with those nations. Lisa was impressed. "Rose among a few others, was selected to spend the winter with the Crow Indians," wrote Holmes, "and was, accordingly, also supplied with such articles of trade as were considered best calculated to promote the interests of the expedition."[1]

As to what articles Rose may have taken with him, his purchases at the Arikara villages a few years later, when he was stocking up on personal supplies and also preparing to trade with Indians, offer some interesting clues. According to Wilson Price Hunt's account book, Rose bought one yard of green cloth, one yard of blue cloth, and one yard of blue flannel; balls and powder; four scalping knives and an ax; a coffee kettle and six pipes; four pounds of beads (some blue and some white); two handkerchiefs; one carrot of tobacco; two dozen brass rings; three fathoms of gartering; a bridle; a cotton shirt; four dozen buttons; four Green River knives; and three horse bells. As one historian pointed out, some of these items were probably intended to gain the favors of Indian women. The prices of various items also reveal something about supply and demand in the Indian nations. Green cloth went for a sky-high $5.00 a yard, while Rose bought three and one-third pounds of balls for $1.75 and one and one-half pounds of powder for $2.25.[2]

The Absaroka (also called Apsáalooke) Indians called themselves "Children of the Large-Beaked Bird," apparently meaning the raven, but early traders, who sometimes called this nation "Rocky Mountain Indians," misinterpreted *raven* as *crow*, and the name stuck. In a creation story somewhat reminiscent of that of the Salish, the Crow told of Old Man Coyote forming the earth and mankind from a clump of earth retrieved by a duck. The Crow, who share common ancestors with the Hidatsa, migrated from the northeast, possibly the Manitoba area, first to the confluence of the Heart and Missouri Rivers (in present southern North Dakota) and then westward. They split into three groups as they migrated—the Mountain Crow, centered in the Bighorn River Valley and the mountains to the southwest (in present northwest Wyoming); the River Crow, settling north of the Yellowstone River; and Kicked-in-Their Bellies, who ranged between the Bighorn River and the Powder River to the east.[3]

"Spent the Day in conversing with them [the Crow], drawing Maps of their Country &c &c.," David Thompson wrote in 1798. "They appeared to be very intelligent, as almost all the Natives of the Mountains are—[they]

fully comprehended with a little explanation the drift of all my Questions, and answered direct to them."[4]

The Crow were horse lovers. Charles McKenzie, a clerk with the North West Company who visited the Crow in 1805, two and a half years before Lisa arrived, recorded a resplendent image of the Crow with their horses:

> About the middle of June the Rocky Mountain Indians made their appearance. They . . . presented the handsomest sight that one could imagine—all on horseback. Children of small size were lashed to the Saddles, and those above the age of six could manage a horse—the women had wooden Saddles—most of the men had none. There were a great many horses for the baggage, and the whole exceeding two thousand covered a large space of ground and had the appearance of an army; they halted on a rising ground behind the Village; formed into a circle—when the Chief addressed them, they then descended full speed—rode through the Village, exhibiting their dexterity in horsemanship in a thousand shapes—I was astonished to see their agility and address:—and I could believe they were the best riders in the world. They were dressed in leather, looked clean and neat—Some wore beads and rings as ornaments. Their arms were Bows and arrows, Lances, and round stones enclosed in leather and slung to a shank in the form of a whip. They make use of shields, and they have a few Guns.[5]

We know nothing of Rose's route, but in light of what is known about the travels of Lisa's three other representatives, it seems possible that he went east and south, to a Crow village lying between the Little Missouri River and Powder River, or east and north, to a Crow village at the mouth of the Powder River.[6]

"No sooner had he arrived," wrote Holmes, "than, as is customary, he had a kind of council, the main object of which, on the part of the whites, was to state their business, and get permission to remain among them, and to cultivate the good will of the Indians, by the distribution of a few presents."[7] Remain among them Rose did, speaking their language and wearing moccasins, leggings, breechcloth, and buffalo robe; marrying a Crow woman and fathering Crow children; becoming a Crow chief and eventually leading his warriors in battle. His name would change from *Nez Coupe* to "the Five Scalps."

Something is thus known about Rose's interaction with the Indians, even though we can only speculate about his location; the opposite is true for Peter Weiser. He was hardly the kind of expedition standout that Colter and Drouillard had been, but he had served the captains faithfully for three years, gaining a depth of experience in canoeing, hunting, scouting, and negotiating with Indians that was invaluable to Lisa. In June of 1806, for example, as the corps headed east across present Idaho, Ordway, Frazer, and Weiser had taken a week-long side trip to obtain salmon from the Nez Perce, interacting considerably with that nation.

In 1810 in present Montana, Reuben Lewis (Meriwether's brother) wrote that "the upper branches of the Columbia are full of Beaver, and the rout by the middle fork on Madison's River is almost without mountains it is about 5 or 6 days travel to an illigable plan [eligible plain] for a fort on that River where the Beavers from the account of Peter Wyzer, is as abundant as in our part of the country."[8]

This tantalizing description indicates that Lisa may have told Weiser to go to Three Forks and then ascend the Madison (the middle fork of the three forks) to the south. Richard Windsor, the only man with Lisa who had traveled from Three Forks to the mouth of the Bighorn (having done so with Clark in 1806), could have instructed Weiser on reaching Three Forks. This required following the Yellowstone until it made a sharp turn to the south (near present Livingston), then continuing west, crossing Bozeman Pass, and heading northwest to the Gallatin River. Weiser, of course, would recognize Three Forks when he got in the vicinity because he had been there in 1804, when the corps came up the Missouri and followed the Jefferson River southwest.

Weiser then followed the Madison south, and Reuben Lewis's succinct summary is quite accurate: avoiding the Madison Range to the east and the Gravelly Range to the west, one can ascend the Madison (past present Ennis) until it turns west into the mountains (heading toward what is now the Earthquake Lake and Hebgen Lake region). At that point, staying on the plain (and continuing south) allows one to cross the Continental Divide at Raynolds Pass—entering present Idaho at the same time—and reach a picturesque mountain lake and an upper branch of the Columbia teeming with beaver (and trout). Andrew Henry reached this area of abundant beaver in 1810 and built a fort (as Lewis had recommended), leaving his name everywhere: Henry's Lake, Henry's Fork (the north fork of the Snake River), and Henry's Fort.

If Weiser did cross into Idaho, he could have seen Indians of the Crow, Shoshone, or Bannock nations, but we have no record of him interacting with any of them. Nor did any other explorers of the time mention any Indian villages in the immediate area.[9]

William Clark's 1810 map corroborates the theory that Weiser reached the area. Clark called the Salmon River the north fork of Lewis's River, and the Snake River (as it forms a crescent through southern Idaho) the south fork of Lewis's River. Clark also showed various rivers merging with the south fork of Lewis's River in present southeastern Idaho, and he labeled one Henry's River and another Wiser's River. The identification of Henry's River was quite accurate because the river now known as Henry's Fork indeed flows from north to south until it converges with the Snake.[10]

Henry's Fork, however, is the only notable tributary of the Snake River in the area, meaning that Henry's River and Wiser's River are quite likely references to the same river (something that probably would have been clear to Clark had he talked to Henry and Weiser at the same time). It is also possible, but less likely, that Wiser's River represented either Fall River or the Teton River, both of which flow into Henry's Fork from Wyoming.[11]

Whatever his exact route, Weiser survived to tell his story and possibly told it to Clark. By all accounts, he lived an active trapping life until he returned to St. Louis in 1810. Two years after that, he apparently went west again, but there is no trace of his activities in the historical record after that. Sometime between 1825 and 1828, Clark noted that Weiser had been killed but offered no details.

Lisa's third emissary was Lewis's right-hand man during the expedition, George Drouillard, whom Lewis called "a man of much merit . . . peculiarly usefull from his knowledge of the common language of gesticulation, and his uncommon skill as a hunter and woodsman; those several duties he performed in good faith, and with an ardor which deserves the highest commendation." Lewis added that Drouillard had encountered "all the most dangerous and trying scenes of the voyage, in which he uniformly acquited himself with honor."[12]

Drouillard made two trips from Fort Raymond, and his routes are rather well established because of a map William Clark created after consulting with Drouillard in 1808. Clark's map specifically identified the dates of each trip: "in the winter 1807–8" and "during the spring 1808." Clark also included symbols on the map that signified "days travel or 30 miles." After analyzing the map, M. O. Skarsten, Drouillard's biographer, estimated that the first journey, which started in 1807 and ended in 1808, was "one of fifteen days," possibly longer, "depending on the duration of his stopovers at the various Indian encampments which he visited."[13]

A fifteen-day (or even twenty-day) trip that extended into 1808 would necessarily mean that Drouillard left in December, quite reasonable because an 1811 deposition given by Lisa shows the men were busy constructing shelters, hunting, and smoking meat in late November (as discussed in chapter 7). Mid-December was thus the earliest that Lisa could have done without the services of three of his best hunters—Rose, Drouillard, and Colter.[14]

On his first trip, Drouillard left the fort and followed the Yellowstone River southwest to Pompeys Pillar, a huge rock outcropping where Clark had carved his name on July 25, 1806. He then went overland to the mouth of Pryor Creek, where he found a Crow village. He continued along the Yellowstone, past the site of present Billings, to Clark's Fork of the Yellowstone (not to be confused with Clark Fork River, in northwestern Montana and northern Idaho, which is on the Pacific side of the Continental Divide and flows into Lake Pend Oreille). He ascended Clark's Fork, possibly to the vicinity of present Edgar, where he found a large Crow camp. In one of the many notes Clark made on the map, he wrote: "Ap-so-roo-kah fork or the camp that the Crow Indians winter—here they find an herb which rises about nine inches high evergreen-smells like sage—small and orbicular leaf— leaves abundant—fall when the horses bite it—this formes the food for the horses and the inducement to the indians to winter here—abundance of buffaloe, Elk, Antelope &c."[15]

Drouillard next followed a creek to the east and then went south. Entering present Wyoming, he came upon the high plain of the Bighorn Basin, reaching Heart Mountain (Clark's "Hart mountain") and the Shoshone River, a tributary of the Bighorn. This stretch of the Shoshone had a foul sulphur smell, prompting Clark to label it "Stinking Water River," probably echoing Crow sentiments. One fascinating spot along this stretch of river, just west of present Cody, would later be called "Colter's Hell." Drouillard stopped in the area, near Cedar Mountain (Clark's "Spirits mountain"), and met another band of Crow Indians.

Now on his return trip, Drouillard followed the Shoshone River northeast, to the approximate site of Byron, Wyoming, and then went north, back into Montana, picking up Sage Creek and passing through the vicinity of present Warren. Then he followed Pryor Creek back to the Yellowstone and traced his outbound route back to the fort, completing a two- or three-week journey.[16]

In the spring of 1808, Drouillard made a second trip, again following the Yellowstone toward Pompey's Pillar. This time, however, he stopped at "Smoke Creek" (in the vicinity of present Kaiser Creek) and cut southeast, to the mouth of the Little Bighorn River, near present Hardin. He ascended this pleasant winding stream through a plain of gently rolling hills, where violence would erupt on June 25, 1876, a Sunday. In striking fulfillment of Hunkpapa Lakota chief and shaman Sitting Bull's vision, where he had seen dead American soldiers falling into Indian camps, two Lakota chiefs, Gall (Hunkpapa) and Crazy Horse (Oglala-Brule) led a mounted force of Lakota and Northern Cheyenne warriors that annihilated Lieutenant Colonel George Armstrong Custer's command of 210 cavalrymen from the "matchless Seventh." As far as is known, Drouillard left no children or grandchildren to read the sensational newspaper reports of Custer's defeat that spawned a nationwide furor and cast suspicion over Major Marcus A. Reno for the rest of his life.[17]

After stopping at a Crow village on the Little Bighorn River, Drouillard went east to the headwaters of Rosebud Creek, where he saw another Crow camp. He then went east again, to another Crow camp on the Tongue River, not far from the Wyoming border. Drouillard's impressive success at finding Crow villages and getting information from the Crow indicates that he enjoyed a friendly relationship with that nation. He had begun communicating via sign language but likely picked up a rudimentary Crow vocabulary as he visited one Crow camp after another.

Drouillard made his way east as far as Otter Creek (southeast of present Ashland), before heading northwest back to Fort Raymond, crossing the Tongue River and Rosebud Creek in the process. He likely followed Tullock Creek toward the end of his journey, which, like the first, lasted at least fifteen days and probably longer.[18]

One problem with Clark's map of Drouillard's travels is that its depiction of key rivers is off-kilter in some ways. For a considerable distance, for example, the Yellowstone River and the Bighorn River are shown following virtually parallel paths. Again, at the mouth of the Shoshone River, the upper Bighorn River is shown trailing off to the southeast, toward a "Spanish Settlement."

The map that Clark completed in 1810, after consulting with Colter, corrects both of these inaccuracies and a number of others. In the 1810 map, for instance, the Bighorn flows north into the east-flowing Yellowstone (which is on a slight angle to the northeast). In addition, instead of originating somewhere in the southeast, the Bighorn starts at a lake (now believed to be Brooks Lake) to the southwest.

Nevertheless, as Skarsten points out, Drouillard had traveled upward of five hundred miles, "had visited several Indian encampments, and had discovered the location of excellent beaver grounds."[19] Moreover, Clark's map of Drouillard's travels in invaluable because it identifies so many known sites, such as Heart Mountain and the confluence of the Bighorn and Little Bighorn Rivers, and because it includes so much information obtained from Indians.

The missions of Rose, Weiser, and Drouillard were all important, and all were documented in some fashion by the 1820s. None ignited controversy. Colter's case is strikingly different. Of all the stories of the early fur trade, his journey presents what is perhaps the most alluring mystery. "Colter's Route" has been a matter of considerable debate for well over a century. Indeed, one historian after another has passionately—sometimes obsessively—spent years chasing Colter's shadow. The upshot is that the story of this quest has become an integral part of Colter's story itself.

It all started with William Clark's map. While Clark's vocation was that of a military officer and public servant, his *avocation* involved geography and cartography. It is safe to say that his real love, outside of his family, was map making. As his biographer William E. Foley points out, Clark developed "skills as a draftsman and cartographer" at a young age, extolling "the importance of trigonometry, astronomy, navigation, geometry, architecture, and land surveying." Clark joined the army in 1789, at age nineteen, and that same year used a "trek across the Indiana wilderness to practice his mapmaking skills. The maps that the novice draftsman sketched already gave hints of an accomplished cartographer in the making."[20]

Clark continued to improve his map-making skills over the years and was thus well prepared to chart his and Lewis's course across the plains and Rocky Mountains. Thomas Jefferson had instructed Lewis and Clark to "take careful observations of latitude & longitude" during their voyage and to record such information, as well as details on the course of rivers and other natural features "with great pains & accuracy."[21]

All of this, of course, was closely related to making maps of the journey, a task that naturally fell to Clark (just as botanical and zoological tasks had fallen to Lewis). "During the expedition," notes Landon Jones, "[Clark] had made fifty route maps, on large sheets of linen paper, and dozens of smaller maps. As early as Camp River Dubois, Clark had begun sketching a comprehensive, or 'connected,' map of the entire Missouri River drainage."[22]

In March of 1807, six months after Lewis and Clark's return, Lewis announced to the public that a map of the expedition (undoubtedly Clark's work) would be published by October of 1807 and that the first volume of the history of the expedition would follow in January of 1808.[23] Lewis was soon overwhelmed by both personal and professional problems, however, and when he died by his own hand in October of 1809, he had made virtually no progress publishing these items.

Although shocked and saddened by Lewis's death, Clark wasted no time taking over the duty of publishing the history of the expedition. In February of 1810, Clark asked Nicholas Biddle (1786–1844), later a prominent financier who served as president of the Second Bank of the United States, to write the history of the expedition based on Lewis and Clark's journals. Biddle accepted, and on December 7, 1810, Clark wrote to Biddle: "I have nearly finished a large Connected Map which I shall send on by the next mail. I wish the whole or such part of it anexed as you may think proper and in such a way as you may think best."[24]

Clark's completed map was four feet wide and more than two feet deep; as Clark scholar Jay H. Buckley has written, this was "the first comprehensive map of the western United States based on field observation . . . a work of superlative craftsmanship and analysis," a map that "remained the best available until Fremont's maps of the 1840s."[25]

Biddle worked hard on the history of the expedition over the next few years and announced in February of 1813 that he had found a publisher. Then, because of pressing duties as a member of the Pennsylvania state legislature, Biddle assigned the final editorial tasks to a colleague named Paul Allen. Despite his dedication to the project, the generous Biddle recommended that Allen be listed as the editor. (Biddle also declined any payment for his labors.)[26]

The History of the Expedition Under the Commands of Captains Lewis and Clark was published early in 1814 and was accompanied by the publication of Clark's 1810 map, prepared by Samuel Lewis, a cartographer; Samuel

Harrison, who assisted with the publication of the history of the expedition; engraver John Vaughn; and Dr. Ferdinand Rudolph Hassler, a leading mathematician and geodetic surveyor who attempted to correct the celestial observations made during the expedition. The map, often called "the Biddle map" by historians, is a beautiful piece of engraving for the times and was titled *A Map of Lewis and Clark's Track Across the Western Portion of the United States, in 1804, 5 & 6. Copied by Samuel Lewis from the Original Drawing of Wm Clark.*[27]

If one looks closely, the dotted line and the four simple words that set off the controversy are clearly visible amid the rivers, mountains, and Indian names: "Colter's route in 1807."[28]

Brackenridge had claimed that Lisa sent Colter to the Indians right after the group arrived at the mouth of the Bighorn, late in 1807. When this claim was added to the winding dotted line (resembling a lopsided figure 8) and accompanying label on the Biddle map, historians understandably assumed that "Colter's route" depicted the single journey described by Brackenridge, when Colter traveled "with a pack of thirty pounds weight, his gun and some ammunition" to bring the Crow nation to trade.

Even that assumption, however, did not solve the puzzle of where Colter had actually gone because Clark had drawn on three different classes of data to construct his map: (1) accurate surveys made by Clark himself during the expedition; (2) information reported by such explorers as Drouillard and Colter; and (3) accounts of the landscape received from Indians. Quite unlike a modern cartographer working with satellite images and precise GPS measurements, Clark did his best to depict country he had never seen—and the upshot was that his finished work resembled a stained-glass window or a patchwork quilt. He filled in the blanks with educated assumptions. Some assumptions turned out to be quite accurate—such as the Yellowstone River flowing from a large lake to the south (Yellowstone Lake, called Lake Eustis by Clark), and some turned out to be not only inaccurate but rather bizarre—such as the Rio del Norte (the Rio Grande) originating in southeastern Idaho when its actual source is hundreds of miles away in southern Colorado.[29]

Moreover, as John Logan Allen has noted, the Biddle version (engraved by Samuel Lewis) "is replete with errors; enough so as to render it nearly useless as a source document." Nevertheless, Allen continues, the Biddle map illustrates "the kind of cartographic information on the West that most Americans had available to them in the early 19th century" and "served as a primary source for maps of the West until the 1840s."[30]

But even when the maps of Fremont and others superseded Clark's map of the West, the Biddle version remained the authoritative source of information on Colter's route for well over a century. And while early publications on Colter (such as those from John Bradbury, Washington Irving, and Thomas James) focused on Colter's Run, later historians became particularly fascinated with Colter's Route. Of the many conundrums these researchers attempted to solve, among the most debated were these:

- Did Colter enter present Yellowstone National Park? (An answer in the affirmative would make him the first known European in the area.)
- Is Colter's Hell located in Yellowstone?
- Did Colter cross the Teton Mountains and enter present Idaho?

The first person to publish his answers to these questions was Hiram Martin Chittenden (1858–1917), a graduate of West Point who eventually achieved the rank of brigadier general. Chittenden became a prominent historian, and although he is now best known for *The American Fur Trade of the Far West* (1902), he served two tours of duty in Yellowstone with the Army Corps of Engineers, then administering the park. One of his key accomplishments was laying out and planning the "Grand Loop Road," which is still the main road in the park today. Another was his 1895 publication of *The Yellowstone National Park: Historical and Descriptive, Illustrated with Maps, Views and Portraits*. In this seminal work (which was regularly revised and reprinted for several decades), Chittenden covered a multitude of topics and devoted an entire chapter to Colter.

To understand Chittenden's proposed route, it is essential to understand crucial assumptions he made about two lakes depicted on the Biddle map—lakes that both fall within the boundaries of "Colter's route in 1807." As Merrill J. Mattes stated so succinctly in 1947, "Colter's precise route is subject to wide differences of opinion, largely revolving about the identification of 'Lake Biddle' and 'Lake Eustis' with Jackson Lake and Yellowstone Lake, respectively, and the true location of a certain 'Boiling Spring and a 'Hot Spring Brimstone.'"[31]

Relying on the American version of the 1814 Biddle map—and assuming that Lake Biddle and Lake Eustis were indeed Jackson Lake and Yellowstone Lake—Chittenden launched a debate about Colter's route that has continued to the present. "The 'route' as traced on the map," he wrote, "starts from a point on Pryor's Fork, the first considerable tributary of the Yellowstone above the mouth of the Bighorn. Colter's intention seems to have been to skirt the eastern base of the Absaroka Range until he should reach an accessible pass across the mountains of which the Indians had probably told; then to cross over the headwater of Pacific or gulf-flowing streams; and then to return by way of the Upper Yellowstone."[32]

According to Chittenden, Colter next "took a south-westerly direction as far as Clark's Fork, which stream he ascended for some distance, and then crossed over to the Stinkingwater [now the Shoshone River at Cody, Wyoming]. Here he discovered a large boiling spring, strongly impregnated with tar and sulphur, the odor of which perceptible for a great distance around, has given the stream its 'unhappy name.'"[33]

Colter then continued along the eastern flank of the Absaroka Range, crossing several tributaries of the Bighorn River, until he reached the Bighorn itself, known as the Wind River at this point.[34]

Colter "ascended this stream to its source, crossing the divide in the vicinity of Lincoln or Union Pass, and found himself upon the Pacific slope. . . . From the summit of the mountains he descended to the westward; crossed the Snake River and Teton Pass to Pierre's Hole, and then turned north."[35]

Chittenden thus answered the question of whether Colter entered present Idaho with an unequivocal *yes*. His answer to the Yellowstone Park question followed almost immediately: Colter recrossed the Teton Range "by the Indian trail in the valley of what is now Conant Creek, just north of Jackson Lake. Thence he continued in his course until he reached Yellowstone Lake, at some point along its southwestern shore."[36]

Yellowstone Lake, of course, lies well within the boundary of Yellowstone Park. Colter next trekked north around the "West Thumb" of the lake and continued north, reaching the Yellowstone River near Alum Creek. "He followed the left bank of the river to the ford just above Tower Falls, where the great Bannock Trail used to cross, and then followed this trail to its junction with his outward route on Clark's Fork." Colter then returned to the boiling spring near present Cody, Wyoming, and descended the Shoshone River "until about south of Pryor's Gap, when he turned north and shortly after arrived at his starting point."[37]

That Colter "was the discoverer of Yellowstone Lake," wrote Chittenden, "and the foremost herald of the strange phenomena of that region, may be accepted as beyond question." As to the location of Colter's Hell, Chittenden curiously claims that Colter "saw too much for his reputation as a man of veracity. No author or map-maker would jeopardize the success of his work by incorporating in it such incredible material as Colter furnished." Colter's stories were not believed, and he "became the object of jest and ridicule; and the region of his adventures was long derisively known as Colter's Hell."[38]

Chittenden thus places Colter's Hell in present Yellowstone Park, implying that William Clark did not identify many "wonders" of Yellowstone on his map because he did not believe Colter's stories. Chittenden adds that although the name "Colter's Hell" early "came to be restricted to the locality where Colter discovered the tar spring," on the Shoshone River, Colter's descriptions "undoubtedly refer in large part to what he saw in the Yellowstone and Snake River Valleys."[39]

One result of Chittenden's claim about Colter's Hell was, as Allen notes, that "an enterprising superintendent of Yellowstone National Park misappropriated the name for Yellowstone in the late 19th century."[40]

Although Chittenden's conclusions about Colter crossing the Tetons and the location of Colter's Hell are now both considered incorrect, other parts of his theory have held up quite well. Regardless, his careful analysis of Colter's route gave others an excellent starting point for conducting their own studies. Quoting Mattes again: "A composite of theories offered by Hiram M. Chittenden, Stallo Vinton, Willam J. Ghent, and Charles Lindsay, to mention only four qualified scholars who have undertaken to prove the ultimately unprovable, is that Colter ascended the Bighorn, followed up the Shoshone River to near present Cody, went south along the foot of the Absaroka Mountains, up Wind River to Union Pass, into Jackson Hole (and possibly across Teton Pass into Pierre's Hole), thence up the Lamar River and Soda Butte Creek, back across the Absarokas, thence south to the Shoshone River, and back to Lisa's Fort by way of Clark's Fork and Pryor's Fork."[41]

Chittenden's influence is clearly manifest because this composite route is so similar to the one he proposed in 1895, with Vinton and Ghent (both of whom wrote biographies of Colter in the 1920s, although only Vinton's was published) as well as Lindsay (author of *The Big Horn Basin*, 1930) largely agreeing with him. Not only that, but other prominent Colter researchers, including Mattes himself ("Behind the Legend of Colter's Hell: The Early Exploration of Yellowstone National Park," 1949), Burton Harris (*John Colter: His Years in the Rockies*, 1952), David J. Saylor (*Jackson Hole, Wyoming; in the Shadows of the Tetons*, 1970), and Barbara Kubik ("John Colter: One of Lewis and Clark's Men," 1983) all interpreted Colter's Route in much the same way. Chittenden's views thus held sway for virtually a century.[42]

Early in the 1900s, however, one passionate Colter researcher proposed a radically different theory about Colter's Route. His name was John G. White. According to the *Encyclopedia of Cleveland History*, John Griswold White (August 10, 1845–August 26, 1928), "lawyer and bibliophile . . . graduated from Western Reserve College and was admitted to the bar in 1868. . . . White practiced largely in real estate, but was also well-versed in maritime, church, and municipal law." White "served on the Cleveland Public Library board of trustees . . . and as president 15 years. . . . Largely through his efforts, [the Cleveland Public Library] grew to national prominence, established a branch library system, introduced the open-shelf policy, and implemented an employee retirement plan." White donated thousands of books on Orientalia to the library and, "upon his death he bequeathed his 12,000-volume chess and checker collection to it. . . . Never married, White died in Jackson, Wyoming, and was buried in Lake View Cemetery."[43]

This brief biography of White offers no clue—except for the site of his death—that he had any interest in Colter. Starting in the mid-1870s, when White was around thirty years old, he began spending his summers in Yellowstone, which had been named the first national park in the United States—and quite possibly in the world—in 1872. White's legal practice was so successful that he was able to continue his regular visits to the park, which then seemed more remote than Alaska does today, until his death. At first White visited Yellowstone for its remoteness, scenic grandeur, and fishing, but over time he became fascinated with the fur trade and John Colter.

White traveled in the greater Yellowstone ecosystem like few people have, first on foot, then by horse and wagon and finally by automobiles and airplanes. He saw the country when it was still young, which brought him in contact with many old-timers who still remembered the later days of trapping and hunting the land before Yellowstone was named a national park. White also began corresponding with Colter scholars like Vinton and Ghent. In 1926, after a good deal of both study and field research, White recorded his thoughts on Colter in a little-known, self-published manuscript titled *A Souvenir of Wyoming: Being a Diary of a Fishing Trip in Jackson Hole and Yellowstone Park, with Remarks on Early History and Historical Geography*.

White's beliefs about Colter's trek were controversial at the time and still are. While he believed, like most other researchers, that Colter went south into present Wyoming and then traveled in a clockwise direction across the Absaroka Range, into the Wind River Valley, and over Union Pass into Jackson Hole, he then parted ways with other Colter enthusiasts. From the Jackson Hole area, he has Colter going anywhere and everywhere—back and forth across the Tetons, up and down the Snake River, even into the Green River Country and southeast along the Wind River Range all the way to South Pass. One of White's most controversial claims was that Colter never saw Yellowstone Lake and that Clark's Lake Eustis was actually a composite of Shoshone and Lewis lakes, to the southwest of Yellowstone Lake. All of this required interpreting Colter's Route as shown on the Biddle map in a radical fashion, as if it only hinted at Colter's true course.

Although Vinton, Ghent, and others were aware of White's research, they never formally reviewed it because it was never published to a general audience. White, for instance, only typed eight copies of "A Souvenir of Wyoming," apparently for friends and relatives. Still, White was in many ways the archetypical "Colter buff"—an unpaid amateur taken by the Colter enigma and unable to leave it alone, spending year after year and dollar after dollar in an engaging but ultimately fruitless effort to track down and understand the first American mountain man.

In the 1930s, a few years after White's death, J. Neilson Barry (1870–1961), a retired Episcopalian minister and a tireless investigator, took up a two-and-a-half decade search for Colter. By that time, Barry had already made a name for himself—he had been publishing articles on Astoria, Astorians, the Columbia River, and the history of the Northwest for more than twenty years. He published frequently in both the *Quarterly of the Oregon*

Historical Society and the *Washington Historical Quarterly* and was especially prolific in the 1920s and 1930s.

Unlike White, Barry had never been closer to the Yellowstone ecosystem
than traveling on a train through Wyoming. But over the years he developed
a keen sense of the geography or drainage patterns in northwestern Wyoming, so much so that he could look at the Biddle map and later the Clark
manuscript map and see things that few other researchers noticed. For several
years, Barry conducted an exhaustive study of the Biddle map and how it
compared to modern maps. One Wyoming researcher wrote to him: "Your
letters rather intrigue me for a man who has never seen Wyoming. . . . I must
confess you are certainly well versed on both its geography and history."[44]

Some tended to discredit Barry, however, because of his obsession of
going over the same material time after time in the hundreds of letters and
maps he sent from his home in Portland, Oregon, a home he had dubbed
"Barrycrest." These letters and maps contain invaluable information on both
history and geography, but the shear volume wore people out, especially
National Park Service employees at Yellowstone and elsewhere. One internal
memorandum of the Park Service made the point quite candidly: "As you
suggest, any attempt to discuss the pros and cons of the Colter question with
Mr. Barry would . . . introduce an endless cycle of burdensome correspondence, since the gentleman is obviously of a highly pugnacious type and is
plainly fanatical on this particular subject."[45]

Scholars at the Wyoming State Department of History appreciated Barry's tenacity, however, and in 1938 devoted half an issue of *Wyoming Annals*
to Colter, including three maps drawn and annotated by Barry and an article
entitled "John Colter's Map of 1814" (relying on the version printed in
England), written by Barry. The other article, "A Sketch of John Colter," was
written by Ghent, the top Colter scholar in the country at the time.

Barry's study of Colter's Route was based chiefly on making enlarge-
ments of the Biddle map and comparing known points, such as Three Forks
and the mouth of the Bighorn River, with current maps. Using known points,
he was able to determine latitudes and longitudes, which he used to plot
Colter's Route. Barry's studies eventually convinced him that Colter, like
Drouillard, drew a number of maps that he gave William Clark in the fall of
1810. He believed that Clark then sent copies of the maps to the engraver of
the Biddle map, Samuel Lewis. However, no such maps have been discovered. Vinton pointed this out to Barry when he wrote: "I notice your discussion of the Colter trip is based on the theory that Colter made three separate
sketch maps. . . . I am not satisfied that this assumption, which apparently is
based only on surmise, is correct."[46]

At the same time, as noted earlier, Barry was correct in concluding that
Clark had sent information—on Henry's River, for example—to Samuel
Lewis after sending the completed map to Biddle in December of 1810.

Barry was also correct when he postulated that Clark eventually revised his master map to include information from Drouillard, Colter, Wilson Price Hunt, Robert Stuart, Andrew Henry, and Peter Weiser (although the case for Weiser is somewhat tentative). Barry simply overstepped the evidence when he theorized that all of these individuals delivered maps to Clark.

As for the actual route of Colter, Barry stated—

- "Colter ascended Pryor's fork to its source at Pryor's Gap, and Colter named the present Sage Creek 'Gap Creek,' but probably went westward from Pryor's gap across Jack and Silvertip creeks and Sand Coulee and then crossed Clark's fork and continued up it to Dead Indian creek."
- "He crossed the rough country to the North Fork of the Shoshone, and . . . there noticed the odor of sulphur and gave that stream an appropriate name. He seems to have found a band of Yeppe Indians and presumably heard from them of the wonders of what is now Yellowstone Park, so made a short sight-seeing trip, going via 'Salt Fork,' our modern Elk or Wapiti river, across the Ishawooa Pass, and around The Thumb of Yellowstone Lake to Sunlight creek."
- "He descended parallel with that creek to where he had previously been, and again ascended along Dead Indian creek and retraced his steps across the rough country to the sulphurous North Fork, which he followed down to the Shoshone branch of the Big Horn, which he assumed was the main stream."
- "Colter traveled along the north side of the branch we now term the Shoshone to Sage creek, which he called Gap creek, and along which he traveled to Pryor's Gap, and then back-tracked his former route via Pryor's Fork to [Fort Raymond]."[47]

Barry maintained that when the first part of the route was compared to a modern map of the Bighorn Basin, the route conformed to actual geography and could be followed like "tracks in the snow." The one caveat was that "on the map of 1814 all places are too far eastward." At the same time, Barry acknowledged that the map's outline of Colter's trek into the Yellowstone country was a confused mishmash: "The writer spent months in analyzing the western portion [of the 1814 map] which is probably the most extraordinary jumble of muddled geography ever drawn and depicts Colter as crossing three tributaries of the Rio Grande del Norte in the immediate vicinity of the Platte and 'Arkansaw.'"[48]

As if to forcefully make his point that the first part of Colter's Route was clear and the second part jumbled, Barry conformed to traditional interpretations in regard to the first part—or until Colter reached the area of present Cody, Wyoming—and advanced a unique theory for the second part. The great majority of previous researchers had argued that Colter reached the Wind River, ascended it to the northwest, and crossed the Continental Divide into the Jackson Hole area. Not so with Barry. Other than agreeing with most others that Colter traveled in a clockwise direction, Barry's scenario is quite different.

By the traditional view, Colter traveled south from present Cody at least as far as present Dubois, possibly even south-southeast to the area near present Crowheart. Barry, by contrast, believed Colter went west from present Cody before ascending Elk Fork (which flows into the North Fork of the Shoshone River), crossing Ishawooa Pass to Pass Creek, and then picking up Thorofare Creek, which took him into the southeast corner of present Yellowstone Park.

Barry's proposed route is somewhat confusing at this point because he was apparently unaware that Thorofare Creek and Atlantic Creek are both tributaries of the Yellowstone River. Regardless, Barry clearly concluded that Colter headed onto Two Ocean Plateau, where streams flowing into the Atlantic are within hundreds of yards from those flowing into the Pacific. [49]

Colter then reached the South Arm of Yellowstone Lake, which (according to Barry) Clark depicted as Lake Biddle, before going northwest around the West Thumb of Yellowstone Lake, which Clark depicted as Lake Eustis. From that point, Barry believed Colter's return to Fort Raymond was roughly similar to the path the traditionalists thought Colter took after reaching the West Thumb from either the Jackson Hole area or from Idaho's Teton Valley.

For years, Barry expressed the belief that Clark had made a number of erasures to the map. (At that time, erasures were often scrapings made with a knife or other sharp instrument.) In Barry's view, these erasures had distorted what was left of John Colter's original drawings in and around the greater Yellowstone area. As noted, however, no maps from Colter have ever been found. But that did not stop Barry—he advocated that color infrared photographs of this section of the map be taken to show what was under the palimpsest that Clark obliterated. [50]

Such photos were never taken, but in 2001, forty years after Barry's death, as planning for the bicentennial of the Lewis and Clark Expedition was making front-page news, archivists at Yale University took a hard look at their copy of William Clark's master map of the American West. Yale had received the map as a gift in 1950 from a Mr. W. R. Coe. For years the map hung on the wall in a small conference room in the Beinecke Rare Book and Manuscript Library, in the dark, seen by few. The map was now quite faded by time and was hard to decipher, but one thing was clear: there were crucial differences between this map and the Biddle versions published in the United States and England in 1814.

In 2003, the Yale archivists took a bold step: using the latest technology, they produced a digitally remastered, full-color copy just as it would have appeared on Clark's drawing table. Allen wrote that viewing the new reproduction of Clark's map was like "listening to a digitally remastered version of an aria sung by Enrico Caruso after listening to the original recording of Caruso's voice on quarter-inch thick black wax, with grooves only on one side."[51]

Dr. Allen continued:

> The new Clark map, unlike the journals of the Expedition, show there were two immediate legacies of the Lewis and Clark Expedition that we often forget in our focus on the accomplishments of the Corps of Discovery. The first legacy, one in which William Clark himself played a key role, was quite simply the first westward probing of the American fur trade as a commercial enterprise. The second legacy, resulting from a combination of geographical lore emerging from the Lewis and Clark travels and the contributions of the fur trade that followed immediately thereafter, was the continuation of a long-held belief in a single source area for major western rivers. It was this belief, as much as anything else, that provided the theoretical basis for Mr. Jefferson's belief that "a practical water route" across the continent of North America existed and, hence, the theoretical basis for the expedition of Lewis and Clark.[52]

Based on his study of Yale's digitally remastered Clark map, Allen proposed the following probable route for Colter:

- "From Lisa's post southwest across the Pryor Mountains (or through Pryor Gap) to the Clark's Fork River, up the Clark's Fork to the canyon, south along the Absaroka/Beartooth front, skirting Heart Mountain on its west side, to the current site of Cody, Wyoming."
- "South along the east face of the Absarokas, crossing Owl Creek Mountains over a low pass to the Wind River (upper Big Horn)."
- "Up the Wind River to its source in Brooks Lake."
- "North from Brooks Lake to the mingled waters of the upper Snake and Yellowstone in the vicinity of Yellowstone Lake."
- "North along the west margins of [Yellowstone Lake], missing the Yellowstone Canyon but crossing Dunraven Pass to the Yellowstone Valley, crossing the Yellowstone at Bannock Ford, then up the Lamar River valley following the Bannock Trail, past Soda Butte (shown on Clark's map as a boiling spring) and across Colter's Pass to the Clark's Fork . . . downstream to the Yellowstone and back down that river to Lisa's fort."[53]

As Allen notes, this proposed route runs contrary to three long-established notions:

(1) Colter was the first European to see the Tetons and Jackson Hole; (2) he crossed the Teton Range into present Idaho; and (3) he carved his name into a stone that was discovered more than a century later by an Idaho rancher. (See Appendix D for a discussion of the so-called "Colter Stone.")

Allen's proposed route has been widely accepted, and rightly so: It is consistent with Clark's original master map and also consistent with accounts of Colter's travels given by two of his associates—Thomas James and John Dougherty (see chapter 10). At the same time, however, a close look at Allen's route shows that Colter scholar W. J. Ghent was right when he concluded that Colter most likely made his trip in 1806–1807 because the given time span during the winter of 1807–1808 did not allow sufficient time for such a long trip.[54]

Like Allen's route itself, this proposal about the timing of Colter's journey runs contrary to a long-established tradition—namely, that Colter departed on this monumental trek late in 1807 and returned in the spring of 1808. As noted earlier in this chapter, the tradition appeared to be based on solid evidence because of its reliance on the Biddle map, which identified "Colter's route in 1807," and Brackenridge's assertion that Colter made a single journey starting late in 1807 and that Colter fought in an Indian battle during his return.

Yale University's digitally enhanced map, however, casts each of these presumed pieces of evidence in a new light. First, in labeling Colter's path, the master map simply says, "Colter's rout," with no date attached. Second, the enhanced map clearly shows Colter beginning and ending his journey at Pryor Creek, which is more than one hundred and fifty miles from where the battle mentioned by Brackenridge took place. (Thomas James, an eyewitness of the bones scattered on the battlefield, reported the fight had occurred along the Gallatin River, one day from Three Forks.) Therefore, the conclusion that Brackenridge's description coincided with Colter's route as identified on Clark's map does not hold water, and one possible explanation is that Brackenridge, who apparently got his information from Lisa, had conflated two different trips by Colter.

All of this is closely related to Ghent's thesis because the question of whether Colter had sufficient time to complete a given journey is tightly bound up with the question of when he departed the mouth of the Bighorn, and, as shown earlier in this chapter, his likely departure time in 1807 was mid-December. Leaving the mouth of the Bighorn at that time would not have presented problems for an explorer traveling to two of the key sites proposed by Allen—Colter's Hell (near present Cody, Wyoming) and the Wind River Valley (which includes present Dubois, Wyoming). Each of these areas has a relatively mild climate, with present average annual snowfalls of less than forty inches.[55]

Allen's list of sites on the proposed map, however, includes Brooks Lake and Colter Pass, both of which would have presented huge challenges to a winter traveler. Reaching Brooks Lake from Dubois may initially seem like a minor task because it is less than twenty-five miles away. However, as Colter ascended the Wind River he would have also ascended a rugged mountain range that simply would not have been passable in winter. The elevation at Brooks Lake is 9,200 feet, and the area is well known for its huge annual snowfall. Togwotee Pass, only a few miles away, reportedly receives an annual snowfall of around six hundred inches.[56]

But, the question might be asked, What if Colter waited in the Wind River Valley until spring and then made his way to Brooks Lake and then the Yellowstone area? There is a serious problem with this theory. Clark's map clearly shows Colter crossing the Yellowstone River, and spring is the worst possible time to attempt such a thing. The spring runoff brings treacherous rapids that sometimes last the entire summer. A savvy explorer like Colter was not at all likely to attempt something so dangerous.[57]

But, the rejoinder might come, Clark's map does not reveal whether Colter traveled clockwise (the direction proposed by Allen and the great majority of previous researchers) or counterclockwise on his trip. Could he have avoided problems with the snow if he had gone counterclockwise. The answer is no, because in that case Colter would have encountered an 8,048-foot pass that now bears his name, Colter Pass, in the dead of winter. Cooke City, Montana, just west of Colter Pass receives an average annual snowfall of two hundred and eight inches.[58] And, since a counterclockwise route would have meant he still had to cross the Yellowstone River, waiting till spring was just as useless as waiting in the Wind River Valley. Nor would Colter have been traveling continuously through gentle meadows once he reached present Yellowstone Park because his route included both a pass over the Continental Divide west of West Thumb (elevation of 8,391 feet) and Dunraven Pass (elevation of 8,859 feet).

Again there's a possible reply: What if Colter had snowshoes? More than one student of Colter's Route has put forth the proposition that he did, but the question is, Where is the evidence? Certainly, many Indian nations in the northern United States and Canada, such as the Cree, the Ojibwa, and the "Rocky Mountain Indians" mentioned by Alexander Mackenzie, used snowshoes, but that does not provide a direct link to Colter. Such a link would most likely be found in Colter's experience with Lewis and Clark. The Corps of Discovery, however, spent three winters together—at Fort Dubois, Fort Mandan, and Fort Clatsop—and there is no mention in the journals that they ever used snowshoes. In fact, the sole reference to snowshoes came when Lewis observed "snowshoes in all the lodges of the natives above the Columbean vally" were necessary because "their snows were frequently breast deep."[59]

Nor is there any mention in the accounts left by Lisa or his partners or his men that they ever used snowshoes. That leaves the question of whether Colter could have obtained snowshoes (or the knowledge of how to make them) from the Crow. There is no evidence of that, either. As a result, no one has yet made a convincing argument that Colter used snowshoes to enter the Yellowstone Park area during winter.[60]

In one sense, however, this entire discussion about winter travel over peaks that no doubt would have prompted Patrick Gass to reconsider his claim about "the most terrible mountains I ever beheld" begs the question because a man on a mission to the Crow Indians had absolutely no reason to venture into present Yellowstone Park. The prominent scholar of the Crow Indians, C. Adrian Heidenreich, has identified a number of Crow camps seen by explorers or trappers between 1804 and 1851. There were Crow camps throughout the region now properly considered Crow country—from Bear Lake (in present southeast Idaho), Teton Pass (near present Jackson, Wyoming), the Yellowstone River (near present Billings, Montana), and the Tongue River (in present southern Montana) to the headwaters of the Powder River (in southern Wyoming), the Bighorn River (near present Thermopolis, Wyoming), and the Wind River (near present Lander, Wyoming), to offer only a partial list. The one region conspicuously missing in this inventory is present Yellowstone National Park. Moreover, two trappers who saw a good deal of the Yellowstone area during the 1820s and 1830s, Daniel Trotter Potts and Osborne Russell, made no mention of seeing Crow Indians there.[61]

The notion that Colter, a shrewd scout and good communicator with Indians, would hazard a trek into Yellowstone in search of Crow camps is simply untenable. He must have gone for some other reason.

Colter and Dickson and Hancock had quite possibly split up not long after they reached the mouth of the Bighorn in September of 1806. Is it possible that Colter's native wanderlust and his admiration for William Clark combined to propel him on a quest for the sources of the great rivers of the West? Throughout the expedition, Colter and his fellows had watched as Clark studied rivers and mountains—and stars; estimated distances by dead reckoning; and used his surveying instruments and skills to sketch one map after another. Colter had been Clark's chief assistant in reconnoitering the treacherous and unnavigable Salmon River, so Colter knew of Clark's particular passion for rivers better than most. In addition, less than three weeks before Colter's departure, Clark had been especially preoccupied with the Yellowstone and Bighorn Rivers. On July 26, 1806, he wrote:

> I am informed by the *Menetarres* Indians and others that this River [the Bighorn] takes its rise in the Rocky mountains with the heads of the river plate and at no great distance from the river Rochejhone [the Yellowstone] and passes between the Coat Nor or Black Mountains and the most Easterly range of Rocky Mountains. it is very long and Contains a great perpotion of timber on which there is a variety of wild animals, perticularly the big horn which are to be found in great numbers on this river. Buffalow, Elk, Deer and Antelopes are plenty and the river is Said to abound in beaver. it is inhabited by a great number of roveing Indians of the Crow Nation, the paunch Nation and the Castahanas all of those nations who are Subdivided rove and prosue the Buffa-

low of which they make their principal food, their Skins together with those of the Big horn and Antilope Serve them for Clothes. [62]

Colter had not been present when Clark made this entry, but it would have been the most natural thing in the world for Clark to go over these details when he granted Colter permission to head up the Missouri and then the Yellowstone with Dickson and Hancock. Besides that, Clark had written these words at the confluence of the Yellowstone and the Bighorn, two of the three rivers he had mentioned in his memorable entry, quite possibly in close proximity to where the three-man company had dissolved their union in 1806 and where Colter was deliberating his next move. [63]

The trapping enterprise had been a bust, but Colter now had an opportunity to repay the man who had not only allowed him to leave but had sent him off with genuine good will and encouragement. The best way to thank the cartographer, Clark, was to make an important contribution to his maps. Clark had not had the chance to follow the Yellowstone or any of its tributaries south, but Colter was now in the perfect position to do so. Could it be a coincidence that Colter's apparently illogical decision to leave Crow country took him to the source of both the Yellowstone and the Bighorn and that Clark identified both on his splendid map of the West?

Merrill J. Mattes was undoubtedly correct when he wrote that trying to describe Colter's precise route was attempting "to prove the ultimately unprovable."[64] Nevertheless, given Allen's analysis of Yale's remastered map and the above examination of when and why Colter was most likely to travel to the Yellowstone country, a modified proposal of Colter's Route becomes possible.

Early in October of 1806, Colter began his journey from the solitary camp he had established on Pryor Creek, near the present town of Pryor, Montana. He ascended Pryor Creek and the Pryor Mountains to Sage Creek, which he followed to the approximate site of present Warren, Montana.

Colter likely wore buckskin, moccasins, and a hat, with a buffalo robe to use as both a coat and blanket. Standard supplies for Colter and the host of trappers who followed him included flint and steel, hooks and fishing line, a pipe and some tobacco, a hefty butcher knife in a sheath of buffalo hide, a tomahawk, and a good supply of pemmican (dried meat mixed with grease and berries—"a high-energy, long-keeping food"). But, most crucial, of course, were the rifle, powder horn, and balls, as well as spare rifle parts and tools for repairing the rifle. It was not a light load. [65]

Colter next went west to Clark's Fork of the Yellowstone, which he ascended into present Wyoming. Going counterclockwise, to reach the source of the Yellowstone before winter hit, he wound to the northwest, crossing present Colter Pass, and then traveling to the headwaters of Soda Butte Creek. Working downstream to the southwest, he found the Bannock

Trail leading to the Lamar River, whereupon he entered present Yellowstone
Park. He descended the Lamar River through a gentle rolling high mountain
plateau. "Thro. this valley ran a small stream in a North direction which all
agreed in believing to be a branch of the Yellow Stone," wrote trapper
Osborne Russell, who saw the Lamar River Valley in 1834. "[July] 29th We
descended the stream about 15 miles thro. the dense forest and at length came
to a beautiful valley about 8 Mls. long and 3 or 4 wide surrounded by dark
and lofty mountains. The stream after running thro. the center in a NW
direction rushed down a tremendous canyon of basaltic rock apparently just
wide enough to admit its waters."[66]

Colter followed the Lamar to its mouth, near Tower Fall (thereby averting
the Grand Canyon of the Yellowstone) and crossed the low-flowing Yellowstone River at that point. He then cut south-southwest, first to Dunraven Pass
and then into Hayden Valley. "Encamped in a beautiful plain which extends
along the Northern extremity of the Lake [Yellowstone Lake]," Russell later
wrote of Hayden Valley. "This valley is interspersed with scattering groves
of tall pines forming shady retreats for the numerous Elk and Deer during the
heat of the day." Next, describing Yellowstone Lake, which Colter took to be
the source of the Yellowstone River, Osborne continued: "The Lake is about
100 Mls. in circumference bordered on the East by high ranges of Mountains
whose spurs terminate at the shore and on the west by a low bed of piney
mountains its greatest width is about 15 Mls lying in an oblong form south to
north or rather in the shape of a crescent."[67]

Colter followed the West Thumb of Yellowstone Lake around to the west
and south. From the southern tip of Yellowstone Lake, he roughly followed
the Continental Divide onto Two Ocean Plateau, then picked up the Yellowstone River once again (although not realizing what river it was) and ascended it out of present Yellowstone Park.

He next took a south-southwest course to Brooks Lake, a key source of
the Wind River. As Colter descended the Wind River and communicated
with Crow Indians in the area, he correctly concluded that he was following
the upper reaches of the Bighorn River. Winter was now coming on, and he
may have wintered with a band of Crow near the present site of Dubois,
Wyoming. With the coming of spring, he continued down the Wind River to
the vicinity of Bull Lake, then crossed a low pass over the Owl Creek Mountains and cut northwest to the South Fork of the Shoshone River, which he
descended to its confluence with the North Fork of the Shoshone. About five
miles downstream, just west of present Cody, Wyoming, Colter noticed a
strange stench in the air and soon discovered the source of it. Washington
Irving offered this description in 1837:

A Volcanic tract . . . is found on Stinking River, one of the tributaries of the
Big Horn, which takes it unhappy name from the odor derived from sulphur-

ous springs and streams. The last mentioned place was first discovered by Colter, a hunter belonging to Lewis and Clark's exploring party, who came upon it in the course of his lonely wanderings, and gave such an account of its gloomy terrors, its hidden fires, smoking pits, noxious streams and the all-pervading "smell of brimstone" that it received and has ever since retained among the trappers the name of "Colter's Hell."[68]

The legend has grown up that when Colter returned to his comrades at Fort Raymond and told them of the wonders he had seen, they laughed him to scorn and labeled his imagined discovery "Colter's Hell." Though often re-peated, this story has no foundation in primary documents. Accounts of Lisa's trapping expedition say nothing at all about Colter's discoveries. In any event, Drouillard had also seen the volcanic tract and could have sup-ported Colter with his testimony. If Colter did describe the spot Clark labeled as "Boiling Spring" (whether based on a conversation with Drouillard, Col-ter, or both, we don't know), he was probably believed.[69]

As for yarns of "Colter's Hell" circulating among the mountain men, here's the amazing thing: The very first known reference to "Colter's Hell" comes from Washington Irving himself. He apparently heard the phrase from Bonneville in the same context he reported it—as a truthful description of the thermal region Colter and Drouillard had both seen. So there is no basis for the notion that "Colter's Hell" was used disparagingly before Irving pub-lished his adventures of Captain Bonneville. Afterward, the phrase was defi-nitely used descriptively. In addition, these early sources never confuse Col-ter's Hell with the Yellowstone geyser region, which lies sixty or seventy miles to the west.[70] In a letter written in 1852, for example, Father Pierre J. De Smet acknowledged Jim Bridger as the source of this information:

Near the source of the River Puante [Shoshone River], which empties into the Big Horn, and the sulphurous waters of which have probably the same medici-nal qualities as the celebrated Blue Lick Springs of Kentucky, is a place called *Colter's Hell*—from a beaver-hunter of that name. This locality is often agitat-ed with subterranean fires. The sulphurous gases which escape in great vol-umes from the burning soil infect the atmosphere for several miles, and render the earth so barren that even the wild wormwood cannot grow on it. The beaver-hunters have assured me, that the underground noises and explosions are often frightful.[71]

Likewise, Joe Meek's biographer, basing her account on personal inter-views with the venerable mountain man and describing events of 1829, ex-plained:

["Stinking Fork"] derives its unfortunate appellation from the fact that it flows through a volcanic tract similar to the one discovered by Meek on the Yellow-stone plains. This place afforded as much food for wonder to the whole camp, as the former had to Joe; and the men unanimously pronounced it the "back door to that country which divines preach about." As this volcanic district had previously been seen by one of Lewis and Clark's men, named Colter, while on a solitary hunt, and by him also denominated "hell," there must certainly have been something very suggestive in its appearance. [72]

Given the popularity of Washington Irving's writings, his assertion that this spot retained the name "Colter's Hell" among trappers may have been in many ways a self-fulfilling prophecy.

Colter concluded his historic, one-man expedition by going north, skirting Heart Mountain, and reaching Clark's Fork of the Yellowstone. Now back in familiar territory, he retraced his steps back to Pryor Creek.

In 1810, William Clark would garner the details of this journey from Colter, just as he had done in 1808, after consulting with Drouillard on his travels, but there was a crucial difference between the two: Colter had traveled to find the source of rivers, Drouillard to invite Indians to trade. Therefore, it made perfect sense that Clark identified Colter's Route on his master map of the West but said nothing of the wanderings of Drouillard.

Chapter Nine

"In the Midst of an Unbounded Wilderness"

Washington Irving and the Legend of Colter's Run

The question naturally arises: If Colter journeyed to the sources of the Yellowstone and Bighorn Rivers from the fall of 1806 to the spring of 1807, what about the trip he reportedly made for Lisa in the winter of 1807–1808? There is every reason to believe he made that trip, as well, although this time he was inviting Crow Indians to trade. In fact, a trek into the Bighorn Basin and the Wind River Valley the previous year would have given Colter unique qualifications to represent Lisa because he would have already known the location of a number of Crow camps.

Clark's 1808 map makes it clear that Drouillard made one expedition to Crow villages in the winter of 1807–1808 and another in the spring of 1808, and there is good evidence that Colter did the same. Not only that, but Drouillard's known route for the winter trip and Colter's likely route complement each other. As noted in chapter 8, Drouillard followed Clark's Fork of the Yellowstone from its mouth to the "Ap-so-roo-kah fork" and then went east and south to the Bighorn Basin. He reached the Shoshone River and Colter's Hell and then followed the Shoshone northeast, cutting north-northwest before reaching the confluence of the Shoshone River and Bighorn River.

Colter, by contrast (as shown on Clark's 1810 map) followed Pryor Creek toward present Wyoming before going west and picking up Clark's Fork of the Yellowstone at a point south of where Drouillard had left it. (The two men thus traveled along completely different sections of Clark's Fork of the Yellowstone.) This was country Colter had seen the previous year, and some-

99

where in the vicinity of Dead Indian Pass he went southeast to the Colter's Hell area.

Did Colter and Drouillard meet in this region of smoking pits and noxious streams? It is certainly possible because Clark's maps show that both men were there. If so, they may have traveled together for a day, following the Shoshone River downstream. As mentioned, however, in the vicinity of Byron, Wyoming, Drouillard went north into present Montana. Colter continued his descent of the Shoshone, soon reaching its confluence with the Bighorn. The dotted line on Clark's map indicates that Colter stayed in the area of the Bighorn until he was almost half-way between the mouth of the Shoshone and the mouth of the Little Bighorn. Then, like Drouillard, he made his way to Pryor Creek, and Clark's dotted line of Colter's Route stops there, as if Colter started and ended his odysseys at a rabbit hole.

Between them, Colter and Drouillard had visited several Crow camps, and there is every indication that the relationship between Lisa's men and the Crow was a friendly one. In the spring, Drouillard departed on a second journey, this time going south and southeast of Fort Raymond and befriending many more Crow Indians. As for Colter, Major Biddle offered this account in his 1819 letter:

> The first party of Lisa's men that were met by the Blackfeet were treated
> civilly. This circumstance induced Lisa to despatch one of his men (Coulter) to
> the forks of the Missouri to endeavor to find the Blackfeet nation, and bring
> them to his establishment to trade. This messenger [Colter] unfortunately fell
> in with a party of the Crow nation, with whom he staid several days. While
> with them, they were attacked by their enemies the Blackfeet. Coulter, in self-
> defense, took part with the Crows.[1]

As noted in chapter 8, claims that Colter got involved in this conflict as he was returning from his trek through the Yellowstone country make no sense because the site of the battle was quite distant from Colter's Route. In addition, Biddle's claim that the Blackfoot Indians were friendly toward Lisa's party is not corroborated by any other source. Thomas James, who heard of the battle directly from Colter, offered a more likely scenario when he wrote that Colter was in the Three Forks area and was leading a combined band of eight hundred Salish and Crow Indians toward Fort Raymond to trade when fifteen hundred Blackfoot Indians "fell upon them in such numbers as seemingly to make their destruction certain. Their desperate courage saved them from a general massacre."[2]

Among those fighting with desperate courage was Colter himself, now—if not before—a fast friend of the Salish (commonly called "Flatheads") and the Crow. "He distinguished himself very much in the combat," wrote Biddle. James added that Colter "was wounded in the leg, and thus disabled from standing. He crawled to a small thicket and there loaded and fired while sitting on the ground."³

James continued: "The battle was desperately fought on both sides, but victory remained with the weaker party. The Black-Feet engaged at first with about five hundred Flat-Heads, whom they attacked in great fury. The noise, shouts and firing brought a reinforcement of Crows to the Flat-Heads, who were fighting with great spirit and defending the ground manfully." The Blackfoot band was "at length repulsed, but retired in perfect order and could hardly said to have been defeated." Seeing the site of the battle two years later, James reported the effects of the "'terrible slaughter'—skulls and bones were lying around on the ground in vast numbers."⁴

Although Colter in one sense had been an innocent bystander—at least initially—in a battle between warring Indian nations, he quickly became a participant and the Blackfoot warriors "plainly observed a white man fighting in the ranks of their enemy."⁵ Colter's presence no doubt took on a symbolic meaning, forging an even closer bond between the trappers and the Salish and Crow and further alienating the Blackfoot from the American traders. This first conflict pitting an American trapper against the Blackfoot set the stage for three years of mistrust, tension, and bloodshed, until the Blackfoot drove Lisa and the others right out of Montana.

Almost three decades later, Washington Irving offered a simple explanation for Blackfoot hostility, calling them "a restless and predatory tribe, who had conceived an implacable hostility to the white men, in consequence of one of their warriors having been killed by Captain Lewis, while attempting to steal horses." A generation of historians accepted and repeated Irving's interpretation, pointing to Lewis's encounter in 1806 as the cause of the trouble. In some circles that trend has continued down to the present. Such researchers as Alvin Josephy and James P. Ronda have shown, however, that the Blackfoot were much more concerned with larger issues, particularly the impact of American trade on the balance of power among the Indians and on the welfare of the Blackfoot people as a whole. Something Lewis said—that he had invited all Indian nations he had met (including Black enemies) to trade with the whites—carried greater weight than what he did, threatening the Blackfoot nation in a way that no skirmish among a few individuals could have done.⁶

Despite his wound, Colter made it back to Fort Raymond, presumably with the help of Crow allies. Not long after his arrival, Lisa, Drouillard, and several others began preparing to return to St. Louis (where Lisa and Drouillard would be acquitted after facing murder charges for Bissonnet's death). Rather than go back to St. Louis, however, most of the trappers were determined to stay and make their elusive fortunes. For some, that meant going further into Lisa's debt for supplies, sold at a healthy profit, of course. In July of 1808 (as noted earlier), Lewis and Clark veterans John Potts and Peter Weiser signed a joint note to Lisa for $424.50, more than their combined pay for almost three years of service with the captains.

Potts had apparently achieved some success as a trader. In the 1808 map Clark created in consultation with Drouillard, he identified "Pots' establishment" about ten miles up the Yellowstone River from Fort Raymond, indicating that Potts set up his own trading post, but nothing further is known.

Just as Lisa was completing his preparations to leave, Edward Rose finally returned from his mission to the Crow. (It's not clear whether he had been given up for dead.) Rose, who had taken a fair number of goods with him, returned with nothing. "Finding himself so much flattered and feasted by the Indians," wrote Captain Holmes, "and learning their language with considerable facility, he became quite satisfied with his situation. He . . . found that he could run a buffalo or a Black-foot as well as they could." The upshot was that Rose gave away all of his trade goods to his new friends.[7]

Not surprisingly, Lisa was quite displeased, and a dispute broke out between him and Rose. Holmes added:

> This quarrel took place between them in the counting room of the establishment, and almost at the moment of Mr. Lisa's departure—the boat, in fact, was waiting for him with the crew on their benches. They were alone, and during the dispute Rose sprang, like a tiger, upon his disputant, and overpowering him before he had noticed such an intention, would probably have killed him, had not the noise of the scuffle brought a man, by the name of Potts . . . to the relief of Mr. Lisa. His coming saved Mr. L., but he suffered severely by the interference.[8]

Lisa ran out to the boat, which promptly swung into the downstream current. He would never have the chance to thank Potts, now taking his punishment. Rose reportedly ran out and fired a "swivel"—a musket filled with buckshot—that was pointed in the boat's direction. Luckily, no one on the boat was injured, and Lisa and his men got safely away with their valuable cargo of beaver pelts. Before Rose could do any more, he was tackled by "about fifteen men, who could barely restrain the effects of his ungovernable passion."[9] But Lisa got away safely, and within a few days Rose had returned to live with his friends, the Crow. Colter would never see him again.

Twenty-five years later, after a lifetime of adventure with trappers and Indians, continually gaining, losing, and then regaining the confidence of prominent men, Rose died a violent death at the hands of his onetime friends, the Arikara—an event that occurred not far from the site of Fort Raymond. In 1833, Indian agent John F. A. Sanford wrote to William Clark:

> During the last winter, a war party belonging to that [Arikara] nation came on the Yellowstone below the Big Horn where they fell in with three men belong-

ing to A. [American] Fur Co. who they treacherously killed. . . . They scalped
them and left part of the scalps of each tied to poles on the grounds of the
murder. A large party of Crows went in pursuit of them the same evening or
next day but could not overtake them. The names of the men killed are Rose,
Menard & [Hugh] Glass. [10]

Colter and Potts, who had experienced that unforgettable moment of running canoes down the Missouri rapids together, were now both convalescing,
Colter from his leg wound and Potts from Rose's beating. After a month or
so, sometime late in the summer of 1808, they left together on a trapping
venture. Considering Colter's recent battle with Blackfoot Indians near Three
Forks, their decision to go there is inexplicable. Beaver were plentiful in
Crow country, along the Bighorn. But west they went, to the Jefferson, the
same river they had followed west three years earlier with Lewis and Clark.
Now the two expedition veterans were about to see what the Blackfoot concern over large issues of trade and power meant on a very personal level.

Potts was killed, of course, but Colter escaped and made his legendary
run, the feat that brought him more fame than either his service with Lewis
and Clark or his exploration of Yellowstone.

As noted in chapter 1, three men talked personally with Colter and left
accounts of his escape—Dr. William H. Thomas, who interviewed Colter in
present North Dakota in the autumn of 1809 and published his version in the
Missouri Gazette in December of that year; John Bradbury, who interviewed
Colter in St. Louis in May of 1810 and published his version in *Travels in the
Interior of America,* 1817; and Thomas James, who interviewed Colter in
March and April of 1810 in present Wyoming and Montana, where Colter's
Run had taken place, and published his version in *Three Years Among the
Indians and Mexicans,* 1846. The writer most responsible for making Colter
famous, however, was Washington Irving, a best-selling author of his day
who, relying on Bradbury's account, included a compelling version of Colter's Run in 1836 in his popular book *Astoria, or Anecdotes of an Enterprise
beyond the Rocky Mountains.* (Appendix A includes all four versions in their
entirety; it is ironic that Thomas, the first to interview Colter and also the first
to publish the story, produced an account far shorter and far less detailed that
the others.)

Like Bradbury, Irving tells the story of Colter's adventure right after a
brief discussion of the legendary American frontiersman, Daniel Boone
(whom Bradbury interviewed). And although neither Bradbury nor Irving
mention it, both were likely aware that Boone himself had made a "run" from
Indians, an episode described in *The Discovery, Settlement and Present State
of Kentucke,* by John Filson, the 1784 book that launched Boone's mythical
persona. (Although Filson based his account on interviews with Boone, he
liberally put words in Boone's mouth—and the mouths of others.)

Daniel Boone's run—thirty years previously and eighteen hundred miles to the east—had been quite a different episode. After his capture by the Shawnee in February of 1778, he had been taken to the Ohio side of the Ohio River and adopted into Chief Blackfish's family. He was given the name Sheltowee. "I became a son," he said, "and had a great share in the affection of my new parents, brothers, sisters, and friends. . . . My food and lodging was in common with them, not so good as I could desire, but necessity made everything acceptable." Boone bided his time, making the most of his life as an Indian—becoming too content in the eyes of fellow prisoner William Hancock (father of Forrest Hancock)—and waiting for the chance to escape. Allowed to hunt, he squirreled away rifle parts and a few supplies. Then, in June, he was "alarmed to see four hundred and fifty Indians, of their choicest warriors, painted and armed in a fearful manner, ready to march against Boonsborough." Boone knew he could wait no longer. "I determined to escape [at] the first opportunity," he said. [11]

Days later, Boone was riding a horse loaded with salt kettles when the Shawnee with him pursued a flock of turkeys. Wasting no time, Boone cut the lashings holding the kettles, shouted a farewell to his Indian mother and sisters, and galloped the horse south, toward the Ohio River, riding hard the entire night. When the horse finally gave out the next morning, Boone set it free and ran on in his bare feet, frequently walking on top of loose timber to disguise his trail. He learned later from a Shawnee friend that the Indians had tracked him for some distance, finally concluding he would get lost and perish in the wilderness. "They all said let you go," the friend recalled, "that you would never get home, you would Starve to death." But Boone's friend knew him much better than that: "I told them that you would get home, for you went as Straight as a leather string." [12]

Boone—like Hancock, who escaped a month later—could only reach Kentucky by swimming the vast Ohio River, much wider than several Madison Rivers combined. Boone reached the river at twilight, tied his precious supplies and his clothes to a log, and pushed off into the powerful, westbound current, collapsing into sleep when he finally stumbled onto Kentucky ground. He woke to feet "scalded" by his run and soothed them with an oak bark poultice. Restoring himself with some jerky he had brought, he also fashioned a stock and then used his spare parts to construct a working musket. "It was June 19, 1778," Boone later said, "being on run from the Indians who had me lately before in captivity, I came to a large open space of ground at the forks of three branches, waters of Johnson's Fork." Here he tested his gun for the first time. "You may depend upon it," he boasted. "I felt proud of my rifle." He soon brought down a buffalo, savoring what he called the one meal of his run and even smoking the buffalo tongue and saving it as a present for his eight-year-old son, Daniel Morgan. [13]

Boone's journey of one hundred and sixty miles took five days. He announced himself before arriving at the fort because his hair had been plucked and he did not want to be mistaken for an Indian. "Bless your soul," one of the settlers said, but many others were suspicious because rumors had already spread that Boone had conspired with the British and the Shawnee. Expecting a reunion with his wife, Rebecca, and his children, Boone heard the dismal news that Rebecca had given him up for dead (apparently preferring that rumor to gossip of his mutiny). "She put into the settlements long ago," he was told, "packed up and was off to the old man's in Carolina."[14] Thinking his entire family had left, the disconsolate Boone went alone to his cabin, but his sorrow was replaced with joy when his married daughter Jemima—the same daughter he had rescued from the Shawnee two years earlier—arrived at his door.

Less than two years after "Boone's Run," another renowned frontiersman, American Revolution hero Samuel Brady (1756–1795), made an escape of his own, known as "Brady's Leap," which bears interesting similarities to Colter's experience. Not published until the 1840s, the story of Brady's escape had spread by word of mouth long before that (which means that Boone's and Colter's experiences are more fully documented than Brady's).

In 1780 in present Ohio, Brady led a group of rangers tracking a band of Sandusky Indians said to have killed settlers in a camp south of Fort Pitt. When Brady and his men attacked, they quickly realized they were vastly outnumbered and retreated. Because the Indians had recognized Brady and desired his capture and torture, they chased him and let his companions escape. He was on the north side of the Cuyahoga River and had to cross the river to escape, but safe crossing points were few. He ran about eight miles toward a crossing spot at Standing Rock, but several Indians were already waiting for him there.

He ran toward another crossing spot but found Indians there as well. He soon found himself surrounded, near a river gorge lined with thirty-foot cliffs. With his pursuers now close behind, he barreled toward a section of river narrower than normal but still seemingly much too wide to jump. Said to be a very athletic man, the exhausted Brady pushed himself harder, picking up speed as he approached the chasm. Then, to the shock of the Indians chasing him, he leaped.

Because the Pennsylvania and Ohio Canal Company widened the river in the 1830s, it is no longer possible to measure the distance of Brady's Leap, in present Kent, but according to popular lore, he leapt twenty-two feet to a ledge on the other side, then pulled himself up to solid ground. Jumping twenty-two feet would have been an incredible though not impossible exploit.[15]

Even then, however, Brady's troubles were not over. An Indian on the other side shot him in the thigh, and as Brady limped away from the river toward a nearby lake (now known as Brady's Lake), he heard the Indians running for the nearest crossing spot. Finding a fallen chestnut tree lying in the lake, Brady submerged himself beneath it and breathed through a reed. Soon the Indians, who had followed his trail of blood, walked above him on the trunk, searching for him. They lingered there for some time, expecting him to come up for air. Brady understood enough Sandusky to comprehend their eventual conclusion that he must have killed himself to avoid being tortured. Even after Brady could no longer hear the Indians, he stayed under water. Finally, when it was dark, he walked shivering to the shore and began his long trek to Fort McIntosh, sixty miles away. [16]

Of course, the tales of Boone and Brady—as well as all other narratives reported by solitary escapees—are simply impossible to corroborate. What is clear is that Colter's Run places him firmly in the tradition of other great American legends. Indeed, the mythical nature of Colter's Run was hardly lost on Washington Irving, who called it a "rugged experience . . . of savage life," observing that Colter "pushed resolutely forward, guiding himself in his trackless course by those signs and indications known only to Indians and backwoodsmen." Not hiding his admiration for Colter, Irving added that "after braving dangers and hardships enough to break down any spirit but that of a western pioneer, [Colter] arrived safe at the solitary post in question." [17]

Because of its widespread distribution, Irving's (and thus Bradbury's) retelling of Colter's Run has become generally known and accepted. When the various narratives are compared, however, a number of questions arise as to which version rings more accurate.

First is the question of where Colter and Potts encountered the Indians. James wrote they were on the Jefferson River, but Irving had them "six miles up a small river that emptied into the [Jefferson] fork." James was clearly the expert because he saw the Three Forks area himself. (Thomas is silent on the issue.) It is therefore reasonable to assume that the conflict occurred on the Jefferson itself and that Colter ran not to the Jefferson but to the Madison, as James said. [18]

When describing Potts's death, James wrote: "In an instant, at least a hundred bullets pierced his body and as many savages rushed into the stream and pulled the canoe, containing his riddled corpse, ashore. They dragged the body up onto the bank, and with their hatchets and knives cut and hacked it all to pieces, and limb from limb." [19]

Irving, by contrast, wrote: "The next moment he fell himself, pierced with innumerable arrows"—"or, as Colter quaintly expressed it, 'he was made a riddle of'" (not mentioning what happened to Potts's body afterward). [20]

Although the Blackfoot Indians had obtained flintlock rifles from British traders, most warriors were still armed with bows and arrows in 1808. (Thomas wrote that Colter and Potts were "fired on by these Indians" but does not offer details on Potts's death.)[21] Therefore, the Irving version is more likely. James's comments about the mutilation of Potts's body, however, are quite consistent with other accounts from the era.

All accounts agree that after Colter's capture, he was given a chance to flee. "He was ordered to run for his life," wrote Thomas in his only comment on the matter. James offered more details, saying a council was held to determine Colter's fate. "After the council, a Chief pointed to the prairie and motioned him away with his hand, saying in the Crow language, 'go—go away.'"[22]

Irving claimed, however, that Colter had "some knowledge of the Blackfoot language" and "overheard a consultation as to the mode of despatching him." Then a chief "seized Colter by the shoulder, and demanded if he could run fast. . . . Though in reality [Colter] was known among his brother hunters for swiftness of foot, he assured the chief that he was a very bad runner."[23]

The best evidence indicates that Irving was wrong on both counts. Colter had had many opportunities to learn the Crow language but virtually no chance to learn Siksika, the tongue of the Blackfoot. In addition, the record offers no mention of Colter being a fast runner. This seems to be a case of Bradbury and Irving taking so-called literary license in their narratives.

The next disagreement among the chroniclers concerns the Indian who ran faster than his companions and reached Colter by himself. Take these accounts:

Thomas:

> Observing one of their young men following at full speed, armed with a spear, he pushed on to some distance, endeavouring to save his life. In a few minutes the savage was near enough to pitch his spear, which he [had] poisoned, and threw with such violence as to break the handle and miss the object. Coulter became the assailant, turned on the Indian and put him to death with the broken spear.[24]

James:

> One solitary Indian, far ahead of the others, was rapidly approaching, with a spear in his right hand, and a blanket streaming behind from his left hand and shoulder. Despairing of escape, Colter awaited his pursuer and called to him in the Crow language, to save his life. The savage did not seem to hear him, but letting go his blanket, and seizing his spear with both hands, he rushed at Colter, naked and defenseless as he stood before him and made a desperate lunge to transfix him. Colter seized the spear, near the head, with his right hand, and exerting his whole strength, aided by the weight of the falling Indian, who had lost his balance in the fury of the onset, he broke off the iron head or blade which remained in his hand, while the savage fell to the ground and lay prostrate and disarmed before him. Now was *his* turn to beg for his life, which he did in the Crow language, and held up his hands imploringly,

but Colter was not in a mood to remember the golden rule, and pinned his adversary through the body to the earth by one stab with the spear head. He quickly drew the weapon from the body of the now dying Indian, and seizing his blanket as lawful spoil, he again set out with renewed strength, feeling, he said to me, as if he had not run a mile.[25]

Irving:

> The sound of footsteps gathered upon him. A glance behind showed his pursuer within twenty yards, and preparing to launch his spear. Stopping short he turned round and spread out his arms. The savage, confounded by this sudden action, attempted to stop and to hurl his spear, but fell in the very act. His spear stuck in the ground, and the shaft broke in his hand. Colter plucked up the pointed part, pinned the savage to the earth, and continued his flight.[26]

There are several interesting puzzles related to this part of the story. First, Thomas is the only one to mention a poisoned spear, a detail that seems oddly out of place. How would Colter know that and why didn't he mention it to James or Bradbury? Second, James's assertion that the Indian was carrying a blanket with him does not ring true. Capturing Colter was a matter of honor for these Indians and they had every reason to rid themselves of anything that might slow them down. No one made that point better than James himself when he wrote that as Colter was getting his head start, "he saw the younger Indians throwing off their blankets, leggings, and other incumbrances, as if for a race."[27] Lastly, James and Bradbury both claimed that the Indian broke the spear head when he fell, which is more likely than Thomas's notion that violently throwing the spear caused it to break.

Irving's version of the event is thus the most convincing.

Colter next sought refuge in the Madison River, but where did he hide? "Naked and tired he crept to the river, where he hid in a beaver dam from the band who had followed to revenge the death of their companion," answered Thomas.[28]

James gave a similar but more detailed answer:

> Dashing through the willows on the bank, he plunged into the stream and saw close beside him a beaver house, standing like a coal-pit about ten feet above the surface of the water, which was here of about the same depth. This presented to him a refuge from his ferocious enemies of which he immediately availed himself. Diving under the water he arose into the beaver house, where a found a dry and comfortable resting place on the upper floor or story of this singular structure. The Indians soon came up, and in their search for him they stood upon the roof of his house of refuge, which he expected every moment to hear them breaking open. He also feared that they would set it on fire. After a diligent search on the side of the river, they crossed over, and in about two hours returned again to his temporary habitation in which he was enjoying bodily rest, though with much anxious foreboding. The beaver houses are

divided into two stories and will generally accommodate several men in a dry and comfortable lodging. In this asylum Colter kept fast till night. [29]

Interestingly, Irving included many of the same details in a different story:

> He swam to a neighboring island, against the upper end of which the drift-wood had lodged in such quantities as to form a natural raft; under this he dived, and swam below water until he succeeded in getting a breathing place between the floating trunks of trees, whose branches and bushes formed a covert several feet above the level of the water. He had scarcely drawn breath after all this toils, when he heard his pursuers on the river bank, whooping and yelling like so many fiends. They plunged in the river, and swam to the raft. The heart of Colter almost died within him as he saw them, through the chinks of his concealment, passing and repassing, and seeking for him in all directions. They at length gave up the search, and he began to rejoice in his escape, when the idea presented itself that they might set the raft on fire. Here was a new source of horrible apprehension, in which he remained until nightfall. [30]

Although Burton Harris claimed that James's account of Colter hiding in a beaver dam was hardly plausible, it is actually more plausible than the claim of Bradbury and Irving that Colter hid under a pile of driftwood and remained half-submerged in the river for several hours. Montana rivers are cold at any time of year, and hypothermia would have set in long before Colter supposedly left the river after darkness fell. It would have been different if Colter had found a large beaver house that allowed him to get his entire body out of the water. The other factor that argues in favor of the beaver dam over the pile of driftwood is that Dr. Thomas and James both reported it, even though they heard and published their accounts independently of each other.

The final issue is straightforward: How long did it take Colter to get back to Fort Raymond? There is no agreement on this. Thomas said nine days, James eleven, and Bradbury seven. (Irving curiously omits this detail, although he follows Bradbury in virtually all others.) Here the nod goes to James, who traveled the same route (but in the opposite direction) with Colter in 1810 and knew perfectly well how long it would have taken a man on foot to reach the mouth of the Bighorn.

Although James gave important clues as to the route taken by Colter from the Madison River to Fort Raymond, no careful study of the subject was conducted until Mark W. Kelly combined James's clues with those given by John Dougherty, also a member of the party traveling with Colter in 1810. According to Kelly, the "extraordinary brevity of the Dougherty Narrative" and the "maddeningly scant details provided by Thomas James . . . renders any attempt to delineate their route with specificity an exercise in futility."

Nevertheless, "assuming veracity as to the comments of Dougherty and James," a tentative route can be proposed.[31]

Given the fact that Fort Raymond was roughly two hundred miles due east of Three Forks, the natural assumption is that Colter headed in that direction. The journey of Dougherty and James made it clear, however, that Colter's first objective had been to get out of Blackfoot country and into Crow country as soon as possible. To that end, he ascended the Gallatin River forty or fifty miles to the south to a breach in the Gallatin Range, where he crossed eastward to the Yellowstone River, possibly in the vicinity of Dome Mountain, near present Miner, Montana.

Colter next ascended the Yellowstone, following it south into present Wyoming and also present Yellowstone Park. Staying with the Yellowstone, he went past the present site of Mammoth Hot Springs and then east to the mouth of the Lamar River, near present Tower Junction. He was now in familiar territory: On his trek to find the sources of the Yellowstone and the Bighorn, he had reached this spot from the opposite direction, and he knew perfectly well how to get back to Fort Raymond. He likely ascended to the headwaters of Soda Butte Creek, then crossed Colter Pass and Dead Indian Pass before reaching Pryor Gap and Pryor Creek and following the Yellowstone back to the fort.

This was a trek of at least three hundred miles; making it in only eleven days would have been an impressive accomplishment.[32]

As for John Potts, the man who saved Lisa's life, he was the second expedition veteran to die and the second to die a violent death. (Joseph Field had been killed about a year earlier.) Potts had been born in 1776 in Dillenburg, Germany, making him about thirty-two when he was killed near Three Forks. When he came to the United States and whether his parents did also is unknown. He enlisted in the army on July 22, 1800, for a five-year term. According to his military record, his hair and eyes were black, his complexion fair, his occupation miller. He did not marry or have children.[33]

Probate proceedings for Potts's estate opened on January 6, 1810, with Rufus Easton, William Russell, and William Massey acting as executors. Potts's assets were appraised at $656.00. Russell bought Potts's land warrant for $325.00. Peter Weiser sued the estate for $499.50 in November of 1810, but it is not known if he ever received any payment. (Weiser also died a violent death, sometime between 1813 and 1825–1828, but no details are known.) Over the next several years, Rufus Easton appeared in court many times, with various parties haggling over what remained. Finally, seventeen years after Potts's death, in December of 1825, his estate was declared insolvent, and the case was closed.[34]

Chapter Ten

"We All Now Became Blind"

West with Menard and Henry

Within months of arriving back at Fort Raymond, Colter set out on a winter journey, but this time he had everything he had needed so desperately on his run: gun, balls, and powder; knife and flint and steel; buckskin clothes and buffalo robe; pemmican and moccasins. Astonishingly, Colter was returning to the Three Forks area. "He wished to recover the traps which he had dropped into the Jefferson Fork on the first appearance of the Indians who captured him," wrote James. "He supposed the Indians were all quiet in winter quarters, and retraced his steps to the Gallatin Fork."[1]

Perhaps this decision by Colter was no more foolhardy than his original decision to trap with Dickson and Hancock. Danger was part of the game, part and parcel of the game, and beaver traps were valuable. He and Potts had presumably dropped several traps into the water when they were confronted by the Indians. So he went back, something that didn't shock James at all. Colter had shot a buffalo and was supping on the bank of the Gallatin when he heard movement near the river, then the cocking of muskets. He jumped over the fire and sought cover. "Several shots followed and bullets whistled around him, knocking the coals off his fire over the ground. Again he fled for life, and the second time, ascended the perpendicular mountain which he had gone up in his former flight fearing now as then, that the pass might be guarded by Indians. He reached the top before morning and resting for the day descended the next night, and then made his way with all possible speed, to the Fort." James next offered a rare insight into Colter's inner life when he reported that Colter "promised God Almighty that he would never return to this region again if he were only permitted to escape once more with his life."[2] His prayers were answered, as Dickson's had been when he was blinded by the snow, and again he made it safely back to Fort Raymond, after his third consecutive encounter with hostile Indians. But the question remained: Would he honor his pledge to the Lord?

The next record of Colter came six or seven months later—in September of 1809, when Dr. Thomas and Thomas James, who went up the Missouri in the same keelboat, met Colter at "the principal trading house," which had been built "a few miles above the upper [Hidatsa] villages,"[3] in present North Dakota.

On February 24, Governor Lewis had signed a contract with the St. Louis Missouri Fur Company "for the safe conveyance and delivery of the Mandan Chief [Sheheke], his Wife, and child, to the Mandan Nation." The company was to "engage and raise One Hundred and Twenty five effective men . . . [to] act in a Military Capacity, on an Expedition from the said Town of Saint Louis, to the Mandan Villages, on the River Missouri." The company was to be paid seven thousand dollars for the successful completion of the mission, and several company officers, including Pierre Chouteau (appointed commander by Lewis), Lisa, Pierre Menard, Andrew Henry, and Reuben Lewis—as well as Dr. Thomas and James—were part of the group that went up the river. It was understood that the company would have ample opportunities for trapping and trade, and Lewis agreed not to authorize any other persons to travel higher than the mouth of the Platte River for the purposes of trade.[4]

As noted, Dr. Thomas heard and recorded Colter's story of his escape from Blackfoot Indians. James's meeting with Colter concerned more practical matters. "We had found a hunter and trapper named Colter, who had been one of Lewis & Clarke's men, and had returned thus far with them in 1807. Of him I purchased a set of beaver traps for $120, a pound and a half of powder for $6, and a gun for $40."[5]

In subsequent years, either six or eight traps constituted a "set," but James likely had the standard Missouri Fur Company definition in mind—five traps per set. In any case, the price James paid for the traps shows rather dramatically how inflated prices were at Fort Mandan. In St. Louis in 1807, Auguste Chouteau had paid the Hunt and Hankinson store $7.50 each for seven beaver traps. Now Colter was charging two or three times that.[6]

The detail not mentioned but implied by James is this: Colter's selling traps, powder, and a gun meant he had decided to keep his vow to God and return to St. Louis. He had already given up three chances to return—when he declined going with the captains in 1806, when he met Lisa at the mouth of the Platte in 1807, and when he opted not to return with Lisa and Drouillard in the summer of 1808—and now, in 1809, he had another golden opportunity to go home and see his son, Hiram, because Pierre Chouteau and

Lisa and a large group of men were then at Fort Mandan making preparations to go down river. [7]

Once again, however, the lure of the West proved too powerful for Colter: He broke his sacred covenant and agreed to return to Fort Raymond and lead a large group of trappers to Three Forks in the spring (of 1810). The group included Pierre Menard, Andrew Henry, Reuben Lewis, John Dougherty, William Weir, Michael Immel, Thomas James, Archibald Pelton, and the famous trio of John Hoback, Jacob Reznor, and Edward Robinson. Expedition veteran George Drouillard was also among the group, and Richard Windsor, Pierre Cruzatte, and Peter Weiser possibly were. Forrest Hancock may have been as well. The stories of even this small group of men are amazing, ranging from those who served distinguished careers in statehouses and business to several who died violent deaths in Montana and Idaho to some who faded into anonymous obscurity to one who went insane in the wilderness. [8]

A promissory note signed by Colter on December 31, 1809, makes several things clear: He had returned to Fort Raymond by that time; he had borrowed thirty-six and a half dollars to restock his personal supplies; and expedition veteran Jean-Baptiste Lepage had died, for the note was payable to his estate. Lepage apparently died from natural causes because Clark later indicated his death was nonviolent. [9]

Thomas James reached Fort Raymond sometime in March of 1810, almost perishing in the process. Within a few days, however, he was ready to leave. Menard wanted to get an early start at Three Forks, and the men left in winter conditions, traveling on horseback. Colter was the guide, taking them over the same ground he had gotten to know so well in his various and sundry wanderings.

Launching what was most likely his fourth consecutive winter exodus, Colter led the band up the Yellowstone River. A friend of James's by the name of Brown became snowblind almost immediately. "His eyes pained him so much that he implored us to put an end to his torment by shooting him," wrote James. "I watched him during that night for fear he would commit the act himself." With the help of James, Brown began to recover. [10]

On the second day out, the group experienced a telling omen of what would follow. An Eastern Shoshone chief, accompanied by two wives and a son, had agreed to assist them, going ahead to kill game. James reported that the men came to an Indian lodge; "stripped, and near by, we saw a woman and boy lying on the ground, with their heads split open, evidently by tomahawk. These were the Snake's elder wife and son, he having saved himself and his younger wife by flight on horseback. Our two men who had started out in company with him, were not molested." The chief's wife and son had been killed by a party of Atsina warriors, who "had come upon them, committed these murders, and passed on as if engaged in a lawful and praise-worthy business."[11]

At Pryor Creek they headed south-southeast into present Wyoming's Big-horn Basin. Before reaching Heart Mountain they cut northwest, over Dead Indian Pass and Colter Pass before following the Lamar River southwest into present Yellowstone Park. Next they descended the Yellowstone to the northwest. Ten or twelve days after leaving Fort Raymond, near Dome Mountain, they entered a gap in the mountains. "It commenced snowing most violently and so continued all night," wrote James. "The morning showed us the heads and backs of our horses just visible above the snow which had crushed down all our tents." Colter led them west, and they "proceeded on with the greatest difficulty." The men with the strongest horses went first, attempting to break a trail, but even those horses "soon gave out and the ablest bodied men took their places as pioneers. A horse occasionally stepped out of the beaten track and sunk entirely out of sight in the snow. . . . By that night we passed the ravine and reached the Gallatin river." James and three others forded the river while Colter led the rest of the men through a pass to the north. As night fell, James and his companions shared a piece of buffalo meat "about the size of the two hands."[12]

Colter and the others were next stricken with what Joseph Dickson had experienced three years earlier: snowblindness.

> During this and the proceeding day we suffered from indistinct vision, similar to Brown's affliction of leaving the Big Horn. We all now became blind as he had been, from the reflection of the sun's rays on the snow. The hot tears trickled from the swollen eyes nearly blistering the cheeks, and the eye-balls seemed bursting from our heads. At first, the sight was obscured as by a silk veil or handkerchief, and we were unable to hunt. Now we could not even see our way before us, and in this dreadful situation we remained two days and nights. Hunger was again inflicting its sharp pangs upon us, and we were upon the point of killing one of the pack horses, when on the fourth day after crossing the Gallatin, one of the men killed a goose, of which, being now somewhat recovered from our blindness, we made a soup and stayed the gnawings of hunger.[13]

Continuing down the river, James and the others soon saw the large group led by Colter on the other side. They had also become blind, enduring even more acute symptoms than James's party had. Unable to hunt, they had staved off starvation by killing two horses and three dogs. Eating dog was hardly unusual, but one of the dogs had been James's pet, a present given to him by the Indians. He didn't give details, but perhaps the Indians had been Sheep Eaters and the dog one of their fine animals. This is a distinct possibility since Shoshone Indians were definitely in the area, with James noting that "thirty Snake Indians" had come among Colter's group while they were all helpless. "Brown and another, who suffered less than the others, saw and counted these Indians, who might have killed them all and escaped with their effects with perfect impunity. Their preservation was wonderful."[14]

The next day they reached the spot where two years earlier Colter had fought with the Salish and Crow against the Blackfoot. James and the others saw the human remains scattered in great numbers over the battlefield as Colter told of the fight. The day after that, April 3, 1810, they at last reached Three Forks. Although Lewis and Clark had noted any number of places in present Montana where beaver were plentiful, the founders of the Missouri Fur Company had concluded that this was the best spot of all. "The resources of this country in beaver fur are immense," Menard wrote.[15] The Gallatin, Madison, and Jefferson Rivers were each fed by lesser rivers, streams, and creeks, in a broad, flat, fertile plain offering a supreme natural habitat for beavers. So Menard and his men came, despite hearing firsthand accounts of hostile Blackfoot warriors from Colter.

Still, Colter's tales had a chilling effect on Menard's trappers. "As we passed over the ground where Colter ran his race," wrote James, "and listened to his story an undefinable fear crept over all. We felt awe-struck by the nameless and numerous dangers that evidently beset us on every side." A trapper by the name of Cheek, who had appeared fearless earlier in the journey, was particularly affected. "Even Cheek's courage sunk and his hitherto buoyant and cheerful spirit was depressed at hearing of the perils of the place." The change in Cheek was dramatic, undoubtedly inspiring fear in several of the men. "He spoke despondingly and his mind was uneasy, restless and fearful. 'I am afraid,' said he, 'and I acknowledge it. I never felt fear before but now I feel it.'"[16]

With this spirit of gloom descending on the camp, the men went about their business, carrying out Colonel Menard's assignments. He sent James, Dougherty, Brown, and Ware down the Missouri (toward Great Falls) to trap. James and Cheek each tried to convince the other to join his party, but neither prevailed. As James and the others left in two freshly built dugout canoes, Cheek "said in a melancholy tone, 'James you are going down the Missouri, and it is the general opinion that you will be killed. The Blackfeet are at the falls, encamped I hear, and we fear you will never come back." Then Cheek said the last words James heard him say: "'But I am afraid for myself as well as you. I know not the cause, but I have felt fear ever since I came to the Forks, and I never was afraid of anything before. You may come out safe, and I may be killed. Then you will say, there was Cheek afraid to go with us down the river for fear of death, and now he has found his grave by going up the river. I may be dead when you return.'"[17]

A group of eighteen men, including Colter and Cheek, went upstream forty miles or so to trap the Jefferson, no doubt led by Colter, who had seen the country with Lewis and Clark in 1805 and with Potts in 1808; another group promptly began constructing a fort between the Jefferson and Madison Rivers. "In 1870 the outlines of the fort were still intact," Lieutenant James H. Bradley wrote in 1876, "from which it appears that it was a double stockade of logs set three feet deep, enclosing an area of about 300 feet square, situated upon the tongue of land (at that point half a mile wide) between the Jefferson and Madison rivers about two miles above the confluence, upon the south bank of a channel now called Jefferson Slough."[18]

James, Dougherty, Brown, and Ware followed the Missouri into territory that James compared to the Garden of Eden, with "the peaks and pinnacles of the Rocky Mountains [shining] resplendent in the sun" and mountainsides that were "dark with Buffalo, Elk, Deer, Moose, wild Goats and wild Sheep; some grazing, some lying down under the trees and all enjoying a perfect millenium of peace and quiet. On the margin the swan, geese, and pelicans, cropped the grass or floated on the surface of the water. . . . Dougherty, as if inspired by the scene with the spirit of poetry and song, broke forth in one of Burns' noblest lyrics, which found a deep echo in our hearts." As the perfect day drew to a close, they set their twenty-three traps and soon found a beaver in each one. The next attempt brought similar results, and they were "cheered with thoughts of making a speedy fortune."[19]

The next day they were jolted back into reality when Brown and Dougherty struck a rock and capsized their canoe, losing their guns, their skins, and most of their ammunition. "Ware and I soon followed them," wrote James, "and we all encamped at the mouth of a small creek on the left side of the river. Here Ware and I remained while the two others went back to the Fort to procure other guns and ammunition, taking with them one of our guns."[20] Taking an overland shortcut, Brown and Dougherty reached the fort after a hard day of travel.

> Early the next morning the whole garrison was aroused by an alarm made by Valle and several Frenchmen who came in, as if pursued by enemies, and informed them that the whole party who had gone up the Jefferson, at the time of our departure down the Missouri, had been killed by the Indians, and that they expected an immediate attack on the Fort. The whole garrison prepared for resistance. The next morning after Valle's arrival, Colter came in unhurt, with a few others, and said there were no Indians near the Fort.[21]

Menard now dispatched Dougherty and Brown back down the Missouri to warn James and Ware and escort them back to assist in the defense of the fort. The four of them saw eight Blackfoot warriors but escaped being detected. Next they came close to being shot when they reached the fort at 2:00 A.M. because "the whole garrison was drawn up with fingers upon triggers . . . expecting at attack every moment . . . all in the greatest consternation." Several of those trapping the Jefferson "had had a very narrow escape themselves, as all but Colter probably considered it; he with his experience, naturally looked upon the whole as an ordinary occurrence."[22]

James soon discovered what had become of his friend Cheek:

> The company consisting of eighteen, had proceeded up the banks of the Jefferson, trapping, and on the third day had pitched their tents for the night, near the river, and about forty miles from the Fort. Cheek, Hull, and Ayers were employed in preparing the camp, while the rest had dispersed in various directions to kill game, when some thirty or forty Indians appeared on the prairie south of them, running a foot and on horses, toward the camp. Valle and two men whose names I forget, came running up to Cheek and others and told them to catch their horses and escape. This Cheek refused to do, but, seizing his rifle and pistols, said he would stay and abide his fate. "My time has come, but I will kill at least two of them, and then I don't care." His gloomy forebodings were about to be fulfilled through his own recklessness and obstinancy. Ayers ran frantically about, paralysed by fear and crying, "O God, O God, what can I do?" Though a horse was within his reach he was disabled by terror from mounting and saving his life. Courage and cowardice met the same fate, though in very different manners. Hull stood coolly examining his rifle as if for battle. The enemy were coming swiftly toward them, and Valle and his two companions started off pursued by mounted Indians. The sharp reports of Cheek's rifle and pistols were soon heard, doing the work of death upon the savages, and then a volley of musketry sent the poor fellow to his long home.[23]

Recalling his and Cheek's farewells to each other, James wrote: "His words made little impression on me at the time, but his tragical end a few days afterwards recalled them to my mind and stamped them on my memory forever."[24]

In a letter to his friend, brother-in-law, and business partner Pierre Chouteau, Menard reflected on the sad events. "A party of our hunters was defeated by the Blackfeet on [April 12]," he wrote. "There were two man killed, all their beaver stolen, many of their traps lost, and the ammunition of several of them, and also seven of our horses. We set out in pursuit of the Indians but unfortunately could not overtake them." Several hunters were now discouraged and refused to trap any more, Menard reported, but a group of thirty was returning to where the others were attacked. "The two persons killed are James Cheeks, and one Ayres. . . . Besides these two, there are missing young Hull . . . and Freehearty and his man who were camped about two miles farther up." It went without saying that these three may have suffered a far worse fate than Cheek or Ayres. Menard and his men had also found a Blackfoot who had been killed and the blood trail of one who had been wounded. "Both of them, if the wounded man dies, came to their death at the hand of Cheeks, for he alone defended himself."[25]

Noting Colter's earlier promise to God Almighty to leave the country forever, James added that Colter "was now again in the same country, court- ing the same dangers, which he had so often braved, and that seemed to have for him a kind of fascination." Waxing philosophical, James continued: "Such men, and there are thousands of such, can only live in a state of excitement and constant action. Perils and dangers are their natural element and their familiarity with them and indifference to their fate, are well illus- trated in these adventures of Colter."[26]

But after six years in the wilderness, even Colter had seen enough. "A few days afterward, when Cheek was killed and Colter had another narrow escape," wrote James, "he came into the Fort, and said he had promised his Maker to leave the country, and 'now' said he, throwing down his hat on the ground, 'If God will only forgive me this time and let me off I *will* leave the country day after tomorrow—and be d—d if I ever come into it again.'"[27]

The night before he left, Colter was given two letters by Menard, one to Chouteau and the other to his wife. "Dear Doll," he wrote, "I am taking advantage of the fact that John Colter leaves for St. Louis tomorrow morning to inform you that I am always in perfect health although at the moment I am the image of a skeleton since I do not have an ounce of fat, but I never felt better." After describing the Blackfoot attack quite candidly, Menard asked his wife to "kiss our dear child for me and tell him to expect me in July."[28]

Reuben Lewis also gave Colter a letter. "Dr. Brother," he wrote to Meri- wether Lewis, "The return of your old acquaintance Coalter, gives me an opportunity of addressing you a few lines." Reuben told of the attack and ruminated on fur trapping prospects on the upper Missouri. Hoping that Lewis was making progress on the journals, he wrote, "I should be glad to get a copy of your travel through this country if it should be published before the next opportunity." Closing by assuring his brother he was in good health—and wanting that news passed on to his mother—he signed, "With high esteem your affectionate Brother."[29]

What Reuben nor no one else at the fort realized, however, was that Meriwether Lewis had died in Tennessee of self-inflicted wounds six months earlier, something that Colter would learn the next month, but Reuben would not learn for another fifteen months.

Colter left the next day, wrote James, "in company with young Bryant of Philadelphia, whose father was a merchant of that city, and one other whose name I forget." Then, adding information presumably gleaned from Colter himself when the two man saw each other at court proceedings in 1811 (see Appendix B), James wrote that Colter, Bryant, and the other man "were attacked by the Blackfeet just beyond the mountains, but escaped by hiding in a thicket, where the Indians were afraid to follow them, and at night they proceeded towards the Big Horn, lying concealed in the daytime. They reached St. Louis safely."[30]

Two or three weeks after Colter's departure, Blackfoot warriors attacked and killed George Drouillard, who went down fighting.[31]

Chapter Eleven

"He Reluctantly Took Leave of Us"

Surviving in Civilization

Thomas James witnessed Colter's departure from Blackfoot country in April of 1810, and John Bradbury witnessed his arrival in St. Louis a month later. Neither indicated that Colter returned with a wealth of beaver plews—quite the contrary, he quite likely came back with nothing other than his rifle and ammunition and a few other necessities he had carried with him on his flight from Three Forks. He paddled down the Missouri in such an incredible hurry that he had little time to hunt, let alone trap beaver, averaging more than one hundred miles a day after reaching the Yellowstone River.

"This man came to St. Louis in May, 1810," wrote Bradbury, "in a small canoe, from the head waters of the Missouri, a distance of three thousand miles, which he traversed in thirty days. I saw him on his arrival, and received from him an account of his adventures after he had separated from Lewis and Clarke's party."[1]

If Colter, who was literate, kept a diary or other records or wrote letters to friends or family, none of those documents has been discovered. But it is reasonable to assume that one of the first things he did on his arrival was ask about Lewis and Clark. Someone—we don't know who—informed him that Governor Lewis had shot and killed himself in Tennessee in October of 1809, just three days after Colter had received the promissory note from Thomas James at Fort Mandan.

Colter delivered Menard's letters; what he did with Reuben Lewis's letter to Meriwether is not known, but he obviously handled it with care because the letter survived.

Colter had stayed in the West to make a fortune but had returned a pauper. This was painfully evident when he learned that the pay he was due

121

from his expedition service—at least $350—would not be forthcoming any time soon because Lewis's estate was a tangled mess, with a host of individuals seeking money Lewis had owed them when he died. Everything was now tied up in probate court, and not a single thing was likely to happen fast. But Colter was still expected to pay his debts, and the note he had signed to Lepage's estate (in December of 1809 at Fort Raymond) had been transferred to prominent St. Louis businessman August Chouteau, with payment due at the end of June.[2]

Nor could Colter find consolation in a reunion with William Clark—always more personable than the withdrawn Lewis—because Clark and his wife Julia and infant son Meriwether Lewis Clark were on a trip to the East. Colter no doubt anxiously awaited Clark's return, and he and his family "arrived back in St. Louis on July 7," with Julia and Lewis "suffering from mosquito bites that had festered into sores on her legs severe enough to cause her to limp."[3]

Unfortunately, no record has been found of Colter's meeting with Clark—the first time they had seen each other in almost four years—and how Colter described his quest to find the sources of the Yellowstone and Bighorn Rivers, which neither man would ever see again. Regardless, at least one and probably several consultations between the two occurred before the end of the year as Clark labored on his master map of the West. As Clark's biographer William E. Foley has written, "Beyond its geographic importance, William Clark's cartographic masterpiece presented the West as a region. His visual depiction helped forge a link in the popular imagination between the West's vast expanses and the American Republic's future destiny."[4]

Hard up for cash, Colter signed over his land warrant of 320 acres (a reward from the U.S. government for his service with Lewis and Clark) to John G. Comegys, a St. Louis entrepreneur and partner in the firm of Falconer and Comegys, on August 20, for "value received." Curiously, a month and a half later, in early October, Colter signed a promissory note to merchant Jacob Philipson for $16, Colter's first known debt after his return. How much did Colter receive for the 320 acres and what did he do with it? We simply don't know.[5]

Also in October, one year after Lewis's death, Colter's attorney, James A. Graham, filed a suit against Edward Hempstead, administrator of Lewis's estate, for $559. This total, which supposedly included $380 for pay and allowances and $179 for the extra pay granted by Congress, made no sense because Colter's pay for the Lewis and Clark Expedition was $178.33 1/3, which Congress doubled, for a total of $356.66 2/3 (the same pay rate received by the other privates with Lewis and Clark). Even this was generous because the captains had decided to pay Colter for the entire period of October 15, 1803 to October 10, 1806, even though Colter left the party on

August 17, 1806. Whatever the reason for the discrepancy, the court proceedings began in November of 1810, and Clark was called as a witness.[6]

But Colter was not done borrowing money. In December he signed a note to Comegys for $18.25.[7]

About this same time, in a bizarre turn of events involving Clark, Colter lost his legal representation." I believe I told you a Duell took place in which I acted as Second," Clark wrote to his brother Jonathan on January 31, 1811. "In this affair the man whome I was actng for wounded his advosary every Shot, which was Close Shooting for a young hand."[8]

The men fighting this duel were "Bernard Gaines Farrar, the Virginia-born surgeon at Fort Bellefontaine and later the first American physician in private practice west of the Mississippi," and James A. Graham, Colter's attorney. That was only half the story, however. Graham had reportedly been watching a card game in which an army lieutenant by the name of John Campbell was a player. Graham boldly announced to the group that he had seen Campbell cheating. The upshot was that Farrar soon appeared on Graham's doorstep with a notice challenging him to a duel with Campbell. "But when Graham spurned Campbell's challenge on the grounds that the officer was not a gentleman, Farrar concluded that as Campbell's designated representative, he too, had been equally insulted."[9]

One thing led to another, and on Christmas Day of 1810, William Clark, acting as second for Farrar, personally delivered a challenge to a duel to Graham, even though Farrar and Graham were—or had been—friends. Farrar apparently qualified as a gentleman because Graham accepted the challenge. "The arrangements were made in Clark's office. The men then rowed through ice floes on the Mississippi to a sandbar later known as Bloody Island, directly opposite St. Louis." As Farrar's second, Clark was present at the duel; Graham's second was Lieutenant Colonel Daniel Bissell of the First U. S. Infantry. "Standing ten paces apart, or about sixty feet, they fired three times."[10]

Graham was hit "in the side, with the ball passing along his ribs and lodging in his back; through both legs; and in the right hand. Farrar was wounded in the second fire in the buttocks." Clark and Bissell called off the fourth shot and later stopped the duel itself because Graham was too injured to continue.[11]

Concerned about his own honor, Clark explained in his letter, "A report got into Circulation that I had gave private Signals which I gave to enable the Gentleman to get the first Shot. This report has vexed me a little, and [I] Caled [on] the opposit Sides for a certificate which is in the paper inclosed, and Shall bring forward the man whome made the report." Interestingly, Clark was apparently not worried about participating in what the *Louisiana Gazette* called a "barbarous custom, hooted at by civilized society."[12]

As historian James J. Holmberg has written, "It is not known whether Clark regretted his role in this unfortunate affair, but it is enlightening as to his apparent adherence to the *code deullo*. I found no information that Clark himself actually ever engaged in a duel."[13]

As for the seriously injured Graham, William Foley reported that "the regretful Dr. Farrar ignored his own wounds and rushed to treat his opponent. Though initially it seemed likely that Graham would survive, a ball lodged in his spine took his life a few days later." Other sources claim that "It took Graham four months to recover enough to leave his room. He attempted to return to the East by horseback, but the effort proved too much for his wound, and he was found dead one morning some one hundred miles from St. Louis."[14]

Whatever the exact circumstances of Graham's death, there is no indication that Colter hired another attorney. He was left to himself to seek his expedition pay. Nor was he providing for himself alone, for he had married by March of 1811 and settled on the south side of the Missouri River about forty-five miles west of St. Louis. His wife was a woman by the name of Sarah Loucy, also called Sally, maiden name unknown. Nor do we know the exact date of their marriage. As noted, Colter had a son, Hiram, almost certainly born by 1804, the year Colter departed with Lewis and Clark. Records indicate that Hiram was an adult by the mid-1820s, for he bought goods at an estate sale in May of 1825 and had a son of his own, John B. Colter, in March of 1827. Both of these details offer solid evidence for Hiram's birth by 1804. (Otherwise, given Colter's return in May of 1810, Hiram could not have been born until 1811, making him only fourteen in 1825.) Nothing is known about Hiram's mother, but she was no longer in the picture when Colter married Sarah Loucy between May of 1810 and March of 1811. Colter also had a daughter, Evelina, presumably born in 1811 or 1812.[15]

How Colter supported his family is not known. He had signed away his land and at any rate was not likely suited for farming. Given his skills, he could have eked out a living by hunting and trapping and raising vegetables on a small plot of land. Eastern Missouri was civilized compared with Colter's wilderness homes, but there were deer hides and beaver pelts to be had. As one who cherished his solitude, Colter would have been quite comfortable going alone, or he may have gone with a companion, as he had with Potts three years earlier.[16]

He could have partnered with a seventy-six-year-old trapper who was a former Indian fighter and explorer and lived just across the Missouri: Daniel Boone. Boone was still active and no doubt restless due to vanishing elbow room. In March of 1811 he was known to have recently returned from a spring hunt with sixty beaver skins. One can easily imagine the two men scouting the nearby streams, creeks, and woods together as they traded tales of the hazards and freedoms of their former lives. They shared much, but not longevity. Although about forty years Colter's senior, Boone would survive him by eight years. Boone lived with his youngest son, Nathan, a few years younger than Colter and considered quite like his father in both temperament and survival skills. Colter and Nathan Boone became good friends, and, as discussed in the next chapter, served together in the War of 1812. Nathan reportedly named a son after the Lewis and Clark veteran.[17]

Neither Boone nor Colter would ever venture into the unknown wilderness again, but one of the most important explorations in the history of the West was about to unfold, and both men would soon learn of it firsthand. The *Louisiana Gazette* announced the mission on March 14, 1811:

> Mr. Wilson P. Hunt, left this place last Monday [March 12], with a well equipped barge, to join his associates, at the Otto village, to proceed on his expedition to the Columbia river. His party amount to about seventy able bodied men, nerved to hardship.
>
> We understand the New York Fur Company, to whom Mr. Hunt is attached, have dispatched a well furnished ship, to meet the party on the shores of the Pacific.
>
> Mr Hunt is accompanied by Mr. Bradbury and a Mr. Nuttall, who are deputed to this country, to explore and make known its riches, in the Animal, Vegetal and Mineral kingdoms.[18]

Born in New Jersey around 1783, Wilson Price Hunt had come to St. Louis in 1804 and had partnered with John Hankinson as a merchant. In 1810, Hunt, along with Canadians Alexander McKay, Duncan McDougal, David Stuart, Robert Stuart, and Donald McKenzie, and Americans Ramsay Crooks, Robert McClellan, and Joseph Miller, had become a partner in John Jacob Astor's Pacific Fur Company. "What Astor proposed," wrote James P. Ronda, "was an ambitious design aimed at controlling the entire fur trade and extending it to the Pacific. Drawing on his Montreal sources of inspiration, Astor envisioned a series of trading posts from the Missouri to the Western Sea. These houses would follow the route pioneered by Lewis and Clark."[19]

Astor, the richest man in America, had the resources and the connections to make anything Lisa or the Chouteaus did look puny in comparison. And he had chosen the unlikely Hunt to lead the enterprise. "Not only was [Hunt], as Irving says, Astor's 'chief agent,' but, without any experience in the fur trade or beyond the frontier, he became head of the Overland Astorians from St. Louis to Astoria."[20]

As the newspaper article noted, Hunt was on his way up the Missouri to meet the rest of his group—they had camped at the mouth of the Nodaway River, in present northwestern Missouri. Bradbury was keeping a journal and five days out, on March 17, he wrote: "After breakfast, we crossed to the north side of the river, and in the afternoon landed at a French village, named

Charette." Next, Bradbury met a famed frontiersman who lived in the area. "On leaving Charette, Mr. Hunt pointed out to me an old man standing on the bank, who, he informed me, was Daniel Boone, the discoverer of Kentucky." Bradbury was carrying a letter of introduction from Boone's nephew Colonel Grant. "I went ashore to speak to him, and requested that the boat might go on, as I intended to walk until evening. I remained with him for some time in conversation with him."[21]

When Bradbury made his way through the woods back to the Missouri, he found that Hunt's keelboat "had disappeared behind an island, and was at too great a distance to be hailed. I got across by swimming, having tied my clothes together, and inclosed them in my deer skin hunting coat, which I pushed before me." The hardy Scottish naturalist, who had been received by Thomas Jefferson upon arriving in the United States in 1809, overtook the boat in about three hours and camped with Hunt and the others on the south side of the river, "at the mouth of a creek called Boeuf, near the house of one Sullens." Bradbury, who had interviewed Colter more than eight months earlier, assumed Colter lived in the neighborhood, information he likely obtained from Clark, because he added: "I enquired of Sullens for Colter, one of Lewis and Clarke's party, whom General Clark had mentioned to me as being able to point out the place on the Missouri where the petrified skeleton of a fish, above forty feet long, had been found." Sullens said that Colter lived about a mile away and sent his son to tell Colter he had visitors, but Colter did not appear that evening.[22]

"At day-break Sullens came to our camp, and informed us that Colter would be with us in a few minutes," continued Bradbury. "Shortly after he arrived, and accompanied us for some miles, but could not give me the information I wished for."[23] There were no men with Hunt who had been permanent members of the Lewis and Clark Expedition, but Colter saw at least one familiar face—that of Pierre Dorion Jr., who had briefly assisted Lewis and Clark in Yankton Sioux country (present South Dakota) in August of 1804. Dorion, son of the well-respected Sioux interpreter Pierre Dorion Sr., was an expert interpreter himself, and Hunt had stolen him away from Lisa, his previous employer. Dorion was accompanied by his wife, an Iowa Indian woman called Marie, and two sons.

More than one historian has speculated that Colter warned the Astorians about Indians. Washington Irving, for instance, opined that Colter "had many particulars to give them concerning the Blackfeet Indians, a restless and predatory tribe, who had conceived an implacable hostility to the white men, in consequence of one of their warriors having been killed by Captain Lewis, while attempting to steal horses." Reaching even farther, Burton Harris conjectured that "Colter's stories of Blackfeet ferocity undoubtedly had a good deal to do with the decision Hunt subsequently made to leave the Missouri at the Arikara Villages, purchase horses, and cross the Rockies south of the area visited by Lewis and Clark."[24]

True, Colter may have talked about the dangers of Blackfoot country, but all such commentary is purely speculative. Besides, Bradbury pretty much said it all when he added that Colter "seemed to have a great inclination to accompany the expedition; but having been lately married, he reluctantly took leave of us."[25]

Hunt certainly would have welcomed Colter, just as he later welcomed Colter's former comrades—Hoback, Reznor, and Robinson—and he presumably pleaded with Lewis and Clark's former hunter and scout to sign on as an employee of the enterprising John Jacob Astor. Considering Colter's passion for frontier life, it is surprising and admirable that he was determined to stay with his family. The sad irony is that Colter, virtually invincible during his six years in the Great Plains and Rockies, would succumb to an illness a little more than a year after resisting the temptation to go west with Hunt.

Did Colter stand at the edge of the water and watch the keelboat until it disappeared? Did he linger even after the image had faded, gazing westward and remembering the unique fellowship of campfire conversations with the captains, the feel of his rifle in his hands when he was out hunting alone, the wondrous sight of a rainbow stretching over the monstrous lake that was the source of the Yellowstone River?

The record is silent.

Nor do we know if Colter knew he had just passed up the opportunity to become the first American to cross the Rockies and reach the Pacific Ocean a second time, but that is not something that would have drawn him.

Even so, Bradbury had given crucial clues as to where Colter and his wife and son and daughter had settled. Burton Harris concluded that Colter's cabin was "near present-day Dundee . . . probably near the Sullens Spring, a short distance above the junction of the Little Boeuf with the Big Boeuf, on the south bank of the Missouri."[26] Harris added in a footnote that he got his information from Dr. E. B. Trail, a Missouri dentist who spent many years researching Colter.

"It seems that if Colter lived a mile from Dundee and that he lived on Boeuf Creek near the house of Sullens, he must have lived near Zachariah Sullens' house, which was near Sullens spring," wrote Dr. Trail, who concluded by adding: "The record in the Bradbury journal of his meeting with Colter at the mouth of Boeuf Creek is one of the few written records that shed any light on Colter's life at Dundee."[27]

The problem with Dr. Trail's statement is that Bradbury never stated that Colter lived on Boeuf Creek—he only said that Sullens told him Colter lived a mile away from Hunt's campsite at the mouth of the Creek. All of this is further complicated by the fact that the course of the Missouri River has shifted considerably over the years. Colter talked to Bradbury and Hunt at the mouth of Boeuf Creek in 1811, but where was the mouth of the creek located at that time? Henry Marie Brackenridge, discussed below, offered an important clue when he wrote: "At this place [the lower point of Boeuf Island] the river makes a considerable bend. Instead of taking the main channel, we entered a small one between the island and the shore, which will shorten the distance; the current is not so strong. The channel is about fifty yards wide, and very handsome having clean even banks, and resembling a small river. It is about four miles in length."[28]

Boeuf Creek and Little Boeuf Creek both flowed into this channel, which ran south of the main part of the Missouri. The area of land that lay between the channel and the river was called Boeuf Island. In the early 1900s, however, the course of the Missouri shifted so much that the channel disappeared and the northern tip of Boeuf Island ended up on the north side of the Missouri in Warren County (while Boeuf Creek and Little Boeuf Creek are both on the south side in Franklin County).

Finding the approximate site of Colter's cabin is thus a more difficult task than Dr. Trail indicated but not an impossible task. The key is using relevant data from both the nineteenth and twentieth centuries. First, a check of official government surveys from both 1852 and 1985 makes it possible to determine where Boeuf Creek entered the main stem of the Missouri in 1811. Next, we turn to Sullens's claim that Colter lived one mile away from the mouth of Boeuf Creek, allow a little leeway, and using that point as the center of a circle, draw a radius one and a half miles from the center. It is reasonable to assume that Colter's cabin fell somewhere within that radius.

Colter's probate file offers the next important clue. We know that Mosias Maupin, John Maupin, and John Sullens recorded the inventory of Colter's estate on December 4, 1813. This is crucial information because an 1807 statute dictated that such appraisers be "respectable householders of the neighborhood of the deceased." Mosias Maupin is buried on his farm in a well-marked grave. John Maupin's farm was just south of Mosias Maupin's place. John Sullens is buried on his farm on the Dundee bluff overlooking the Missouri River. These men were close neighbors of Colter, and each of them owned property in or near the radius described above.[29]

Local history, both written and oral, also provides important evidence. In 1972, for example, Mabel Maupin, the wife of a descendant of John Maupin, reported that "Grandfather [Maupin] said the John Colter home was across from the New Port Church and school (which of course were not there then). This is the property where the Galbraith's now live." In addition, the property of John Sullens has been handed down through the family for the past two hundred years, and an oral tradition among the Sullens, Bailey, and Humphrey families (which are all inter-related) placed Colter's cabin at the same spot. The location in question falls within the given radius, and Mosias Maupin, John Maupin, and John Sullens all lived close by.[30]

The best evidence thus indicates that Colter's cabin was about a half-mile east of Little Boeuf Creek and about a mile from the present channel of the Missouri River, just north of the junction of the Newport Road and Bluff Road—and roughly halfway between Washington and New Haven, Missouri. So why wasn't a cabin listed in the inventory of Colter's estate? Because in 1812 John Colter had no legal right to the land on which his cabin was located. These lands were not surveyed and opened to homesteading by the government until 1818. Anyone on the land before then would have been a squatter.

Hunt's and Bradbury's meeting with Colter therefore seems to have been a happy coincidence. Hunt chose the camp site independently of Bradbury, who was either talking with Boone or swimming across the river at the time, and, by all appearances, Bradbury was the person most interested in talking with Colter, as well as the one with some knowledge of where Colter had settled.

After bidding Colter farewell, Bradbury "walked along the bluffs, which were beautifully adorned with *anemone hepatica*. We encamped near the lower end of Lutre (Otter) Island."[31]

Perhaps Colter concluded for the time being that he had seen his last visit from an explorer traveling up the Missouri. If so, he was wrong.

On April 13, the *Louisiana Gazette* made another announcement: "A few days ago, Mr. Manuel Lisa sailed from here, on a voyage to Fort Mandan. Should Mr. Lisa join Mr. Hunt's party, on the head waters of the Missouri, they will form an army able to oppose any number of Blackfeet which may attack them. It is thought there will be upwards of 300 Americans on the Columbia River next year."[32]

Lisa's group had departed St. Charles on April 2. Like Hunt, Lisa had an observer onboard—the twenty-five-year-old lawyer and writer, Henry Marie Brackenridge, who, like Bradbury, was keeping a record of the trip. Brackenridge himself observed another similarity between the two expeditions: a French-Canadian interpreter and his Indian wife were present. "We had on board a Frenchman named Charboneau, with his wife, an Indian woman of the Snake nation, both of whom had accompanied Lewis and Clark to the Pacific, and were of great service."[33]

The Frenchman's wife, of course, was Sacagawea, destined to become one of the most famous women in American history. And while the Indian woman onboard Hunt's boat, Marie Dorion, would not achieve the same kind of fame, she would leave her own mark—as the second woman known to cross the Great Plains and reach the Pacific and as the first woman to give birth along what would become the Oregon Trail. Not only that, but she would also endure a sojourn in the wild unlike anything her Shoshone counterpart had experienced.

"We are in all, twenty-five men, and completely prepared for defence," continued Brackenridge. "There is, besides, a swivel on the bow of the boat, which, in case of attack, would make a formidable appearance; we have also two brass blunderbusses in the cabin, one over my berth, and the other over that of Mr. Lisa." Such precautions were "absolutely necessary," said Brackenridge, "from the hostility of the Sioux bands, who, of late had committed several murders and robberies on the whites."[34]

Brackenridge next summed up quite precisely what was remembered most about the spring of 1811: "Mr. Wilson P. Hunt had set off with a large party about twenty-three days before us, on his way to the Columbia, we anxiously hoped to overtake him before he entered the Sioux nation; for this purpose it was resolved to strain every nerve, as upon it, in a great measure depended the safety of our voyage."[35]

Thus began the Great Race up the Missouri. Lisa, known to push his men even under normal circumstances, would now push them to the limit, continually gaining a day here and a day there on Hunt, and would make his way upstream faster than anyone before or after him—at least until steamboats arrived on the Missouri. But this race was also deeply ironic. As Ronda has noted, all of Lisa's "hurried preparations were unknown to Hunt as he plodded against the Missouri current. Tangles of rushes and brambles along the river flats kept Bradbury and Nuttall from much botanizing. And the torrential rains continued."[36]

Nor did Hunt have any interest in traveling with Lisa—he had great distrust for the man and wanted nothing to do with him. To compound the conflict, two of Astor's partners who were with Hunt—Crooks and McClellan—were bitter enemies of Lisa and believed he had encouraged Indians to delay them or even attack them in the past. McClellan had vowed more than once to kill Lisa.

Then there was Dorion, who had run up a huge whiskey bill with Lisa at Fort Mandan. Lisa had every intention of leveraging that debt to get the Frenchman—who not only spoke the Sioux language but was on good terms with that nation—back in his service in time to avoid conflicts with the Sioux and others.

The final irony was that in 1807, when Ensign Pryor had hurried up the Missouri in hopes of catching Lisa, Lisa had successfully stayed ahead of Pryor and had reportedly turned the Arikara nation against him.

Brackenridge was naturally not aware of most of this and viewed Lisa as a sort of noble dictator. Dutifully keeping up his journal, Brackenridge noted that on April 8 they "came in sight of a little village N. E. Side called Charette. There are about thirty families here, who hunt, and raise a little corn." Nothing was said of Daniel Boone. "A very long island lies in the bend in which this village is situated," he added. "About this island, passed under a gentle breeze, some very handsome bluffs."[37] The group was now in

Colter's neighborhood and even spent the night near the upper end of the island—and thus not far from where Hunt's party had camped—but Brackenridge's journal made no mention of Colter.

At the same time he had been keeping his journal, however, the prolific Brackenridge had been busy writing a series of articles called "Sketches of the Territory of Louisiana" for the *Louisiana Gazette*. (Brackenridge would subsequently publish a popular book entitled *Views of Louisiana* [1814].) On April 18, nine or ten days after he obviously talked with Colter, Brackenridge included a paragraph on the course of the Rocky Mountains, and, as discussed earlier, casually mentioned that "At the head of the Gallatin Fork, and of the Grosse Corne of the Yellowstone [Bighorn River], from discoveries made since the voyage of Lewis & Clark, it is found less difficult to cross than the Allegheny mountains; Coulter, a celebrated hunter and woodsman, informed me, that a loaded waggon would find no obstruction in passing."[38]

Why Brackenridge mentioned this key bit of information (not mentioned by Clark, James, or Bradbury) in his article but not in his journal is unclear. Perhaps he already intended to publish both works (which he did) and wanted to avoid duplication.[39] Nor did he say if Lisa tried to enlist Colter, a man he obviously trusted and respected, a second time. If so, Colter, now apparently resolute to take care of his family and keep his vow to the Almighty, declined, likely realizing he wouldn't get another chance to go West. And another chance never came.

So, rather than confronting the perils of mad rivers and mad bears, Colter turned to the mundane but hostile world of financial quagmires and endless rounds of litigation that his former employer Lisa knew so well. Thomas James was back in Missouri and had sued the St. Louis Missouri Fur Company for back wages. Lisa, Menard, Reuben Lewis, and William Clark were among the defendants. The company quickly countersued, and both sides called Colter (spelled "Caulter" in court documents) as a witness. He was summoned to testify in March, June, and October of 1811. No record of that testimony has been found.[40]

James had the final word:

> I sued [the St. Louis Missouri Fur Company] on my contract, and was the only one who did so. After many delays and continuances from term to term, I was glad to get rid of the suits and them, by giving my note for one hundred dollars to the Company. This, with my debt to Colter, made me a loser to the amount of three hundred dollars by one years trapping on the head waters of the Missouri. Some of the Americans, however, fared much worse, and were deterred from returning to the settlements at all, by their debts to the Company, which they were hopeless of discharging by any ordinary business in which they could engage. Such is one instance of the kind and considerate justice of wealth, to defenceless poverty, beautifully illustrating the truth of the senti-

ment uttered by somebody, "take care of the rich and the rich will take care of the poor."[41]

Luckily, Colter's suit against Lewis's estate was drawing to a successful close. William Clark testified in March of 1811, strengthening Colter's case, and two months after that the court awarded Colter $375.60, almost twenty dollars more than he was actually due (although almost two hundred dollars less than Graham had requested). This was the best Colter could have hoped for, and he received payment from Edward Hempstead on May 28, within days of the one-year anniversary of his return from the West.[42]

Things seemed to be looking up.

Chapter Twelve

"As Fine a Body of Hardy Woodsmen as Ever Took the Field"

Colter's Final Days

When Colter reached St. Louis fresh from frontier violence, he must have hoped for tranquility in Missouri, but what he found was all too familiar. In July of 1810, only weeks after his arrival, a post rider on his way from Vincennes, Indiana, to St. Louis was killed by Indians and the mail lost. Then, as militia general William Clark wrote to the War Department, "four men who reside near the Missouri . . . who had been in pursuit of horses which had been stolen from them were killed in their camp . . . by the Indians."[1]

The brutality continued, and one particular incident triggered alarm throughout the area. In the early morning hours of June 2, 1811, three Indians attacked a family by the name of Cox who lived on Shoal Creek in Illinois. The Indians killed the family's young son and kidnapped his sister. "From travellers, from spies, and from every other source of information direct from the hostile indian country," wrote the editor of the *Louisiana Gazette*, "we have every reason to expect a general attack as soon as the corn is ripe enough for food."[2] Like other government officials, Clark placed the ultimate blame for this hostility not on an Indian nation but on a group he had distrusted and detested from his youth— the British.

Tension between the United States and its former mother country had been rising steadily for several years, and a group of Republican congressmen known as the war hawks were now demanding war with England. At the same time, several Indian tribes in the Missouri Territory and surrounding areas, including the Shawnee, Winnebago, Potawatomi, Miami, and Kickapoo, all of whom had a long list of grievances against the United States, had aligned themselves with the British. The Americans and Indians were intent on war, so it came as no surprise that a conflict broke out between William Henry Harrison's troops and the Shawnee in November of 1811 at the Battle of Tippecanoe, often considered the start of the War of 1812.

Settlers in the western territories lived in constant fear of Indian attacks. Early in January, Clark received word that one hundred Winnebago warriors, eager to revenge their comrades killed at Tippecanoe, had attacked a lead-smelting operation on the Galena River. Two men were "butchered in a most horrid manner," although George Hunt and Lewis and Clark veteran Nathaniel Pryor (who had resigned from the military in 1810) were allowed to escape after claiming they were British.[3]

Only a month later, Indians attacked another of Colter's fellow expedition veterans, Alexander Willard, who was "coming down the [Mississippi] river in a sleigh on the ice, [and] was fired on above Salt river and repeatedly chased by war parties." Willard was fleeing after finding the bodies of nine members of an O'Neal family killed by Indians upstream from St. Louis. "The Winnebagos are Deturmined for War," Clark wrote to Secretary of War William Eustis.[4]

Despite the violence more and more common throughout the previous year, the gruesome murder of the O'Neal family pushed the settlers to the brink. Clark urged Benjamin Howard, governor of the Missouri Territory, to use federal funds to recruit rangers to patrol both sides of the Mississippi, and on March 19, 1812, Howard wrote to Eustis:

> On the 10th of last month, nine persons of murder'd, in the most barbarous manner on the Mississippi, within the limits of our settlements; It is believed, that this michief was done by the Kickapoos, or Pawtawatimies of the Illinois—about the same time an express, from Fort Madison, was fired on, but escaped, and on the 3d Inst a soldier was kill'd near Fort-Madison.—Strong apprehensions, are entertain'd there, that the Fort will soon be attack'd by a combination of Wenebagoes, Kickapoos, Pawtawatimies and Shawanese; The commanding officer had called for a reinforcement.—Since Christmass—12 persons have been killed certainly. More are now missing, and from various circumstances, there is little doubt of their having, fallen into the hands of the enemy, besides this, there has been a considerable loss of both, public, and private property. . . . I think nothing can prevent a strong combination among the Indians against us now, but a succession of quick campaigns, against those that are avowedly hostile, or a display of efficient, defensive measures. . . . Being apprehensive of future difficulties, early in the winter, I encouraged the raising a company of mounted riflemen, to act as rangers, to be commanded, by Capt Boon, (Son of the celebrated Colo Daniel Boon). . . . On the 6th ulto [of the previous month—February] I authorized Capt Boon to raise his company, upon the principle that it should go into actual service, so soon as it was raised, for three months, unless sooner discharged.[5]

The Captain Boone appointed commander of the rangers was Colter's friend, Nathan Boone, and Colter was among the forty-one men who enlisted at St. Charles on March 3. "We went into Building forts in Different places over the country to keep the Indians from murdering our helpless women and children," remembered one of the rangers decades later.[6]

A week before signing on with Nathan Boone, Colter had stopped in St. Louis to see Clark, who would have said good things about Boone. In 1808, when he launched an expedition to build Fort Osage three hundred miles upstream from the mouth of the Missouri, Clark had entrusted Boone with a key role in the mission. Now, Clark and Colter reminisced for the final time—this was also the last known contact between Colter and any veteran of the Corps of Discovery. Clark also loaned Colter forty-five dollars, which Colter probably used to prepare for his enlistment, because "the rangers were to equip themselves with good rifles or muskets and side arms as well as with clothing, horses, and provisions."[7]

The three hundred, seventy-five dollars and sixty cents received from Lewis's estate ten months earlier was apparently gone.

"Nathan Boone's company of Mounted Rangers . . . marched immediately to the northern frontier," wrote Kate L. Gregg, "where they instituted their famous patrol . . . and helped the regulars of Lieutenant John Campbell's company in erecting blockhouse forts."[8]

Less than three weeks after Colter and his fellows enlisted, the *Louisiana Gazette* warned that Kickapoo and Winnebago warriors had massacred settlers to the north and that the Potawatomi chief Main Poc intended to wage war against the Osage nation and attack whites while doing so. There would be no peace, reported the *Gazette*, "as long as there is a British subject suffered to trade within the lines of our territories." However, the editorial continued, "The new company of rangers now doing duty in the district of St. Charles are perhaps as fine a body of hardy woodsmen as ever took the field. They cover, by constant and rapid movements, the tract of country from Salt River on the Mississippi to the Missouri near Loutre."[9]

According to a history published in 1816, Indians besieged Fort Mason, around eighty miles north of St. Louis, about this time. "Captain Boone, who commanded a company of rangers, succeeded in getting into the fort, by which it was rendered completely secure against their forces." The history added that the Indians "remained before it 8 or 10 days, and succeeded once in setting fire to some of the cabins, which were burnt down, and at the same time a violent assault was made on the fort, which was gallantly repulsed by the garrison without much loss."[10]

As Nathan Boone's biographer, R. Douglas Hurt, aptly wrote:

> Boone's rangers, who began patrolling the Missouri frontier between Loutre Island and the Illinois River country, were a group of fifty-three hard men,

including the officers, who knew how to sit a horse for hours over rough terrain, and who often had more familiarity with their rifles than with their families. They were also a tough-handed lot, with calluses testifying to their practical knowledge of the workings of an ax and saw. During the fifteen months that Boone led the rangers across the frontier they would have cause to use all their skills.[11]

Early in May, Boone's rangers spotted a band of Indians about ten miles from Fort Mason and pursued them but lost the trail in darkness and a rain squall. "Captain Boone has given a good account so far of those have visited the frontier, and no doubt will continue to do so," commented the *Gazette.*

At a July 4, 1812, celebration in St. Louis, thankful settlers paid tribute to Boone and his men: "Our Frontiers—watched and protected by a hardy band of Spartan Warriors—the Rangers deserve well of their country."[12] Colter was not there to enjoy the celebration, however; he had died two months earlier.

Colter's military record answers certain questions about his death but raises others. He enlisted as a private on March 3 and was due payment of one dollar per day until May 6, the day he was released. Then follows this note: "Died 7 May 1812."[13] There is no mention of the cause of death, but he was apparently too sick to complete his nine-day enlistment term. Nor is there reason to believe he died from wounds suffered in battle. What was the nature of his illness? How long had he been sick? Did he see his wife and children before he died? All of these questions must go unanswered. Thomas James estimated that Colter was about thirty-five in 1809, which would have made him about thirty-eight at his death—the best information available on that subject.

James, also the sole source concerning the cause of Colter's death, wrote that "a few years after [Colter left Three Forks in 1810] I heard of [his] death by jaundice."[14] Jaundice is a yellowish discoloration of the skin that can have any number of causes, including pancreatic cancer, malaria, kidney disease, and liver disease caused by alcoholism or hepatitis (which in turn can be caused by ingesting contaminated food or water). Whatever Colter's malady, it came on quickly because a sick man could hardly have enlisted in Boone's company.

Probate proceedings for Colter's estate began on November 27, 1813, leading such historians as Stallo Vinton, Burton Harris, and Charles G. Clarke to conclude he must have died earlier that month. Subsequent historians accepted this assumption, and November 1813 thus became the de facto date for Colter's death. While the original military record states unequivocally that Colter died on May 7, 1812, the printed copy of that record—and the indexes that followed, as well as *Territorial Papers of the United States*—

mistakenly reprinted the name as "Cotter" (understandable because the person who wrote the original record crossed both the "l" and the "t"). The actual date of Colter's death was thus lost to the world until Ruth Colter-Frick and Shirley Winkelhoch identified the correct date in an article in the *New Haven* (Missouri) *Leader* on June 29, 1988.

It is not known why Colter's probate proceedings were delayed for almost a year and a half, but such a situation was not uncommon in Missouri at the time. Legal machinery turned slowly on the frontier, and official measures to settle the estates of expedition veterans George Drouillard, Thomas Howard, John Potts, and even Meriwether Lewis (all of whom died between 1808 and 1814) did not begin for at least a year after their deaths.[15]

On December 4, 1813, the following notice appeared in the *Louisiana Gazette*:

> All persons having demands against the estate of John Coulter, deceased, will please to exhibit their claims within a year from the date hereof, to the undersigned who has obtained letters of administration on the said estate, or they will not be entitled to receive any dividend of the assets in the hands of the administrator, if the said estate should prove insolvent; and those who are indebted to the said estate will please to make immediate payment to the undersigned.
> Daniel Richardson
> Administrator
> St. Louis, Nov. 26th, 1813

Colter's estate papers show that his wife Sarah Loucy, also called Sally, had remarried by November of 1813 because her husband, James Brown, participated in the proceedings from the start. On December 4, three neighbors and friends of Colter, John Maupin, Mosias Maupin, and John Sullens (quite likely the man who arranged the meeting between Hunt's party and Colter), appraised Colter's property as follows:

one Dark Bay mare $45.60
one brown Cow and Calf 9.00
one two year old heifer 7.00
one Cow and Calf 13.00
one set of plough Irons 5.00
one flax wheel 4.00
four Chears 2.00
one feather [Bed?] 18.00
one feather Bed 12.00
one feather Bed 8.00
two tinpans .75
one puter Dish and Six plates 5.50
three puter Basons 6.00
one womans saddle 18.00

one pot and oven 5.50
one hoe .75
one flat Iron 1.50
one Cotton Wheel 1.75
one pare Cotton Cards .75
one year old Colt past 16.50
three histories 3.00
one Coffee pot .75
one piggan and six Cups 1.25
one tumbler .25
two quart Bottles .50
three knives and four forks and seven spoons 1.50

$187.25 [actually $187.85]

June 15th, 1814, Labbadie Township, the appraisement of two fillies the property of John Colter, deceased by us:

to one filly $35.00
to one filly $35.00
to one book .25

$70.25

The life of the great explorer was thus reduced to a list of mundane objects valued at around two hundred and fifty-eight dollars. Two references are particularly poignant: "three histories" and "one book," appraised at a grand total of $3.25, another affirmation, along with his confident signature on a variety of documents, that Colter was a literate man. (His widow, by contrast, signed probate documents with an "x.") What were the titles of these volumes? Were all four published books, or could one have contained Colter's handwritten account of his travels along the Missouri, Jefferson, Gallatin, Yellowstone, Bighorn, Shoshone, Snake, or Columbia rivers? We will never know, for rather than being secured in an archive, the books were sold at auction. Benjamin Heatherly bought one for 64 cents, Samuel Cantly another for 86 cents, Mosias Maupin one for 75 cents, and John Maupin the last for 25 cents. The coffee pot brought in more than any of the books— Enoch Greenstreet bought it for $1.62 ½.

Like most of his neighbors, Colter was a poor man, but he had a roof over his head, three horses for work and travel, and a cow for milk and cheese. Sarah Loucy had a cotton wheel and a flax wheel to make clothes. Each of the four people in the family had a feather bed to sleep on, a chair to sit on, and their own plate, cup, and knife, fork, and spoon.

Conspicuously missing from the inventory were Colter's absolute necessities: his rifle and ammunition. Also missing from the probate papers is any mention of the sixty-five dollars that the United States government owed Colter for his service as one of Boone's rangers. No evidence has ever been found that either Colter or his heirs received any of that money. Nor is there any mention in the probate file of Colter's land warrant and whether any cash was ever paid for it. These are three items to add to the long list of Colter mysteries.

After being sued, Thomas James paid $176.00 to Colter's estate in 1816. There was also income from the sales of the inventory listed above. One sale brought in $213.48 ½ and another $53.35. Hartley Sappington bought the mare for $42.75, John Woollums the "little spinning wheel" for $7.12 ½, Zachariah Sullens the plow iron for $8.00, and James Kiggins the weeding hoe for $1.43 3/4. As Harris wrote, "The sale bill of [Colter's] personal property reveals with appalling clarity the austerity of life on the frontier." Over the years, the estate made payments to William Clark, Edward Hempstead, Sheriff Thompson, Joseph Charless (editor of the *Louisiana Gazette*), John Sullins, Elizabeth Maupin, Auguste Chouteau, and a host of others.[16]

On October 22, 1821, more than nine years after Colter's death, and eighteen years and one week after he enlisted with Lewis and Clark, the probate proceedings were finally closed. The original administrator, Daniel Richardson, had died himself, and his sons Richard and Amos Richardson handled the filing. Colter's widow received $124.11.[17]

Despite the kind of intense research so common in the Colter world, no historian or enthusiast or descendant has identified Colter's burial site with any certainty, something that is somehow fitting for a man surrounded by so much mystery.[18] Although Colter's probate papers are quite detailed, no information is included concerning his burial. In fact, not a single nineteenth-century record related to the burial has been found. Early in the twentieth century, however, with the celebration of the centennial of the Lewis and Clark Expedition, renewed interest in Colter surged, no doubt spurred on by Hiram Martin Chittenden's successful book, The American Fur Trade of the Far West, which included an entire chapter on Colter. Chittenden said nothing about Colter's burial, but given the unending allure of the Colter story—and the irresistible urge to fill in the blanks—amateurs and professionals alike began telling parts of the Colter legend not mentioned in primary documents. And, just as his birth in Virginia and the family's move to Maysville, Kentucky, had been added to the known "facts," one tale after another of his burial—or lack thereof—soon complemented the narratives of a horse stolen by Lakota Indians and a thrilling escape from Three Forks.

Chittenden wrote that in 1811, at the time Colter talked with the westbound Astorians, he had "lately married and was living near the river above the point where the little creek La Charette empties into the main stream."[19]

Chittenden failed to note, however, that La Charette was across the Missouri from Colter's residence and that there was no record of his ever having lived in La Charette. Nevertheless, a number of writers, beginning with Eva Emery Dye in 1904, concluded that since Colter lived in La Charette, he must have died there. Dye even added that he married an Indian squaw, which, as seen, has no basis in the historical documents. The theory that Colter died in La Charette, with the clear implication that he was also buried there, is thus based on a misunderstanding, but it has been propagated into the twenty-first century.[20]

Another hypothesis concerning Colter's burial site appeared in 1926 and has become the best-known theory. In the spring of that year, the Missouri Pacific Railroad had begun work to bypass an old tunnel that had become a train bottleneck. The railroad had built the tunnel through a bluff in the 1850s–the first tunnel west of St. Louis–and the construction project had given rise to the community of Dundee. The bluff became known as Tunnel Hill. The remarkable increase in traffic on the Missouri Pacific during the World War I and the early 1920s placed a heavy burden on the operation mainly because of inadequate double-track mileage. A study was conducted, and the railroad decided to double-track a number of sections, including the area near Tunnel Hill. As construction crews started work on the top of the bluff, they accidentally unearthed human skeletal remains. Word quickly spread of the discovery. On May 21, 1926, the Washington Citizen reported: "Workers employed by Sprague and Nisely Construction Company at Dundee say that eight or ten graves on Dundee Hill above the tunnel have been unearthed so far. . . . Skull bones from two graves were black. Trees several feet in diameter were over some graves. It was said that it was generally believed that the graves were of Indians. Human bones and remains of one box (coffin) were dumped in a car at one time."[21]

A month later a St. Louis newspaper published a feature story describing the incident–as well as Colter's exploring and trapping career. It read in part:

New Haven, Missouri. The other day at Dundee, a village just down the Missouri River from here–New Haven is 67 miles from St. Louis–a steam shovel bit into the side of a bluff, swung around and dumped its contents into a "gondola" car. Then it did the same thing again. One of the construction gang shouted, "Heh, what are you doing there?"

The natural answer was that they were cutting down the side of the bluff, and anybody ought to know it. A halt was called, and some whitish-yellow things examined. They were human bones, parts of skeletons that had been resting in rough wooden boxes.

The steam shovel had eaten its way into a little cemetery of a half a dozen graves, a cemetery of Missouri of the old days. That little cemetery was distributed in three or four dirt cars; the business was simply an unknowing desecration, an unexpected happening, an accident; it could not be mended.

Somebody in New Haven said that was where John Colter had been buried, high on the bluff overlooking the grand sweep of the muddy Missouri and the country for miles around.[22]

The reporter added that there were about fifteen Colter (or Coulter) families in Franklin County and that the oldest Colter was seventy-year-old Sam, a great-grandson of the explorer. Dr. E. B. Trail, a longtime Colter researcher, heard about the discovery and went to the construction site. In his investigation he visited with Sam Coulter, who signed the following notarized affidavit in November of 1926: "About 1883, I was talking with Mr. Jacob Krattli of Dundee, Missouri. He told me that sometime prior to this time he had been talking to a group of old time settlers at Dundee, Missouri, and that they had told him that John Colter, the famous trapper and guide, was buried on Tunnel Hill."[23]

In 1942, Dr. Trail added more information:

> During the summer of 1926, the Missouri Pacific railroad opened an immense cut through Tunnel Hill. Several graves were unearthed. Since 1850, several known men have been buried on the summit of this hill. The story of Colter's supposed last resting place on this hill was relayed to the men employed in the excavation. We questioned them carefully as to the probability of finding and identifying the grave of Colter. They unearthed several graves but found no identification leading to a discovery of the grave of Colter. The huge steam shovel working at night possibly scooped up several graves and emptied the contents into the dump cars unobserved. The foreman in charge said that he was confident that had happened. There is a possibility that a few fragments of the bones of John Colter now lie embedded in the new embankment of the Missouri Pacific railroad.[24]

Maupin family tradition also offers support for the Tunnel Hill theory. (As noted, John Maupin helped appraise property for the estate sale.) In a 1972 letter to researcher Ralph Gregory, Mabel Maupin stated that her husband had told her "John Colter was buried over the old Pacific tunnel. I believe this would all fit in with Dr. Trails account, which, I believe reported that his farm was 1½ miles from the mouth of the Boeuf–is the right distance S. W. I doubt that there were any markers at the graves over the tunnel. When the [1926] cut was made there were not too many skeletons–but the men did report some Indian graves, which contained some Indian's artifacts. My husband was there and saw this and so were some of the [neighbors] . . . . I recall that my husband and the other neighbor men helped dig graves two or three times in the Richardson Cemetery, which is much nearer New Haven."[25]

Several historians have repeated this story. Burton Harris's treatment is typical: "Colter was buried in the graveyard on the top of what is now called Tunnel Hill, according to trustworthy old-time residents around Dundee. . . .

the Missouri Pacific dug a tunnel through the hill, directly under the graves, when its lines were first extended westward in 1850."[26]

This oral tradition is significant because it has been so widely reported. In addition, the site is close to the likely site of Colter's cabin–.98 miles to be exact. However, since the account is thus far uncorroborated and is both late (not recorded for more than a century after Colter's death) and third hand (the parties who reported the story heard it from someone who heard it from someone else) it proves nothing in and of itself.[27]

The Tunnel Hill theory still holds interest, however, because a skull found at the site has been retained. In 1972, Ralph Gregory interviewed William Harold Bailey, who obtained a skull from the hill when it was excavated in 1926. Bailey, who later became a dentist, was in his twenties at the time; his interest in human anatomy motivated him to keep the skull. The Bailey family still has the skull, and in 2003 a graduate student in forensic anthropology examined it and concluded it belonged to a white, middle-aged male who died of unknown causes.[28]

An unbroken male lineage back to Colter exists, and DNA samples could be collected from one of Colter's male descendants and compared to the DNA of the skull. A match would indicate that Colter's body (or the body of a close relative—and there are no likely candidates) had indeed been buried at Tunnel Hill.

Forty years after the Tunnel Hill story appeared, in 1966, the most bizarre conjecture concerning Colter's final resting place was published. As this story goes, after his return from the West, Colter settled on Boeuf Creek and married a Missouri "Corn Cracker" by the name of Nancy Hooker. When he died, Nancy was so poor that she did not have enough money to bury John. She reportedly left his remains in their bed and went to live with her brother. In 1926, someone stumbled upon a fallen-down cabin and found a skeleton with a leather pouch that had "Colter" branded on it. Various other sources say the leather pouch had "J C" branded on it. The pouch had papers from the fur-trade era inside, but no one knows what became of the pouch.[29]

This whole story, and its variations, is undoubtedly the figment of an active imagination. Colter was a man with family and friends, including the powerful William Clark and an administrator responsibly handling his estate, none of whom would have tolerated such a thing.[30]

In 1970, Lewis and Clark scholar Charles G. Clarke offered yet another account of Colter's burial:

> In the collections of the St. Charles Historical Society are the books of the Fee Fee Baptist Church Records. An entry is written, "John Colter–a fur trader with Manuel Lisa." A tombstone, said to have been in the church cemetery, read:

Here lies John Colter
of Lewis and Clark Expedition
Born in 1775 in Va.
Died 1813 of jaundice

This church and cemetery are at Bridgeton, Missouri, not far from Colter's farm at Charette. No trace of the tombstone has yet been found.[31]

This claim is problematic for a variety of reasons. The supposed inscription, for example, gives every appearance of having been written many years after Colter's death. As discussed earlier, the first known mention of Colter's having been born in Virginia appeared in the early 1900s, with the work of Dye and Thwaites. Thomas James was the first to claim that Colter died of jaundice, and his book was not published until 1846. (That edition, however, was quickly taken out of circulation, and James's views were not commonly known until the book was reprinted in 1916.) Moreover, a tombstone inscribed shortly after Colter's death would have given 1812 as the year of his death, not 1813, (the year generally accepted until the 1990s).

Concerned about these issues, Gregory wrote a letter to Clarke, which reads in part: "I did not find the grave of Colter at the Fee Fee cemetery and the only record I saw was a typewritten one that Mrs. Olson [apparently an employee or volunteer at the cemetery] had. I believe the record is spurious and wish you had not said anything about it."[32]

Clarke replied: "I had run across this and the inscription on the headstone, many years ago–long before Mrs. Olson had mentioned it. Some early writer had mentioned this headstone, perhaps in a newspaper account, and it has been repeated since. I can find no other mention of where they knew he died of jaundice. It seems to have come from the headstone inscription. Now this headstone could have been erected at the Tunnel Hill site, and probably Colter was not buried at Fee Fee Baptist Church."[33]

Subsequent research has further weakened the case against the Fee Fee Baptist Church theory. A check of the Fee Fee Cemetery records showed that the first internment there took place in 1822, ten years after Colter's death. In addition, in 2005, archivists at the St. Charles Historical Society were unable to locate any records mentioning Colter's burial.[34]

In 1984, Ruth Colter-Frick became interested in the old cemeteries located along the river bluffs between Dundee and New Haven. She reported that she and her brother Forrest were searching for Colter's tombstone when Forrest

found a spring area between two hills with a natural access to the Missouri River. He turned over a flat stone and thought that he saw the initials J C on it. He laid it down again. When we joined him, he randomly turned over several stones for us. When Forrest lifted the J C stone, both of us saw the initials and we all were excited about the discovery. The spring area was definitely not a cemetery, so we continued to search with renewed enthusiasm. That day we found three cemeteries, but did not find a tombstone for John Colter.

Several days later . . . we found a grave marker for Hiram Coalter who had died in Gasconade Country, Missouri, 12 to 15 miles from the cemetery. The stone had been mostly covered with leaves and . . . had not been discovered . . . earlier.

Next to Hiram's grave was a plain fieldstone shaped like a mountain that was used as a headstone. Both headstones probably were less than a footl high with even shorter footstones. . . . In 1988, a memorial monument to John Colter was donated by a small group of men known as the Tavern Bluff Party and was placed at the cemetery. . . . The J C stone was removed from the spring area by my husband Bill and me, with pictures to document its removal.

The stone may have been used to mark Colter's proposed land claim. . . . The location would have been a desirable place for John Colter to live. . . . I believe that John Colter lived near the Missouri River and that he is buried in the cemetery on a bluff overlooking the Missouri River, and that he is REST-ING IN PEACE by his son Hiram.[35]

The stone marked "JC" and the grave marker for Hiram Coalter are the key evidence for this site, but whether "JC" referred to John Colter is unknown. Furthermore, after the death of Hiram Colter (John's son), each of his sons named one of their sons Hiram, and those sons did likewise. The Hiram buried on the bluff has not been positively identified. Also, the site proposed by Colter-Frick does not have an oral tradition associated with it. Finally, in an era where individuals were often buried in small cemeteries close to their homes, this cemetery is relatively distant from the likely site of Colter's cabin–about eight or nine miles upriver.

Research within the last few years, however, has brought a possible Colter burial place to light that carries a strong family tradition and is also located close (.45 miles) to the likely cabin site. When the Astorians camped at the mouth of Boeuf Creek in March of 1811, a man by the name of Sullens put them in touch with Colter. Is is possible that a Sullens descendant has likewise offered crucial details as to Colter's whereabouts?

The property owned by Sullens in 1812 has stayed continually with the family and is now owned by Harold Humphrey, a descendant of John Sullens, and his wife, Janet. Their son, Kurt D. Humphrey, said in a 2009 interview that John Colter is buried in the family cemetery and that the family has kept that secret for two hundred years to allow Colter to rest in peace. Now, however, in deference to Colter's descendants, Humprey has announced the details of where he believes Colter is buried.[36]

Clearly, Colter's burial spot is likely to remain a mystery of mysteries because this entire discussion of possible sites deals with oral tradition, educated speculation, and pure guesswork but lacks the true stuff of history: primary documents. That lack of certainty is somehow fitting for a man surrounded by so much mystery. A newly discovered document is the most likely way this conundrum—or those linked to Colter's birth, his youth, his run, his route, and his death—would be resolved. Perhaps, some day, the discovery of a trunk of old letters stowed away in the attic of an old house will suddenly be announced–as was the case with William Clark's letters published in *Dear Brother*.

Until that time, the monument erected by the Tavern Bluff Party in 1998 will serve quite nicely as a headstone of sorts:

JOHN COLTER
MEMBER OF
U.S. MOUNTED VOLUNTEER RANGERS
NATHAN BOONE'S CO.
MAR. 3, 1812 TO MAY 6, 1812
DIED MAY 7, 1812

Wherever John Colter is buried, one can only hope the grave sits at the edge of a bluff overlooking the wide Missouri River because the Missouri was Colter's River.

Who more than Colter would have appreciated the retrospections of John C. Nierhardt?

"The Missouri is unique among rivers. I think God wished to teach the beauty of a virile soul fighting its way toward peace—and His precept was the Missouri." [37]

Along the Missouri, Colter had watched Clark taking notes, estimating distances, and sketching maps; he had seen Lewis taking "long, solitary walks, collecting specimens, animal and plant, noting the physical character- istics of the land, judging the fertility of the soil, the presence of springs of good water, like sites for homesteads, trading posts, and fortifications." [38]

"The Missouri—my brother—is the eternal Fighting Man! . . . the Mis- souri is more than a sentiment—even more than an epic. It is the symbol of my own soul, which is, I surmise, not unlike other souls. In it I see flung before me all the stern world-old struggle become materialized." [39]

Along the Missouri, Colter had watched Sergeant Floyd suffer and die. "A little before his death he said to Captain Clark, 'I am going to leave you'; his strength failed him as he added, 'I want you to write me a letter.' He died with a composure which justified the high opinion we had formed of his firmness and good conduct." [40]

"Here is the concrete representation of the earnest desire, the momentar- ily frustrate purpose, the beating at the bars, the breathless fighting of the half-whipped but never-to-be-conquered spirit, the sobbing of the wind-brok- en runner, the anger, the madness, the laughter. And in it all the unwearying urge of a purpose, the unswerving belief in the peace of a far away ocean." [41]

Along the Missouri, Colter had seen a band of Lakota warriors "on a hill, hooting, jeering, and proclaiming their readiness to kill the Americans"; he had gazed on the "earth lodges, fortifications, and extensive fields of corn, beans, and squash" that "were all signs of the culture of the Missouri Valley villagers" called the Arikiara; and he had met the congenial Mandan chief called Sheheke, who told the captains, "If we eat you Shall eat, if we Starve you must Starve also."[42]

"Not only in its physical aspect does the Missouri appeal to the imagination. From Three Forks to its mouth—a distance of three thousand miles—this zigzag watercourse is haunted with great memories. Perhaps never before in the history of the world has a river been the thoroughfare of a movement so tremendously epic in its human appeal, so vastly significant in its relation to the development of man." [43]

Along the branches of the Missouri, Colter had traveled westward with the captains, searched for and found Yellowstone Lake and Brooks Lake, and run for his life from Blackfoot warriors.

"In the building of the continent Nature fashioned well the scenery for the great human story that was to be enacted here in the fullness of years. She built her stage on a large scale, taking no account of miles; for the coming actors were to be big men, mighty travelers, intrepid fighters, laughers at time and space. . . . And that the arrangements might be complete, she left a vast tract unfinished, where still the building of the world goes on—a place of awe in which to feel the mighty Doer of Things at work." [44]

But what spot along the Missouri would have been more memorable to John Colter than the gentle bluff spotted with timber rising on the west side of the mouth of the Bighorn, where Fort Raymond stood, the home he had returned to time and again, where a group of friends could swap tales, savor pipes stuffed with tobacco, rest their bones around a fire, and imagine ways to spend their fortunes? But as good as any fortune was seeing the swans and pelicans and geese landing on the water, the gangs of buffalo coming down to the river to drink, and the sound of friendly Crow warriors approaching on their magnificent horses.

Epilogue

The legend of Colter's Run initiated by Bradbury and boosted by Irving has not lagged in the more than two centuries since Colter ran into the history books. Newspaper reprints of the story seemed to continually pop up in the late 1800s. In the first half of the twentieth century, serious scholars like Hiram Martin Chittenden, Stallo Vinton, W. J. Ghent, Burton Harris, and others kept the episode alive. In the 1950s, Pulitzer-Prize winner A. B. Guthrie published a short story about Colter's adventure called "Mountain Medicine." Fifty years after that, Stephen T. Gough and Don Amiet both published novels about the Run.

In 1966, Cornel Wilde directed and acted in *The Naked Prey*, a retelling of Colter's Run set in the African veldt, with Mel Gibson's *Apocalypto* (2006) likewise depicting a lone hero outrunning a band of vicious pursuers—this time in ancient Mesoamerica.

When the celebration of the two hundredth anniversary of the Lewis and Clark Expedition began in 2004, thousands heard the story of Colter's Run for the first time, not a few of them reading about it in the *Wall Street Journal* or some such.

Each year in September at Three Forks, Montana, two or three hundred runners charge up and down rugged trails in the John Colter Run, a seven-and-a-half-mile race that even takes them across the waist-deep Gallatin River.

Colter turns up everywhere: When the nationally known sales and marketing consultant Patrick Henry Hansen enhanced a presentation on customer sales with descriptions of Colter's survival tactics, he was surprised at the enthusiastic response to his account of the legendary explorer. Hansen went on to publish *Power Prospecting: Cold Calling Strategies for Modern Sales People*, a book that teaches dynamic sales principles by relating "some of history's most compelling moments," including "John Colter's miraculous escape" from Blackfoot Indians. Colter's story has been reprinted or re-imagined countless times, and whether applied to a cold sales call or a drug deal gone bad in an urban ghetto, the storyline always remains the same: one man's survival against overwhelming odds.

One man's survival: Colter's accomplishing his feat alone is inexorably linked to the universal appeal of his story.

"The mountain man had no back up systems. If his reflexes failed, if he erred, he was dead and his hair was gone. And he found the final solitude of an unknown grave," wrote Don D. Walker. "If John Glenn had been attacked by the Blackfeet of outer space, the whole world would have known almost as the arrows were beginning to fall. But if John Colter had stumbled or run out of breath, no one would have known but the Blackfeet, and they kept no record books. At best some historian of the fur trade could later have noted obscurely: John Colter, who had been with Lewis and Clark, went trapping in the Blackfoot country and was never heard of again."[1]

So it's not surprising that even historians who are not Lewis and Clark specialists have given Colter his due. "He was, and one of the greatest, of the fur-trading explorers of the northern Rocky region of the United States," wrote one; "the most likely candidate for the title of archetypical mountain man," said another.[2]

In Colter's day when the extraordinary was considered the norm, his contemporaries looked upon him as a man out of the ordinary. He was a celebrity of his time like Daniel Boone, Simon Kenton, and later, Jim Bridger and Kit Carson. Colter was one of the nine young men from Kentucky with the "right stuff," hand picked by Meriwether Lewis and William Clark for their Journey of Discovery into some of the most unknown territory on the continent, finally reaching across two thousand miles of primitive land all the way to the Pacific Ocean and back again. Every step of the way across the steep cold spine of the Rockies or the barren prairie deserts carried unexpected dangers that could only be met by men with an exceptional sense for survival. He and his comrades were the Special Operations men of their time, soldiers and explorers with instincts ahead of even their very capable skills. But of them all, Colter, even in his own time, was always the one to inspire the most imagination and mystery. He turned his back on civilization and retraced a path into darkness that most men, even today still fear to face on their own.

Ken Kamper, founder and historian for the Daniel Boone and Frontier Families Research Association, compared Colter to Boone:

> What I see for better understanding our subject of the frontier types is to separate them a bit into categories. In my case I see the Boones and Colters at the top of their kind. They have mastered the wilderness. Then there are others

who are close with some of the traits such as with courage and wanting to live in the frontier for the benefits that the frontier offers, such as land to live on and land to speculate with. Some of these latter are quite mature thinking types and some are the opposite, being spontaneous. Of these two types I see them as single men or as the head of a family, with the male family members usually less frontier oriented. Such as if the males in a family were old enough when the family left for the frontier, some would go along, and some would stay back in the settlements. This little exercise narrows down the Boones and Colters to a more or less unique or rare breed of men. Of the Boones, only Nathan came close to his father's image, with sons-in-law Capt. William Hays and Flanders Callaway a significant notch or two below. Mainly what they lacked was the natural leadership attribute or characteristic, and the depth of understanding of the wilderness and nature as a whole, and an understanding of the ways of the Indians, which were of course major issues that set Colter and Boone apart.[3]

If Colter had lived to the same moderately old age that William Clark did (sixty-eight), he would have seen the actual declaration of war for the conflict he was a part of, the War of 1812; he would have celebrated Missouri's admission as a state in the Union; he would have seen his son and daughter marry; he would have played with his grandchildren and likely would have been interviewed by Washington Irving, who would have written a thrilling book on the archetypical mountain man. On the flipside, if Colter had lived as long as Patrick Gass (ninety-eight), he would have seen the terrible strife in Missouri before, during, and after the Civil War.

But none of that was to be. Colter's illness took him only months after James Madison began his second term in office, when Kit Carson was two years old, Abraham Lincoln three, and Jim Bridger eight. The potential of Colter's future was lost, but not all was lost. The genuine goodwill Colter had shown to Indians was not lost, nor was Thomas James's declaration that Colter was an honest man. But the ultimate tribute came from Clark: "We were disposed to be of Service to any one of our party who had performed their duty as well as Colter had done."[4]

As for John Colter's legacy, the great historian Edgeley W. Todd may have said it best:

"Today no monument marks his grave. . . . But, though his name never achieved the popular fame of a Kit Carson, his place in history has long been assured even as his exploits were long the talk of the mountain men. And it is as a hero in the history and mythology of the West that Colter still has his appeal and finds a more fitting monument than a cemetery headstone."[5]

Chronology

October 15, 1803

John Colter, one of the "nine young men from Kentucky," enlists in the Lewis and Clark Expedition in present Kentucky.

October 26, 1803

Joins other members of the Corps of Discovery in traveling together for the first time as the corps sets out from the Falls of the Ohio (near Clarksville, Indiana).

December 30, 1803

Kills a deer and a turkey (in first contemporary record mentioning him).

Winter 1803–1804

Spends first winter with the rest of the corps at Camp Dubois, in present Illinois.

March 29, 1804

Tried—but not punished—by court-martial for drinking and threatening Sergeant Ordway.

April 1, 1804

Listed as a member of the permanent party.

May 14, 1804

Heads up Missouri River with fellow explorers, across present Missouri.

June 29, 1804

Serves on court-martial that tries Collins and Hall, along the present border of Missouri and Kansas.

August, 1804

Searches unsuccessfully for Shannon, who is lost (but later found), along the present border of Nebraska and South Dakota.

September 24, 1804

Horse is stolen by Lakota Sioux, in present South Dakota; a violent confrontation with the Lakota is narrowly avoided.

Winter 1804–1805

Spends winter at Fort Mandan, in present North Dakota.

April 16, 1805

Catches "a verry large fat beaver in a Steel trap" (according to Ordway), in present North Dakota.

June 13, 1805

Reaches Great Falls of the Missouri (in present Montana) with fellow explorers.

August 1805

Explores Salmon River country in present Idaho with Clark and delivers important letter to Lewis.

September 10, 1805

Befriends three members of Salish tribe after laying down gun and signing in friendly manner, in present Montana.

Winter 1805–1806

Spends winter at Fort Clatsop, in present Oregon.

May 6, 1806

Quarrels with Drouillard when the two of them are assigned by Lewis to lead an unbroken horse, in present Idaho.

June 18, 1806

Takes serious fall with horse and is driven a "considerable distance" down the creek but "fortunately [escapes without] much injurey or the loss of his gun" (according to Clark), in present Idaho.

July 1806

Travels with Ordway's party up the Missouri River from Three Forks, in present Montana (as Lewis's party explores northern Montana and Clark's party southern Montana, with the corps eventually splitting into five groups).

July 26, 1806

Shows ability as boatman when he and Potts "[go] at running the canoes down the rapids" (according to Ordway), in present Montana.

August 3, 1806

Leaves Lewis's group to hunt with John Collins; by August 9, Lewis fears "that some missfortune has happened to them."

August 12, 1806

Still traveling with Collins and safe and sound, reaches Lewis's group to find that Lewis has been wounded (the previous day) and that members of the corp have met two trappers headed west—Joseph Dickson and Forrest Hancock.

August 17, 1806

Receives permission from Clark to leave the corps (now in present North Dakota) and head back up the Missouri River to trap with Dickson and Hancock.

October 1806–Spring 1807

Apparently makes solitary journey (after he and Hancock have a falling out with Dickson) in search of the sources of the Yellowstone and Bighorn Rivers, both of which he finds—at Yellowstone Lake and Brooks Lake, respectively.

Summer 1807

Traveling alone, meets Lisa's trapping party near the mouth of the Platte River (along present border of Iowa and Nebraska) and joins them in their journey up the Missouri.

Winter 1807–1808

Sent out by Lisa to befriend Crow Indians and invite them to trade at Fort Raymond, at the mouth of the Bighorn River.

Spring 1808

Fights with Crow and Salish—and is wounded—in battle against Blackfoot near Three Forks, in present Montana; returns safely to fort.

Summer 1808

Recovers from wound and is at Fort Raymond when Edward Rose attacks Lisa (who is saved when John Potts intervenes).

Late summer or early fall 1808

Escapes from Blackfoot warriors in legendary run after companion John Potts is killed; again makes way safely to fort.

Winter 1808–1809

Spends winter at Fort Raymond but makes trip to Three Forks to retrieve traps lost at time Potts was killed; once again escapes Blackfoot attack.

September 1809

Meets Dr. William H. Thomas, Thomas James, and others when they arrive at Mandan and Hidatsa villages (in present North Dakota) from St. Louis and safely return Mandan chief Sheheke and family to their home.

October 7, 1809

Sells a set of traps, gun, and powder to Thomas James and receives a promissory note for $140, apparently intending to accompany Chouteau and Lisa's party to St. Louis.

Winter 1809–1810

Joins Menard and Henry's trapping party and spends winter at Fort Raymond.

December 31, 1809

Signs promissory note with Reuben Lewis for $36.50 to the estate of Jean Baptiste Lepage.

March 1810

Leads the group west toward Three Forks, following same route (but in the opposite direction) he followed in his legendary run.

April 3, 1810

Arrives with others at Three Forks after harrowing trek through snow; soon begins trapping with several others on Jefferson River.

April 12, 1810

Survives Blackfoot attack that leaves five fellow trappers dead or taken prisoner; vows to leave West forever.

April 22, 1810

Departs Three Forks and heads east with William Bryant and one other man, carrying letters from Pierre Menard and Reuben Lewis.

May 1810

Reportedly reaches St. Louis thirty days after leaving Three Forks (after six years in the wilderness); interviewed by Bradbury upon arrival.

Around 1810

Marries Sarah Loucy (maiden name unknown) and fathers a daughter, Evelina; a son, Hiram, had most likely been born by 1804 (nothing is known about Hiram's mother).

August 24, 1810

Sells land warrant to John G. Comegys.

November 1810

Sues Meriwether Lewis's estate for expedition pay totaling $559.00.

March 18, 1811

Meets Wilson Price Hunt's party of westbound Astorians near his home along the Missouri River.

May 28, 1811

Settles with Lewis's estate for $375.60.

February 24, 1812

Signs a promissory note to William Clark for $45.00.

March 3, 1812

Enlists as a private in Captain Nathan Boone's Company of U.S. Mounted Rangers.

May 7, 1812

Dies in Missouri Territory of unknown illness that reportedly caused jaundice.

Appendix A

Accounts of Colter's Run

1. DR. WILLIAM H. THOMAS, 1809

Information was received here, that the Blackfoot Indians, who reside at the foot of the mountains, were hostile; that the British had factories all over the country, and had impelled them to cut off Mr. Manuel Lisa's party. One of the survivors, of the name of Coulter, who had accompanied Lewis and Clark, says, that he, in company with another was fired on by these Indians; that his companion, who made resistance, was killed; that his canoe, cloathing, furs, traps and arms were taken from him, and when expecting to receive the same fate of his comrade, he was ordered to run off as fast as possible; which he coldly complied with. Observing one of their young men following at full speed, armed with a spear, he pushed on to some distance, endeavouring to save his life. In a few minutes the savage was near enough to pitch his spear, which he [had] poisoned, and threw with such violence as to break the handle and miss the object. Coulter became the assailant, turned on the Indian and put him to death with the broken spear. Naked and tired he crept to the river, where he hid in a beaver dam from the band who had followed to revenge the death of their companion. Having observed the departure of the enemy, he left the river and came to the Gros Ventres, a tribe of the Mandans, a journey of nine days, without even mowkasons to protect him from the prickly pear, which covered the country, subsisting on such berries as providence threw in his way.*

* Here is the first published account of one of the most famous incidents in all of western history, John Colter's escape from the Blackfeet. The story agrees substantially with the longer account published by Bradbury (op. cit.,

155

17–20). Dr. Thomas apparently saw and talked to Colter, who had come east to the establishment at the Gros Ventres. Bradbury did not see Colter until May 18, 1810, on the lower Missouri, and the Bradbury version was not published until 1817. His more detailed story is quoted in full in Oglesby (op. cit., 86–88), and in Burton Harris, *John Colter: His Years in the Rockies*, New York, 1952, 124–27.

[Source: Jackson, "Journey to the Mandans," 191–92, including Jackson's original footnote (identified by an asterisk). On February 24, 1809, Meriwether Lewis, governor of the Upper Louisiana Territory, had signed an agreement with the St. Louis Missouri Fur Company for the return of Mandan chief Sheheke to his home in present North Dakota (see Jackson, *Letters*, 2:446–50). Dr. Thomas was in the group (commanded by Pierre Chouteau) that left St. Louis on May 17, 1809; the second group (which included Manuel Lisa and Thomas James) left on June 17, and the two groups traveled together after meeting at the mouth of the Osage River in present western Missouri. James reported that the combined group totaled around 350 men. Dr. Thomas thus met Colter near the Mandan and Hidatsa (called Gros Ventres in Jackson's note, above) villages in North Dakota at the same time Sheheke was safely returned to his village. When Thomas came back down the river, Charbonneau, Sacagawea, and Pomp were apparently with the group (see Morris, *Fate of the Corps*, 107). As Jackson notes, Thomas gave an account of his travels to Joseph Charless, publisher of the *Missouri Gazette* ("Journey to the Mandans," 179). The first installment appeared in the *Missouri Gazette* on November 30, 1809, with the second and final installment (which includes Thomas's report on Colter) presumably appearing in the December 7 issue. However, no extant copies of the December 7 or December 14 issues of the *Missouri Gazette* have been found. Luckily, the Pittsburgh *Gazette* reprinted the articles, and the excerpt quoted above is taken from the July 13, 1810, issue of that paper, via Jackson.]

A final and sad postscript to this fascinating story is that Lewis naturally incurred a number of expenses in his effort to return Sheheke to his home (a matter that had been quite important to Thomas Jefferson). The Madison administration, however, rejected some of the charges, plunging Lewis further into debt and prompting him to travel to Washington, D.C., in an attempt to settle the matter. By the time Dr. Thomas reached St. Louis, on November 20, 1809, Lewis had died from self-inflicted wounds in present Tennessee (see Morris, *Fate of the Corps*, 54–74, and Guice, *By His Own Hand?*, which put forth detailed arguments both for and against the position that Lewis committed suicide).

2. JOHN BRADBURY, 1817

This man [Colter] came to St. Louis in May, 1810, in a small canoe, from the head waters of the Missouri, a distance of three thousand miles, which he traversed in thirty days. I saw him on his arrival, and received from him an account of his adventures after he had separated from Lewis and Clarke's party: one of these, from its singularity, I shall relate. On the arrival of the party on the head waters of the Missouri, Colter, observing an appearance of abundance of beaver being there, he got permission to remain and hunt for some time, which he did in company with a man of the name of Dixon, who had traversed the immense tract of country from St. Louis to the head waters of the Missouri alone.

Soon after he separated from Dixon, and *trapped* in company with a hunter named Potts; and aware of the hostility of the Blackfeet Indians, one of whom had been killed by Lewis, they set their traps at night, and took them up early in the morning, remaining concealed during the day. They were examining their traps early one morning, in a creek about six miles from that branch of the Missouri called Jefferson's Fork, and were ascending in a canoe, when they suddenly heard a great noise, resembling the trampling of animals; but they could not ascertain the fact, as the high perpendicular banks on each side of the river impeded their view. Colter immediately pronounced it to be occasioned by Indians, and advised an instant retreat; but was accused of cowardice by Potts, who insisted that the noise was caused by buffaloes, and they proceeded on. In a few minutes afterwards their doubts were removed, by a party of Indians making their appearance on both sides of the creek, to the amount of five or six hundred, who beckoned them to come ashore.

As retreat was now impossible, Colter turned the head of the canoe to shore; and at the moment of its touching, an Indian seized the rifle belonging to Potts; but Colter, who is a remarkably strong man, immediately retook it, and handed it to Potts, who remained in the canoe, and on receiving it pushed off into the river. He had scarcely quitted the shore when an arrow was shot at him, and he cried out, *"Colter, I am wounded."* Colter remonstrated with him on the folly of attempting to escape, and urged him to come ashore. Instead of complying, he instantly leveled his rifle at an Indian, and shot him dead on the spot. This conduct, situated as he was, may appear to have been an act of madness; but it was doubtless the effect of sudden, but sound reasoning; for if taken alive, he must have expected to be tortured to death, according to their custom. He was instantly pierced with arrows so numerous, that, to use the language of Colter, *"he was made a riddle of."*

They now seized Colter, stripped him entirely naked, and began to consult on the manner in which he should be put to death. They were first inclined to set him up as a mark to shoot at; but the chief interfered, and seizing him by the shoulder, asked him if he could run fast? Colter, who had been some time amongst the Kee-kat-saw, or Crow Indians, had in a considerable degree acquired the Blackfoot language, and was also well acquainted with Indian customs. He knew that he had now to run for his life, with the dreadful odds of five or six hundred against him, and those armed Indians; therefore cunningly replied that he was a very bad runner, although he was considered by the hunters as remarkably swift. The chief now commanded the party to remain stationary, and led Colter out on the prairie three or four hundred yards, and released him, bidding him *to save himself if he could.* At that instant the horrid war whoop sounded in the ears of poor Colter, who, urged with the hope of preserving life, ran with a speed at which he was himself surprised. He proceeded towards the Jefferson Fork, having to traverse a plain six miles in breadth, abounding with the prickly pear, on which he was every instant treading with his naked feet. He ran nearly half way across the plain before he ventured to look over his shoulder, when he perceived that the Indians were very much scattered, and that he had gained ground to a considerable distance from the main body; but one Indian, who carried a spear, was much before all the rest, and not more than a hundred yards from him.

A faint gleam of hope now cheered the heart of Colter; he derived confidence from the belief that escape was within the bounds of possibility; but that confidence was nearly being fatal to him, for he exerted himself to such a degree, that the blood gushed from his nostrils, and soon almost covered the fore part of his body. He had now arrived within a mile of the river, when he distinctly heard the appalling sound of footsteps behind him, and every instant expected to feel the spear of his pursuer. Again he turned his head, and saw the savage not twenty yards from him. Determined if possible to avoid the expected blow, he suddenly stopped, turned around, and spread his arms. The Indian, surprised by the suddenness of the action, and perhaps at the bloody appearance of Colter, also attempted to stop; but exhausted with running, he fell whilst endeavoring to throw his spear, which stuck in the ground, and broke in his hand. Colter instantly snatched up the pointed part, with which he pinned him to the earth, and then continued his flight.

The foremost of the Indians, on arriving at the place, stopped till others came up to join them, when they set up a hideous yell. Every moment of this time was improved by Colter, who, although fainting and exhausted, succeeded in gaining the skirting of the cotton wood trees, on the borders of the fork, through which he ran, and plunged into the river. Fortunately for him, a little below this place there was an island, against the upper point of which a raft of drift timber had lodged. He dived under the raft, and after several efforts, got his head above water amongst the trunks of trees, covered over with smaller wood to the depth of several feet. Scarcely had he secured himself, when the Indians arrived on the river, screeching and yelling, as

Colter expressed it, "like so many devils." They were frequently on the raft during the day, and were seen through the chinks by Colter, who was congratulating himself on his escape, until the idea arose that they might set the raft on fire. In horrible suspense he remained until night, when hearing no more of the Indians, he dived from under the raft, and swam silently down the river to a considerable distance, when he landed, and travelled all night.

Although happy in having escaped from the Indians, his situation was still dreadful: he was completely naked, under a burning sun; the soles of his feet were entirely filled with the thorns of the prickly pear; he was hungry, and had no means of killing game, although he saw abundance around him, and was at least seven days journey from Lisa's Fort, on the Bighorn branch of the Roche Jaune River. These were circumstances under which almost any man but an American hunter would have despaired. He arrived at the fort in seven days, having subsisted on a root much esteemed by the Indians of the Missouri, now known by naturalists as *psoralea esculenta*.

[Source: Bradbury, *Travels in the Interior of America*, first published in 1817 and reprinted in Thwaites, ed., *Early Western Travels*, 5:44–47 n 18, emphasis in original, paragraphing added for readability. As Bradbury explains, he first met Colter in 1810, shortly after the latter's return to St. Louis. Interestingly, the excerpt reproduced above is actually Bradbury's footnote to his narrative of meeting Colter a second time, in 1811, which is included in appendix B. Bradury's account became the standard version of Colter's run, and, as shown below, was heavily relied on by Washington Irving, who further popularized Colter's adventure.]

3. THOMAS BIDDLE, 1819

Coulter returned to the trading-house. In traversing the same country, a short time after, in company with another man, a party of the Blackfeet attempted to stop them, without, however, evincing any hostile intentions; a recounter ensued, in which the companion of Coulter and two Indians were killed, and Coulter made his escape.

[Source: Thomas Biddle to Colonel Henry Atkinson, October 29, 1819. See appendix B for the context of this letter and for the other excerpts dealing with Colter.]

4. WASHINGTON IRVING, 1836

The next morning early, as the party were yet encamped at the mouth of a small stream, they were visited by another of these heroes of the wilderness, one John Colter, who had accompanied Lewis and Clarke in their memorable expedition. He had recently made one of those vast internal voyages so characteristic of this fearless class of men, and of the immense regions over which they hold their lonely wanderings; having come from the head waters of the Missouri to St. Louis in a small canoe. This distance of three thousand miles he had accomplished in thirty days. Colter kept with the party all the morning. He had many particulars to give them concerning the Blackfeet Indians, a restless and predatory tribe, who had conceived an implacable hostility to the white men, in consequence of one of their warriors having been killed by Captain Lewis, while attempting to steal horses. Through the country infested by these savages the expedition would have to proceed, and Colter was urgent in reiterating the precautions that ought to be observed respecting them. He had himself experienced their vindictive cruelty, and his story deserves particular citation, as showing the hairbreadth adventures to which these solitary rovers of the wilderness are exposed.

Colter, with the hardihood of a regular trapper, had cast himself loose from the party of Lewis and Clarke in the very heart of the wilderness, and had remained to trap beaver alone on the head waters of the Missouri. Here he fell in with another lonely trapper, like himself, named Potts, and they agreed to keep together. They were in the very region of the terrible Blackfeet, at that time thirsting to revenge the death of their companion, and knew that they had to expect no mercy at their hands. They were obliged to keep concealed all day in the woody margins of the rivers, setting their traps after nightfall and taking them up before daybreak. It was running a fearful risk for the sake of a few beaver skins; but such is the life of the trapper.

They were on a branch of the Missouri called Jefferson's Fork, and had set their traps at night, about six miles up a small river that emptied into the fork. Early in the morning they ascended the river in a canoe, to examine the traps. The banks on each side were high and perpendicular, and cast a shade over the stream. As they were softly paddling along they heard the trampling of many feet upon the banks. Colter immediately gave the alarm of "Indians!" and was for instant retreat. Potts scoffed at him for being frightened by the trampling of a herd of buffaloes. Colter checked his uneasiness and paddled forward. They had not gone much further when frightful whoops and yells burst forth from each side of the river, and several hundred Indians appeared on either bank. Signs were made to the unfortunate trappers to come on shore. They were obliged to comply. Before they could get out of their canoe, a savage seized the rifle belonging to Potts. Colter sprang on shore, wrested the weapon from the hands of the Indian, and restored it to his companion, who was still in the canoe, and immediately pushed into the stream. There was the sharp twang of a bow, and Potts cried out that he was wounded. Colter urged him to come on shore and submit, as his only chance for life; but the other knew there was no prospect of mercy, and determined to die game. Leveling his rifle, he shot one of the savages dead on the spot. The next moment he fell himself, pierced with innumerable arrows.

The vengeance of the savages now turned upon Colter. He was stripped naked, and, having some knowledge of the Blackfoot language, overheard a consultation as to the mode of despatching him, so as to derive the greatest amusement from his death. Some were for setting him up as a mark, and having a trial of skill at his expense. The chief, however, was for nobler sport. He seized Colter by the shoulder, and demanded if he could run fast. The unfortunate trapper was too well acquainted with Indian customs not to comprehend the drift of the question. He knew he was to run for his life, to furnish a kind of human hunt to his persecutors. Though in reality he was noted among his brother hunters for swiftness of foot, he assured the chief that he was a very bad runner. His stratagem gained him some vantage ground. He was led by the chief into the prairie, about four hundred yards from the main body of savages, and then turned loose to save himself if he could. A tremendous yell let him know that the whole pack of bloodhounds were off in full cry, Colter flew rather than ran; he was astonished at his own speed; but he had six miles of prairie to traverse before he should reach the Jefferson Fork of the Missouri; how could he hope to hold out such a distance with the fearful odds of several hundred to one against him! The plain, too, abounded with the prickly pear, which wounded his naked feet. Still he fled on, dreading each moment to hear the twang of a bow, and to feel an arrow quivering at his heart. He did not even dare to look around, lest he should lose an inch of that distance on which his life depended. He had run nearly half way across the plain when the sound of pursuit grew somewhat fainter, and he ventured to turn his head. The main body of his pursuers were a considerable distance behind; several of the faster runners were scattered in the advance; while a swift-footed warrior, armed with a spear, was not more than a hundred yards behind him.

Inspired with new hope, Colter redoubled his exertions, but strained himself to such a degree, that the blood gushed from his mouth and nostrils, and streamed down his breast. He arrived within a mile of the river. The sound of footsteps gathered upon him. A glance behind showed his pursuer within twenty yards, and preparing to launch his spear. Stopping short he turned round and spread out his arms. The savage, confounded by this sudden action, attempted to stop and to hurl his spear, but fell in the very act. His spear stuck in the ground, and the shaft broke in his hand. Colter plucked up the pointed part, pinned the savage to the earth, and continued his flight. The Indians, as they arrived at their slaughtered companion, stopped to howl over him. Colter made the most of this precious delay, gained the skirt of cottonwood bordering the river, dashed through it, and plunged into the stream. He swam to a neighboring island, against the upper end of which the drift-wood had lodged in such quantities as to form a natural raft; under this he dived, and swam below water until he succeeded in getting a breathing place between the floating trunks of trees, whose branches and bushes formed a covert several feet above the level of the water. He had scarcely drawn breath after all this toils, when he heard his pursuers on the river bank, whooping and yelling like so many fiends. They plunged in the river, and swam to the raft. The heart of Colter almost died within him as he saw them, through the chinks of his concealment, passing and repassing, and seeking for him in all directions. They at length gave up the search, and he began to rejoice in his escape, when the idea presented itself that they might set the raft on fire. Here was a new source of horrible apprehension, in which he remained until nightfall. Fortunately the idea did not suggest itself to the Indians. As soon as it was dark, finding by the silence around that his pursuers had departed, Colter dived again and came up beyond the raft. He then swam silently down the river for a considerable distance, when he landed, and kept on all night, to get as far as possible from this dangerous neighborhood.

By daybreak he had gained sufficient distance to relieve him from the terrors of his savage foes; but now new sources of inquietude presented themselves. He was naked and alone, in the midst of an unbounded wilderness; his only chance was to reach a trading post of the Missouri Company, situated on a branch of the Yellowstone River. Even should he elude his pursuers, days must elapse before he could reach his post, during which he must traverse immense prairies destitute of shade, his naked body exposed to the burning heat of the sun by day, and the dews and chills of the night season, and his feet lacerated by the thorns of the prickly pear. Thought he might see game in abundance around him, he had no means of killing any for his sustenance, and must depend for food upon the roots of the earth. In defiance of these difficulties he pushed resolutely forward, guiding himself in his trackless course by those signs and indications known only to Indians and backwoodsmen; and after braving dangers and hardships enough to break down any spirit but that of a western pioneer, arrived safe at the solitary post in question.*

Such is a sample of the rugged experience which Colter had to relate of savage life; yet, with all these perils and terrors fresh in his recollection, he could not see the present band on their way to those regions of danger and adventure, without feeling a vehement impulse to join them. A western trapper is like a sailor; past hazards only stimulate him to further risks. The vast prairie is to the one what the ocean is to the other, a boundless field of enterprise and exploit. However he may have suffered in his last cruise, he is always ready to join a new expedition; and the more adventurous its nature, the more attractive is it to his vagrant spirit.

Nothing seems to have kept Colter from continuing with the party to the shores of the Pacific but the circumstances of his having recently married. All the morning he kept with them, balancing in his mind the charms of his bride against those of the Rocky Mountains; the former, however, prevailed, and after a march of several miles, he took a reluctant leave of the travellers, and turned his face homeward.

* Bradbury. *Travels in America*, p. 17.

[Source: Irving, *Astoria*, the 1836 edition, unabridged, in two volumes, reprinted by J. B. Lippincott in 1961, including Irving's original footnote (identified by an asterisk). Born in 1783, Washington Irving was only a decade younger than Lewis and Clark. By 1820, Irving, the author of such stories as "The Legend of Sleepy Hollow" and "Rip van Winkle," had become a respected and well-known author. *Astoria* offered a history of the American fur trade, with particular emphasis on John Jacob Astor (Irving's good friend) and his employees, the "Astorians." As Edgeley W. Todd has written,

"Not only is *Astoria* generally dependable as history, but it also has literary merit. There is no necessary reason why history should not be well written, and Irving's style has been probably the quality of his work that has been most persistently praised. It is the chief literary and creative element in *Astoria*, for after mentally digesting the raw material of his sources, Irving presented it in the dress of clear and graceful prose.

"*Astoria* has literary importance in still other ways. By the time it appeared, only one other major American writer [James Fenimore Cooper] had used the American wilderness for creative purposes. . . . *Astoria*, along with Irving's two other books on the West [*A Tour on the Prairies* and *The Adventures of Captain Bonneville*], must have done much, however difficult it is to determine the extent, to awaken an interest in the West as a literary resource and hence to stimulate a gradually emerging frontier literature which attained culmination in Mark Twain thirty years and more later." (Irving, *Astoria*, edited and with an introduction by Edgeley W. Todd, xli-xlii.)]

5. THOMAS JAMES, 1846

When Colter was returning in 1807 with Lewis and Clark from Oregon he met a company of hunters ascending the Missouri, by whom he was persuaded to return to the trapping region, to hunt and trap with them. Here he was found by Lisa in the following year, whom he assisted in building the fort at the Big Horn. In one of his many excursions from this post to the Forks of the Missouri, for beaver, he made the wonderful escape adverted to in the last chapter, which I give precisely as he related it to me. His veracity was never questioned among us and his character was that of a true American backwoodsman. He was about thirty-five years of age, five feet ten inches in height, and wore an open, ingenuous, and pleasing countenance of the Daniel

Boone stamp. Nature had formed him, like Boone, for hardy endurance of fatigue, privations, and perils.

He had gone with a companion named Potts to the Jefferson river, which is the most western of the three Forks, and runs near the base of the mountains. They were both proceeding up the river in search of beaver, each in his own canoe, when a war party of about eight hundred Black-Feet Indians suddenly appeared on the east bank of the river. The chiefs ordered them to come ashore, and apprehending robbery only, and knowing the utter hopelessness of flight and having dropped his traps over the side of the canoe from the Indians into the water, which was here quite shallow, he hastened to obey their mandate. On reaching the shore he was seized, disarmed and stripped entirely naked. Potts was still in his canoe in the middle of the stream, where he remained stationary, watching the result. Colter requested him to come ashore, which he refused to do, saying he might as well lose his life at once as to be stripped and robbed in the manner Colter had been. An Indian immediately fired and shot him about the hip; he dropped down in the canoe, but instantly rose with his rifle in his hands. "Are you hurt," said Colter. "Yes, said he, too much hurt to escape; if you can get away, do so. I will kill at least one of them." He leveled his rifle and shot an Indian dead. In an instant, at least a hundred bullets pierced his body and as many savages rushed into the stream and pulled the canoe, containing his riddled corpse, ashore. They dragged the body up onto the bank, and with their hatchets and knives cut and hacked it all to pieces, and limb from limb. The entrails, heart, lungs, &c., they threw into Colter's face. The relations of the killed Indian were furious with rage and struggled, with tomahawk in hand, to reach Colter, while others held them back. He was every moment expecting the death blow or the fatal shot that should lay him beside his companion. A council was hastily held over him and his fate quickly determined upon.

He expected to die by tomahawk, slow, lingering, and horrible. But they had magnanimously determined to give him a chance, though a slight one, for his life. After the council, a Chief pointed to the prairie and motioned him away with his hand, saying in the Crow language, "go, go away." He supposed they intended to shoot him as soon as he was out of the crowd and presented a fair mark to their guns. He started in a walk, and an old Indian with impatient signs and exclamations, told him to go faster, and as he still kept a walk, the same Indian manifested his wishes by still more violent gestures and adjurations. When he had gone a distance of eighty or a hundred yards from the army of his enemies, he saw the younger Indians throwing off their blankets, leggings, and other incumbrances, as if for a race. Now he knew their object. He was to run a race, of which the prize was to be his own life and scalp.

Off he started with the speed of the wind. The war-whoop and yell immediately arose behind him; and looking back, he saw a large company of young warriors, with spears, in rapid pursuit. He ran with all the strength that nature, excited to the utmost, could give; fear and hope lent a supernatural vigor to his limbs and the rapidity of his flight astonished himself. The Madison Fork lay directly before him, five miles from his starting place. He had run half the distance when his strength began to fail and the blood to gush from his nostrils. At every leap the red stream spurted before him, and his limbs were growing rapidly weaker and weaker. He stopped and looked back; he had far outstripped all his pursuers and could get off if strength would only hold out. One solitary Indian, far ahead of the others, was rapidly approaching, with a spear in his right hand, and a blanket streaming behind from his left hand and shoulder.

Despairing of escape, Colter awaited his pursuer and called to him in the Crow language, to save his life. The savage did not seem to hear him, but letting go his blanket, and seizing his spear with both hands, he rushed at Colter, naked and defenseless as he stood before him and made a desperate lunge to transfix him. Colter seized the spear, near the head, with his right hand, and exerting his whole strength, aided by the weight of the falling Indian, who had lost his balance in the fury of the onset, he broke off the iron head or blade which remained in his hand, while the savage fell to the ground and lay prostrate and disarmed before him. Now was *his* turn to beg for his life, which he did in the Crow language, and held up his hands imploringly, but Colter was not in a mood to remember the golden rule, and pinned his adversary through the body to the earth by one stab with the spear head. He quickly drew the weapon from the body of the now dying Indian, and seizing his blanket as lawful spoil, he again set out with renewed strength, feeling, he said to me, as if he had not run a mile. A shout and yell arose from the pursuing army in his rear as from a legion of devils, and he saw the prairie behind him covered with Indians in full and rapid chase.

Before him, if anywhere was life and safety; behind him, certain death; and running as never man before sped the foot, except, perhaps, at the Olympic Games, he reached his goal, the Madison River and the end of his five mile heat. Dashing through the willows on the bank, he plunged into the stream and saw close beside him a beaver house, standing like a coal-pit about ten feet above the surface of the water, which was here of about the same depth. This presented to him a refuge from his ferocious enemies of which he immediately availed himself. Diving under the water he arose into the beaver house, where he found a dry and comfortable resting place on the upper floor or story of this singular structure. The Indians soon came up, and in their search for him they stood upon the roof of his house of refuge, which he expected every moment to hear them breaking open. He also feared that they would set it on fire. After a diligent search on the side of the river, they crossed over, and in about two hours returned again to his temporary habitation in which he was enjoying bodily rest, though with much anxious foreboding. The beaver houses are divided into two stories and will generally accommodate several men in a dry and comfortable lodging. In this asylum Colter kept fast till night. The cries of his terrible enemies had gradually died away and all was still around him when he ventured out of his hiding place, by the same opening under the water by which he had entered and which admits the beavers to their building.

He swam the river and hastened towards the mountain gap or ravine, about thirty miles above on the river, through which our company passed in the snow with so much difficulty. Fearing that the Indians might have guarded this pass, which was the only outlet from the valley, and to avoid the danger of a surprise, Colter ascended the almost perpendicular mountain before him, the tops and sides of which a great way down were covered with perpetual snow. He clambered up the fearful ascent about four miles below the gap, holding on by the rocks, shrubs, and branches of trees, and by morning had reached the top. He lay there concealed all that day, and at night proceeded on in the descent of the mountain, which he accomplished by dawn. He now hastened on in the open plain towards Manuel's fort on the Big Horn, about three hundred miles ahead in the north-east. He travelled day and night, stopping only for necessary repose, and eating roots and the bark of trees, for eleven days. He reached the Fort, nearly exhausted by hunger, fatigue, and excitement. His only clothing was the Indian's blanket, whom he had killed in the race, and his only weapon, the same Indian's spear which he brought to the Fort as a trophy. His beard was long, his face and whole body were thin and emaciated by hunger, and his limbs and feet swollen and sore. The company at the Fort did not recognize him in this dismal plight until he had made himself known.

[Source: James, *Three Years Among the Indians*, the 1846 edition, unabridged, with an introduction by A. P. Nasatir, 29–34, paragraphing added for readability. Like William Thomas, James traveled up the Missouri River in the summer of 1809 and met Colter at the Hidatsa villages in present North Dakota in September. James is a particularly valuable witness because he traveled the route of Colter's run (in the opposite direction) with Colter himself and had the chance to query Colter on various aspects of the adventure. Also, since he spent several months with Colter, he possibly heard Colter's account more than once. James, however, did not publish his account until 1846, almost four decades after he first met Colter. The time lapse, as well as James's style, leaves the impression that he may have embellished the story. For information on James and on the interesting publishing history of his narrative, see the Quaife edition of *Three Years Among the Indians*, xi–xxxii.]

Appendix B

The Documentary History of John Colter, 1803–1846

1803–1806

Journals of the Lewis and Clark Expedition. Colter is mentioned hundreds of times, and Lewis, Clark, Ordway, Gass, and Whitehouse all make numerous references to him. Floyd, who died on August 20, 1804 (and whose journal dates from May 14 to August 18), does not mention Colter by name. The first contemporary record of Colter is Clark's journal entry of December 30, 1803 (at Camp Dubois, Illinois), which states that Colter had killed a deer and a turkey; the last expedition references to Colter were made on August 17, 1806 (at the Mandan villages in North Dakota) by Clark and Ordway, who both recorded that Colter headed back up the Missouri River with trappers Joseph Dickson and Forrest Hancock. (See Moulton, *Journals*, vols. 2–11 and 13, the comprehensive index.)

1804

Meriwether Lewis to William Clark, May 6, 1804. Lewis wrote this letter from St. Louis to Clark at Camp Dubois. The excerpt mentioning Colter reads as follows: "I send you by Colter and Reed 200 lbs. of tallow which you will be so good as to have melted with 50 lbs. of hog's lard." The corps departed Camp Dubois on May 14. (Jackson, *Letters*, 1:179–80)

1807

Meriwether Lewis to Henry Dearborn, January 15, 1807. Lewis's letter to Secretary of War Dearborn included a roll of men who accompanied Captains Lewis and Clark on their late tour to the Pacific Ocean. Colter is listed in alphabetical order with the other privates. Although Lewis gave special praise to certain individuals (such as the Field brothers and John Shields), he simply listed the name and rank of most of the men, including Colter. (Jackson, *Letters*, 364–69)

1807

The Act Compensating Lewis and Clark, March 3, 1807. The U.S. House and Senate passed the bill, which granted land warrants to Lewis and Clark and those who served with them, on February 28, 1807. Lewis and Clark received 1,600 acres each, and Colter and thirty others received 320 acres each on any of the public lands of the United States, lying on the west side of the Mississippi. The act also doubled the pay to each of the before named persons. (Jackson, *Letters*, 2:377)

1807

Clark's roster [March], 1807. Clark listed John Colter seventh, with the rank of private, serving from October 15, 1803 to October 10, 1806 (for a total of 35 months and 25 days) at $5 per month, for a total of $179.33 1/3. Clark's notation provides some interesting information. First, this is the first document telling us when Colter actually enlisted—October 15, 1803; second, Colter was the only person who enlisted on that day (Gibson, Shields, and Shannon enlisted on October 19 and Pryor and Bratton on October 20); third, Lewis and Clark made sure that Colter, like the others, was paid through October 1806 even though he had left the expedition in August. (Jackson, *Letters*, 2:378)

1807

Messrs. Lewis & Clarke's Donation Lands [March 6, 1807]. As Donald Jackson points out, this bound book deals with the land warrants and contains both blank and executed forms, with stubs indicating that similar forms have been torn out. Colter is the ninth person named in a list of thirty-three people that includes Richard Warfington and John Newman (temporary members of the party who returned to St. Louis in the spring of 1805). (Jackson, *Letters*, 2:380–82)

1807

Clark's receipt to Lewis, March 10, 1807. Clark wrote: "Received of Meriwether Lewis the sum of six thousand eight hundred and ninety six dollars and thirty four cents, the same being in full of the sum of one thousand two hundred and twenty eight dollars and six cents . . . including also the gratuitous donations under the said act to all the men who were with us on our late expedition to the Pacific Ocean except John Ordway and John Colter." Lewis did not give Colter's pay to Clark because Colter had not yet returned to St. Louis. (Jackson, *Letters*, 2:384)

1807

Final summation of Lewis's account, August 5, 1807. This record includes the following paragraph:

"1661

Bounties to Soldiers, 1803. For bounty in full paid by him to Charles Floyd, Nathl. Pryer, Wm. Bratton, John Colter, Reuben Fields, Joseph Fields, George Gibson, Geo. Shannon & Jno. Shields [the nine young men from Kentucky] men whom he inlisted in 1803 for 5 Years or during the expedition up the Missouri—9 men 12 drs. each.108.00." (Jackson, *Letters*, 2:425)

1809

Clark's list of Lewis's protested bills [August 24, 1809]. This list was drawn up shortly before Lewis left on his ill-fated trip to the east (he died on October 11 in Tennessee). Although most of the list is in Clark's hand and deals with protested bills, the following line was written by Lewis and was not among the disputed debts:

"To John Colter
$320.00"
(Jackson, *Letters*, 2:723)

1809

Thomas James's promissory note to John Colter for $140.00. James signed this note on October 7, 1809 in present North Dakota, near the Mandan and Hidatsa villages. Colter's estate later sued James for the debt. Interestingly, James says he bought the following from Colter: a set of beaver traps, at $120; a pound and a half of powder, at $6; and a gun, at $40; for a total of $166. (James, *Three Years Among the Indians*, 14.) However, Colter's probate file includes mention that a cash payment of $176 was received from Thomas James. (A photocopy of the document, which apparently is a copy of an original, can be found in Colter-Frick, *Courageous Colter*, 98; no source is listed.)

1809

Publication of Dr. William H. Thomas's account of Colter's run (see appendix A).

1809

John Colter and Reuben Lewis's promissory note to the estate of Jean Baptiste Lepage for $36.50. Colter and Lewis signed this document, which states that Lepage is deceased, on December 31, 1809 at Fort Raymond, Lisa's post at the confluence of the Yellowstone and Bighorn Rivers, in present Montana. (John Colter's Estate Papers, Franklin County Courthouse, Union, Missouri, original note in French)

1809

John Colter's promissory note to Auguste Chouteau, with $36.00 and $36.50 both listed as totals. Colter signed this document, like the preceding one, on December 31, 1809, at Fort Raymond. The two documents apparently represent the same debt. Colter promised to make the payment to the estate of Jean Baptiste LePage by June of 1810. Jean Baptiste Champlain signed as a witness and was apparently representing Chouteau, who was not present at Fort Raymond. Chouteau's son-in-law Rene Paul collected principal and interest of $46.18 from Colter's estate in 1816. (John Colter's Estate Papers, Franklin County Courthouse, Union, Missouri)

1810

Reuben Lewis to Meriwether Lewis, April 21, 1810. This letter was written from the Three Forks of the Missouri (in present Montana) and was given to Colter, who was about to depart for St. Louis. Not realizing his brother Meriwether had died six months earlier, Reuben wrote: "The return on your old acquaintance Coalter, gives me an opportunity of addressing you a few lines." (Missouri History Museum, St. Louis)

1810

Pierre Menard to His Wife, Angelique, April 21, 1810. Like Reuben Lewis, Menard wrote this letter from Three Forks and asked Colter to deliver it. "Dear Doll," he wrote, "I am taking advantage of the fact that John Colter leaves for St. Louis tomorrow morning to inform you that I am always in perfect health." (Pierre Menard Letterbook, 1785–1818, Abraham Lincoln Presidential Library and Museum, Springfield, Illinois, original in French; transcript of translation in Colter-Frick, *Courageous Colter*, 107–8)

1810

John Colter's assignment of his land warrant. On August 20, 1810, Colter assigned his land warrant for 320 acres to "John G. Comegys or his assigne [hole in document] my right and title in and to the within Three hundred and twenty acres of land for value received of them." The document does not say how much Colter received from Comegys, a prominent merchant. (Colter-Frick, *Courageous Colter*, 112–13; the source cited is the U.S. Land Office.) Comegys subsequently surrendered the warrant for land in 1824 (see the entry for 1841, below).

1810

John Colter's promissory note to Jacob Philipson for $16.00. Colter signed this document in St. Louis on October 4, 1810. After Colter's death, the debt was paid by Daniel Richardson, administrator of Colter's estate. (Meriwether Lewis Collection, Missouri History Museum, St. Louis)

1810

John Colter's suit against Lewis's estate. In November of 1810, Colter's attorney, J. A. Graham, filed suit against Edward Hempstead, administrator of Meriwether Lewis's estate, for $559.00 ($380.00 for Colter's service with the Corps of Discovery and $179.00 for the extra pay allowed by Congress). A summons had been served to Hempstead on September 3, 1810. William Clark was called as a witness (although the record does not include his actual testimony), and William H. Thomas was among those making claims against Lewis's estate. The matter was taken up in two separate cases during the

November term. As shown below, the suit was settled in May 1811. (*John Colter v. Edward Hempstead*, November 1810, Case No. 35 and Case No. 38, Circuit Court Case Files, Office of the Circuit Clerk—St. Louis, Missouri State Archives—St. Louis [September 2, 2013,http://stlcourtrecords.wustl. edu])

1810

John Colter summoned as a witness in *Thomas James v. St. Louis Missouri Fur Company*. James filed the suit in November 1810, and in March, June, and October of 1811, Colter (spelled Caulter in court documents) was summoned as a witness. During the same term, the St. Louis Missouri Fur Company also sued James, discussed next. The final disposition of these cases is not known, although James wrote three decades later that he was "glad to get rid of the suits" by giving the company a note for one hundred dollars. (James, *Three Years Among the Indians*, 55; *Thomas James v. St. Louis Missouri Fur Company*, November 1810, Case No. 62, Circuit Court Case Files, Office of the Circuit Clerk—St. Louis, Missouri State Archives—St. Louis [September 2, 2013,http://stlcourtrecords.wustl.edu])

1810

John Colter summoned as a witness in *St. Louis Fur Company v. Thomas James*. In an interesting flipside to the preceding record, Colter was called to testify for the defendant (James) on the same days in March, June, and October, 1811. (*St. Louis Missouri Fur Company v. Thomas James*, November 1810, Case No. 36, Circuit Court Case Files, Office of the Circuit Clerk—St. Louis, Missouri State Archives—St. Louis [September 2, 2013, http://stlcourtrecords.wustl.edu])

1810

John Colter's promissory note to John G. Comegys for $18.25. Colter signed this document in St. Louis on December 12, 1810. (Meriwether Lewis Collection, Missouri History Museum, St. Louis)

1811

John H. Marks on Lewis's debts [1811]. Jackson states that this document is in the hand of John H. Marks, Meriwether Lewis's stepbrother, and was probably written in 1811, when Marks was attempting to settle Lewis's financial affairs. The following line mentioning Colter is listed under Debts:

"John Coalter open [. . .] judgment entered March 1811 . . 397.60"

A similar document, also in the hand of Marks and also presumably written in 1811 includes this line under Debts:

"Jon. Coalter
320.00"
(Jackson, *Letters*, 2:729, 730)

1811

Bradbury's reference to John Colter. John Bradbury, who had first met
Colter in May 1810, interviewed him again on March 18, 1811, when Bradbury was on his way up the Missouri River with Wilson Price Hunt's trapping party. Bradbury recorded the experience at the time and published it in
1817. The complete reference reads as follows:

"I enquired of Sullens for John Colter, one of Lewis and Clarke's party,
whom General Clark had mentioned to me as being able to point out the
place on the Missouri where the petrified skeleton of a fish, above forty feet
long, had been found. Sullens informed me that Colter lived about a mile
from us, and sent his son to inform him of our arrival; but we did not see him
that evening.

"18th. At day-break Sullens came to our camp, and informed us that
Colter would be with us in a few minutes. Shortly after he arrived, and
accompanied us for some miles, but could not give me the information I
wished for. He seemed to have a great inclination to accompany the expedition; but having been lately married, he reluctantly took leave of us."
(Thwaites, *Early Western Travels*, 5:44–46; Bradbury's account of Colter's
run is a footnote to this reference)

1811

Brackenridge's reference to John Colter. Henry Marie Brackenridge, who
traveled up the Missouri River in 1811, shortly after Bradbury (but in Lisa's
party, which was trying to catch Hunt), also interviewed Colter, quite possibly as Lisa's party passed near Colter's residence in St. John's township. In
a series of articles for the *Missouri Gazette*, Brackenridge described the
Louisiana Territory. In a paragraph offering general information on the
Rocky Mountains, Brackenridge wrote:

"At the head of the Gallatin Fork, and of the Grosse Corne of the Yellow
stone, from discoveries since the voyage of Lewis and Clark, it is found less
difficult to cross than the Allegheny Mountains. Coulter, a celebrated hunter
and woodsman, informed me that a loaded wagon would not find obstruction
in passing." (*Missouri Gazette*, April 18, 1811)

1811

John Colter's receipt to Edward Hempstead, May 28, 1811. Colter, who
had quite a difficult time being paid for his expedition service, had originally
sought $559. The complete document reads as follows:

"John Colter
vs.
Edward Hempstead, admr.
of Meriwether Lewis dec.
Judgment of the Court of Common Pleas, St. Louis district, March Term 1811.

Received of Edward Hempstead the sum of three Hundred & Seventy five Dollars and Sixty Cents in full of the Judgment in the above case: Witness my hand & Seal May 28. 1811.

Witness
John Colter [Seal]
John Kerr"
(Jackson, *Letters*, 2:567)

1812

John Colter's promissory note to William Clark for $45.00. Colter signed this note on February 24, 1812, one week before enlisting in the U.S. Rangers. On January 31, 1816, almost four years after Colter's death, Clark received principal and interest, for a total of $49.50. The complete document reads as follows:

"On Demand I promise to pay or license to be paid unto William Clark of his Order the just and full Sum of Forty five Dollars Currency of the United States for the Payment of which Sum I bind myself, my heirs Executor, or Assigns & for Witness whereof I have Set my hand and Seal the Twenty fourth Day of February One Thousand and Eight hundred & twelve

Witness
John Colter
Seal"
(John Colter's Estate Papers, Franklin County Courthouse, Union, Missouri)

1812

John Colter's enlistment in the U.S. Mounted Rangers. Colter enlisted as a private in Captain Nathan Boone's company on March 3, 1812 and was scheduled to serve until June 7, 1812, but his term ended on May 6, presumably because of poor health. He was paid $65 dollars ($1 dollar per day for 65 days). (National Archives, War of 1812 Military Records; also in Carter, *Territorial Papers*, 14:560–62 [which mistakenly has the name as "Cotter"])

1812

John Colter's death. The Muster Roll and Company Pay Roll for Captain Nathan Boone's Company of U.S. Rangers both contain this note for Colter, with no further explanation: Died 7 May 1812. (National Archives, War of 1812 Military Records; also in Carter, *Territorial Papers*, 14:560–61.)

1813

Newspaper notice concerning John Colter's estate, December 1813. The notice reads as follows:

"All persons having demands against the estate of John Coalter deceased, will please to exhibit their claims within a year from the date hereof, to the undersigned who has obtained letters of administration on the said estate, or they will not be entitled to receive any dividend of the assets in the hands of the administrator, if the said estate should prove insolvent; and those who are indebted to the said estate will please to make immediate payment to the undersigned.

> *Daniel Richardson.*
> Administrator.
> St. Louis, Nov. 26th, 1813."
> (*Missouri Gazette*, December 4, 1813)

1813–1821

John Colter's estate papers. This packet consists largely of a series of vouchers and statements created after Colter's death. All of the documents in this packet created before Colter's death are discussed above. Settlement of Colter's estate did not begin until November 1813, a year and a half after his death. Daniel Richardson, John Morrow, and James Brown (husband of Colter's widow, variously referred to as Loucy, Sarah, and Sally) committed to a bond of $275.00 on November 26, 1813, and letters of administration were granted to Richardson, administrator of the estate. As Ruth Colter-Frick notes, "One appraisal was made December 4th, 1813. Six days later on December the 10th, 1813, there was a public estate sale of [Colter's] personal property. That was fast work considering the fact that the Probate Court was in St. Louis, about sixty miles from his home" (*Courageous Colter*, 17). The estate was finally settled on October 22, 1821, in Franklin County, Missouri, and Colter's widow received a final payment of $124.11. By that time, Daniel Richardson had died, and his sons Richard and Amos Richardson were handling his affairs (John Colter's Estate Papers, Franklin County Courthouse, Union, Missouri, discussed in detail in Colter-Frick, *Courageous Colter*, 148–73). A compilation of St. Louis probate records published by the St. Louis Genealogical Society contains the following statement on Colter's estate papers: "John Colter, a veteran of the Lewis & Clark Expedition n 1804, set up a trading post on presumed bounty land at Bouef Creek and the Missouri River, then in the far reaches of St. Louis County. When Colter died intestate in the fall of 1813 (he was only 37 years old), his estate was filed for probate (F. 160) in St. Louis. Due to lawsuits, debts, and remarriage of Colter's widow, the case dragged on for years. It was still unsettled in December 1818, when Franklin County was formed from St. Louis County, and the newer county requested and received transfer of Colter's file." (*St. Louis and St. Louis County, Missouri, Probate Records,* Volume 1, 1804 1849 [St. Louis: St. Louis Genealogical Society, 1985], ii)

1814

Brackenridge's references to Colter. In 1814, Brackenridge published *Views of Louisiana: Together with a Journal of a Voyage up the Missouri River, in 1811*, which included the following two references to Colter:

"At the river Platte, Lisa met one of Lewis and Clark's men, of the name of Coulter, who had been discharged at the Mandan villages, at his own request, that he might make a hunt before he returned. Coulter was persuaded to return; his knowledge of the country and nations rendered him an acquisition." (90)

"He [Lisa] shortly after dispatched Coulter, the hunter before mentioned, to bring some of the Indian nations to trade. This man, with a pack of thirty pounds weight, his gun and some ammunition, went upwards of five hundred miles to the Crow nation; gave them information, and proceeded from thence to several other tribes. On his return, a party of Indians, in whose company he happened to be, was attacked, and he was lamed by a severe wound in the leg; notwithstanding which, he returned to the establishment, entirely alone and without assistance, several hundred miles." (91–92)

1817

Bond obligating Thomas, John, and Joseph James to appear and answer to Daniel Richardson, administrator of John Colter's estate, October 8, 1817. (Missouri History Museum)

1817

Publication of John Bradbury's account of Colter's run (see appendix A).

1819

Major Thomas Biddle to Colonel Henry Atkinson, October 29, 1819. In this report, written from Camp Missouri River (near present Council Bluffs, Iowa), Biddle discussed Indian trade on the Missouri, briefly reviewed Lisa's 1807 expedition, and mentioned that the first party of Lisa's men that were met by the Blackfeet were treated civilly. (However, other records make no mention of Lisa's men being treated civilly by the Blackfoot, either before or after he sent the four emissaries out to the Crow.) Biddle continued:

"This circumstance induced Lisa to despatch one of his men (Coulter) to the forks of the Missouri to endeavor to find the Blackfeet nation, and bring them to his establishment to trade. This messenger unfortunately fell in with a party of the Crow nation, with whom he staid several days. While with them, they were attacked by their enemies the Blackfeet. Coulter, in self-defense, took part with the Crows. He distinguished himself very much in the combat; and the Blackfeet were defeated, having plainly observed a white man fighting in the ranks of their enemy. Coulter returned to the trading-house." See appendix A for Biddle's account of Colter's run. (American State Papers, 202)

1825–1828

Clark's List of Expedition Members. In this document, entitled Men on Lewis & Clarks Trip, Clark's reference to Colter reads, J. Colter do. (The do. stands for *ditto*, a reference to Dead after the name of P. Gass; Gass, however, was not dead and was, in fact, the last surviving veteran of the expedition when he died in 1870 at the age of ninety-eight.) As Donald Jackson explains, "This document appears on the front cover of Clark's cash book and journal for 1825–1828 and seems, according to internal evidence, to have been written during these years." The most controversial item on the list is Clark's note that Sacagawea was dead—this after certain 20th-century researchers had concluded she lived until the 1880s. (See Jackson, *Letters*, 2:638–39, for the document itself and Morris, *Fate of the Corps*, 149–61, for a discussion of the list.)

1836

Publication of Washington Irving's account of Colter's run (see appendix A).

1841

R. R. H. Frazer and Hiram Colter to Jas. Whitcomb, June 18, 1841. In this letter, the sons of expedition veterans Robert Frazer (who died in 1836 or 1837) and John Colter wrote to Whitcomb, an official at the Franklin County, Missouri, Land Office requesting information about their fathers' land warrants. Whitcomb replied that Frazer's warrant had been surrendered at the Land Office by John Vivian, assignee, in 1818, and that Colter's warrant had been surrendered at the Land Office by John G. Comegys, assignee, in 1824. (Colter-Frick, *Courageous Colter*, 113–14; the source cited is the U.S. Land Office.)

1846

Thomas James's account of his experiences with Colter. James's book *Three Years Among the Indians and Mexicans* was published in 1846. See Appendix A for James's account of Colter's run; the other sections concerning Colter read as follows:

"On Arriving at the Gros-Ventre village we had found a hunter and trapper named Colter, who had been one of Lewis & Clarke's men, and had returned thus far with them in 1807. Of him I purchased a set of beaver traps for $120, a pound and a half of powder for $6, and a gun for $40." (14)

"Our guide on this route [from Fort Raymond to Three Forks] was Colter, who thoroughly knew the road, having twice escaped over it from capture and death at the hands of Indians. In ten or twelve days after leaving the Fort we re-entered an opening or gap in the mountains, where it commenced snowing most violently and so continued all night. The morning showed us the heads and backs of our horses just visible above the snow which had crushed down all our tents. We proceeded on with the greatest difficulty. As we entered the ravine or opening of the mountain the snow greatly increased in depth being in places from fifty to sixty feet on the ground, a third of which had fallen and drifted in that night. The wind had heaped it up in many places to a prodigious height. The strongest horses took the front to make a road for us, but soon gave out and the ablest bodied men took their places as pioneers. A horse occasionally stepped out of the beaten track and sunk entirely out of sight in the snow. By night we had made about four miles of that day's travel. By that night we passed the ravine and reached the Gallatin river, being the eastern fork of the Missouri. The river sweeps rapidly by the pass at its western extremity, on each side of which the mountain rises perpendicularly from the bank of the river; and apparently stopped our progress up and down the east side of the stream. I forded it and was followed by Dougherty, Ware, and another, when Colter discovered an opening through the mountain on the right or north side, and through it led the rest of the company. We, however, proceeded down the left bank of the river till night, when we encamped and supped (four of us) on a piece of buffalo meat about the size of the two hands.

"During this and the proceeding day we suffered from indistinct vision, similar to Brown's affliction of leaving the Big Horn. We all now became blind as he had been, from the reflection of the sun's rays on the snow. The hot tears trickled from the swollen eyes nearly blistering the cheeks, and the eye-balls seemed bursting from our heads. At first, the sight was obscured as by a silk veil or handkerchief, and we were unable to hunt. Now we could not even see our way before us, and in this dreadful situation we remained two days and nights. Hunger was again inflicting its sharp pangs upon us, and we were upon the point of killing one of the pack horses, when on the fourth day after crossing the Gallatin, one of the men killed a goose, of which, being now somewhat recovered from our blindness, we made a soup and stayed the gnawings of hunger. The next day our eyes were much better, and we fortunately killed an elk, of which we ate without excess, being taught by experience, the dangers of gluttony after a fast.

"We continued on down the river and soon came in sight of our comrades in the main body on the right bank. They, like ourselves, had all been blind, and had suffered more severely than we from the same causes. They had killed three dogs, one a present to me from an Indian, and two horses to appease the demands of hunger before they had sufficiently recovered to take sight on their guns. Which in this distressed situation enveloped by thick darkness at midday, thirty Snake Indians came among them, and left without committing any depredation. Brown and another, who suffered less than the others, saw and counted these Indians, who might have killed them all and escaped with their effects with perfect impunity. Their preservation was wonderful. When we overtook them they were slowly recovering from blindness and we all encamped together, with thankful and joyous hearts for our late narrow escape from painful and lingering death. "We proceeded on in better spirits. On the next day we passed a battle field of the Indians, where the skulls and bones were lying around on the ground in vast numbers. The battle which had caused this terrible slaughter, took place in 1808, the year but one before, between the Black-Feet to the number of fifteen hundred on the one side, and the Flat-Heads and Crows, numbering together about eight hundred on the other. Colter was in the battle on the side of the latter, and was wounded in the leg, and thus disabled from standing. He crawled to a small thicket and there loaded and fired while sitting on the ground. The battle was desperately on both sides, but victory remained with the weaker party. The Black-Feet engaged at first with about five hundred Flat-Heads, whom they attacked in great fury. The noise, shouts and firing brought a reinforcement of Crows to the Flat-Heads, who were fighting with great spirit and defending the ground manfully. The Black-Feet, who are the Arabs of this region, were at length repulsed, but retired in perfect order and could hardly be said to have been defeated. The Flat-Head are a noble race of men, brave, generous and hospitable. They might be called the Spartans of Oregon. Lewis & Clark had received much kindness from them in their expedition of the Columbia, which waters their country; and at the time of this well fought battle, Colter was leading them to Manuel's Fort to trade with the Americans, when the Black Feet fell upon them in such numbers as seemingly to make their destruction certain. Their desperate courage saved them from a general massacre.

"The following day we reached the long sought Forks of the Missouri, or the place of the confluence of the Gallatin, Madison and Jefferson Rivers. Here at last, after ten months of travel, we encamped, commenced a Fort in the point made by the Madison and Jefferson forks, and prepared to begin business. This point was the scene of Colter's escape in the fall of the year, but one before, from the Indians and a death by torture; an event so extraordinary and thrilling, as he related it to me, that it deserves a brief narration." (24–27)

"Early the next morning the whole garrison was aroused by an alarm made by Valle and several Frenchmen who came in, as if pursued by enemies, and informed them that the whole party who had gone up the Jefferson, at the time of our departure down the Missouri, had been killed by the Indians, and that they expected an immediate attack on the Fort. The whole garrison prepared for resistance. The next morning after Valle's arrival, Colter came in unhurt, with a few others, and said there were no Indians near the Fort." (39)

"Lieutenant Emmel [Immel] with those before mentioned of the trapping party up the [Jefferson] river, had come in and they supposed that all the rest had been killed. They had had a very narrow escape themselves, as all but Colter probably considered it; he with his experience, naturally looked upon the whole as an ordinary occurrence." (40–41)

"Colter now with me passed over the scene of his capture and wonderful escape, and described his emotions during the whole adventure with great minuteness. Not the least of his exploits was the scaling of the mountain, which seemed to me impossible even by the mountain goat. As I looked at its rugged and perpendicular sides I wondered how he ever reached the top—a feat probably never performed before by mortal man. The whole affair is a fine example of the quick and ready thoughtfulness and presence of mind in a desperate situation, and the power of endurance, which characterise the western pioneer. As we passed over the ground where Colter ran his race, and listened to his story an undefinable fear crept over all. We felt awe-struck by the nameless and numerous dangers that evidently beset us on every side. Even Cheek's courage sunk and his hitherto buoyant and cheerful spirit was depressed at hearing of the perils of the place. He spoke despondingly and his mind was uneasy, restless and fearful. I'm afraid, said he, and I acknowledge it. I never felt fear before but now I feel it. A melancholy that seemed like a presentiment of his own fate, possessed him, and to us he was serious almost to sadness, until he met his death a few days afterwards from the same Blackfeet from whom Colter escaped.

"Colter told us the particulars of a second adventure which I will give to the reader. In the winter when he had recovered from the fatigues of his long race and journey, he wished to recover the traps which he had dropped into the Jefferson Fork on the first appearance of the Indians who captured him. He supposed the Indians were all quiet in winter quarters, and retraced his steps to the Gallatin Fork. He had just passed the mountain gap, and encamped on the bank of the river for the night and kindled a fire to cook his supper of buffalo meat when he heard the crackling of leaves and branches behind him in the direction of the river. He could see nothing, it being quite dark, but quickly he heard the cocking of guns and instantly leaped over the fire. Several shots followed and bullets whistled around him, knocking the coals off his fire over the ground.

"Again he fled for life, and the second time, ascended the perpendicular mountain which he had gone up in his former flight fearing now as then, that the pass might be guarded by Indians. He reached the top before morning and resting for the day descended the next night, and then made his way with all possible speed, to the Fort. He said that at the time, he promised God Almighty that he would never return to this region again if he were only permitted to escape once more with his life. He did escape once more, and was now again in the same country, courting the same dangers, which he had so often braved, and that seemed to have for him a kind of fascination. Such men, and there are thousands of such, can only live in a state of excitement and constant action. Perils and danger are their natural element and their familiarity with them and indifference to their fate, are well illustrated in these adventures of Colter.

"A few days afterward, when Cheek was killed and Colter had another narrow escape, he came to the Fort, and said he had promised his Maker to leave the country, and now said he, throwing down his hat on the ground, If God will only forgive me this time and let me off I *will* leave the country day after tomorrow—and be d—d if I ever come into it again. He left accordingly, in company with young Bryant of Philadelphia, whose father was a merchant of that city, and one other whose name I forget. They were attacked by the Blackfeet just beyond the mountains, but escaped by hiding in a thicket, where the Indians were afraid to follow them, and at night they proceeded towards the Big Horn, lying concealed in the daytime. They reached St. Louis safely and a few years after I heard of Colter's death by jaundice." (34–36)

"After many delays and continuances from term to term, I was glad to get rid of the suits and them [the Missouri Fur Company], by giving my note for one hundred dollars to the Company. This, with my debt to Colter, made me a loser to the amount of three hundred dollars by one years trapping on the head waters of the Missouri." (55)

Appendix C

The Colter Stone and Other Graffiti

According to the Lewis and Clark Journals the explorers burned, carved, or painted their names or initials or in the modern term "tagged" the landscape more than fourteen times. All over what are now the western United States early explorers left their mark to prove they were there first. But just as often those who followed would mark an object as a joke or to bring recognition to their property or to bring fame to their town or community by claiming some early explorer had been in their area. The authenticity of the mark was easy to discount if the explorer was not known, or even suspected, to have been in the area, but a different matter if the explorer could have been in the area. Then it would be difficult to either prove or disprove the authenticity of the initials or signature. That's what we have with John Colter.[1]

Stallo Vinton was the first to bring attention to graffiti presumed to have been made by Colter along Coulter Creek, near the boundary of Yellowstone National Park. He wrote about a blaze found on a tree, in September 1889, by Tazewell Woody (Theodore Roosevelt's hunting guide), John H. Dewing (also a hunting guide), and Philip Ashton Rollins, a western writer of the day. Vinton stated that Rollins told him that the blaze was found on the left side of Coulter Creek, some fifty feet from the water and about three-quarters of a mile above the creek's mouth. Here he said, "a large pine tree on which was a deeply indented blaze, which after cleared of sap and loose bark was found to consist of a cross 'X' (some five inches in height), and, under it, the initials 'J C' (each some four inches in height). They thought the blaze appeared to be approximately eighty years old, and they refused to cut the tree down because they felt the blaze had been made by Colter himself."[2]

181

These men reported their findings to the Yellowstone Park authorities. Park employees then cut the tree down to salvage the portion bearing the initials. The log was to be placed in the park museum, but, as luck would have it, it disappeared in transit, or so the story goes. Vinton went on to use the blaze to promote his theory that Colter traveled along Coulter Creek in the winter of 1807 on his great trek through Yellowstone. J. Neilson Barry, the great curmudgeon, had problems with Vinton's theory from the beginning. First, he argued, how would anyone know how old a blaze was by just looking at the tree, and secondly, "J C" could stand for anything from James Carter to Jiminy Cricket.

In 1957, a detailed search of the park's files was made at the behest of the park superintendent in response to a letter from a Mr. Frederic E. Voelker dated September 18, 1957, concerning the location of the tree with the blaze. On October 11, 1957, Park Superintendent Lemuel A. Garrison wrote:

- "Coulter Creek, as you may know, was named after the Botanist John M. Coulter, who accompanied the Hayden Survey of 1872, not John Colter. Botanist Coulter was thrown from his horse into the waters of the creek, and it has since borne his name. Stallo Vinton is incorrect in stating that the creek was named after John Colter.
- "From Mr. Rollins' account it would appear that the tree stood a short distance outside the boundaries of Yellowstone NP. The Park boundary is 3/8 to ½ mile south of the mouth of Coulter Creek.
- "We do not have knowledge of a stump, which could definitely be identified as the one remaining from the tree in question. . . .
- "None of our present personnel have been acquainted with this tree or its exact location, nor have they any written data concerning it in Park records.
- "A thorough search of the Yellowstone Research Library, which includes all of the Superintendent's Annual Reports, the Hayden Reports, Hague's Geology of the YNP, and many other sources, reveals not [one] reference whatever to the tree in question except those of Stallo Vinton and Burton Harris. There are no clippings or articles by Rollins, Woody, or Dewing in our library or in any bibliographies which we have. We have also checked the army letter files for the years 1889 and 1890 and could not located any correspondence between the superintendent and Mr. Rollins relating to the disposition of the section of tree trunk. We hope that this information, while largely of a negative character, will be helpful to you in your study of the life and explorations of John Colter."[3]

So, did John Colter carve his initials on a tree near the mouth of Coulter Creek? Nothing can be proven, but the answer is most likely a resounding NO.

The next artifact attributed to John Colter is the so-called "Colter Stone." In the summer of 1931, William Beard and his son Richard were clearing scrub timber from a section of their homestead. The latter was located three or four miles east of Tetonia, Idaho, just east of the state line, on the Wyoming side of the line, in the rolling foothill country along the west base of the Teton Range. They had cut away the dense lodge-pole pines and aspens at the intersection of two shallow ravines and were plowing the land when they found a piece of rhyolite (lava rock) stone about the size and shape of a human head.

Geologist Fritiof Fryxell, Grand Teton National Park's naturalist, was the first to view and write a report on the Colter Stone, on May 8, 1934, to Director Arno B. Cammerer of the National Park Service, Washington, D.C.: He wrote the following:

"Early last summer Mr. Aubrey Lyon, who operates the saddle horse concession in the Grand Teton National Park, chanced to mention that one of his neighbors over in Teton Basin had a few years prior found a stone on which was carved the name John Colter. Realizing that this relic would, if authentic, be of great historical significance, I asked Mr. Lyon to make an effort to borrow or purchase it for the park. A week later Mr. Lyon . . . having secured the Colter Stone from the owner . . . presented it to the museum."

Within weeks, excellent photographs were made of the stone by Park authorities and Fryxell wrote the first description of what is now referred to as "The Colter Stone": "The Colter Stone is a slab of weathered rhyolite lava, about three inches thick, one edge of which has been rudely carved (probably with a hunting knife or some such instrument) into the form of a human face, approximately life-sized. On one surface is the inscription (scarcely legible now) '1808,' and on the reverse, in letters which are still very easy to decipher, appears the inscription John Colte 'r' lower than the other letters." It should be noted at this time that Fryxell did not write "COULTER," the importance of which will become apparent later in this discussion.

Mr. Fryxell continued: "The question of authenticity of the relic seemed to hinge also on the circumstances attending its finding, so on August 19th [1933?] in company with Mr. George Grant I made a trip over into Teton Basin to get further information on this subject. . . . It is perhaps unnecessary now to go into detail as to the investigation we made, and it may suffice to say that so far as Mr. Grant and I were concerned, our doubts as to the genuineness of the Colter Stone were dismissed. . . .

"It appears that the stone was found in the summer of 1931 when Mr. Beard and his son were clearing scrub timber from a section of their homestead. . . . So far as we could tell the finders did not know who John Colter was and had no interest whatever in the inscription. Their curiosity grew solely out of the fact that they had found a 'stone head' as they put it." Fryxell concluded: "It was hard to believe in the authenticity of the relic to begin with, but after careful study I became convinced that it couldnot be a fake."[4]

Regional Historian Merrill J. Mattes in a letter to Dwight Stone wrote on October 16, 1957: "William Richard Beard, the man who actually found the Colter Stone, is now employed at West Yellowstone by Kiewit Construction Company, and he was interviewed by Dr. Merrill D. Beal of Idaho State College and a member of our seasonal ranger staff at Yellowstone National Park. Mr. Beard reiterated the circumstances surrounding the find, including the great interest shown in the stone by his father (now dead). The odd thing is that his father's interest was stimulated by the fact that the stone was in the shape of a human head, and it was not until later that the lettering was discovered.

"The principal reason to suspect the stone is the simple fact that it is almost too good a thing to be true and, therefore, one naturally suspects a hoax. Yet we have been unable to figure out who would be capable of perpetrating a hoax of this type. The inscription itself is quite old, and it is difficult to imagine a practical joker of 50 to 100 years ago having enough historical knowledge to perpetrate a hoax. In any event, we are now inclined to give the stone the benefit of the doubt, and it will be exhibited in our new museum which will probably not be constructed and open until the summer of 1959."[5]

It did not take long for Stallo Vinton and later Burton Harris in his book and scores of other historians and writers to seize upon the Colter Stone as the missing link in an almost total enigma of what happened to John Colter in the winter of 1807–1808. The Colter Stone was offered as proof that Colter crossed the Tetons and entered present Idaho's Pierre's Hole (Teton Valley). But there are a few problems with this line of reasoning (laid out in detail in chapter 8), mainly that the enhanced version of Clark's map indicated that Colter did not go as far west as present Jackson Hole, let alone Teton Valley. There is also the little problem of the five other stones found within a fifty-mile radius of where the Colter Stone was found. These five other stones also have questionable graffiti on their surface; which leads to considerable doubt of the authenticity of any of them. These other five are as follows:

1. A stone with the inscription "Clark 1805," found by Mr. M. D. Yeaman of Irwin, Idaho. This stone was found near a pile of other stones built up as a monument and close to Longitude 111' 30", Latitude 43' 30", and close to the baseline. The stone was found soon after 1890 when that part of the country was starting to be settled

2. A second "Clark 1805" stone found about five miles from the first by Dr. Samuel Clongee (about fifty-five miles up the South Fork of the Snake River). (These Clark stones are far removed from the route followed by Captain Clark. We can be quite certain of this for the

maps drawn by William Clark are quite accurate. If Clark carved these stones, somebody then moved them a considerable distance from where he traveled.)

3. A stone with the inscription "Fort Henry 1811 by Cap Hunt," found in 1933 below the ground where Elgin, Idaho, now stands. Previously an old settler had stated this was the site of Fort Henry. In 1927 some excavating was conducted at the site. Nothing was concluded with this first excavation, so in 1933 a second excavation was started. During this excavation the outline of the walls of a cabin were found and what was presumed to be the floor. Here they found charcoal, a broken piece of pottery, and a few other objects, along with a third stone, this one was marked "Cap Hunt." This stone was ascribed to Wilson Price Hunt's group of westbound Astorians.

4. A stone inscribed with "Al the Cook but Nothing to Cook"—also found at the Fort Henry site.

5. A stone inscribed with "Gov't Camp 1811 H. Wells," found at the same site.

It did not take long for J. Neilson Barry to jump feet first into the debate over the authenticity of these stones, and for years he badgered the National Park Service to the point that they voluntarily removed the Colter Stone from public display.[6] But the controversy did not start or end with Barry. A writer by the name of Nolie Mumey, for whatever reason, could not leave the Colter Stone alone. Apparently, someone involved with the writing or publishing of Mumey's book *The Teton Mountains: Their History and Tradition* altered the National Park Service 1934 photo of the stone. Whereas the 1934 photo clearly shows the inscription as "COLTER," the photo published in the book shows the spelling to "COULTER." One has to wonder who made this change and why because Mumey had made a detailed search of all the available Colter signatures and would have known that John Colter always signed his name "COLTER." The National Park Service in their review of Mumey's book pointed these and many other errors out in an internal Memorandum for the Director dated March 18, 1947.[7]

William Barrett II in a letter to Merrill Mattes also pointed out Mumey's carelessness, when he wrote: "In mentioning Dr. Mumey, I noticed many of his works while at the [Missouri Historical Society]. . . . I was astonished to find a picture of the Colter Stone which had been touched up. . . . Perhaps I should have heeded your warning regarding his scholarship long ago. I cannot imagine someone trying to alter historical pieces such as the stone."[8]

In the mid-1960s Don Holm (outdoors editor for *The Oregonian*), now deep into his research into John Colter, wrote to Grand Teton National Park, now the trustee of the Colter Stone, requesting photographs. The Park Service at that time made a startling discovery, which they shared with Holm.

"While my assistant Mr. Victor L. Jackson was printing these pictures, he noticed that there are two dates carved on the left side of the stone. The '1808' date has long been recognized. There also appears to be the reverse of '1852' located below the eye and to the right of the nose. It can be read by holding the photograph up to a bright light source and looking through the back side. This discovery may again throw suspicion on the authenticity of the Colter Stone," wrote Chief Naturalist Willard E. Dilley.[9]

On November 4, 1974, a Mr. Forrest H. Coulter wrote the superintendant of Yellowstone National Park a curious letter in which he described (and drew a sketch of) a Colter Stone he claimed to have seen in the museum at Moose, Wyoming, in 1950. The sketch he drew did not look anything like the original Colter Stone. The Park Service in their reply to Mr. Coulter, on November 21, 1974, responded: "To the best of our knowledge there is no other 'Colter Stone' and we are perplexed as to the one you referred to in you letter."[10] One has to wonder what Mr. Coulter thought he saw? The only reason for even discussing Mr. Forrest's letter is that Ruth Colter-Frick made it an issue in her book *Courageous Colter and Companions* and in a subsequent paper she wrote on the subject, and in the future someone might believe the Park Service is hiding something, which they are not.[11]

In 2010, Jim Hardee in his very well-researched book *Pierre's Hole! The Fur Trade History of Teton Valley* wrote: "More worrisome is evidence that the original inscription [he is referring to the Colter Stone] has been tampered with since its discovery. A comparison between the circa 1947 Mumey photo of the Colter stone and a modern snapshot exhibits alteration of the rock's inscription."[12] As noted, however, it was the photo that was altered; there is no evidence that the original Colter Stone has been tampered with. It now can be viewed each summer at the Teton Valley Museum in Driggs, Idaho, on loan from the Colter Bay Museum in Grand Teton National Park.

While there is no question that the stone was found (not made and planted) by the Beard family, there is no way to prove John Colter actually inscribed it. Rather, the Colter Stone and the other five stones are in all likelihood the work of a joker traveling with the Hayden Geological Survey expedition of 1871 to explore the region of northwestern Wyoming that became Yellowstone National Park the next year. Merrill Mattes probably addressed the issue best when he wrote: "Our position [speaking for the Park Service] is that the Colter Stone, even though its authenticity cannot be proven in an absolute sense, is an historic object in its own right which plays a legitimate role in interpretation. . . . Finally, the National Park Service is the rightful owner . . . by virture of donation by the finder and subsequent . . . possession.[13]

The last piece of questionable graffiti attributed to John Colter was found at the mouth of the Bighorn River, in present Montana, where, on the second terrace up from the river, sits a sandstone boulder with at least two inscriptions. The first reads "M Lisa 1808" and the second "Colter 1810." There is no question that Manuel Lisa established a fur-trading post called Fort Raymond at this spot and also no question that John Colter lived, worked, and operated from this post for much of the period from late fall 1807 to April 1810 when he left the area for good. The first known photo was taken by Bob Edgar and is found in a book he coauthored in 1996.[14] In the fall of 2008, Ron Anglin made a trip to the site, where he met the current owner of the property, Mr. John Sjostrom. Mr. Sjostrom said his family had owned the property since the late 1930s and he had known of the inscriptions from since about that same time. He also said the inscriptions were found in the 1920s by someone from Billings and that he would get the name. Although Anglin has made subsequent requests for information, to date no additional information has been provided.[15]

In 2009, the National Park Service conducted an archeological investigation of the area at the mouth of the river and of the sandstone boulder and reported:

- "A relative clustering of nine historic artifacts from a 20-acre area within the plowed terrace," although it is not presumed "that this apparent artifact cluster is the result of a single event occupation."
- The various "data sets suggest [Fort Raymond] was situated west of the Big Horn River and south of the main channel of the Yellowstone River."
- "Data was not obtained in 2009 that would allow a conclusive determination of the precise location of the fort."[16]

Therefore, the archeological study did not clarify the question of whether the inscriptions could be genuine. Moreover, the year 1996 is thus far the earliest that the inscriptions can be solidly verified. Thus, making a convincing case for or against the authenticity is not likely at present.

Notes

1. "OFF HE STARTED WITH THE SPEED OF THE WIND"

1. Meriwether Lewis's journal entry, July 27, 1805, Moulton, *Journals*, 4:434; William Clark's journal entry, July 25, 1805, Moulton, *Journals*, 4:428.

2. Potts signed a series of notes in 1808 (for $14.00, $424.50, $120.00, and $170.00) that left him with a debt of more than seven hundred dollars at the time of his death. Several lawsuits were filed against his estate, which was proclaimed insolvent. The items specifically mentioned in the court documents include "one half of a Kettle, one half of a Rifle, and sundry other goods wares and merchandizes." The other items listed above were commonly purchased by trappers leaving for a prolonged hunt. (See the Meriwether Lewis Collection, Missouri History Museum; and the list of items purchased from the Pacific Fur Company by Joseph Miller during October of 1811 [Morris, *The Perilous West*, 219n26].)

3. John Ordway's journal entry, July 26, 1806, Moulton, *Journals*, 9:340; Coues, *History of the Expedition*, 2:442, 2:447, 2:448. Blackfoot oral histories often mention instances of whites being unaware they were being watched by Indians. In the late 1800s, Robert Vaughn recorded: "While on my recent visit to the home of Edward A. Lewis a pleasant evening was passed listening to the family telling Old Indian stories which were told to them by Black Bear (Sikey-kio), an old Indian woman who lived with them for many years. . . . When the century was young, while she was in camp with her people at the mouth of the Sun river, where now the city of Great Falls is located, she saw several members of the Lewis and Clarke expedition, who were the first white men she ever saw." (Vaughn, *Then and Now*, 395.) Lewis and Clark, however, made no mention of seeing Indians at Great Falls.

4. For Colter's and Potts's pay for their service with Lewis and Clark, see Morris, *Fate of the Corps*, 190, 197.

5. Bradbury, *Travels in the Interior*, 45n18. If Potts called Colter a coward, as reported by Bradbury, it may have shamed Colter into ignoring his own best judgment. Calling a man a coward in the early nineteenth century was an extreme insult, something that may have cost Daniel Boone his son's life at the battle of Blue Licks on August 19, 1782. (See Faragher, *Daniel Boone*, 218.) As for either Colter's or Bradbury's claim that the war party consisted of five or six hundred Indians, known population sizes for the Blackfoot nation indicate this is a gross exaggeration.

6. Bradbury, *Travels in the Interior*, 45n18.

7. James, *Three Years Among the Indians*, 30.

8. James, *Three Years Among the Indians*, 31.

9. James, *Three Years Among the Indians*, 31.

10. Bradbury, *Travels in the Interior*, 46n18.

11. James, *Three Years Among the Indians*, 32–33.

12. James, *Three Years Among the Indians*, 33. See chapter 9 for a detailed analysis of the route Colter likely took back to Fort Raymond.

13. Lewis's journal entry, August 22, 1805, Moulton, *Journals*, 5:143.

14. Lewis's journal entry, July 17, 1805, Moulton, *Journals*, 4:392.

15. Clark's journal entry, May 8, 1805, Moulton, *Journals*, 4:128; Lewis's journal entry, May 8, 1805, Moulton, *Journals*, 4:126; Bradbury, *Travels in the Interior*, 47 n. 18. Some thought *Psoralea esculenta*, or "Prairie Turnip," delicious, others tolerable, and still others hardly tolerable. The Indians ate it raw or dried it and crushed it to powder to make soup. They also boiled it or roasted it in embers.

16. Clark's journal entry, July 18, 1806, Moulton, *Journals*, 8:200–1.

17. James, *Three Years Among the Indians*, 33–34.

2. "ONE OF THE SURVIVORS, OF THE NAME OF COULTER"

1. Jackson, "Journey to the Mandans," 182.

2. Ibid., 191.

3. The first installment of Dr. Thomas's narrative was published in the *Missouri Gazette* on November 30, 1809. The second and last installment, which includes Thomas's discussion of Colter, presumably ran in the same newspaper early in December. However, complete copies of the December 7 and December 14 issues–as well as Thomas's second install-ment–have never been found. Luckily, the first and second installments were found in the July 6 and July 13, 1810, issues of the *Pittsburgh Gazette*, respectively, apparently reprints of what had originally run in the *Missouri Gazette*. See Jackson, "Journey to the Mandans."

4. Ambrose, *Undaunted Courage*, 389.

5. Thomas James lost his 1809 journal when a trunk fell overboard and did not publish his account of Colter's adventure until 1846.

6. Clark's journal entry, December 30, 1803, Moulton, *Journals*, 2:142.

7. Browne, *Eva Emery Dye*, 6; Barber, review of *Eva Emery Dye: Romance with the West*, by Browne, 493.

8. Cited in Cutright, *History of the Journals*, 127.

9. Reuben Gold Thwaites to Eva Emery Dye, March 26, 1903, Dye Collection, Oregon Historical Society.

10. Eva Emery Dye to Dr. Hosmer, April 4, 1904, Dye Collection, Oregon Historical Society.

11. Thwaites, *Bradbury's Travels*, 44 n. 17.

12. Vinton references his correspondence with Logan and others in Yellowstone, 27. In addition, a series of 1925–1927 letters written to or from Vinton or Ghent reveal the complex communications that took place between the two historians and supposed Colter relatives. See the Organization of American Historians Records, 1906–2003, Ruth Lilly Special Collections and Archives, IUPUI University Library, Indiana University–Purdue University Indianapolis.

Katherine G. Bushman, a leading genealogist of August County, Virginia (which includes Staunton), found no evidence—in her thirty years of researching local genealogy records—that the John Colter of the expedition was born in Virginia. (See Katherine G. Bushman to Mr. Gough, November 9, 1993, Katherine Gentry Bushman Papers, 1961–1997, Accession 35743, Box 15, Folder 9–10, Coalter Family, The Library of Virginia, Richmond.)

Many genealogists became interested in Colter's possible connection to the Staunton area. Take, for example, the following correspondence in 1981 between Joseph Coulter and J. William Barrett:

"I discount the Staunton, VA, area as an origin for John Colter because the Coulter family that settled there was a well-educated family (it produced an early VA Supreme Court Justice) and I do not believe they would have dropped the "U" from the name "Coulter." I've been through the Virginia records and they do not seem to be the type of family that would produce a trapper-hunter such as John Colter of Yellowstone.

"I have pretty well accounted for all the Coalters from the Staunton area and find no room for John of Yellowstone . . . I told [Frank] Dickson that, at this late date, I don't think it possible to identify the family to which he belonged. (I adhere to this thought). I told him that long before he was attributed to the Augusta County, VA, family, he was attributed to a Brown Country, Ohio, family and referred to History of Brown County, Ohio, published 1883, p. 576 . . . I said the men with whom John Colter (of Yellowstone was associated are the same as the names of families associated with one Pennsylvania Coulter family (not mine)." (Joseph Coulter to J. William Barrett, January 20, 1981, in Ron Anglin's possession.)

"First of all, let me tell you that I have also examined the Augusta Co., Virginia records first-hand. The original documents are very revealing and I find much support for my beliefs there. . .I can definitely agree with you that at this late date, we will probably never positively know or prove the ancestry of John Colter. I can also agree that his direct progenitors were not Joseph and Ellen (Shields) Colter. However, I have yet to be conclusively strayed from my conviction that he was of the Augusta Co., Virginia families. . .I refer to history rather than genealogy. On the Lewis & Clark expedition were many Virginia originated men, three of whom are definitely traced to the Augusta Co. area, Robert Frazier, John Shields, William Bratton and I also believe John Colter. The Brattons and Shields' intermarried with the Coulter-Coalter clan and here is the reference to Joseph and Ellen (Shields) Colter. Ellen shield came from the family to which John Shields belonged but Joseph was not the father of John Colter. I do believe that he may have been an uncle. Also, Nancy Bratton was a sister of Joseph and it was the same Bratton family she was a member of by marriage which harbored William Bratton. This Nancy seems the aunt of John Colter, as the information I have about the Maysville, Kentucky connection of the families leads me to believe his father name was James, the brother of Joseph and Nancy and one of the eight children. This James varies from the Brown Co, Ohio James Coulter in that he was known to have lived in Kentucky as early as 1797. This also supports my contention that John Colter lived in and around Maysville some time prior to his enlistment with Lewis and Clark and that was in all likelihood known to William Clark (who resided in Louisville) as well as Simon Kenton, Pierre Drouillard (Father of George Drouillard, also of L & C fame) . . . In regards to John Colter's children . . . It is also possible that John Colter fathered a daughter, who may have been born shortly before or after his death . . . but what I feel is most important proof of his childrens' birthright is a letter regarding the soldiers land grant. . .which his son, Hiram, was making painstaking inquiry into during 1841 . . . gives a clue that perhaps the Coulter-Coalter families of Virginia were somehow intertwined with Fraziers of Augusta Co., as Hiram Colter and H.H. Frazier each sought information regarding their fathers rightul land grants and each resided in the same general area of Missouri. While this is not conclusive prooft, it is old to see that two so close. Could there have been a real relationship?" (J. William Barrett to Joseph Coulter, January 29, 1981, in Ron Anglin's possession.)

13. Ghent, "Sketch of Colter,"111; Vinton, *Yellowstone*, 28.

14. Clarke, "Roster"; Harris, *John Colter*, 12; Clarke, *Men of the Expedition*, 46; Moulton, *Journals*, 2:515.

15. Colter-Frick, *Courageous Colter*, 181. Editorial note: Shortly before this book went to press, Timothy Forrest Coulter published an important article entitled "Discovering John Colter: New Research on His Family and His Death." In the article, Coulter, a fourth great-grandson of John Colter, discusses how recent yDNA testing suggests "a high probability" that either John Colter or his father "was fathered by a Cannon, but raised as a Colter." See *We Proceeded On* 40 (May 2014): 25–28.

3. "IN QUEST OF THE COUNTRY OF KENTUCKE"

1. Coues, *History of the Expedition*, 2; bracketed insertions added by Coues. The financial records of the expedition make it clear that the "nine young men from Kentucky" were the

following: Charles Floyd, Nathaniel Pryor, William Bratton, John Colter, Reubin Field, Joseph Field, George Gibson, George Shannon, and John Shields. These men, the only members of the expedition to enlist in 1803, are listed in this order in the final summation of Lewis's account, recorded on August 5, 1807. (Jackson, *Letters*, 425.)

2. Jones, *William Clark*, 51.

3. Foley, *Wilderness Journey*, 20.

4. The claim (made by Donald Jackson, Gary Moulton, and many others) that Colter was already with Lewis when he reached Louisville is apparently based on the unsupported assumption that Colter enlisted at Maysville.

5. James, *Three Years Among the Indians*, 56.

6. On April 24, 1777, Kenton and a few others were attacked by Indians outside the Boonesborough palisades. Boone and about twelve others rushed out to help. When Boone saw that they were surrounded by scores of Shawnee warriors, he yelled, "Boys, we are gone–let us sell our lives as dearly as we can!" and ordered a charge back to the fort. When Boone fell from a gunshot to the ankle, Kenton ran to his defense and fought off two attackers. Then he hoisted the wounded man on his shoulder and ran for the fort. (Lofaro, *Daniel Boone*, 79). The two were fast friends ever after. Kenton lived a long life, like Boone, and died at the age of eighty-one. George Rogers Clark was so closely associated with Boone, Kenton, and others that such stories would have been commonplace to young Billy Clark. It is hardly an exaggeration to say that among Kentucky frontiersmen, everyone knew everyone else. (Eva Emery Dye points out another possible connection when she writes that Pierre Drouillard, George's father, saved Simon Kenton from being killed by Shawnee Indians. As with the rest of her claims in her historical novel, however, she offers no documentary support for the story. See Dye, *The Conquest*, 46.)

7. Jones, *William Clark*, 42; background from *William Clark*, 3-48.

8. Josiah Herndon to Jonathan Clark, October 23, 1779, cited in Jones, *William Clark*, 42.

9. Elizabeth A. Perkins, "Distinctions and Partitions amongst Us: Identity and Interaction in the Revolutionary Ohio Valley," in *Contact Points*, 232–33, cited in Jones, *William Clark*, 20.

10. Jones, *William Clark*, 22.

11. Ibid.

12. Fischer, *Albion's Seed*, 638.

13. Elizabeth Semancik, "Albion's Seed Grows in the Cumberland Gap," http://xroads. virginia.edu/~ug97/albion/albion3.html, accessed on March 3, 2012. The village of Hannastown, Pennsylvania, was founded in 1773 as the seat of the newly created Westmoreland County and was settled primarily by Irish and Scotch-Irish though the surrounding area was mostly Pennsylvania Dutch. In 1782, the settlement was completely destroyed by a combined force of British soldiers and Indians. The village was rebuilt, but after Forbes Road was rerouted through Greensburg, the settlement grew little, and eventually most of it became farmland. There were a number of Coulters living around Hannastown at the time of the attack who dispersed to Ohio and Kentucky. For more on Hannastown, see George Albert Dallas, *The Frontier Forts of Western Pennsylvania* (Harrisburg: C. M. Busch, state printer, 1896), 2:290–92.

14. Fischer, *Albion's Seed*, 615.

15. Coulter, *The Charles Coulter Ancestry*, 1. The surname Colter in its various forms— including Coulter, Coalter, and Colther—is of ancient origin. It first appears in Scotland during the twelfth century and is the Scottish form of Vrusk Kaldr, a Viking name that arrived with the Norse Vikings, who invaded Scotland and Ireland in the eleventh and twelfth centuries.

16. See Miller, *History of the Families of Miller, Woods, Harris, Wallace, Maupin, Oldham, Kavanugh, and Brown*.

17. Elizabeth Semancik, "Albion's Seed Grows in the Cumberland Gap."

18. Faragher, *Daniel Boone*, 111–12.

19. John Floyd to Thomas Jefferson, April 16, 1781, cited in Jones, *William Clark*, 42.

20. Cited in Jones, *William Clark*, 41.

21. Cited in Lofaro, *Daniel Boone*, 114. Indian retaliation for such atrocities brought about the death of George Washington's friend William Crawford. "In 1782, Crawford led a com-

bined force of Virginians and Pennsylvanians in an attack on Mingo Indians and Delaware Indians along the Sandusky River. David Williamson and a number of the men who had participated in the Gnadenhutten Massacre were among his troops. Crawford and his men fought off the natives and their British allies at the Battles of the Sandusky and Olentangy on June 4–6, 1782, but the following day the American forces were divided and Crawford and a number of his men were captured. In revenge for the Gnadenhutten Massacre, the natives tortured Crawford before burning him at the stake." (Ohio History Central website, http://www.ohiohistorycentral.org/w/William_Crawford, accessed on January 7, 2014.) Crawford's horrific execution was widely publicized in the United States, worsening the already strained relationship between American Indians and European Americans.

22. Cited in Lofaro, *Daniel Boone*, 131.

23. William Clark to Jonathan Clark, August 18, 1794, cited in Jones, *William Clark*, 79.

24. Jones, *William Clark*, 79.

25. Meriwether Lewis to William Clark, June 19, 1803, Jackson, *Letters*, 1:57, 58.

26. Clark to Meriwether Lewis, August 21, 1803, Jackson, *Letters*, 1:117.

27. Colter-Frick, *Courageous Colter*, 34.

28. Clark to Lewis, August 21, 1803, Jackson, *Letters*, 1:117.

29. Cited in Kercheval, *Valley of Virginia*, 283.

30. Cited in Payne, *Indian Warfare*, 1.

31. Doddridge, *Notes on the Settlement and Indian Wars*, 94.

32. Jones, *William Clark*, 52.

33. Anthony Wayne to Henry Knox, May 9, 1793, cited in Jones, *William Clark*, 69.

34. Wayne to Knox, July 13, 1792, cited in Richard Clark Knopf, *Anthony Wayne and the Founding of the United States Army*, dissertation, Ohio State University, 1960. The skill of reloading at a dead run applied to expert frontiersmen and was not taught to the average soldier. The marksmen who did learn the ability used it in battle when they found themselves fighting against overwhelming odds.

35. Knopf, *Wayne and the Founding of the Army*, 130.

36. Clark's journal entry, May 6, 1804, Moulton, *Journals*, 1:212.

37. See Clark's journal entry, January 6, 1804, Moulton, *Journals*, 2:152.

38. See Clark's journal entry, March 29, 1804, Moulton, *Journals*, 2:182; Lewis's detachment orders, March 3, 1804, Moulton, *Journals*, 178-79; undated notes, Moulton, *Journals*, 2:195; Clark's journal entry, March 30, 1804, Moulton, *Journals*, 2:183; Clark's detachment order, April 1, 1804, Moulton, *Journals*, 2:187; and Clark's journal entry, June 29, 1804, Moulton, *Journals*, 2:329.

39. John Ordway to his Parents, April 8, 1804, Jackson, *Letters*, 1:176.

40. Jones, *William Clark*, 86. Clark may have met Manuel Lisa for the first time on one of his missions down the Ohio for General Wayne. In October of 1795, a witness reported Clark's "taking Don Manuel Lisa with his *bercha* in his escort of ships to protect him in the transit of the Ohio." (Douglas, *Manuel Lisa*, 11.)

41. Whitehouse's journal entry, July 7, 1804, Moulton, *Journals*, 11:36.

42. Payne, *Indian Warfare*, 1.

43. Clark's journal entries, August 28, 1804, and September 3, 1804; Ordway's journal entry, September 6, 1804, Moulton, *Journals*, 3:20, 3:45, and 9:55, respectively. Clark apparently saw impressive potential in Shannon and recruited him as one of the nine young men even though at eighteen he was quite inexperienced and was the youngest man on the expedition. Clark's confidence eventually proved to be well placed because Shannon became one of the best hunters in the group.

44. Faragher, *Daniel Boone*, 271; Filson, *The Discovery, Settlement, and Present State of Kentucke: . . .* , 55, cited in Lofaro, *Daniel Boone*, 34; Faragher, *Daniel Boone*, 54.

45. "When the captives, who were restored under the treaty of 1763, came in, those who were at the Mingo towns when the remnant of Kiskepila's were returned, stated that the Indians represented Gibson as having cut off the Little Eagle's head with a *long knife*. Several of the white persons were then sacrificed to appease the name of Kiskepila; and a war dance ensued, accompanied with terrific shouts and bitter denunciations of revenge on "*the Big knife warrior*." This name was soon after applied to the Virginia militia generally; and to this day they are

known among the northwestern Indians as the *"Long Knives,"* or *"Big Knife Nation."* The term *"Big Knives"* or *"Long Knives"* may have had reference either to the long knives carried by early white hunters, or the swords worn by backwoods militia officers. (Withers, *Chronicles of Border Warfare*, 79–80.)

46. Buchanan, *Sketches*, 102–3.

47. Dillon, *Meriwether Lewis*, 88. Dillon was the first prominent historian to claim that Colter had blue eyes. At the authors' request, David L. Williams (MA, MLS, and former reference librarian at the Chicago Public Library) conducted an extensive search for records of Colter at the Draper Collection, Wisconsin Historical Society. Because of Colter's reported involvement with Simon Kenton during the Ohio Indian wars and his known involvement in the War of 1812, the historical periods and geographical regions referenced in Harper's Guide to the Draper Manuscripts that were searched were primarily those dealing with (1) Northern Kentucky and southern Ohio in the early- to mid-1790s and (2) the early months of the War of 1812 as it unfolded in the Upper Mississippi River region, particularly in what later became the state of Missouri where Colter served briefly with Nathan Boone's Mounted Rangers. The following Draper notebooks (or volumes)—identified by their Draper Collection alphanumeric series numbers—were examined: Series C Daniel Boone Papers volumes 7, 11, 12, 13, 15, 26, 27, 30, 31; Series E Samuel Brady and Lewis Wetzel Papers volumes 4, 8, 9, 10, 11, 12; Series S Draper's Notes 6, 7, 8, 9, 19, 20, 21, 22, 23, 24, 25, 26; Series NN Pittsburgh and Northwest Virginia Papers volume 8NN; Series BB Simon Kenton Papers Series volumes 4, 5, 10, 11, 12, 13; Series CC Kentucky Papers volumes 2, 33, 34. Draper apparently searched for information on Colter because two correspondents told him they knew nothing about Colter. Otherwise, however, nothing was found on Colter. Other volumes could be searched, but all obvious leads have been exhausted. In addition to the Draper collection a search was made of some of the papers of Reuben Thwaites in the WHS for any notes or correspondence about Colter. Thwaites worked closely with Draper at the WHS for a number of years and was Draper's handpicked successor as its superintendent in 1887. Specifically searched were Thwaites General Correspondence Box 1 Folders 3–9 1885–1903, Box 2 1904–1905, Box 3 1906–1910, and Box 4 April 1910–August 1928 plus some undated; Thwaites writings in these papers including Box 5 Folder 11 1904–1905; Box 6 Folders 1, 3, 4, 5, 6, 8, and 9; and Miscellaneous Notebooks and Fragments in Box 7 Folders 6 and Box 8 Folder 1. Nothing of significance was found concerning JC's early life, possible military service in the early- to mid-1790s, or the circumstances of his death or location of his grave in Missouri. As a follow-up to the above work, much time was spent in examining book sources in the WHS Library including genealogical registries and compilations and histories of the relevant regions of Virginia, Kentucky, Ohio, and Missouri. These searches turned up numerous Coulters and a few Colters along with a few standard historical narratives about John Colter, but nothing of significance was found.

48. Faragher, *Daniel Boone*, 170.

49. Barrows, *Brady*, 26.

50. Hartley, *Wetzel*, 108.

4. "COLTER CAME RUNNING ALONG THE SHORE"

1. Moulton, *Journals*, 2:209–12.

2. Clark's journal entry, September 22, 1804, Moulton, *Journals*, 3:102. As Gary Moulton notes, because of incomplete records and the complexities of French names, it is not perfectly clear how many men were present for the first part of the journey; a number of scholars agree that fifty is the most likely number. By September, however, Charles Floyd had died, leaving forty-nine. Thirty-three individuals made the journey from Fort Mandan (in present North Dakota) to the Pacific coast and back.

3. Clark's undated list of estimated distances, Moulton, *Journals*, 8:380.

4. Clark's field notes, September 23, 1804, Moulton, *Journals*, 3:104.

5. Wishart, "Sioux," *Great Plains*, 601.

6. Thomas Jefferson to Meriwether Lewis, January 22, 1804, Jackson, *Letters*, 1:166.

7. Clark's field notes, September 23, 1804, Moulton, *Journals*, 3:104, emphasis in original. The Titunwan, or Teton, one of seven divisions of the Great Sioux Nation, is itself divided into seven subgroups: Oglala (Scatter One's Own), Sicangu or Brule (Burnt Thigh), Hunkpapa (Those Who Camp At the Entrance), Mnikowoju or Minneconjou (Those Who Plant By the Stream), Itzipco or Sans Arcs (Without Bows), Oohenupa (Two Kettles), and Sihasapa (Black Feet)–an entirely separate group from the Algonquian-speaking Blackfoot nation that inhabited Montana and Alberta, Canada. Lewis and Clark had encountered the Brule. (Wishart, "Sioux," *Great Plains*, 601.)

8. Clark's field notes, September 23, 1804, Moulton, *Journals*, 3:104. Such languages as Mandan, Hidatsa, Crow, Omaha, and Osage are all part of the Siouan family, but members of the Great Sioux Nation, or "Seven Council Fires," speak three mutually intelligible dialects: Dakota, Nakota, and Lakota. The Teton are also known as Lakota, the dialect they speak. (Wishart, "Native Languages," "Sioux," *Great Plains*, 581–82, 601.)

9. Clark's field notes, September 3, 1804, Moulton, *Journals*, 3:44.

10. The pronghorn is a unique animal, neither antelope nor goat. Lewis and Clark recorded the first scientific description of the pronghorn, which inhabit the western part of North America, from Saskatchewan to Mexico, on September 14, 1804. Interestingly, they also offered the first description of a white-tailed jackrabbit the same day.

11. Ordway's journal entry, September 24, 1804, Moulton, *Journals*, 9:65. Interestingly, not even two of the four diarists who mentioned Colter's hunting trip can agree on how many elk or deer Colter killed. Clark says four elk, Gass three elk, Ordway two elk and a deer, and Whitehouse two elk.

12. Hassrick, *The Sioux*, 91.

13. Horses were spreading from Mexico to Missouri on the east, California on the west, and Canada on the north (and to many points in-between) at the same time that Indians were migrating in all directions. See Calloway, *Winter Count*, 267–312, for a fascinating discussion of the impact of the horse on Native American society and culture (with a graphic on p. 271 showing the spread of horses and Indian migrations).

14. Hassrick, *The Sioux*, 88.

15. Herbert E. Bolton, ed., *Athanase de Mezieres and the Texas-Louisiana Frontier, 1768–1780*, 2 vols. (Cleveland: Arthur H. Clark, 1914), 2:280, cited in Calloway, *Winter Count*, 274. As Calloway points out, this enhanced ability to hunt buffalo was a two-edged sword. "Despite an ethos that required restraint and respect in hunting, the Indians' annual harvest of buffalo began to exceed the herds' natural increase in periods when the toll taken by wolves, fire, habitat degradation, and drought was high. Buffalo populations were falling even before American soldiers, hunters, and ranchers began to destroy the herds in the second half of the nineteenth century." *Winter Count*, 311–12.

16. Utley, *Last Days*, 13.

17. Utley, *Last Days*, 14–15.

18. Hassrick, *The Sioux*, 88.

19. Clark's journal entry, September 24, 1804, Moulton, *Journals, 3:108.*

20. Ordway's journal entry, September 25, 1804, Moulton, *Journals*, 9:67.

21. Coues, *History*, 138-39; Hassrick, *The Sioux*, 227, 226.

22. Ronda, *Among the Indians*, 30. According to Ronda, "With its tangle of economic, military, and imperial interests, the Teton Sioux negotiation was perhaps the most demanding piece of Indian diplomacy assigned to Lewis and Clark." Lewis and Clark certainly had imperialist motives, but, as Jeffrey Ostler points out, "European Americans did not have a monopoly on expansion. . . . Using guns acquired through trade, [the Lakota] displaced Omahas, Otoes, Iowas, Missouris, and Poncas." (Ostler, *The Plains Sioux*, 23, 22.)

23. Clark's field notes, September 25, 1804, Moulton, *Journals*, 3:111..

24. Lewis and Clark to the Oto Indians [August 4, 1804], Jackson, *Letters*, 1:205, emphasis in original.

25. Clark's journal entry, September 25, 1804, Moulton, *Journals*, 3:112. Of course, the captains' failure to communicate with the Lakota may have worked in their favor. As Joseph Marshall III points out, if "Lewis and Clark had been able to communicate accurately the message they carried with them from President Jefferson, their expedition might well have

ended at the Bad River confluence. The message was that the United States now owned the land, and the tribes had a Great Father in Washington, and this new Great Father wanted his 'red children' to make peace with their neighbors and trade only with Americans. After a good laugh, the warrior leaders might well have turned their men loose against the explorers." (Marshall, *The Day the World Ended*, 109.)

26. Ordway's journal entry, September 25, 1804, Moulton, *Journals*, 9:67.

27. See Ronda, *Among the Indians*, 31.

28. Clark's field notes, September 25, 1804, Moulton, *Journals*, 3:113.

29. Ordway's journal entry, September 25, 1804, Moulton, *Journals*, 9:68.

30. Thwaites, "William Clark: Soldier, Explorer, Statesman," 6.

31. Dr. James O'Fallon to Colonel Jonathan Clark, May 30, 1791, in Draper, MSS., 2L28, cited in Thwaites, "William Clark: Soldier, Explorer, Statesman," 6. The encounter mentioned took place on May 31, 1794, about two months before Clark's twenty-fourth birthday. Eight of his men were killed and two wounded. "The Indians hastily retreated, leaving behind a half-dozen rifles, forty blankets, and one fallen warrior, to be scalped by the Americans." (Jones, *William Clark*, 75; see also Foley, *Wilderness Journey*, 33–34.)

32. Ordway's journal entry, September 25, 1804, Moulton, *Journals*, 9:68.

33. Ordway's journal entry, September 25, 1804, Moulton, *Journals*, 9:68.

34. In describing the event, Clark added the parenthetical explanation, "all this time the Indians were pointing their arrows blank," which Moulton takes to mean "that the Sioux warriors were pointing their arrows straight at [Clark] because they were at 'point blank' range–so close that they did not need to elevate their aim to allow for dropping of the missile due to gravity." Clark's journal entry, Moulton, *Journals*, 3:114n5.

35. Nicholas Biddle, assisted by George Shannon, paraphrased Clark's description of the Omaha prisoners thus: "Their appearance is wretched and dejected; the women too seem low in stature, coarse, and ugly–though their present condition may diminish their beauty. We gave them a variety of small articles, such as awls and needles, and interceded for them with the chiefs, to whom we recommended to follow the advice of their great father, to restore the prisoners and live in peace with the Mahas, which they promised to do." (Coues, *History of the Expedition*, 1:137.) Cloud Shield's winter count for the year presumed to be 1804-5 indicates that the Lakota kept that promise: "The Omahas came and made peace to get their people, whom the Dakotas held as prisoners." (Greene and Thornton, *Year the Stars Fell*, 136.)

36. Ambrose, *Undaunted Courage*, 170.

37. Clark's journal entry, September 25, 1804, Moulton, *Journals*, 3:113.

38. Pryor, Colter, Gibson, Shannon, the Field brothers, and Drouillard all displayed a definite spirit of adventure, and all eventually fought Indians and proved themselves brave under fire. The Field brothers, Drouillard, and Meriwether Lewis had a violent skirmish with Blackfoot Indians in Montana in July 1806 (the only time that gunfire actually broke out between the Corps of Discovery and Indians); Pryor, Gibson, and Shannon were attacked by the Arikara in South Dakota, in September 1807, with Gibson and Shannon both being wounded; and by 1810 Colter and Drouillard, now trappers with Manuel Lisa, had both fought–and the latter was killed by–Blackfoot warriors in Montana.

39. "Black Buffalo continued to be a major chief of the Brule Teton Lakota until his death in July 1813. Highly influential in the Missouri River trade, he was, as Pierre-Antoine Tabeau described him, 'of good character, although angry and fierce in his fits of passion'—something Lewis and Clark learned firsthand. . . . The Partisan continued to be a powerful spokesman for the Teton Lakota in the years following the expedition. It is thought that he may have met Zebulon Pike in September 1805, and he undoubtedly took part in a conference arranged by Manuel Lisa at Prairie du Chien in July 1815." Woodger and Toropov, *Encyclopedia*, 53, 269.

40. Meriwether Lewis to Thomas Jefferson, April 7, 1805, Jackson, *Letters*, 1:233.

41. Moulton, *Journals*, 3:418. Clark's "Estimate of the Eastern Indians" was separate from his regular journal.

42. Hassrick, *The Sioux*, 8–9.

43. Greene and Thornton, *Year the Stars Fell*, 138, 142. Iron Shell's count is now presumed to describe 1807, American Horse's 1805–1806, and Cloud Shield's 1807–1808. But the Indians, of course, did not use a European dating system and did not have a strict notion of a 365-

day year, and therefore a perfect one-to-one correspondence between the winter counts and western calendars can hardly be expected. (Even the winter counts are not perfectly consistent among themselves.) We believe all three descriptions are referring to Lewis and Clark's visit of 1804.

44. Danker, "Wounded Knee Interviews," 193–97.

45. Among the many controversies swirling around the Wounded Knee Tragedy is the question of how many Lakota were killed. Some historians, including Yenne, have followed Utley in placing the number of dead at 153. Based on Richard E. Jensen's excellent research, many have revised the number upwards. Michael L. Tate and Jo Lea Wetherilt Behrens believe that more than 250 were killed, and Ostler puts the number at between 270 and 300 total and between 170 and 200 women and children. Jensen shows quite conclusively that conflicting accounts make a final, solid count impossible. Jensen, "Big Foot's Followers"; Wishart, "War," *Great Plains*, 817–22; Ostler, *The Plains Sioux*, 345.

46. Utley, *Last Days*, 230.

47. In 1884, the Lake Mohonk Conference of Friends of the Indian (which met every year from 1883 to 1916) stated that "the organization of the Indians in tribes is, and had been, one of the most serious hindrances to the advancement of the Indian toward civilization, and that every effort should be made to secure the disintegration of all tribal organizations." Prucha, *Indian Policy*, 163. Perhaps, Cyrus Brady expressed the prevailing sentiments of the nineteenth century best when he wrote of the closing days of the Indian Wars: "The war with the Indians was about the ownership of territory, as most of our Indian wars have been. Indeed, that statement is true of most of the wars of the world. The strong have ever sought to take from the weak . . . the westward-moving tide of civilization has at last pressed back from the Missouri and the Mississippi the Sioux and their allies the Cheyenne's, the largest and most famous of the several groups of Indians who have disputed the advance of the white man. . . . It cannot be said the Indians [did not enjoy] a quasi-legal title to this land. But if a comparatively small group of nomadic and savage tribes insists upon reserving a great body of land for a mere hunting ground . . . [which] would easily support a great agricultural and urban population of industrious citizens . . . experience has shown that in spite of treaties, purchases and other peaceful means of obtaining it, there is always bound to be a contest about that land. The rights of savagery have been compelled to yield to the demands of civilization, ethics to the contrary notwithstanding. And it will always be so, sad though it may seem to many." (Cyrus Townsend Brady, *Indian Fights and Fighters*, American Fights and Fighters Series [New York: Double-day, Page and Company, 1912], 4–6.)

5. "COLTER HAD JUST ARRIVED WITH A LETTER FROM CAPT. CLARK"

1. Clark's group included Gass, Pryor, Collins, Colter, Cruzatte, Shannon, Windsor, and four others who have not been identified. Charbonneau and Sacagawea accompanied them to a Shoshone village near present Tendoy, Idaho. Clark called the Salmon Lewis's River. Moulton, *Journals*, 5:116 n. 4.

2. The Salmon flows into the Snake River at the Idaho/Oregon border west of Grangeville, Idaho, and the Snake flows into the Columbia near the Tri-cities of Washington (Richland, Pasco, and Kennewick). A navigable river would have offered Lewis and Clark a quick, straight shot across Idaho, saving them weeks of travel time, not to mention the most difficult part of their journey. Even if Lewis and Clark had known they could avoid the Salmon by going southeast to the Snake, that waterway did not offer safe passage to the Pacific because several stretches including Hells Canyon—the deepest river gorge in North America—were certainly not passable in dugout canoes. Wilson Price Hunt and the westbound Astorians would find out the hard way just how treacherous the Snake River was. (See, Ronda, *Astoria and Empire*, 180–94.)

3. Clark's journal entry, August 23, 1805, Moulton, *Journals*, 5:155, our bracketed insertion.

4. Clark's journal entry, August 23, 1805, Moulton, *Journals*, 5:155, 156. Although Clark does not name the three men who accompanied him and Old Toby, Ordway's journal entry of August 26 (discussed below) makes it clear that Colter was one of them. Clark turned back near the site of present Shoup. One would be hard-pressed to find a more wild country in the lower forty-eight states than Idaho's Salmon River Mountains. Even today it is not possible to cross the state by vehicle from east to west anywhere near this point. To reach western Idaho from the town of Salmon, you must first go south to Stanley (about 110 miles) or north to Lolo, Montana (about 130 miles), which is the route Lewis and Clark eventually took.

5. Clark's journal entry, August 23, 1805, Moulton, *Journals*, 5:155–57.

6. Clark's journal entry, August 24, 1805, Moulton, *Journals*, 5:163.

7. Ibid., emphasis in original, our bracketed insertion. Clark proposed a third plan, which involved some of the men going back to the Missouri River to collect provisions but crossed it out. See Moulton, *Journals*, 5:164 n. 8.

8. Clark's journal entry, August 24, 1805, Moulton, *Journals*, 5:162, our bracketed insertions.

9. Harris, *John Colter*, 24; the trouble with Harris's theory is that Colter had been asked throughout the Expedition to carry out assignments—such as hunting, searching for lost horses, or tracking down missing men—on his own.

10. See Colter-Frick, *Courageous Colter*, 27–28. The packet actually contained Lewis's letter, a letter to Clark from the Secretary of War, and Clark's commission as an officer. Both Lewis and Clark were quite displeased that Clark had not been named a captain, as expected, but a second lieutenant (even though he had been a first lieutenant when he resigned from the army in 1796). See Lewis to Clark, May 6, 1804, Jackson, *Letters*, 1:179–80

11. Lewis's journal entry, August 26, 1805, Moulton, *Journals*, 5:170.

12. Ibid.

13. Lewis's journal entry, August 12, 1805, Moulton, *Journals*, 5:74.

14. Lewis's journal entry, August 26, 1805, Moulton, *Journals*, 5:171, 173.

15. Ordway's journal entry, August 26, 1805, Moulton, *Journals*, 9:211.

16. Clark's journal entry, September 1, 1805, Moulton, *Journals*, 5:182.

17. Whitehouse's journal entry, September 1, 1805, Moulton, *Journals*, 11:29.

18. Ordway's journal entry, September 2, 1805, Moulton, *Journals*, 9:216.

19. Clark's journal entry, September 2, 1805, Moulton, *Journals*, 5:183.

20. Ordway's journal entry, September 2, 1805, Moulton, *Journals*, 9:216.

21. Clark's journal entry, September 3, 1805, Moulton, *Journals*, 5:186.

22. Ordway's journal entry, September 3, 1805, Moulton, *Journals*, 9:217. As Moulton points out, The party's traverse of September 3 and the camp of that night is one of the most disputed areas of the trip through the mountains. *Journals*, 5:186 n. 1.

23. Ordway's journal entry, September 4, 1805, Moulton, *Journals*, 9:217–18. "[Flathead] was a misnomer, since it actually applied to Salishan-speaking nations on the northwest coast who had the custom of flattening the foreheads of babies." Woodger and Toropov, *Encyclopedia*, 140.

24. Background information taken from The Salish-Pend d'Oreille Committee, *The Salish People*, 19–32.

25. Account of Francois Saxa *via* Jerome D'Aste S. J. and Olin D. Wheeler, The Salish-Pend d'Oreille Committee, *The Salish People*, 103–104. The two men at the head of the party may have actually been hunters—perhaps Drouillard and Colter—for, as Joseph Whitehouse explained, "2 of our men who were a hunting came to their [Salish] lodges first." Whitehouse's journal entry, September 4, 1805, Moulton, *Journals*, 11:299.

26. The Salish-Pend d'Oreille Committee, *The Salish People*, 103–104; our bracketed insertion.

27. Clark's journal entry, September 4, 1805, Moulton, *Journals*, 5:187. The river mentioned by Clark is the Bitterroot.

28. Whitehouse's journal entry, September 4, 1805, Moulton, *Journals*, 11:299.

29. The Salish-Pend d'Oreille Committee, *The Salish People*, 81–82.

30. Ordway's journal entry, September 5, 1805, Moulton, *Journals*, 9:219. "The origin of the legend lies in Welsh folklore and was promulgated in a 15th-century Welsh poem. . . . While it seems strange to modern eyes, many educated Americans of the 18th and 19th centuries gave credence to the legend." Woodger and Toropov, *Encyclopedia*, 361.

31. The definitions and classifications of Indian languages are controversial matters among linguists, with various sources disagreeing. See Lamar, Indian Languages, *New Encyclopedia*, 522–25.

32. The Salish-Pend d'Oreille Committee, *The Salish People*, 158, with A Brief Guide to Written Salish on 157–61.

33. Clark's journal entry, September 5, 1805, Moulton, *Journals*, 5:188.

34. Account of Sophie Moiese *via* Louie Pierre and Ella Clark, The Salish-Pend d'Oreille Committee, *The Salish People*, 102.

35. Clark's journal entry, September 6, 1805, Moulton, *Journals*, 5:189.

36. Ordway's journal entry, September 10, 1805, Moulton, *Journals*, 9:221.

37. Lewis's journal entry, September 10, 1805, Moulton, *Journals*, 5:196.

38. Ordway's journal entry, September 10, 1805, Moulton, *Journals*, 9:221.

39. Harris, *John Colter*, 24. "Indian sign language evolved among Native American Indian tribes and was practiced extensively in the eighteenth and nineteenth centuries so that members of different linguistic groups were able to converse with each other." Tubbs, *Lewis and Clark Companion*, 281.

40. Lewis's journal entry, September 10, 1805, Moulton, *Journals*, 5:196–97. Moulton writes that "the Indians' description of their country matches the Nez Perce homeland in Idaho, and they were probably of that tribe, not Flatheads (Salish)." Moulton, *Journals*, 198 n. 3. Ronda, however, describes the Indians as Flatheads and says Lewis and Clark did not meet the Nez Perce until September 20. Ronda, *Among the Indians*, 157, 158.

41. Gass's journal entries, September 12, 16, and 17, 1805, Moulton, *Journals*, 10:141, 143.

6. "COLTER EXPRESSED A DESIRE TO JOIN SOME TRAPPERS"

1. Lewis's journal entry, August 2, 1806, Moulton, *Journals*, 8:146.

2. See Lewis's journal entry for July 27, 1806, Moulton, *Journals*, 8:133-37; and Ronda, *Among the Indians*, 241-43. Although historians have criticized the captains for splitting into so many groups, this part of the expedition also makes for fascinating historical study because of the multiplicity of routes and adventures. On July 3, 1806, at Travelers Rest Camp, south of present Missoula, Montana, the corps split into three groups, with Lewis (accompanied by Drouillard and Joseph and Reubin Field) going northeast, Gass (accompanied by Frazer, Goodrich, McNeal, Thompson, and Werner) going east, and Clark and everyone else going southeast. On July 13, at Three Forks, Ordway (accompanied by Collins, Colter, Cruzatte, Howard, Lepage, Potts, Weiser, Whitehouse, and Willard) headed down the Missouri River, while Clark's group crossed overland toward the Yellowstone River. Ordway met Gass near Great Falls on July 19, and Lewis joined them at the confluence of Marias River and the Missouri, on July 28. Meanwhile, Pryor (accompanied by Hall, Shannon, and Windsor) split from Clark (accompanied by Bratton, Gibson, Labiche, Shields, York, and Charbonneau, Sacagawea, and Jean-Baptiste) near present Billings, with the intent of taking horses all the way to the Mandan (a plan cut short when Crow Indians stole the horses). Clark and Pryor were reunited on August 8, east of the confluence of the Yellowstone and the Missouri (in North Dakota), and Lewis's group caught up with them on August 12, after the corps had crossed virtually all of Montana in various parties. The successful reuniting of these thirty-three people is just one more delightful element in the amazing journey of Lewis and Clark.

3. See Lewis's journal entry, July 27, 1806, Moulton, *Journals*, 8:133-39.

4. Lewis's journal entry, August 3, 1806, Moulton, *Journals*, 8:146.

5. Lewis's journal entries, August 5 and August 6, 1806, Moulton, *Journals*, 8:148, 149.

6. Ordway's journal entry, August 5, 1806, Moulton, *Journals*, 9:346.

7. Lewis's journal entry, August 6, 1806, Moulton, Journals, 8:149, bracketed explanation added.

8. Lewis's journal entry, August 7, 1806, Moulton, *Journals*, 8:149-50.

9. The Yellowstone River originates in Wyoming southeast of Yellowstone Lake and flows 670 miles across much of lower Montana, ending when it reaches the Missouri River in North Dakota. According to Woodger and Toropov, Clark's exploration of the Yellowstone "was more worthwhile than Lewis's dramatic journey up the Marias River. Clark conscientiously recorded what he was; charted the river, its tributaries, and its landmarks on maps that were to remain in use for 40 years. . . . it is the longest free-flowing river in the United States." *Encyclopedia*, 380. "Yellowstone" is a translation of the French *Roche Jaune*, which Clark rendered *Rochejhone* and Ordway *Roshjone*.

10. Lewis's journal entry, August 7, 1806, Moulton, *Journals*, 8:150. This habit of leaving messages for other expedition members shows how important it was for Lewis and Clark's men to be able to read and write, even though that ability was not explicitly mentioned by the captains as they recruited their men.

11. Lewis's journal entry, August 7, 1806, Moulton, *Journals*, 8:150.

12. See Clark's journal entry, August 8, 1806, Moulton, *Journals*, 8:283–84.

13. Lewis's journal entry, August 8, 1806, Moulton, *Journals*, 8:152.

14. Ordway's journal entry, August 9, 1806, Moulton, *Journals*, 9:347.

15. Lewis's journal entry, August 9, 1806, Moulton, *Journals*, 8:153. As Moulton notes, "Evidently Collins's 'deportment' had improved greatly since the early days of the expedition," *Journals*, 153n2. The same could be said of Colter.

16. Lewis's journal entry, August 11, 1806, Moulton, *Journals*, 8:155. Of course, Lewis's almost comical aside that the one-eyed Cruzatte could not see well begs the question, Why was Cruzatte hunting in the first place? Nevertheless, the expedition journals indicate that Cruzatte was a reasonably good hunter (better than about half the men). See Large, "Expedition Specialists," 5.

17. Lewis's journal entry, August 11, 1806, Moulton, *Journals*, 8:156; Lewis had wisely applied a poultice of Peruvian bark, a medicine he had obtained prior to the expedition. "Taken from the cinchona tree, this substance contains quinine (known nowadays to be effective against the malarial parasite) and other alkaloids used for treating high temperatures, aches, and pains," Tubbs, *Lewis and Clark Companion*, 243.

18. Ibid.

19. Gass's journal entry, August 12, 1806, Moulton, *Journals*, 10:266.

20. Lewis's journal entry, August 12, 1806, Moulton, *Journals*, 8:157.

21. Ordway's journal entry, August 12, 1806, Moulton, *Journals*, 9:348, bracketed explanations added.

22. Lewis's journal entry, August 12, 1806, Moulton, *Journals*, 8:157.

23. Ordway's journal entry, August 12, 1806, Moulton, *Journals*, 9:348. If Colter had sold thirty-one beaver pelts in St. Louis at $5 each, a reasonable expectation, he could have made $155. By contrast, his pay for the entire three-year expedition was $178.33 1/3. By the standards of the day, Colter, Dickson, and Hancock really could have made a "fortune."

24. Lewis's journal entry, August 12, 1806, Moulton, *Journals*, 8:157.

25. Ordway's journal entry, August 12, 1806, Moulton, *Journals*, 9:348.

26. Clark's journal entry, August 12, 1806, Moulton, *Journals*, 8:290.

27. Gass's journal entry, August 12, 1806, Moulton, *Journals*, 10:266.

28. Joseph Dickson was born January 13, 1775 in Cumberland County, Pennsylvania to George and Sarah Dickson. He married Susan (reportedly born October 19, 1775 in Ireland, maiden name unknown) in 1798. She died December 5, 1841. Joseph died June 12, 1844 in Illinois. The couple reportedly had at least five children, among them sons Joseph Jr. and Missouri and a daughter whose name is not known. Dickson has known living descendants. General information from Dickson, "Joseph Dixon" and "Hard on the Heels of Lewis and Clark" and from the International Genealogical Index.

29. Forrest Hancock was born in 1774 in Bedford County, Virginia to William and Mary Merchant Hancock. He married Emily Boone, daughter of Jesse Boone (son of Daniel Boone) and Cloe Van Bibber, about 1795, and they had a child in 1797. (Emily was born in Kentucky

and reportedly died before 1818.) Forrest died before April 9, 1847 in Warren County, Missouri; he has no known descendants. General information from Kenneth R. Jordan, "The Hancock Family History," Missouri State Archives, Jefferson City, Missouri and from the International Genealogical Index.

30. Boone's relationship with the Shawnee aroused a good deal of controversy, with some concluding he had actually betrayed his American companions and sided with the Shawnee and their British allies. Boone was subsequently court-martialed for treason by the Kentucky Militia. Although he was acquitted, Boone considered the incident terribly humiliating and did not mention it to his biographer or his children. William Hancock was among those who thought Boone's life among the Shawnee was suspiciously easy. Nevertheless, the two of them remained friends. Boone's granddaughter Delinda recalled that she many times heard Hancock "complain of Boone surrendering the salt boilers" and that Boone would argue that had he not done so, everyone at Boonsborough would have been killed. They would debate the matter, with Hancock always conceding that Boone "had done more than any one else would have under similar circumstances" and that Hancock "was well satisfied Boone acted from the best of motives." Faragher, *Daniel Boone*, 199–202.

31. Lofaro, *Daniel Boone*, 105–6.

32. Faragher, *Daniel Boone*, 179–80, 81.

33. Jordan, "Hancock Family History," 50.

34. Lofaro, *Daniel Boone*, 152.

35. Forrest Hancock is the sole Hancock specified by Lofaro as being in the group that went west in 1799 with Daniel Boone. Moulton notes that Boone came to Missouri "in 1799 and received a grant of 1,000 arpents of land from the Spanish government, having been preceded there by his son, Daniel Morgan Boone, in 1797. The old frontiersman was appointed judge and commandant of the Femme Osage district in 1800 and held the post until the American takeover. The site of his cabin is a few miles northwest of Matson, in southwest St. Charles County." *Journals*, 2:249n8.

36. Cartwright, *Autobiography*, 255. Cartwright's entertaining narrative is valuable because he heard the story directly from Dickson himself; the drawbacks are that he talked to Dickson twenty years after the events in question took place and that he may not have recorded those events for another thirty years after that. As will be evident throughout the rest of this chapter, Cartwright gets any number of details wrong. For starters, he states that Dickson had two companions from the start and describes Dickson's two winters in the wild when Dickson actually spent three winters on the Missouri. At the same time, Clark and others confirm certain events described by Cartwright, such Dickson and Hancock caching their furs and being attacked by Indians. We believe that like other late, second-hand sources, this one is best used to corroborate other documents and that any claims that cannot be double-checked should be viewed with caution.

37. Clark's journal entry, August 11, 1806, Moulton, *Journals*, 8:288; emphasis in original. Moulton explains that Dixon was apparently struck by a patch of leather or other material used to pack a ball tightly into a musket. Journals, 8:289n3.

38. When Lewis and Clark had sent Warfington's team down river in April of 1805, they had been quite concerned that the Lakota Sioux might attack; from hearing that Dickson and Hancock had seen Warfington near the Kansas River, Clark knew (for the first time) that Warfington had successfully passed through Lakota country. Thanks to Clay Jenkinson for pointing this out in *A Vast and Open Plain*, 399n106.

39. See Morris, "The Mysterious Charles Courtin and the Early Missouri Fur Trade," *Missouri Historical Review* 104/1 (2009): 21–39, for more information on Courtin.

40. Clark's journal entry, September 15, 1804, Moulton, *Journals*, 3:74. Moulton's use of a word followed by a question mark inside brackets, such as [Clintens?], represents his conjectural reading of the original journal entry.

41. Ordway's journal entry, August 14, 1806, Moulton, *Journals*, 9:350.

42. Ordway's journal entry, August 14, 1806, Moulton, *Journals*, 9:351. Clark wrote that the offer to join Dickson and Hancock was "very advantagious" for Colter, that "his Services Could be dispenced with from this down and as we were disposed to be of Service to any one of our party who had performed their duty as well as Colter had done, we agreed to allow him the

prvilage provided no one of the party would ask or expect a Similar permission who which they all agreed." Clark's journal entry, August 15, 1806, Moulton, *Journals*, 8:302.

43. Dickson's wife, Susan, had two children before he left, and she gave birth to another child a few months afterwards. Hancock's wife, Ellen, had a child in 1797, but whether that child was male or female and how long he or she survived is not known. Colter's son Hiram was almost certainly born before Colter left with Lewis and Clark. Dickson, "Hard on the Heels of Lewis and Clark," 16, 24; Jordan, "Hancock Family History,"18; Colter-Frick, *Courageous Colter*, 174-77.

44. Clark's journal entry, August 15, 1806, Moulton, *Journals*, 8:302.

45. Coues, *History*, 3:1182.

46. Lavender, *Westward Vision*, 127. As Lavender notes, "During that long [trapping] period many individuals, both red and white, protested the trespasses. But there is no indication that anyone who really wanted to trap was ever dissuaded by the objections or by the laws, or that anyone was ever given more than token punishment for violation." *Westward Vision*, 128.

47. Hudson's Bay Company is now the oldest business in North America and one of the oldest in the world. It now owns the largest chain of department stores in Canada. The Bay, Zellers, Home Outfitters, Designer Depot, and Fields are all part of Hudson's Bay. The British government forced the North West Company to merge with Hudson's Bay in 1821, even though the "Nor'westers' outtraded and outfought the men of Hudson's Bay." Lamar, "Hudson's Bay Company," *New Encyclopedia*, 502.

48. See Lamar, "Fur Trade in the United States," *New Encyclopedia*, 413–16.

49. See Lamar, "Manifest Destiny," *New Encyclopedia*, 676–77.

50. As for the inaccurate claim that Colter had traveled the Yellowstone during the expedition, David Lavender, for example, writes that Colter "chose to follow the Yellowstone branch of the river. Having just descended it with Clark, he knew that it offered the quickest approach to the spurs of the Rockies." *The Rockies*, 65.

51. Clark's journal entry, August 3, 1806, Moulton, *Journals*, 8:277, 78.

52. Cartwright, *Autobiography*, 255, bracketed explanation added.

53. Cartwright, *Autobiography*, 255–56.

54. In 1821, Dickson donated five acres of farmland for church and cemetery purposes. He was also one of the key supporters behind the construction of a chapel and at one time opened his home for sermons. Dickson, "Joseph Dickson," 78.

7. "UNRULY HANDS TO MANAGE"

1. Henry Dearborn to James Wilkinson, April 9, 1806, Jackson, *Letters*, 1:303. Dearborn did not name any of the other chiefs who died, but their deaths raise the possibility that the group of Indians were all exposed to a common disease during their travels.

2. Thomas Jefferson to the Arikaras [April 11, 1806], Jackson, *Letters*, 1:306. There were several chiefs among the Arikara, and some were identified by multiple names, creating a certain level of confusion about exact identities. Arketarnarshar was presumably the chief who accompanied Lewis and Clark to the Mandan and also the one who died in Washington, but the record leaves some ambiguity on that question. See Moulton, *Journals*, 3:156n5.

3. Henry Dearborn to James Wilkinson, April 9, 1806, Jackson, *Letters*, 1:303-5. We know that Gravelines had a family that remained in the St. Louis area because Dearborn made provisions for them: "I have agreed with Graveline, to request you to assign a building, at the Cantonement, left by the Troops, for his family to reside in during his absence, with the privilege of a piece of Ground for a garden." (Jackson, *Letters*, 1:304.)

4. Clark's journal entry, August 21, 1806, Moulton, *Journals*, 8:312. Rivet was one of the engages who went up the Missouri with the expedition in 1804; he may have left Warfington's return party when they reached Arikara territory. Grenier was possibly an employee of Gravelines and may have been one of the two men Lewis and Clark met on October 18, 1804, who had been robbed by the Mandan. (Moulton, *Journals*, 2:528, 8:316n1.)

5. Clark's journal entry, August 21, 1806, Moulton, *Journals*, 8:312, 13.

6. Clark's journal entry, September 12, 1806, Moulton, *Journals*, 8:357. Robert McClellan was a colorful individual who knew both Lewis and Clark, and, like both of them, had served under General Wayne in the Indian wars of the Northwest Territory. He later entered the Indian trade and had serious disputes with Lisa, one time threatening to kill him. With Ramsay Crooks, he formed the company Crooks and McClellan, which was active on the Missouri from 1807 to 1811. He went west with the overland Astorians in 1810 and returned in 1812 with Robert Stuart's party, the first to cross South Pass in Wyoming. He died in 1815 and was buried on William Clark's farm. According to Chittenden, Robert McClellan was "one of the most romantic characters in the annals of the Western fur trade. He was a man of many perilous exploits and hairbreadth escapes, a sure shot, a daring hunter, and altogether a superb example of frontier manhood." (Moulton, Journals, 8:358n1; Chittenden, *The American Fur Trade*, 1:160.)

7. Clark's journal entry, September 14, 1806, Moulton, *Journals*, 8:360. Clark concluded his entry for the day with this memorable passage: "Our party received a dram and Sung Songs untill 11oClock at night in the greatest harmoney." Lewis and Clark passed through Kaw country without incident.

8. Robert McClellan to Meriwether Lewis, April 5, 1807, Clark Papers, Missouri History Museum, bracketed explanation added. When Clark mentioned a small party setting out from the Omaha Indians (Clark to Dearborn, May 18, 1807), he may have been referring to Courtin. The letter was addressed to Lewis, who had not yet arrived in St. Louis, so it is not clear if Clark saw it or not. Clark himself had arrived from Virginia earlier in May. (Foley, *Wilderness Journey*, 160.)

9. Charles Courtin to "Gentlemen," June 22, 1807, entry 18, Letters Received, 1801-1870, Records of the Office of the Secretary of War, Record Group 107, National Archives, College Park, Maryland. The letter was intended for the governing officials of the Louisiana Territory. Territorial secretary Frederick Bates was essentially acting as governor because Meriwether Lewis had not yet arrived in St. Louis (and would not arrive until March of 1808, thirteen months after his appointment as governor by Jefferson). Bates had Courtin's letter (written in French) translated into English and sent the English transcription to Secretary of War Henry Dearborn. "Sir," he wrote, "I do myself the honor of enclosing the translation of a letter which I have lately received from a French Trader at the Ricaras' village. As this letter contains all of the evidence which I have of the insecurity of the navigation of the Missouri, I forbear to make comments.–Of Courtin I know nothing;–It is said he is respectable." (Frederick Bates to Henry Dearborn, August 2, 1807, Marshall, *Papers of Frederick Bates*, 168.)

10. Courtin to "Gentlemen," June 22, 1807. Courtin was a first-hand witness who recorded the event within days, so his account trumps Cartwright, who offered a version decades later depicting his friend Dickson in a more heroic light: "When the weather opened for trapping he said he had astonishing good luck; took a great amount the very best furs; and collecting them, began to descend the river. He had an Indian village to pass the bank of the river, and as they were a deceitful, sly, bad tribe of Indians, he determined to keep his canoe as far from their shore as possible. They made many friendly signs for him to stop, so he concluded to land and trade a little with them. He had his rifle well loaded, and was a very strong man. When his canoe struck the bank a large, stout Indian jumped into it, and others were following. He, accordingly, shoved off, when one on the bank raised his rifle and aimed to shoot him. As quick as thought Dixon jerked the Indian that was in the canoe between him and the other that raised his rifle; the gun fired, and lodged its contents in the heart of the large Indian in the canoe, who fell overboard dead. Dixon paddled with all speed down the river, and escaped being robbed or killed." (Cartwright, *Autobiography*, 256-57.)

11. Courtin to "Gentlemen," June 22, 1807.

12. Brackenridge, *Views of Louisiana*, 141. Although Lisa's party left St. Louis on April 19, 1807, Lisa himself did not leave until at least April 28. The party must have therefore waited, or traveled slowly, until Lisa caught up. (Expedition veteran Jean Baptiste Lepage was apparently one of the men who left St. Louis with Lisa.) Assuming an April 28 departure date, Lisa was about three weeks ahead of Lewis and Clark, who left St. Charles on May 21 (three years previously, of course). This pattern seems to have held true because Lisa reached the Kansas River on June 3, twenty-three days ahead of Lewis and Clark (who reached it on June 26). The

same rate of travel would place Lisa at the Platte River on June 28 (the captains arrived there on July 21). Such estimates are not certain, but they do provide valid ranges. Douglas, *Manuel Lisa*, 249n30. Assuming that traveling alone allowed Colter to travel faster than Lewis and Clark, who in 1806 had gone from the Arikara villages to the Platte River in eighteen days, he may have made the same distance in sixteen days. This calculation would place Colter at the Arikara towns on June 12.

13. Oglesby makes this assumption, which seems quite reasonable, in *Manuel Lisa*, 46.

14. Contract (translated from French) drawn up in 1809 between Alexis Doza and Pierre Menard, agent for the Missouri Fur Company. (Noy, *Distant Horizon*, 43-44.)

15. Cartwright, *Autobiography*, 17. Cartwright's mention that Dickson had been "absent nearly three years" looks to be quite accurate. He and Hancock left in August of 1804, and he may have reached home late in July of 1807. Douglas says that Dickson probably enlisted with Lisa, and Josephy–in a rare error–writes that Dickson definitely did. To date, however, no trace of Dickson has been found in the records associated with Manuel Lisa's various expeditions up the Missouri. (Douglas, "Manuel Lisa," 251; Josephy, *Opening of the Northwest*, 661n11.) Born September 8, 1772 in New Orleans, Manuel Lisa married three times and had five children. He was active in the Mississippi River trade by the 1790s and attempted unsuccessfully to enter the Santa Fe trade in the early 1800s. He founded the St. Louis Missouri Fur Company with several partners in 1809 and led expeditions up the Missouri River in 1809, 1811, 1812, and 1814 (as well as in 1807, before the company was founded). He served as an Indian agent during the War of 1812. He died August 12, 1820 of an unidentified illness. (Oglesby, "Manuel Lisa," in Hafen, *Mountain Men*, 5:179-201.)

16. Since Lisa started up the Missouri in April of 1807, reached the confluence of the Yellowstone and Bighorn Rivers–where he built Fort Raymond–in the fall, and remained there until July of 1808, and since no organized group associated with Lisa came up the Missouri in 1808, we assume that anyone who was with Lisa in 1808 necessarily came with him in 1807. Forrest Hancock fits in that category because on July 6, 1808, at Fort Raymond, he signed a document witnessing Potts and Weiser's promissory note to Manuel Lisa and Company. Meriwether Lewis Papers, Missouri Historical Society. As discussed below, Grenier is one possible exception.

17. Oglesby, *Manuel Lisa*, 40. Pierre Menard was born in Quebec around 1766 and arrived in the Indiana territory in the mid-1780s. He soon became a prominent merchant. He was appointed a major in the Randolf County, Illinois, militia and later appointed a judge of the Court of Common Pleas. Menard was one of the founding partners of the St. Louis Missouri Fur Company and went up the Missouri with Lisa in 1809, leading group of trappers (including Colter and Drouillard) to Three Forks (covered in detail later in this book). Menard was elected the first lieutenant governor of the state of Illinois and enjoyed a distinguished public career. He died on June 13, 1844. Oglesby, "Pierre Menard." William Morrison was born in Bucks County, Pennsylvania, on March 14, 1763. He partnered with an uncle in the dry goods business and arrived in Kaskaskia, Illinois, in 1790. Later that decade, he developed key contacts with the powerful Chouteau family in St. Louis, trading with the Osage Indians after the Louisiana Purchase. Like Menard, Morrison was a founding partner in the St. Louis Missouri Fur Company. In 1810, however, he and Lisa had a public dispute over business matters. During the War of 1812, Morrison became involved in mail delivery and lead mining, but his business activities diminished after 1815. He died on April 9, 1837. Governor John Reynolds described him as "kind and benevolent," "honest and upright," and a "self-made man." Oglesby, "William Morrison."

18. Colter and Drouillard were undisputably with Lisa in 1807, and their experiences are well documented. Legal documents from 1809 make it clear that Cruzatte was also with Lisa in 1807. The case for Lepage is more circumstantial. He sold the rights to his land warrant to John Ordway in 1806 and then signed a promissory note to Auguste Chouteau on April 25, 1807. (He could have been purchasing supplies to head up the river with Lisa, who left within a few days.) Lepage, who had lived among the Mandan and Hidatsa before signing up with Lewis and Clark in the fall of 1804, apparently spent the rest of his life on the upper Missouri, dying at Fort Raymond in 1809. (A promissory note signed to his heirs on December 31, 1809 shows he died by this date.) The fact that he never collected his expedition pay from Meriwether Lewis is

further evidence that he departed St. Louis in 1807 and never returned. Several legal documents in the Missouri Historical Society, as well as Colter's reminiscences, show that Potts was at Fort Raymond in 1808. He had incurred considerable debt before he was killed by Blackfoot warriors in the fall of 1808. Legal documents in the Missouri Historical Society also place Weiser (often spelled Wiser or Wyzer) at Fort Raymond in 1808. Windsor is the lone expedition veteran listed in "List of Notes of the 'Men' on the Missouri Belonging in Part to Pierre Menard." See Morris, *Fate of the Corps*, 150–52; Colter-Frick, *Courageous Colter*, 391–97; promissory notes of Lepage, Colter, and Weiser, Missouri History Museum; Jackson, *Letters*, 2:384, 385n1, 462, 723; Menard Family Papers, Abraham Lincoln Presidential Library.

19. Irving, *Astoria*, 176. If Robinson were indeed sixty-six in 1811, he was born around 1745, making him a fairly close contemporary of Daniel Boone, who was born in 1734.

20. Irving, *Astoria*, 215; Irving and Pilcher as cited in Chittenden, *The American Fur Trade*, 2:676. Pilcher's comment was confirmed by Holmes, who said that Rose was "brought in irons to St. Louis." "The Five Scalps," 42.

21. Holmes, "The Five Scalps," 6–7.

22. See Moulton, *Journals*, 7:312n6; Brackenridge, *Views of Louisiana*, 141. According to some reports, Lisa had between fifty and sixty men. As discussed below, however, Lisa himself said that he had only forty-two men when he reached Lakota country in July. Lisa was in the habit of recruiting men along the way, so the exact number quite possibly varied. We believe the following men signed on with Lisa: Antoine Bissonnet (died after being shot by Drouillard), Michel Bourdon, ———— Bovais, Etienne Brant, Joseph Brazeau, Francois Bouche, Jean-Baptiste Bouche, V. Bourbouois, Joseph Cayona, Jean Baptiste Champlain fils, John Colter (joined at Platte River), ———— Cousin, John Crump, Pierre Cruzatte, Pierre Deseve, George Drouillard, Antoine Dubriel, Bazil Eakey, Joseph Grenier, Forrest Hancock (joined somewhere on the Missouri River), John Hoback, Jean La Farque, Joseph Laderout dit Casse, Joseph Lafarque, Francois Lame, Francois LeCompt (enlisted at the Kansas River), Jean-Baptise Lepage, Jean-Baptiste Lusignan (also spelled Lusingman), John McPherson, ———— Machecon, Baptiste Marie, Jean-Baptiste Mayette, R. Miller, Calliste Montardy, Joseph Morin, Jean Muriz, Daniel Murray, Adam Philippe, ———— Poitras, John Potts, Paul Primeau, Jacob Reznor, Edward Robinson, Edward Rose (replaced Bissonett at the Osage River), Charles Sanquinet fils, Francois Solas dit Sansquartier, Baptiste Tibeau, Benito Vasquez, Peter Weiser, Richard Windsor, and Jacob Wiser. This list combines our research (primarily with "List of Notes of the 'Men' on the Missouri Belonging in Part to Pierre Menard") with the research of Walter Douglas and a Mrs. Hayden of Jackson, Wyoming. Grenier was probably the same trapper who met Lewis and Clark in August of 1806; he may have joined Lisa at the Knife River villages in the fall of 1807, or, theoretically, he could have gone up the Yellowstone in the spring of 1808 and joined then. Bourdon is the subject of a biographical sketch (Merle Wells, "Michael Bourdon," in Hafen, *Mountain Men*, 3:55-60) but that sketch makes no mention of his service with Lisa. One final note: *Fils* is French for "son," and *dit* is French for "called" or "known as." (Oglesby, *Manuel Lisa*, 40; Menard Family Papers, Illinois State Historical Society; Douglas, "Manuel Lisa," 250; Hayden's handwritten notes, Missouri History Museum; see Abel, *Tabeau's Narrative*, 168n22 for information on various men named Grenier.)

23. "The United States vs. George Drouillard," *Louisiana Gazette*, October 12, 1808. In August of 1804, when Moses Reed deserted, Clark wrote that he and Lewis were "deturmind to Send back 4 men to take reede Dead or alive." Drouillard was one of those sent after Reed, "with order if he did not give up Peaceibly to put him to Death." Desertion was therefore no more serious to Lisa than it had been to the captains. The difference was that Reed was returned without violence while Bissonnet was not, truly a life-altering distinction for Drouillard. (Clark's field notes, August 6, 1804, Moulton, *Journals*, 2:452; emphasis in original; Clark's journal entry, August 7, 1804, Moulton, *Journals*, 2:455.)

24. Wheeler, *The Trail of Lewis and Clark*, 1:110–11, cited in Skarsten, *George Drouillard*, 274, 79. For details on Drouillard's trial, see Skarsten, *George Drouillard*, 271–79; Oglesby, *Manuel Lisa*, 3–7; and Morris, *Fate of the Corps*, 49–53.

25. Lewis's journal entry, May 6, 1806, Moulton, *Journals*, 7:216.

26. Cohen, *Mapping the West*, 92.

27. Deposition of Manuel Lisa, March 18, 1811, Lisa Papers, Missouri History Museum.
28. Deposition of Manuel Lisa, March 18, 1811.
29. Brackenridge, *Views of Louisiana*, 141–42.
30. William Clark to Henry Dearborn, May 18, 1807, National Archives. See also Foley, *Wilderness Journey*, 163.
31. Potter, *Sheheke*, 139. As Potter points out, it is not clear whether the entire group consisted of 102 or 108 people. Auguste Pierre Chouteau (1786-1838), who had graduated from West Point and served as an aide to General James Wilkinson, was the son of Jean Pierre (1758-1849), the nephew of Auguste (1749–1829), and the brother of Pierre Jr. (1789-1865, also called Cadet) Chouteau. See Lamar, "Chouteau Family," *New Encyclopedia*, 211–12. Pierre Dorion Jr. was the son of Pierre Dorion Sr., who interpreted for Lewis and Clark in 1804 and traveled part way up the Missouri with McClellan in 1806. Pierre Jr. went west with Wilson Price Hunt's group of Astorians in 1811 and was killed by Shoshone Indians in present Idaho in 1814. (Jackson, *Letters*, 2: 414n1.)
32. Nathaniel Pryor to William Clark, October 16, 1807, Jackson, Letters, 2:432, bracketed explanation added. Jackson points out that this letter is in Frederick Bates's hand as well as in his style. He apparently helped Pryor write it. (*Letters*, 2:437, unnumbered note.)
33. Pryor to Clark, October 16, 1807, Jackson, *Letters*, 2:432; emphasis in original. Sheheke and Jusseaume had quarreled over something, and the latter was riding on Chouteau's keelboat as a result. He may have come over from Chouteau's boat to translate for the Mandan woman. He was back with Chouteau when violence ultimately broke out, and that choice proved disastrous for Jusseaume.
34. Pryor to Clark, October 16, 1807, Jackson, *Letters*, 2:433, emphasis added.
35. Pryor to Clark, October 16, 1807, Jackson, *Letters*, 2:433, bracketed explanation added.
36. Pryor to Clark, October 16, 1807, Jackson, *Letters*, 2:435.
37. See Morris, *Fate of the Corps*, 28–37, 75–77, and 82–88, for information on Pryor, Gibson, and Shannon, respectively. Pryor and Chouteau reached St. Louis a few days after October 20.
38. Various records make it clear that Joseph Field died between June 27 and October 10, 1807, and William Clark reported that he was killed. Jim Holmberg perceptively suggested the possibility that Field died in Pryor and Chouteau's encounter with the Arikara. See *Dear Brother*, 93–96n10. Patrick Gass, the last surviving member of the Lewis and Clark Expedition, was born on June 12, 1771. With the help of an editor who was also a ghost writer of sorts, Gass published his journal of the expedition in 1807, something not authorized and even criticized by Lewis. Gass served in the War of 1812 and lost an eye in an accident. He later settled in present West Virginia and at age fifty-nine married a twenty-year-old bride, having several children and surviving his wife by many years. Gass died on April 2, 1870, two months shy of his ninety-ninth birthday.
39. Jusseaume lived among the Mandan for decades but was never considered a competent interpreter. Such traders as David Thompson and Alexander Henry the Younger–as well as Lewis and Clark–tended to have a negative opinion of him. After his injury, he petitioned Thomas Jefferson for a pension. He was still living at the Knife River villages when Maximilian arrived there in 1833-34. (Moulton, *Journals*, 3:205n1; Jackson, *Letters*, 2:438n8.)
40. Pryor to Clark, October 16, 1807, Jackson, *Letters*, 2:436.
41. Oglesby, *Manuel Lisa*, 53. Even Bates, who may have helped Pryor write his letter, failed to mention Lisa is his own summary of the event: "The escort of the Mandane-chief, commanded by Lt. Pryor, returned with their illustrious charge, a few days ago. Prior's party has been defeated by the Ricaras, with the loss of four men killed and nine wounded." (Frederick Bates to The Hon. Aug. B. Woodward, October 20, 1807, "Miscellaneous Documents," *Michigan Historical Collections* 8 [1885]: 559.)
42. René Jusseaume to Thomas Jefferson, December 3, 1807, Missouri History Museum, cited in Potter, *Sheheke*, 146.
43. Brackenridge, *Views of Louisiana*, 142.
44. William Clark to Henry Dearborn, May 18, 1807, National Archives.
45. Brackenridge, *Views of Louisiana*, 142–43. The Assiniboine originally lived near Lake Superior but migrated westward in the 1600s. "Once they acquired horses, their range extended

even further through western Manitoba, up into Saskatchewan, and down into Montana and North Dakota." By the time Lewis and Clark met the Mandan, they had already established a solid trading relationship with the Assiniboine, though the latter sometimes resorted to intimidation. Since the Assiniboine were based in Canada, with strong ties to British traders, Lewis and Clark did not attempt to negotiate with them or present them with gifts like they had with other Great Plains nations. The captains, who were happy not to see the Assiniboine on their return journey, encouraged the Mandan and Hidatsa to break off ties with the Assiniboine—and the British—but that was not to be. Woodger and Toropov, *Encyclopedia*, 35–37.

46. Of the Lewis and Clark veterans traveling with Lisa, Richard Windsor was the only one who had accompanied Clark on his journey down the Yellowstone in 1806. Part of that time, he had been with Pryor, Hall, and Shannon, going overland with horses, but after the horses were stolen, the men made their way back to the Yellowstone, built canoes from buffalo skins and wood, and re-entered the river near Pompeys Tower. Windsor had thus traveled the Yellowstone all the way from its confluence with the Bighorn to its mouth at the Missouri. See Clark's journal entry, August 8, 1806, Moulton, *Journals*, 8:283–86.

47. Cited by Harris, *John Colter*, 71.

48. Deposition of Manuel Lisa, March, 18, 1811, Missouri History Museum; Oglesby, *Manuel Lisa*, 54. Lisa's son Remon was born December 4, 1805, and died July 15, 1811. The mouth of the Bighorn had been a meeting place and part of a key trail for more than ten thousand years. With Lisa's arrival, the site gradually took on a role as a route for commerce in the fur industry. Mountain men made their way from widely dispersed trapping grounds or from rendezvous finally arriving at the mouth of the Shoshone River. From there, the fur traders followed the trail, now commonly referred to as the "Bad Pass Trail" until they reached the mouth of Grapevine Creek where they unloaded pelts from pack animals and built bullboats on the spot. Once the boats were built, they loaded their pelts into them and could float down river all the way to St. Louis. Fort Raymond (also called "Lisa's Post," "Fort Manuel," "Fort Lisa," and "Big Horn Post") was the first of a number of forts built in the area. A town was laid out in the 1860s or 1870s but nothing came of it since the head of navigation on the Yellowstone was a little farther up river and was called Coulson and later became Billings, Montana.

49. Brackenridge, *Views of Louisiana*, 91–92.

8. "LONELY WANDERINGS"

1. Holmes, "The Five Scalps," 8.
2. Hunt's account book, July 1811, cited in Irving, *Astoria*, 214-15n11.
3. Wishart, *Great Plains Indians*, 55; Lamar, *New Encyclopedia*, 276..
4. David Thompson's journal, January 5, 1798, Wood and Thiessen, *Early Fur Trade*, 116.
5. Charles McKenzie's narrative, 1805, Wood and Thiessen, *Early Fur Trade*, 245. As noted below, McKenzie met Lewis and Clark at Fort Mandan in November of 1804.
6. See Heidenreich, *Smoke Signals*, 48, 113.
7. Holmes, "The Five Scalps," 8.
8. Reuben Lewis to Meriwether Lewis, April 21, 1810, Meriwether Lewis Papers, Missouri History Museum, bracketed explanation added.
9. In 1805, Lewis and Clark had noted a Shoshone village about eighty miles northwest of Henry's Lake, near present Dillon, Montana, and in 1812, Robert Stuart had mentioned a Crow village about seventy miles to the southwest, near Teton Pass on the Wyoming/Idaho border. See Heidenreich, *Smoke Signals*, 48, 113.
10. Clark's identification of Henry's River on his so-called 1810 map is hardly a straightforward matter. As John Logan Allen points out, although Clark sent the map off for publication in December of 1810, he continued to add information to the map (or to a copy he himself made) until at least 1813. (Allen, "The Forgotten Explorers," 26.) After 1810, for example, Clark obtained information from Andrew Henry, who returned to St. Louis in October of 1811, and from the eastbound Astorians, who reached St. Louis in April of 1813. This means that the

map sent for publication could not have included data from Henry, such as the name and location of Henry's River. However, the version of the map published in 1814 did identify Henry's River. It seems, therefore, as Allen has speculated, that "Clark continued to add information up to the time of the engraving of the copper plate for the Biddle edition and somehow transmitted cartographic data to the engraver (Samuel Lewis). We just don't have the correspondence to support that contention." (Correspondence between Larry Morris and John Logan Allen, November 2013.) Decades earlier, in an unpublished manuscript, J. Neilson Barry had also speculated that the identification of Henry's River "must have been sent by Clark as a revision of what [he] had previously sent." (Barry Files, 1955, Yellowstone National Park Archives.)

11. The question naturally comes up, What connection did Peter Weiser have with the river and town in western Idaho reportedly named after him? The town of Weiser lies at the confluence of the Weiser River and the Snake River, about seventy-five miles northwest of Boise. In 1812, as Robert Stuart was leading a small group of Astorians back to St. Louis, he identified "Wisers River, a Stream 60 yards wide; well stocked with small wood and Beaver." Since William Clark had identified a Wiser's River on his 1810 map, the natural conclusion would be that Stuart somehow got his information from Clark. There are two problems with such a speculation, however. First, Stuart was a Canadian who sailed for the Oregon Coast in 1810 and is not known to have had any possible connection with Clark before that time. (Before leaving St. Louis in 1811, Wilson Price Hunt, leader of the westbound Astorians, had the opportunity to consult with Clark, but in his account of the westbound journey, Hunt did not use any of Clark's names for Idaho rivers. Nor was Hunt present with Stuart's eastbound party.) Second, the waterway called Wiser's River by Stuart was clearly not in the same vicinity as Clark's river of the same name. Indeed, the name given by Clark to the present Weiser River was "Nemo River." (Nor would it be reasonable to assume that the Weiser River was named after Peter Weiser because he somehow reached the area on his mission for Lisa. As the westbound Astorians sadly discovered, the Snake River is extremely treacherous and not navigable after the Burley, Idaho, area.) Therefore, Stuart's reason for using the name "Wiser" remains a mystery. Philip Ashton Rollins adds that Wiser's River "was the 'river Wuzer' of Alexander Ross, the 'Wazer's River' of Peter Skene Ogden in 1827, the 'Wazer' and 'Waser' River of John Work, the 'Wagner or Waze River' of Albert in 1838." (Rollins, *Discovery of the Oregon Trail*, 83, 100n143.) Peter Weiser was of German extraction, and the German pronunciation of his name employs a long *i*, as in *wise*. His contemporaries apparently pronounced the name that way, because they usually spelled it *Wiser*, *Wyser*, or *Wyzer*. The name of the current river and town in Idaho, however, is pronounced with a long *e*, as in *weep*.

12. Meriwether Lewis to Henry Dearborn, January 15, 1807, National Archives, Jackson, *Letters*, 1:368.

13. Skarsten, *George Drouillard*, 266. Skarsten also speculates that Colter left "in early November, or possibly in late October," but offers no support for that claim. (*George Drouillard*, 260.) See Allen, *Passage Through the Garden*, 375–79, for information on Drouillard's routes.

14. Deposition of Manuel Lisa, March 18, 1811, Lisa Papers, Missouri History Museum. We do not know the exact date of Lisa's arrival at the mouth of the Bighorn, but he chronicled much of the journey in the deposition and implied that the group arrived sometime between October 10 and November 21. According to Burton Harris, "the first map drawn by William Clark, August 5, 1808, on the basis of information supplied by George Drouillard," gave October as the date of the arrival. (Harris, *John Colter*, 69–70; Harris's endnote number 16 on p. 169 adds: "The map is in the possession of the Library of Congress, Washington, D. C.")

15. Clark's 1808 map.

16. See Skartsten, *George Drouillard*, 260–67 and Harris, *John Colter*, 82–89.

17. Background on the Battle of Little Bighorn drawn from Lamar, *New Encyclopedia*, 280–81, and Wishart, *Great Plains Indians*, 117–18.

18. See Skarsten, *George Drouillard*, 267–70, and Heidenreich, *Smoke Signals*, 48, 113. In 1805, North West Company trader Francois-Antoine Larocque, only twenty-one years old, had traveled through some of the same country as Drouillard. His positive relations with the Crow helped lay a good foundation for Drouillard's visits. Larocque was with Charles McKenzie

when he met Lewis and Clark on November 27, 1804 at Fort Mandan. See Clark's journal entry, November 27, 1804, Moulton, *Journals*, 3:241.

19. Skarsten, *George Drouillard*, 269.

20. Foley, *Wilderness Journey*, 19, 24.

21. Jefferson's Instructions to Lewis, [June 20, 1803], Jackson, *Letters*, 1:61, 62.

22. Jones, *William Clark*, 192.

23. Lewis to the Public, March 14, 1807, Jackson, *Letters*, 2:386.

24. William Clark to Nicholas Biddle, December 7, 1810, Jackson, *Letters*, 2:562.

25. Jones, *William Clark*, 193; Buckley, *William Clark*, 84. To understand the early maps of the western United States, it is important to realize that every drop of moisture that falls from the sky in whatever form is controlled by a "divide" once it reaches the ground. These divides, the most prominent of which is the Continental Divide, control whether the moisture runs to the Atlantic Ocean or the Pacific, or to a closed basin such as the Great Basin. Early travelers paid close attention to how these drainages related to the landscape. Lewis and Clark, for example, knew they were crossing the Continental Divide when they reached Lemhi Pass (along the present Montana/Idaho border) in August of 1805. Therefore, cartographers such as Clark based maps on impressions of streams and mountains, as well as on measurements taken by sextents, compasses, artificial horizons, and chronometers.

26. See Cutright, *A History of the Lewis and Clark Journals*, 53–72.

27. To add one more complication to the picture, two different versions of Biddle's map were published–one in the United States and one in England. Although the two maps are quite similar in most regards, certain features, particularly mountain ranges, are sometimes conspicuously different. In addition, the lake now believed to be Brooks Lake is called "Lake Riddle" on the U.S. map and "Lake Riddle" on the English. How two different maps were printed is not clear. John G. White, a Colter researcher discussed later in this chapter, thought it curious "that when the only communication . . . was by sailing vessels, there should, in the same year be published [two] . . . editions." He speculated that "arrangements were made for simultaneous publication . . . in which even the one [publisher] would have the same authority as the other." (White, "A Souvenir of Wyoming.") Luckily, the U.S. and English versions offer the same dotted line for Colter's Route.

28. Both Clark and Biddle had noted discrepancies between the journal entries and the original drawings, but no related corrections were made before printing began. The format of the published map is small (12 inches by 28 inches) for such a large area, and the "Colter's route in 1807" section covers approximately 1.5 inches by 4 inches. Concerning the widely held belief that Clark consulted with Colter before sending his map for publication in December of 1810, the only evidence directly confirming that assumption is the note "Colter route in 1807" on the map itself. Even the note, however, offers persuasive evidence that Clark and Colter (both of whom were in the St. Louis area during the second half of 1810) did meet and discuss the map, a conclusion reached by such prominent Clark scholars as Landon Y. Jones and Jay H. Buckley. In addition, while it is certainly possible that Colter drew his own map and gave it to Clark, no document supporting this notion has yet been discovered.

29. As for Clark inaccurately compressing much of Wyoming and Colorado into the same space, it is important to note that Clark was relying on Pike, who "made the assertion that the sources of the Platte and Arkansas were in the same chain of mountains that gave birth to the Red River of the Missouri (Yellowstone), the Rio Colorado of California, and the Rio del Norte (Rio Grande)." (Harris, *John Colter*, 102.) Clark's understandable assumption was that one key area–in present northwest Wyoming–contained the source of the major rivers of the West. He was half right, because the Gallatin, Madison, Bighorn, Yellowstone, Sweetwater, Snake, and Green rivers all rise in that region. The other key source of western rivers–and the region actually seen by Pike–is central Colorado, where the Rio Grande, Colorado, Arkansas, and South Platte rivers all originate.

30. Allen, "The Forgotten Explorers," 26.

31. Mattes, "Behind the Legend of Colter's Hell," 253. Lake Biddle was named after Nicholas Biddle, editor of Lewis and Clark's history, and Lake Eustis after William Eustis, who succeeded Henry Dearborn as secretary of war.

32. Chittenden, *Yellowstone*, 22–23.

33. Chittenden, *Yellowstone*, 23, bracketed explanation in original.

34. During the American fur trade era, trappers and explorers considered the Bighorn River to be divided into three sections. The longest section begins at Brooks Lake and flows down to the first canyon, and was known as the "Wind River." The central part, from this upper (southern) canyon to the lower (northern) canyon was called the "Horn River." The lowest (most northern) and longest section, which flows to the Yellowstone River, has always been called the "Bighorn River." The Indian name was "na e Ar-sar-tah" for the mountain sheep. The French fur trader Francois Larocque in 1805 called the river the "Grosse Corne," French for *big horn*, after the sheep he saw along its banks. Today the two rivers are sometimes referred to as the "Wind/Bighorn." The Wind River officially becomes the Bighorn River at the "Wedding of the Waters" on the north side of Wind River Canyon near the town of Thermopolis, Wyoming. J. Neilson Barry liked to write that the Wind/Bighorn canyon was like a church, where a woman went in with one name and came out with another.

35. Chittenden, *Yellowstone*, 23–24.

36. Chittenden, *Yellowstone*, 24.

37. Chittenden, *Yellowstone*, 24. Today, tourists are told almost from the first moment they enter Yellowstone Park that John Colter was the first European to view its wonders: "A member of the Lewis and Clark Expedition, John Colter, left the group during its return journey to join trappers in the Yellowstone area. During his travel, Colter probably skirted the northwest shore of Yellowstone Lake near Tower Fall, where he noted the presence of 'Hot Spring Brimstone.'" (Yellowstone Resources and Issues Handbook, 2012, 22.)

38. Chittenden, *Yellowstone*, 27–28.

39. Chittenden, *Yellowstone*, 28n.

40. Allen, "The Forgotten Explorers," 32. About this same time, the historian Olin Wheeler wrote a number of articles promoting Yellowstone National Park as an ideal destination in publications of the Great Northern and Milwaukee railroads.

41. Mattes, "Behind the Legend of Colter's Hell," 253–54.

42. See the works cited section for complete bibliographical information on these books and articles.

43. The Encyclopedia of Cleveland History, http://ech.case.edu/cgi/article.pl?id=WJG, accessed on November 29, 2013.

44. W. D. Green to J. Neilson Barry, April 13, 1950, J. Neilson Barry Collection, Albertsons Library, Boise State University.

45. Memorandum NP, October 19, 1943, American Heritage Center, University of Wyoming.

46. Stallo Vinton to J. Neilson Barry, June 16, 1938, J. Neilson Barry Collection, Albertsons Library, Boise State University. Barry's assumption that George Drouillard made maps of the area and gave them to Clark is also based on a surmise because no map drawn by Drouillard has been found.

47. Barry, "Colter's Map of 1814," 108, bracketed explanation added.

48. Barry, "Colter's Map of 1814," 105, 107.

49. At Two Ocean Pass, just south of the southeast corner of Yellowstone Park, one stream, North Two Ocean Creek, actually splits into Pacific Creek and Atlantic Creek, each of which flows into its namesake ocean.

50. J. Neilson Barry to Merrill J. Mattes, December 5, 1950, Barry Papers, Albertsons Library, Boise State University.

51. Allen, "The Forgotten Explorers," 27. It is important to note, however that while the remastered map shows "what would have appeared on Clark's drawing table," that means Clark's final image–which was created in 1813 or sometime thereafter–and not the version he sent to Biddle in December of 1810. Moreover, as Allen has pointed out, "a letter from Clark to Thomas Jefferson in 1816 suggests that the map at Yale from which the new reproduction was made is a second copy of the map sent to Biddle for publication." (Allen, "The Forgotten Explorers," 28.) This in turn means that it is impossible to say exactly what the December 1810 version looked like.

52. Allen, "The Forgotten Explorers," 27.

53. Allen, "The Forgotten Explorers," 32–33.

54. William J. Ghent to John G. White, October 1, 1926, Ghent Papers, Bancroft Library.

55. Average annual snowfall statistics from the Western Regional Climate Center website, http://www.wrcc.dri.edu/, accessed on January 9, 2014.

56. The Western Regional Climate Center website, http://www.wrcc.dri.edu/, the Brooks Lake Campsite website, http://www.fs.usda.gov/recarea/shoshone/recarea/?recid=36419, and the Togwotee Mountain Lodge website, http://www.togwoteelodge.com/, all accessed on January 9, 2014. Little wonder that the Brooks Lake Campground does not open until July 4.

57. Conclusions about the path and direction taken by Colter and about winter travel in the Yellowstone Park area are drawn in part from conversations between Ron Anglin and Bob Richard as they traveled Colter's Route together during the summer of 2013. A longtime Wyoming resident, Richard is uniquely qualified as an expert on Yellowstone. Since the early 1900s, his family has been guiding people to the wonders and beauty of the greater Yellowstone region. His father Jack Richard, the region's best-known photojournalist, passed on his love of the high country and taught Richard skills he still uses as a professional photographer. Richard has a broad range of knowledge based on his experience as a cattle rancher, military veteran, school teacher, civic leader, and author. At the behest of Superintendent Lemuel "Lon" Garrison, he became the only Designated Mounted Ranger in Yellowstone National Park in the 1950s (meaning he was the only ranger authorized to travel the park by horseback and deal with the public). His years as a mounted ranger gave him an unparalleled opportunity to see virtually any section of Yellowstone at any time of year and to talk with visitors about their experiences.

58. The Western Regional Climate Center website, http://www.wrcc.dri.edu/, accessed on January 9, 2014.

59. Mackenzie, *Voyages from Montreal Through the Continent of North America*, 18; Lewis's journal entry, April 11, 1806, Moulton, *Journals*, 7:106. The artist George Catlin depicted Ojibwa Indians wearing snowshoes.

60. Sources checked include Oglesby, *Manuel Lisa*; Douglas, *Manuel Lisa*; James, *Three Years Among the Indians*; Rollins, *Discovery of the Oregon Trail*; Chittenden, *American Fur Trade*; Wishart, *Fur Trade*; Lowie, *The Crow Indians*; and Linderman, *Plenty Coups: Chief of the Crow*.

61. Heidenreich, *Smoke Signals*, 48, 113; see Bagley, *The First Known Man in Yellowstone*, and Haines, *Osborne Russell's Journal of a Trapper*.

62. Clark's journal entry, July 26, 1806, Moulton, *Journals*, 8:232.

63. After getting permission from Lewis and Clark to leave the expedition, Colter started up the Missouri with Dickson and Hancock from a Mandan village on August 15, 1806. If the trio traveled up the Yellowstone River—as is widely and reasonably believed—they could have reached the mouth of the Bighorn by late September. As noted earlier, none of the three left a firsthand account of what happened next, but Dickson's friend Peter Cartwright wrote in the 1850s that Dickson and his partners split up in the fall, before the approach of winter. This only known account (other than pure hearsay) of what happened that fall thus leaves open the possibility that Colter could have departed on his journey in early October. Again, as noted, his likely departure time in 1807 was mid-December. That significant difference makes a trip into the Yellowstone country quite possible in 1806 and virtually impossible in 1807.

64. Mattes, "Behind the Legend of Colter's Hell," 254.

65. Hartley, *Lexicon*, 125; background information from Noy, *Distant Horizon*, 50. Colter likely carried one of the "short rifles" obtained from Harper's Ferry by Meriwether Lewis in March of 1803. Now generally referred to as "1792–94 Contract Rifles," these were flintlocks with 42-inch octagonal barrels that fired .49-caliber balls. Lewis requested the barrels shortened (although the length he specified is unknown). When Colter left with Dickson and Hancock, Lewis and Clark gave him one or more waterproof lead canisters that contained four pounds of powder each. Powder for immediate use was carried in the powder horn. Colter would have also carried forty or fifty lead balls in his pouch and, if possible, would have retrieved them after shooting an animal so they could later be remelted for future use. (Clark's journal entry, August 15, 1806, Moulton, *Journals*, 8:320; Tait, "The U.S. Contract Rifle Pattern of 1792," *Man at Arms* 21/3 (May/June 1999), 33–45; Tait, response to letter, *Man at Arms* 21/6 (November/December 1999), 7–8; S. K, Wier, "The Firearms of the Lewis and

Clark Expedition," http://www.westernexplorers.us/Firearms_of_Lewis_and_Clark.pdf, accessed on January 11, 2014.)

66. Russell, *Journal of a Trapper*, 26, bracketed explanation added.

67. Russell, *Journal of a Trapper*, 44, bracketed explanation added. Although the Yellowstone River actually begins in the southeastern corner of present Yellowstone Park and then flows in and out of Yellowstone Lake, Colter's identification of Yellowstone Lake as the source of the Yellowstone River was essentially correct and provided sufficient information for Clark's map.

68. Washington Irving, *The Rocky Mountains*, Philadelphia, 1837, 1:223, cited in Vinton, *John Colter*, 69.

69. Take this typical example: "When, back at the fort, Colter told his companions of these incredible sights, the mythology of the early West got under way, for to be sure, Colter must only be telling tall tales, they thought. Here was the first of the legends that formed around Colter and gained currency among the mountain men yarning around innumerable mountain and prairie campfires" (Todd, "John Colter," 86). According to Harris, Clark's manuscript version of the map says "Boiling Spa," but the printed version reads "Boiling Spring" (*John Colter*, 90).

70. Benjamin Louis Eulalie de Bonneville (1796–1878) was born in France, came to the United States in 1803, and graduated from West Point in 1815. By 1830 he became interested in founding his own fur trading concern and was granted a two-year leave from the military. He brought more than one hundred men and built a fort in the Green River country, but his financial efforts failed, and the fort became known as "Fort Nonsense" to veteran trappers. He fought to be reinstated in the army and was befriended by Washington Irving, who recorded— and idealized—Bonneville's adventures. (Lamar, *New Encyclopedia*, 115.)

The boundary of Yellowstone Park itself is approximately forty-five miles from Cody. Throughout his article, "Behind the Legend of Colter's Hell," Mattes demonstrates convincingly that early sources clearly distinguished between the Yellowstone region and Colter's Hell and that confusion between the two actually developed with later historians.

It is also important to note that although many have described Colter's Hell as a *volcanic* area, the related hot springs, steam, and gas actually originate from underground friction involving rock and water, which is *thermal*, not volcanic, activity.

71. Pierre Jean De Smet, *Western Missions and Missionaries*, 1863, cited in Mattes, "Behind the Legend of Colter's Hell," 258–59, emphasis in original, our bracketed insertion.

72. Frances Fuller Victor, *The River of the West: Life and Adventure in the Rocky Mountains and Oregon*, 1870, cited in Mattes, "The Legend of Colter's Hell," 258, emphasis added by Mattes, bracketed explanation added by the authors. Osborne Russell, who had already seen the amazing sights of the Yellowstone area, described Colter's Hell in a rather matter-of-fact way: "This stream is called Stinking River a branch of the Bighorn which after running about 40 mls thro. the big plain enters the above river about 15 mls. above the lower Bighorn Mountain. It takes its name from several hot Springs about 5 miles below the forks producing a sulphurous stench which is often carried by the wind to the distance of 5 or 6 Mls." (Russell, *Journal of a Trapper*, 25.)

9. "IN THE MIDST OF AN UNBOUNDED WILDERNESS"

1. Major Thomas Biddle to Colonel Henry Atkinson, October 29, 1819, *American State Papers*, Class II, Indian Affairs, 2:202, bracketed information added.

2. James, *Three Years Among the Indians*, 26. Considering the common tendency of the time to use the term *Flathead* rather generically, and also considering the Salish strategy of forming multi-tribal parties when going east to hunt buffalo, it is quite possible that this band of what James called Flathead actually consisted of Salish proper as well as members of any of these nations: upper and lower Pend d'Oreille, Nez Perce, Spokane, Coeur d'Alene, Colville, Kutenai, and Shoshone. (Salish-Pend d'Oreille Culture Committee, *The Salish People*, 83; Josephy, *The Opening of the Northwest*, 44.) It is also likely that whoever reported the numbers

of fifteen hundred warriors vs. eight hundred exaggerated considerably. This is hardly surprising–in both ancient and modern history, participants and witnesses of great battles have exaggerated the numbers of people involved. After his victory at the Battle of Alesia in 52 B.C., for example, Julius Caesar reported an enemy force of a quarter million Gauls when the actual figure was more like eighty thousand.

3. Biddle to Atkinson, October 29, 1819, 2:202; James, *Three Years Among the Indians*, 26.

4. James, *Three Years Among the Indians*, 26.

5. Biddle to Atkinson, October 29, 1819, 2:202.

6. Irving, *Astoria*, 147; see Ronda, *Among the Indians*, 243-44. The Blackfoot nation (*Nitsi-ta-pi-ksi*, "Real People") was actually a confederation of three tribes sharing a common language and culture: the Kainai, also called Blood; the Pikani, also called Piegan; and the Siksika, also called Blackfoot proper or Northern Blackfoot. The Atsina nation, or Gros Ventre of the Prairie, was a longtime ally of the confederation. Traditional Blackfoot territory was bordered on the west by the Rocky Mountains, on the east by the Great Sand Hills in present Saskatchewan, and stretched more than five hundred miles from north to south, from the North Saskatchewan River to the Yellowstone (thus encompassing major portions of present Alberta, Saskatchewan, and Montana). Far to the north, Blackfoot people had successfully traded with the British for several years, calling them "Northern White Men."

7. Holmes, "The Five Scalps," 8.

8. Holmes, "The Five Scalps," 9.

9. Holmes, "The Five Scalps," 10.

10. John F. A. Sanford to William Clark, July 26, 1833, National Archives, cited in Betts, *In Search of York*, 138. There were a number of Menards involved in the fur trade; the identity of this one is not clear, but he was not the Pierre Menard discussed elsewhere in this book. Hugh Glass (birth date unknown), of course, is most famous for surviving a grizzly bear attack in South Dakota and crawling many miles along the Grand River before meeting other trappers. He also had more than one narrow escape from Indians. See Morgan, *Jedediah Smith*, 96–109, for good information on Glass. The Arikara who killed Rose, Menard, and Glass were later killed by Johnson Gardner and a group of trappers. (Lamar, "Hugh Glass," *New Encyclopedia*, 432).

11. Filson, *The Discovery, Settlement, And Present State of Kentucke*, 65, 66, cited in Lofaro, *Daniel Boone*, 91, 92.

12. John C. Boone to Lyman C. Draper, November 20, 1890, Draper Manuscripts, cited in Faragher, *Daniel Boone*, 175.

13. Deposition of Daniel Boone, September 28, 1795, and Lyman C. Draper interview with Henry Wilson, n.d., Draper Manuscripts, cited in Faragher, *Daniel Boone*, 175.

14. Lyman C. Draper, "The Life of Boone," manuscript, cited in Faragher, *Daniel Boone*, 175–76.

15. The world record in the long jump in 1901 (when records were first kept) was twenty-four feet, eleven and a half inches; as of 2013, the record is twenty-nine feet, four and a fourth inches.

16. Background on Brady's Leap from Brad Bolton, "About Captain Samuel Brady," Kent, Ohio, Historical Society, http://www.oocities.org/heartland/park/9580/brady.html, accessed on December 20, 2013. Brady's father and brother were both killed by Indians, and Brady became particularly vengeful in his attitude and actions toward Indians. In 1771 he was tried and acquitted in the murder of several innocent Indians.

17. Irving, *Astoria*, 150.

18. Irving, *Astoria*, 148. David A. Miller has suggested that if the encounter occurred on a tributary of the Jefferson, a likely candidate would be Willow Creek. (*Call of the Headwaters*, 30–31.)

19. James, *Three Years Among the Indians*, 30.

20. Irving, *Astoria*, 148, 148n25.

21. Jackson, "Journey to the Mandans," 191.

22. Jackson, "Journey to the Mandans," 191; James, *Three Years Among the Indians*, 30–1.

23. Irving, *Astoria*, 148.

24. Jackson, "Journey to the Mandans," 191–92.

25. James, *Three Years Among the Indians,* 31–32.

26. Irving, *Astoria*, 149. This is the only recorded instance of Colter killing an Indian.

27. James, *Three Years Among the Indians*, 31.

28. Jackson, "Journey to the Mandans," 192.

29. James, *Three Years Among the Indians*, 33–33.

30. Irving, *Astoria*, 149–50.

31. Kelly, "The Dougherty Map," 156.

32. Word of the Blackfoot attack on Colter and Potts apparently reached North West Company trader Alexander Henry the Younger (1765–1814), who wrote in 1809 at Fort Vermilion (in present Alberta, Canada): "Last year it is true we got some Beaver from them [a band of Blackfoot Indians Henry called the "Slave Indian Tribe"], but it was the spoils of War. Having fell upon a party of Americans on the Missouri. They stripped them of everything they had, and brought off a quantity of Beaver Skins." (*Journals of Alexander Henry the Younger*, 397.) The attack also found its way into Indian oral tradition. A 1934 newspaper article from Mineral County, Montana, included the following account: "A striking development of the observance was brought about by Lon Cook, publicity director, Milwaukee railroad . . . [while] engaged in conversation with Chief Ta-Wah of the Flatheads in an effort to verify reports in history of the feats of John Colter . . . the chief, now 92 years old, was unable at first to identify Colter by name. . . . Cook then recounted feats of Colter . . . suddenly the face of Chief Ta-Wah lit up with understanding 'Ah, I know of whom you speak,' said the chief. 'His story has come down through our Indian traditions, they were told me by my father. They had come to him from his own father, for the incidents of which you speak, were in 1808 before even the birth of my father. Your story of Colter agrees with our tribal traditions except in one respect. You call the man Colter. In our traditions he was Sis Se Use Al Cheman, meaning 'brave white man.'" (*The Mineral Independent*, March 15, 1934.) A search by the authors for mention of Colter's Run in Blackfoot oral history or in Blackfoot winter counts has thus far been fruitless.

33. Morris, *Fate of the Corps*, 197.

34. St. Louis County Probate Records, 1804–1849, File 69; Colter-Frick, *Courageous Colter*, 262–71; Morris, *Fate of the Corps*, 197, 199–200.

10. "WE ALL NOW BECAME BLIND"

1. James, *Three Years Among the Indians*, 34.

2. James, *Three Years Among the Indians*, 35. James implies that Colter was traveling on foot. If so, he would been carrying his supplies as well and could not likely have transported more than a few traps. The typical beaver trap weighed between two and five pounds, and a complement of six or eight traps and the associated chains generally weighed fifty or sixty pounds. Still, even a single trap was quite valuable–as noted later in this chapter. (Russell, *Firearms, Traps, and Tools*, 127.)

3. Jackson, "Journey to the Mandans," 191. Based on a November 1810 court case, some argue that Colter may have returned to St. Louis in May of 1809 and met with Meriwether Lewis. (See Colter-Frick, *Courageous Colter*, 69-71.) The case in question reads in part, "the said John [Colter] saith that whereas the said Meriwether [Lewis] on the fourth day of May in the Year of our Lord one thousand eight hundred and nine at the [District of St. Louis], was indebted to the said John in the sum of Five hundred and fifty nine dollars lawful money." (John Colter v. Edward Hempstead, Administrator, November, 1810, Case Number 35, Circuit Court Case Files, Office of the Circuit Clerk-St. Louis, Missouri State Archives-St. Louis, Office of the Secretary of State, accessed December 28, 2013, http://stlcourtrecords.wustl.edu; Lewis and Clark Papers, Missouri History Museum, St. Louis.)

Although the reference to May 4, 1809 is admittedly confusing, the document does not actually say that Colter and Lewis met or appeared in court that day. Moreover, no court record or any of Lewis's estate papers mention any such meeting. Most problematic are the statements by Dr. Thomas and James that Colter was already in the Hidatsa country when they arrived.

Therefore, the theory that Colter traveled down the river after the ice broke and then hurried back up the river ahead of Chouteau's armada is untenable.

4. Agreement for Return of the Mandan Chief, [February 24, 1809], Jackson, *Letters*, 2:446-50. Dr. Thomas wrote that the group left on May 17, 1809, with ten barges, or keelboats, and one hundred and sixty men. (Jackson, "Journey to the Mandans," 182.) James claimed there were thirteen keelboats and three hundred and fifty men and that they left in June. (James, *Three Years Among the Indians*, 3-4.) The number of men listed by Thomas is consistent with Lewis's instructions; James's total is therefore likely an exaggeration. James, however, was right about the departure date: a letter from Lewis to Chouteau shows that the group did not leave before June 8. (Meriwether Lewis to Pierre Chouteau, June 8, 1809, Jackson, *Letters*, 2:451–56.)

5. James, *Three Years Among the Indians*, 14. James signed his promissory note to Colter on October 7, 1809. (Colter-Frick, *Courageous Colter*, 98, 142.)

6. Alexis Doza, an independent trapper, had come up the Missouri in the same group and had signed a contract with the Missouri Fur Company in May of 1809 with the agreement that the company would "furnish him with five traps which will be in good condition & repaired at the expense of the said Society." (Noy, *Distant Horizon*, 44.) Robert Campbell, who trapped in the Rocky Mountains during the 1820s and 30s, wrote that "the trappers generally set out from camp with eight traps each." (Maguire, Wild, and Barclay, *A Rendezvous Reader*, 80.) George Ruxton, an Englishman who spent time with American trappers in 1847, wrote that they usually had "six traps, which are carried in a bag of leather called a trapsack." (Noy, *Distant Horizon*, 50.) See Russell, *Firearms, Traps, & Tools*, 128, for information on the transaction between Chouteau and Hunt and Hankinson.

7. As explained in chapter 11, there is good evidence that Colter's son, Hiram, was born by 1804. Chouteau and Lisa and their party, which included Toussaint Charbonneau, Sacagawea, and their son Baptiste, left around October 9 and arrived in St. Louis on November 20, only to learn that Meriwether Lewis had died of self-inflicted gunshot wounds on October 11. (*Missouri Gazette*, November 16, 1809, and November 23, 1809; see also Morris, *The Perilous West*, 45-46.)

8. Oglesby estimates there were close to eighty men in the group although James said there were thirty-two. (Oglesby, *Manual Lisa*, 93n71; James, *Three Years Among the Indians*, 22.)

9. See Morris, *Fate of the Corps*, 77–78, 149–50.

10. James, *Three Years Among the Indians*, 23–24.

11. James, *Three Years Among the Indians*, 23.

12. James, *Three Years Among the Indians*, 24–25. As noted, important information on the route is provided in Kelly, "The Dougherty Map," 156–57.

13. James, *Three Years Among the Indians*, 25.

14. James, *Three Years Among the Indians*, 25.

15. Pierre Menard to Pierre Chouteau, April 21, 1810, Montana Historical Society Research Center Archives, Helena.

16. James, *Three Years Among the Indians*, 34.

17. James, *Three Years Among the Indians*, 36.

18. Journal of Lieutenant James H. Bradley, March 26, 1876, cited in Hardee, "The Fort at the Forks," 102-3. See the complete article for more information. As Hardee points out, "While Bradley's information aids in pinpointing these particular log remains, as many questions are raised as answered." (Hardee, "The Fort at the Forks," 103.) David A. Miller offered another perspective when he wrote: "There is some disagreement as to where [the] old Fort Three Forks was located. The Fort was built in the matter of weeks by a contingent of twelve army soldiers, while the rest of the men, numbering thirty-two in all, trapped for beaver before the fur became unprimed. . . . Either the soldiers burned the Fort before they left or the Blackfeet put a torch to it shortly thereafter as it was burned to the ground that fall, after only a few months occupancy. The post was described as having been located about two miles above the confluence the Madison and Jefferson rivers between the two streams. It was apparently built closer to the Jefferson, as the shifting course of the Jefferson River was identified as having eaten away at the land on which the fort or post stood." (Miller, *Call of the Headwaters*, 34.)

19. James, *Three Years Among the Indians*, 37–38.

20. James, *Three Years Among the Indians*, 38.

21. James, *Three Years Among the Indians*, 39.

22. James, *Three Years Among the Indians*, 40.

23. James, *Three Years Among the Indians*, 41.

24. James, *Three Years Among the Indians*, 36.

25. Menard to Chouteau, April 21, 1810, 120.

26. James, *Three Years Among the Indians*, 35.

27. James, *Three Years Among the Indians*, 35.

28. Pierre Menard to his wife, Angelique, April 21, 1810, Abraham Lincoln Presidential Library and Museum, Springfield, Illinois.

29. Reuben Lewis to Meriwether Lewis, April 21, 1810, Missouri History Museum, St. Louis.

30. James, *Three Years Among the Indians*, 35–36. An interesting issue related to the fort at Three Forks is the statement from Lieutenant James H. Bradley (also discussed above), who visited the site of the fort in 1876, that "when Henry abandoned the fort, a blacksmith's anvil was left behind.") (Cited in Hanson, "Mystery of the Anvil," 133.) Some have also questioned if Lewis and Clark could have left the anvil behind when they were in the area in 1804. At the 2010 Fur Trade Conference held in Three Forks, however, James A. Hanson offered several factors indicating that the anvil could not date to either 1804 or 1809. (See Hanson, "Mystery of the Anvil.")

31. Drouillard continued to trap by himself, insisting he was "too much of an Indian to be caught by Indians." But one day James and several others found two Shawnee members of the trading party dead. "Further on, about one hundred and fifty yards, Druyer [Drouillard] and his horse lay dead, the former mangled in a horrible manner; his head was cut off, his entrails torn out and his body hacked to pieces. We saw from the marks on the ground that he must have fought in a circle on horseback, and probably killed some of his enemies, being a brave man, and well armed with a rifle, pistol, knife and tomahawk. We pursued the trail of the Indians till night, without overtaking them, and then returned, having buried our dead, with saddened hearts to Fort." (James, *Three Years Among the Indians*, 46. See also Morris, *Fate of the Corps*, 95.)

11. "HE RELUCTANTLY TOOK LEAVE OF US"

1. Bradbury, *Travels in the Interior*, 44-45n18. Bradbury likely got the figure of three thousand miles from Clark, who had calculated the distance from the mouth of the Missouri to Three Forks at 2953 miles. (Moulton, *Journals*, 8:392-3.) Clark, however, had reached the Yellowstone River from Three Forks by way of Bozeman Pass, and Colter's normal route (which took him into present Wyoming rather than across Bozeman Pass) would have increased the total by approximately one hundred miles.

2. See Colter-Frick, *Courageous Colter*, 155–57.

3. Foley, *Wilderness Journey*, 185–86.

4. Foley, *Wilderness Journey*, 188.

5. Colter-Frick, *Courageous Colter*, 112-14; Holmberg, Dear Brother, 236n6; Meriwether Lewis Papers, Missouri History Museum, St. Louis. Jacob and Joseph Philipson were both St. Louis businessmen. (Jackson, *Letters*, 2:729n1.) They were apparently related because Colter's debt to Jacob was paid to Joseph after Colter's death. (Colter's probate papers, Franklin County Probate Court, Union, Missouri.) Colter's land grant was for property on the west side of the Mississippi, and at the time he signed it over to Comegys, the area where Colter lived had not been surveyed and was thus not open to homesteading. It is therefore difficult to say what the grant would have been worth.

6. A summons had been served to Hempstead on September 3, 1810. See John Colter v. Edward Hempstead, Administrator, November 1810, Case Number 38, Circuit Court Case Files, Office of the Circuit Court Clerk, City of St. Louis, Missouri, accessed on 12/28/2013 at

http://stlcourtrecords.wustl.edu; Colter's receipt to Edward Hempstead, Jackson, *Letters*, 2:567; and the act compensating Lewis and Clark, Jackson, Letters, 2:377–78. Edward Hempstead (1780–1817) was the attorney general for Upper Louisiana at the time and was a friend of Clark's. In 1812 he was elected a delegate to Congress from the newly formed Missouri Territory. He died in St. Louis from injuries received when he was thrown from a horse. (Jones, *William Clark*, 208; Biographical Dictionary of the United States Congress, accessed on 12/28/2013 at http://bioguide.congress.gov/scripts/biodisplay.pl?index=H000472.)

7. Lewis Papers, Missouri History Museum.

8. William Clark to Jonathan Clark, January 31, 1811, Holmberg, *Dear Brother*, 254. Clark inserted the phrase "3 fires" into this text.

9. Jones, *William Clark*, 191, 92; Holmberg, *Dear Brother*, 255–56.

10. Jones, *William Clark*, 192.

11. Holmberg, *Dear Brother*, 256.

12. William Clark to Jonathan Clark, January 31, 1811, Holmberg, *Dear Brother*, 254; Jones, *William Clark*, 192.

13. Holmberg, *Dear Brother*, 256n2. William E. Foley points out Clark was a changed man by 1816. When newly elected territorial delegate John Scott was insulted in a derogatory handbill, he challenged the author, Charles Lucas, to a duel. "Governor Clark, perhaps remembering all too well the tragic duel that had taken the life of James Graham, proposed mediation as an alternative to bloodshed." Scott subsequently withdrew his challenge and bloodshed was indeed avoided. "Lucas, who afterward taunted Scott for withdrawing, foolishly got himself killed the following year on the field of honor following a similar election-day imbroglio." (Foley, *Wilderness Journey*, 211.)

14. Foley, *Wilderness Journey*, 190; Holmberg, *Dear Brother*, 256, citing the following sources: Colter-Frick, *Courageous Colter*, 472-75; Houck, *A History of Missouri*, 3:75–76; Billon, *Annals of St. Louis*, 81–82, 242–43; and *Louisiana Gazette*, January 2, 31, 1811. It is one of those interesting quirks of history that the man who killed Colter's attorney was the same man that saved George Shannon's life. When Ensign Nathaniel Pryor's party was attacked by Arikara Indians in 1807 as they attempted to return Sheheke and his family to their Mandan village, Lewis and Clark veteran George Shannon, who had been shot in the leg, was among the wounded. When the group finally reached Fort Bellefontaine, Dr. Bernard G. Farrar reported that he found Shannon's leg "in a state of gangrene caused by a ball having passed through it, and that to save his life I was under the necessity of amputating the limb above the knee, the loss of which constitutes in my opinion the first grade of disability." (William Clark to Henry Clay, September 11, 1816, Jackson, *Letters*, 2:620.)

15. Colter-Frick, *Courageous Colter*, 174-80. By the time papers were filed (in the St. Louis Court of Common Pleas in November of 1813) to settle Colter's estate, his widow had married a man by the name of James Brown. Hiram Colter married Margaret Davis, and they had at least nine children. Hiram died by 1845, survived by Margaret and the following children: John B., 17; James, 16; Absolam, 12; William, 10; Mary Ann, 9; Jefferson, 7; Joseph, 5; Nathan, 3; and Lucy Jane, 1. The 1870 Franklin County, Missouri, census record includes a John Colter, age 41. Other family records, however, make it clear that this was James Colter, Hiram's second son. (Perhaps his middle name was John.) The 1880 Gasconade County, Missouri, census record includes a John Colter, age 53 (Hiram's first son) and his son Hiram Colter, age 27. This Hiram had a 7-year-old son named John B. Colter, a great-great-grandson of the explorer. Colter's daughter, Evelina, married John Blize in 1830, and they had at least one child, a daughter named Sarah Blize (apparently named after her grandmother). Ruth Colter-Frick and Shirley Winkelhoch pointed out that this John Blize may have been related to the man (called *Bly* and *Blight*) who deserted from Lisa's 1809 expedition. "It is interesting that all these names are intertwined by place of residence, i.e., close neighbors, intermarriage and as witnesses etc." (*New Haven Leader*, June 22, 1988.) Most of Colter's grandchildren had several children themselves, so his descendants rapidly increased. Today, he has quite a number of known descendants. (Genealogical information from Colter-Frick, *Courageous Colter*, 174–80; the E. B. Trail papers, Western Historical Manuscripts Collection, University of Missouri, Columbia; the Giulvezan genealogical file, Missouri History Musem; and the Colter file, St. Charles, Missouri, Historical Society.)

16. A publication produced by the St. Louis Genealogical Society in 1985 claims that "John Colter, a veteran of the Lewis and Clark Expedition in 1804, set up a trading post on presumed bounty land at Bouef Creek and the Missouri River, then in the far reaches of St. Louis County." (St. Louis Genealogical Society, *St. Louis and St. Louis County Missouri Probate Records*, Vol. 1, 1804–1849, 1985, ii.) However, no record corroborating this claim has been found; nor did Bradbury mention such a post when he and other members of Hunt's party visit with Colter in March of 1811.

17. Boone's recent trapping excursion is mentioned in Bradbury, *Travels in the Interior*, 43. Given the proximity of the residences of Daniel Boone and John Colter and the latter's friendship with Nathan Boone, it is hard to believe that Boone and Colter did not become well acquainted. Speculation regarding their association, however, is based on circumstantial rather than direct evidence. Boone family genealogy records and the Ancestral File database both state that Nathan Boone had a son named John Colter Boone.(And, as mentioned above, Hiram Colter named one of his sons Nathan, possibly after Nathan Boone.) There is some confusion concerning John Boone's middle name. Nathan Boone's biographer lists it as Coburn. (See Hurt, *Nathan Boone and the American Frontier*, 218.) Some genealogical databases agree that John Boone's middle name was Coburn.

Another resident of the area was "the elusive and colorful Indian Phillips. Not a local resident by birth, he was representative of the Native Americans recently displaced from east of the Mississippi. His presence at La Charrette Village spanned as much as forty years as a visitor, a famous trapper, hunter, hunting guide, and local resident. In fact, he lived to see the initiation of present-day Marthasville. By 1805, he and his Osage wife lived on United State Survey 975 near the mouth of Little Boeuf Creek in Franklin Country, immediately across the Missouri from La Charrette. John Colter his friend and America's first mountain man of the west lived nearby. (Lowell M. Schake, *La Charrette: Village Gateway to the American West* [New York: iUniverse, 2003], 36.

"Most considered Phillips 'a dirty fellow– of no account and only fit for the woods as servant or campkeeper' [which] no doubt explains why 85-year old Boone hired him in 1816 to assist on one of his last extended hunting ventures. . . . Can you imagine the topics discussed when Charles 'Indian' Phillips, Daniel Boone, his black slave Derry and America's First Mountain Man John Colter sat about a campfire telling tales? Chewing a plug of tobacco . . . spitting, now and again. Such was the mix of cultures fueling the intellect at La Charrette." (Schake, La Charrette Village website, accessed at http://lacharrettevillage.blogspot.com/2005/07/indian-phillips-shawnee-at-la.html on January 12, 2014.

18. *Louisiana Gazette*, March 14, 1811.

19. Ronda, *Astoria and Empire*, 39.

20. Irving, *Astoria*, 36n41 (text written by Edgeley W. Todd, editor of the volume).

21. Bradbury, *Travels in the Interior*, 43.

22. Bradbury, *Travels in the Interior*, 44. Daniel Boone lived on the north side of the Missouri, near present Marthasville, Warren County, Missouri. The site of the French village La Charette, mentioned by both Bradbury and Lewis and Clark, is now covered by mud and part of the bottom land in Warren County. Colter lived in present Franklin County, Missouri, on the south side of the Missouri, east of present New Haven. (See Moulton, *Journals*, 8:368n3.)

23. Bradbury, *Travels in the Interior*, 44–45.

24. Irving, *Astoria*, 147; Harris, *John Colter*, 159.

25. Bradbury, *Travels in the Interior*, 45–46.

26. Harris, *John Colter*, 193, 157.

27. E. B. Trail, "Bits of Franklin County History: Giving the Life and Adventures of John Colter," *Washington Citizen*, March 16, 1928.

28. Brackenridge, *Journal of a Voyage*, 19.

29. Ralph Gregory, "Charette Village, St. John's Have Their Place in History," *Washington Missourian*, March 11, 1992. Section 42, Chapter 39 of the Territorial Laws of Louisiana for 1807 reads in part as follows: "Every judge of probate granting letters testamentary or of administration, shall nominate three respectable householders of the neighborhood of the deceased, as appraisers, who being sworn or affirmed before the judge probate, or any justice of

the peace for that purpose, shall truly and justly to the best of their judgment, view and appraise all the slaves, and all the personal estate to them produced."

30. Mrs. Charles Maupin to Ralph Gregory, March 20, 1972, copy in Ron Anglin's possession; Ron Anglin interview with Kurt D. Humphrey (a direct descendant of John Sullens) 2009. For more information on the inter-relationships of the Sullens, Bailey, Humphrey, and Maupin families, see Anna B. Sartori, *Among My Pioneer Ancestors* (St. Louis: Missouri Historical Society, 1942) and Kurt Douglas Humphrey, *The Father Side of Kasha Lucinda Humphrey*, Washington, MO: K. D. Humphrey, 1993).

31. Bradbury, *Travels in the Interior*, 46–47.

32. *Louisiana Gazette*, April 11, 1811.

33. Brackenridge, *Journal of a Voyage*, 10. Although he did not mention her name, Brackenridge left one of the most memorable descriptions of Sacagawea when he called her "a good creature, of a mild and gentle disposition, greatly attached to the whites, whose manners and dress she tries to imitate, but she had become sickly, and longed to revisit her native country; her husband, also, who had spent many years among the Indians, had become weary of civilized life." (Brackenridge, *Journal of a Voyage*, 10.)

34. Brackenridge, *Journal of a Voyage*, 8.

35. Brackenridge, *Journal of a Voyage*, 9.

36. Ronda, *Astoria and Empire*, 142.

37. Brackenridge, *Journal of a Voyage*, 19.

38. *Louisiana Gazette*, April 18, 1811.

39. Although Brackenridge did not say explicitly that he interviewed Colter around March 8, 1811, the publication of the details ten days later makes it certain that Brackenridge saw him at that time or sooner, and there is no evidence that Brackenridge had the opportunity to talk to Colter at any other time.

40. Thomas James v. St. Louis Missouri Fur Company, November 1810, Case Number 62 and St. Louis Missouri Fur Company v. Thomas James, November 1810, Case Number 38, Circuit Court Case Files, Office of the Circuit Clerk, City of St. Louis, Missouri, accessed on 12/31/2013 at http://stlcourtrecords.wustl.edu/.

41. James, *Three Years Among the Indians*, 55.

42. John Colter's receipt to Edward Hempstead, May 28, 1811, Jackson, *Letters*, 2:567.

12. "AS FINE A BODY OF HARDY WOODSMEN AS EVER TOOK THE FIELD"

1. William Clark to the War Department, September 12, 1810, U. S. War Department, Extracts of Letters about Indian Affairs, 1807-1811, Ohio State Historical Society, Columbus.

2. *Louisiana Gazette*, July 4, 1811, cited in Gregg, "The War of 1812," 10.

3. Capt. Horatio Stark to Col. Daniel Bissell, January 6, 1812, *Territorial Papers*, 14:506, cited in Jones, *William Clark*, 204.

4. Gregg, "War of 1812," 11; William Clark to the Secretary of War, February 13, 1812, *Territorial Papers*, 8:161, cited in Jones, *William Clark*, 204.

5. Governor Howard to the Secretary of War, March 19, 1812, *Territorial Papers*, 14:531-32. Regarding the slaughter of the nine members of the O'Neal family, one witness of the carnage wrote, "The youngest child, about one year old, was thrown alive into a large oven and baked." (Walter Williams, *History of Northeast Missouri*, 513.)

6. Boone Manuscript Collection, Vol. 15, 1782-1815, No. 82, Wisconsin Historical Society, Madison. Documents in the National Archives, the William Henry Collection at the Indiana Historical Society, and *Territorial Papers* (vol. 14, p. 567) discuss the pay roll of Captain Boone's company both during and after Colter's enlistment, but no mention has been found of Colter's pay being made to his widow or anyone else.

7. Hurt, *Nathan Boone*, 86–87.

8. Gregg, "War of 1812," 12.

9. *Louisiana Gazette*, March 21, 1812, cited in Gregg, "War of 1812," 14, and Hurt, *Nathan Boone*, 87.

10. McAfee, *History of the Late War*, 320.

11. Hurt, *Nathan Boone*, 87.

12. *Louisiana Gazette*, May 9, 1812, cited in Hurt, *Nathan Boone*, 89.

13. *Louisiana Gazette*, July 11, 1812, cited in Gregg, "War of 1812," 15.

14. Muster Roll and Company Pay Roll, Captain Nathan Boone's Company of U.S. Mounted Rangers, War of 1812, National Archives. See Colter-Frick, *Courageous Colter*, 137-38, for reprints of these documents.

15. James, *Three Years Among the Indians*, 36.

16. See Morris, *Fate of the Corps*, 191–99.

17. Colter's probate papers, Franklin County Probate Court, Union, Missouri; Harris, *John Colter*, 163.

18. Colter-Frick, *Courageous Colter*, 170. As Colter-Frick points out, the surviving estate papers and totals listed therein make it impossible to trace the amounts received and paid out over the years and reach a sum anywhere near the total of $121.11. (*Courageous Colter*, 148–73.) Interestingly, Colter's estate was settled in a courthouse in the newly formed county seat of Franklin County, Missouri, on land where his cabin likely stood.

19. Chittenden, *The American Fur Trade*, 2:712.

20. Eva Emery Dye to Dr. Hosmer, April 4, 1904. "Yes," Dye wrote, "Coalter died at Charrette, married a squaw there and lived near Daniel Boone." (Dye Collection [Mss 1089, Box F 45], Oregon Historical Society.) As late as 2003, Lowell M. Schake wrote that "Colter died of jaundice two years later at Charrette, Missouri." (La Charrette: Village Gateway to the American West [Lincoln, Nebraska: Universe, Inc., 2003], 137.) La Charette was located approximately sixty miles beyond St. Louis on the north banks of the Missouri River, across the river from the community of St. John's. It existed for approximately thirty years. During the short life of the village it played a vital role in shaping the American West. Located in a transition zone between the frontier and the more civilized east, it was a melting pot where French, English, Whites, Blacks, Indians, and later German immigrants interacted. Daniel Boone and his family had moved to the area in 1799. After it ceased to exist, a new community called Marthasville developed in a narrow valley immediately to the north of where La Charette once stood. Today Marthasville is recognized as the oldest town of continual habitation in Warren County, Missouri.

21. *Washington Citizen*, May 21, 1926. Although Colter's military record lists the dates of his discharge and death, it says nothing about his burial. One contemporary account shows how a burial was handled by the rangers during this period. In July 1813, Captain David Musick's Company of United States Rangers had a skirmish with a party of Winnebago Indians near Fort Mason on the Mississippi in which a soldier named John M. Duff was fatally wounded; a few days later he was buried with military honors in St. Louis. (Louis Howard Conrad, *Encyclopedia of the History of Missouri* [1901], 1:384.) Colter's burial was less likely to find its way into the official record because he was discharged before his death and because he was not wounded in action. If he were buried near Fort Mason, the related military record has been lost.

22. Julius Kleimann, "A Steam Shovel Digs Up Old John Colter," *Sunday Magazine–St. Louis Post-Dispatch*, June 27, 1926. Courtesy of Western Historical Manuscript Collection, University of Missouri, Columbia.

23. E. B. Trail Papers, Western Historical Manuscript Collection, University of Missouri, Columbia. Although Sam Coulter cited Jacob Krattli as his source, Krattli seems to have had two opinions on the matter and reportedly told his son that he thought there were only four or five graves on the hill and that they all belonged to riders atop box cars killed when the trains entered the tunnel. (There was very little room between the top of a train car and the ceiling of the tunnel, and any riders sitting on top of a car and unaware of the upcoming tunnel could have been killed.) (Jim Miller to Ralph Gregory, March 10, 1972, copy in Ron Anglin's possession.)

24. E. B. Trail, "The Life and Adventures of John Colter," *Old Travois Trails*, Vol. 2 No. 5, January and February, 1942, 20.

25. Mrs. Charles Maupin to Ralph Gregory, March 20, 1972, bracketed explanation added, copy in Ron Anglin's possession.

26. Harris, John Colter, 162-63.

27. Ron Anglin visited Tunnel Hill in 2003 and found evidence that a cemetery had indeed been there at one time. He wrote: "I made a measurement from the high point to the approximate location of Colter's cabin at New Port (using Garmin Global Position System [GPS] map 76S receiver). The distance was approximately one mile. The only thing I found unusual on Tunnel Hill was some yucca plants. I asked Marc Houseman, Director of the Washington, Missouri, Historical Society Museum, if there was any significance about the yucca plants, since they are not native to Missouri. He told me at the time, 'I don't have any specific information on yucca plants as they relate to graveyards, other than the tradition of the nineteenth century to plant the nonnative plants in cemeteries. The old timers called them "century plants" since they virtually last forever. The fact that they stay green year round was looked upon as symbolic of eternal life–"forever green!" It's the same with cedar trees and periwinkle, myrtle or vinca; all are green year round and found in many early Missouri cemeteries. Also, the yucca blooms once annually so it's a way of "decorating" the grave with flowers without visiting the cemetery.'"

28. Ralph Gregory, "A Paper on the Life of John Colter in Franklin County, Missouri," 1972, unpublished, copy in Ron Anglin's possession. Heather Shawver, the graduate student who examined the skull, reported: "The skull is complete and intact, except for a few anterior teeth, which were lost postmortem. The skull has not been cut, which means that this not an anatomy specimen. It was either dug out of the ground from an archaeological or historic site, or it was never buried. There is no evidence of surface weathering or bleaching, so it is unlikely that the skull lay on the ground exposed. The lack of insect or carnivorous activity indicates that the individual was sheltered, either in a sturdy coffin or in (for example) a basement. The entire skull has been covered in some sort of glue or varnish, which was a common preservation technique in the past. The skull is of a man . . considered to be a Caucasian. He has a high forehead and very little prognathism. His nose is narrow and tall, with a deviated septum. His chin is square and projecting, and his palate is narrow, with fairly crowded teeth. He has a few traits that are considered Native American, such as shovel-shaped incisors and curved, "Tented" nasals. However, his teeth are barely worn for his age, indicating a Western diet . . . Aging is again difficult, perhaps even more so for this individual. Almost all of his sutures are fused, indicative of advanced age. However, his teeth show wear more suggestive of someone in their thirties or forties . . . Therefore, all we can say about this individual is that he was a white male (with some Native American traits) who died of unknown causes sometime during mid-life, sometime in the (not particularly recent) past." (Shawyer, "A Tale of Two Crania [Inherited Skulls with No Provenance]," December 26, 2003, unpublished, copy in Ron Anglin's possession.)

29. Raymond W. Thorp, "Colter's Bones," *Old West* magazine, Summer 1966.

30. One of the variations, included as a "follow-up" to a 1913 account of Colter's Run written by Edwin Sheldon, read as follows: "In 1812 the United States declared war on Great Britain, and Colter enlisted. Fighting under Nathan Boone, he died while in the service of his country. However, after such an eventful life, he died, not by the hand of the British soldiers or the many Indians he encountered in his travels, but by jaundice. After his death, his remains were shipped back to Missouri to his wife. However, Sallie was unable to provide a proper burial. Leaving him lying in state in their cabin, she moved into her brother's home. Amazingly, John Colter's body continued to lie in the cabin for the next 114 years, the house slowly falling to ruins around him. In 1926, the land on which the cabin once sat was being cleared and during the process his bones, as well as a leather pouch portraying his name, was found. Afterwards, his remains were gathered and buried on a bluff in New Haven that overlooks the Missouri River." (Posted on the "Legends of America" website in 2009, http://www.legendsofamerica.com/ne-johncolter.html, accessed on 1/5/2014.)

31. Clarke, *Men of the Expedition*, 47.

32. Ralph Gregory to Charles G. Clarke, January 8, 1972, copy in Ron Anglin's possession.

33. Charles G. Clarke to Ralph Gergory, January 15, 1972, copy in Ron Anglin's possession.

34. Margaret Wherry, Historical Sketch of the Old Fee Fee Baptist Church, 5; n. d. Larry Morris visited the St. Charles Historical Society in 2005 and an archivist reported that no records related to Colter's burial could be found.

35. Colter-Frick, *Courageous Colter*, 210-12.

36. Kurt Humphrey signed the following statement now in Ron Anglin's possession: "To Whom It May Concern: I can attest to and do solemnly swear before almighty God & to my ancestors spirits that John Colter of the Lewis & Clark Expedition of the Missouri River in 1804 is buried here in our family cemetery (TWP 44 N Range 2 West). He is buried in the SE section of said cemetery burial plot # 34 on map that I gave copy to county assessor office in 1990 here in Franklin, County, MO. I listed him as unknown for same reason I left the Indian Mound that joins the West end of said cemetery. For it had been a family secret as my family had and still is John Colter's burial guardians. One can note that other cemetery plot maps I gave to County I showed their Indian mounds. I now speak up for I believe every one has a right to know where their fore father's and fore mothers are at on this earth. I have nothing to gain or lose in making this info public on this 23rd day of October 2009 Sincerely Kurt D. Humphrey"

37. Neihardt, *The River and I*, 8.

38. Ambrose, *Undaunted Courage*, 141.

39. Neihardt, *The River and I*, 8.

40. Coues, *History of the Expedition*, 1:79.

41. Neihardt, *The River and I*, 8.

42. Ronda, *Among the Indians*, 27, 23; Clark's journal entry, November 1, 1804, Moulton, *Journals*, 3:225.

43. 25. Neihardt, *The River and I*, 8.

44. Neihardt, *The River and I*, 8.

EPILOGUE

1. Walker, "The Mountain Man as Literary Hero," 16.

2. Phillips, *The Fur Trade*, 264; *Literary History of the American West*, 79.

3. Ken Kamper to Ron Anglin, March 8, 2010 (email), copy in Ron Anglin's files.

4. Clark's journal entry, August 15, 1806, Moulton, *Journals*, 8:302.

5. Todd, "John Colter, Mountain Man," 90.

APPENDIX C

1. William Clark's signature at Pompeys Pillar in Wyoming is a good example of a piece of frontier graffiti that can be verified because Clark recorded making the signature in his journal and also because the signature is still in the same location, which he also identified. See the website, http://en.wikipedia.org/wiki/Pompeys_Pillar_National_Monument, accessed on January 13, 2014.

2. Stallo Vinton, *John Colter*, 61–62.

3. Box 19, File H18 Biographical Data and Accounts 1954–1962, Yellowstone National Park Archives.

4. F. M. Fryxell to Arne B. Cammerer, May 8, 1934, Yellowstone National Park Archives.

5. Mattes, October 16, 1957 (H2215), Yellowstone National Park Archives.

6. See the J. Neilson Barry files in the Yellowstone National Park Archives for a long series of letters back and forth between the National Park Service and Mr. Barry concerning the authenticity of the Colter Stone

7. United States Department of the Interior National Park Service, Chicago Illinois Memorandum for the Director, March 18, 1947: "Possibly this new book, Teton Mountains, by Dr.

Nolie Mumey, has already come to your attention. . . . Over the past weekend I read it. . . . Dr. Mumey has provided a very useful account of the more recent history of the Teton region. Unfortunately, his chapters on early history are marred by numerous small but rather noticeable errors. (The review is three pages in length and marked "Chief Naturalist," Carl Parcher Russell Papers, 1920–1967, Washington State University.)

8. J. William Barrett II to Merrill J. Mattes, April 14, 1979, copy in Ron Anglin's possession.

9. Willard E. Dilley to Don Holm, October 15, 1968, Colter Stone files, Grand Teton National Park, Moose, Wyoming.

10. Colter Stone files, Grand Teton National Park, Moose, Wyoming.

11. Colter-Frick, *Courageous Colter*, 51–52; see also "Forty-Four Years with John Colter: The Colter Stone," *Yellowstone Newspaper,* May 11, 1998, Volume 2, Number 51.

12. Hardee, *Pierre's Hole*, 65–66.

13. Memorandum to Director, Midwest Region, from Manager, Historic Preservation, Denver Service Center, Subject: Colter Stone, Grand Teton NP 7/11/72, Colter Stone files, Grand Teton National Park, Moose, Wyoming.

14. Jeannie Cook, *Buffalo Bill's Town,* 22.

15. Ron Anglin to John Sjostrom October 13, 2008, copy in Ron Anglin's possession.

16. Haecker and Wegman-French, "Manuel Lisa's Fort," 49.

Sources Cited

MANUSCRIPT COLLECTIONS

Abraham Lincoln Presidential Library and Museum, Springfield
Pierre Menard Collection

Bancroft Library, University of California at Berkeley
W. J. Ghent Papers

Boise State University, Albertson's Library
J. Neilson Barry Collection

Huntington Library
Unpublished Colter biography by William Ghent

Indiana University–Purdue University Indianapolis, Ruth Lilly Special Collections and
   Archives
Organization of American Historians Records, 1906–2003,

Missouri History Museum, St. Louis
William Clark Papers
Meriwether Lewis Papers (which includes Colter documents)
Lisa Papers
St. Louis Circuit Court Papers
St. Louis Missouri Fur Company Record Book, 1809–1812

Missouri State Archives, Jefferson City

Montana Historical Society Research Center Archives, Helena

Ohio Historical Society, Columbus
U.S. War Department, Extracts of Letters about Indian Affairs, 1807–1811

Oregon Historical Society
Dye Collection

National Archives
General Land Office Records
Letters Received by the Secretary of War Relating to Indian Affairs, 1800–1816
Veterans Records
War Department Records

State Historical Society of Wisconsin, Madison
Draper Manuscripts
Dye Collection

University of Wyoming
American Heritage Center

Western Historical Manuscript Collection, Columbia, Missouri
Barry Papers
Thomas Smith Letterbook
Trail Collection

In Ronald M. Anglin's Possession: papers of J. William Barrett II, Charles G. Clarke, Frank
     Dickson, and Don Holmes

Yellowstone National Park Archives

MISSOURI PUBLIC RECORDS

Franklin County Probate Records, Union

FEDERAL PUBLIC RECORDS

Bureau of the Census, "Population Schedules of the United States," 1790–1870. National
     Archives and Records Service, Washington, D.C.

DISSERTATIONS

Knopf, Richard Clark. *Anthony Wayne and the Founding of the United States Army.* Ohio State
     University, 1960.

NEWSPAPERS

Louisiana Gazette, St. Louis
New Haven Leader, New Haven
Pittsburgh Gazette, Pittsburgh
St. Louis Post-Dispatch, St. Louis

Washington Citizen, Washington
Washington Missourian, Washington

PUBLISHED PRIMARY AND SECONDARY SOURCES

Abel, Annie Heloise. *Tabeau's Narrative of Loisel's Expedition to the Upper Missouri*. Norman: University of Oklahoma Press, 1939.

Allen, John L. "The Forgotten Explorers." In Hardee, *Selected Papers*, 26–39.

———. *Passage Through the Garden: Lewis and Clark and the Image of the American Northwest*. Urbana: University of Illinois Press, 1975.

Ambrose, Stephen E. *Undaunted Courage: Meriwether Lewis, Thomas Jefferson, and the Opening of the American West*. New York: Simon and Schuster, 1996.

American State Papers. 38 vols. Washington, D.C.: Gales & Seaton, 1834.

Bagley, Jerry. *The First Known Man in Yellowstone*. Rigby, Idaho: Old Faithful Eye-Witness Publishing, 2000.

Betts, Robert B. *In Search of York: The Slave Who Went to the Pacific with Lewis and Clark*. University Press of Colorado, 1985, 2000.

Billon, Frederick L. *Annals of St. Louis in Its Territorial Days from 1804 to 1821*. St. Louis: Privately printed, 1888.

Brackenridge, Henry M. *Views of Louisiana: Containing Geographical, Statistical and Historical Notices of That Vast and Important Portion of America*. Baltimore: Schaeffer & Maund, 1817.

Bradbury, *John. Travels in the Interior of America*. Thwaites, *Western Travels*, volume 5.

Brown, Sheri Barlett. *Eva Emery Dye: Romance with the West*. Corvallis: Oregon State University Press, 2004.

Buchanan, James. *Sketches of the history, manners, and customs of the North American Indians with a plan for their melioration*. New York. Borradaile, 1824.

Buckley, Jay A. *William Clark: Indian Diplomat*. Norman: University of Oklahoma Press, 2008.

Calloway, Colin G. *One Vast Winter Count*. Lincoln: University of Nebraska Press, 2003.

Carter, Clarence E., comp. and ed. *The Territorial Papers of the United States*, 25 vols. Washington, Government Printing Office, 1943–1960.

Cartwright, Peter. *The Backwoods Preacher: Being the Autobiography of Peter Cartwright, the Oldest American Methodist Traveling Preacher*. London: Daldy, Isbister & Co., 1878.

Chittenden, Hiram M. *The American Fur Trade of the Far West*. 2 vols. New York: The Press of the Pioneers, 1935. Reprint, Lincoln: University of Nebraska Press, 1986.

———. *The Yellowstone National Park*. Cincinnati: R. Clarke Co., 1895.

Clarke, Charles G. *Men of the Lewis and Clark Expedition*. Glendale, CA: Arthur H. Clark Co., 1970. Reprint, Lincoln: University of Nebraska Press, 2002.

———. "A Roster of the Lewis and Clark Expedition." *Daughters of the American Revolution Magazine* (November 1965): 878–82, 921.

Cohen, Paul E. *Mapping the West: America's Westward Movement, 1524–1890*. New York: Rizzoli, 2002.

Colter-Frick, Ruth. *Courageous Colter and Companions*. Washington, MO: Privately printed, 1997.

Cook, Jeannie. *Buffalo Bill's Town in the Rockies: a Pictorial History of Cody, Wyoming*. Virginia Beach, VA: Donning Co., 1996.

Coues, Elliott, ed. *The History of the Expedition under the Command of Lewis and Clark*. 1893. Reprint. 3 vols. New York: Dover Publications, 1965.

Cutright, Paul Russell. *A History of the Lewis and Clark Journals*. Norman: University of Oklahoma Press, 1976.

Danker, Donald F., ed. "The Wounded Knee Interviews of Eli S. Ricker." *Nebraska History* 62 (1981): 151–243.

Dickson, Frank H. "Hard on the Heels of Lewis and Clark." *Montana* 26 (January 1976): 14–25.

228 Sources Cited

────. "Joseph Dickson." In Hafen, *Mountain Men*, 3:71–79.

Dillon, Richard. *Meriwether Lewis: A Biography*. Santa Cruz, CA: Western Tanager Press, 1965, 1988.

Doddridge, Joseph. *Notes, on the Settlement and the Indian Wars, of the Western Parts of Virginia & Pennsylvania*. Wellsburgh, VA: By the author, 1824.

Douglas, Walter B. *Manuel Lisa*. New York: Argosy-Antiquarian Ltd., 1964.

Dye, Eva Emery. *The Conquest: the True Story of Lewis and Clark*. Chicago: McClurg, 1903.

Faragher, John Mack. *Daniel Boone: The Life and Legend of an American Pioneer*. New York: Henry Holt and Company, 1992.

Fischer, David Hackett. *Albion's Seed: Four British Folkways in America*. New York: Oxford University Press, 1989.

Foley, William E. *Wilderness Journey: The Life of William Clark*. Columbia: University of Missouri Press, 2004.

Ghent, William. "Sketch of John Colter." *Annals of Wyoming* 10 (July 1938): 111–16.

Greene, Candace S. and Russell Thornton. *The Year the Stars Fell: Lakota Winter Counts at the Smithsonian*. Lincoln: University of Nebraska Press, 2007.

Gregg, Kate L. "The War of 1812 on the Missouri Frontier." *Missouri Historical Review* 33 (1938): 3–22, 184–202, 326–48.

Gregory, Ralph. "Charrette Village, St. John's Have Their Place in History." *Washington [Missouri] Historical Society Newsletter* 9 (2002).

Hafen, LeRoy R., ed. *The Mountain Men and the Fur Trade of the Far West,* 10 vols. Glendale, CA: A. H. Clark Co., 1965–1972.

Haines, Aubrey L., ed. *Osborne Russell's Journal of a Trapper* [1834–1843]. Reprint, Lincoln: University of Nebraska Press, 1965.

Hanson, James A. "The Mystery of the Three Forks Anvil." In Hardee, *Selected Papers*, 133–39.

Hardee, Jim. "The Fort at the Forks: 'A Good State of Defense.'" In Hardee, *Selected Papers*, 98–111.

────, ed. *Selected Papers of the 2010 Fur Trade Symposium at the Three Forks*. Three Forks, MT: Three Forks Historical Society, 2011, 98–111.

────. *Pierre's Hole! The Fur Trade History of Teton Valley, Idaho*. Pinedale, WY: Sublette County Historical Society, 2010.

Harris, Burton. *John Colter: His Years in the Rocky Mountains*. New York: Scribner, 1952. Reprint, Lincoln: University of Nebraska Press, 1993.

Hartley, Alan H. *Lexicon of Discovery*. Pullman: Washington State University Press, 2004.

Hartley, Cecil B. *Life and Adventures of Lewis Wetzel*. Philadelphia: G. G. Evans, 1860.

Hassrick, Royal B. *The Sioux: Life and Customs of a Warrior Society*. Norman: University of Oklahoma Press, 1964.

Heidenreich, C. Adrian. *Smoke Signals in Crow (Apsáalooke) Country: Beyond the Capture of Horses from the Lewis and Clark Expedition*. Billings, MT: By the Author, 2006.

Holmberg, James J. *Dear Brother: Letters of William Clark to Jonathan Clark*. New Haven: Yale University Press, 2002.

Holmes, Reuben. "The Five Scalps." *Missouri Historical Society Glimpses of the Past*, 5 (January–March 1938): 19–22.

Houck, Louis. *A History of Missouri from the Earliest Explorations and Settlements until the Admission of the State into the Union*. 3 vols. Chicago: R. R. Donnelley, 1908.

Hurt, R. Douglas. *Nathan Boone and the American Frontier*. Columbia: University of Missouri Press, 1998.

Irving, Washington. *Astoria, or Anecdotes of an Enterprise Beyond the Rocky Mountains*. Ed. Edgeley Todd. Norman: University of Oklahoma Press, 1964.

Jackson, Donald. "Journey to the Mandans, 1809; the Lost Narrative of Dr. Thomas." *Bulletin of the Missouri Historical Society* 20 (April 1964): 179–92.

────, ed. *Letters of the Lewis and Clark Expedition with Related Documents*. 2 vols. Urbana: University of Illinois Press, 1963. Reprint, 1978.

James, Gen. Thomas. *Three Years Among the Indians and Mexicans*. The 1846 edition, reprinted unabridged, introduction by A. P. Nasatir. Philadelphia: J. B. Lippincott Company, 1962.

———. *Three Years Among the Indians and Mexicans*. Edited by Walter B. Douglas. St. Louis, 1916. Reprint, edited with an introduction by Milo Milton Quaife. New York: The Citadel Press, 1966.

Jenkinson, Clay S. *A Vast and Open Plain: The Writings of the Lewis and Clark Expedition in North Dakota, 1804–1806*. Bismark: State Historical Society of North Dakota, 2003.

Jensen, Richard E. "Big Foot's Followers at Wounded Knee." *Nebraska History* 71 (1990): 194–212.

Jones, Landon Y. *William Clark and the Shaping of the West*. New York: Hill and Wang, 2004.

Kelly, Mark W. "The Evacuation of the Three Forks—per the Doughterty Map." In Hardee, *Selected Papers*, 149–82.

Kercheval, Samuel. *A History of the Valley of Virginia*. Woodstock, VA: J. Gatewood, 1850.

Kleimann, Julius. "A Steam Shovel Digs Up Old John Colter." *St. Louis Post-Dispatch*, June 27, 1926.

Kubik, Barbara. "John Colter: One of Lewis and Clark's Men." *We Proceeded On* 9 (May–June 1983): 10–14.

Lamar, Howard R., ed. *The New Encyclopedia of the American West*. New Haven: Yale University Press, 1998.

Large, Arlen J. "Expedition Specialists: The Talented Helpers of Lewis and Clark," *We Proceeded On* 20 (February 1994): 4–10.

Lavender, David S. *The Rockies*. New York: Harper & Row, 1968.

———. *The Westward Vision: The Story of the Oregon Trail*. New York: McGraw-Hill, 1963.

Loendorf, Lawrence L. and Nancy Medaris Stone. *Mountain Spirit*. University of Utah Press, 2006.

Lofaro, Michael A. *Daniel Boone: An American Life*. Lexington: The University Press of Kentucky, 2003.

Lowie, Robert H. *The Crow Indians*. New York: Farrar and Rinehart, 1935. Reprint, Lincoln: University of Nebraska Press, 2004.

Maguire, James H. and Peter Wild and Donald A. Barclay. *A Rendezvous Reader: Tall, Tangled, and True Tales of the Mountain Men, 1805–1850*. Salt Lake City: University of Utah Press, 1997.

Marshall, Joseph M. III. *The Day the World Ended at Little Bighorn: A Lakota History*. New York: Penguin Books, 2008.

Marshall, Thomas Maitland, ed. *The Life and Papers of Frederick Bates*. St. Louis: Missouri Historical Society, 1926.

Mattes, Merril J. "Behind the Legend of Colter's Hell: The Early Exploration of Yellowstone Park," *Mississippi Valley Historical Review* 36 (September, 1949): 251–82.

McAfee, Robert B. *History of the Late War in the Western County*. Bowling Green, OH: Historical Publications Company, 1919. (Originally published in 1816.)

Michigan Historical Collections 8 (1885).

Miller, David A. *Call of the Headwaters*. Kearny, Nebraska: Morris Publishing, 1988.

Morgan, Dale. *Jedediah Smith and the Opening of the West*. Bobbs-Merrill, 1953. Reprint, Lincoln: University of Nebraska Press, 1964.

Morris, Larry E. *The Fate of the Corps: What Became of the Lewis and Clark Explorers After the Expedition*. New Haven: Yale University Press, 2004.

———. "The Life of John Colter. *We Proceeded On* 34 (November 2008): 6–15.

———. "The Mysterious Charles Courtin and the Early Missouri Fur Trade." *Missouri Historical Review* 104 (October 2009): 21–39.

———. *The Perilous West: Seven Amazing Explorers and the Founding of the Oregon Trail*. Lanham: Rowman and Littlefield Publishers, 2013.

Moulton, Gary, ed. *The Journals of the Lewis and Clark Expedition*. 13 vols. Lincoln: University of Nebraska Press, 1986–1997.

Neihardt, John C. *The River and I*. New York: Macmillan and Company. 1927.

Noy, Gary. *Distant Horizon: Documents from the Nineteenth-Century American West*. Lincoln: University of Nebraska Press, 1999.

Oglesby, Richard E. "Manuel Lisa." In Hafen, *Mountain Men*, 5:179–201.

———. *Manuel Lisa and the Opening of the Missouri Fur Trade*. Norman: University of Oklahoma Press, 1963.

———. "Pierre Menard." In Hafen, *Mountain Men*, 6:307–18.

———. "William Morrison." In Hafen, *Mountain Men*, 3:197–203.

Ostler, Jeffrey. *The Plains Sioux and U.S. Colonialism from Lewis and Clark to Wounded Knee*. New York: Cambridge University Press, 2004.

Phillips, Paul C. *The Fur Trade*. Norman: University of Oklahoma Press, 1961.

Potter, Tracy. *Sheheke, Mandan Indian Diplomat: The Story of White Coyote, Thomas Jefferson, and Lewis and Clark*. Helena, MT: Farcountry Press and Fort Mandan Press, 2003.

Prucha, Francis Paul, ed. *Documents of United States Indian Policy*. Lincoln: University of Nebraska Press, 1975.

Rollins, Philip Ashton, ed. *The Discovery of the Oregon Trail*. New York: Charles Scribner's Sons, 1935.

Ronda, James P. *Astoria and Empire*. Lincoln: University of Nebraska Press, 1990.

———. *Lewis and Clark among the Indians*. Lincoln: University of Nebraska Press, 1984

Russell, Carl P. *Firearms, Traps, and Tools of the Mountain Men*. New York: Knopf, 1967.

The Salish Pend d'Oreille Culture Committee and Elders Cultural Advisory Council, Confederated Salish and Kootenai Tribes. *The Salish People and the Lewis and Clark Expedition*. Lincoln: University of Nebraska Press, 2005.

Schake, Lowell M. *La Charrette: Village Gateway to the American West*. New York: iUniverse, 2003.

Skarsten. M. O. *George Drouillard, Hunter and Interpreter for Lewis and Clark*. Glendale, CA: Arthur H. Clark Co., 1964. Reprint, Lincoln: University of Nebraska Press, 2005.

Thwaites, Reuben Gold, ed. *Early Western Travels, 1748–1846*. 32 vols. Cleveland, OH: A. H. Clark, 1904–1907.

Todd, Edgeley W. "John Colter, Mountain Man." *The Colorado Quarterly* 2 (Summer 1953): 79–91.

Tubbs, Stephanie Ambrose and Clay S. Jenkinson. *The Lewis and Clark Companion: An Encyclopedic Guide to the Voyage of Discovery*. New York: Owl Books, 2003.

Utley, Robert M. *The Last Days of the Sioux Nation*. New Haven: Yale University Press, 1963.

Vaughn, Robert. *Then and Now, or Thirty-Six Years in the Rockies*. Minneapolis: Tribune Printing Company, 1900.

Vinton, Stallo. *John Colter, Discoverer of Yellowstone Park*. New York: E. Eberstadt, 1926.

Wheeler, Olin D. *The Trail of Lewis and Clark, 1804–1094*. New York: G. P. Putnam's Sons, 1904.

———. *Wonderland 1900*.

Wishart, David J., ed. *Encyclopedia of the Great Plains*. Lincoln: University of Nebraska Press, 2004.

———, ed. *Encyclopedia of the Great Plains Indians*. Lincoln: University of Nebraska Press, 2007.

———. *The Fur Trade of the American West, 1807–1840: A Geographical Synthesis*. Lincoln: University of Nebraska Press, 1992.

Wood, W. Raymond, and Thomas D. Thiessen, eds. *Early Fur Trade on the Northern Plains: Canadian Traders among the Mandan and Hidatsa Indians, 1738–1818*. The American Exploration and Travel Series, no 68. Norman: University of Oklahoma Press, 1985.

Woodger, Elin and Brandon Toropov. *Encyclopedia of the Lewis and Clark Expedition*. New York: Checkmark Books, 2004.

Yenne, Bill. *Indian Wars: The Campaign for the American West*. Yardley, PA: Westholme, 2006.

Index

About the Authors

Ronald M. Anglin is the author of *Forgotten Trails: Historical Sources of the Columbia's Big Bend Country*. He is retired from the U.S. Fish and Wildlife Service, where he spent thirty years in land management in the National Wildlife Refuge System. He feels strongly that to be a good steward of an area, one must first understand its history, so that one's mark on the land will be with love and respect, not cruelty or disdain. He and his wife, Kathy, live in Fallon, Nevada, and have two sons who are happily married with six children between them.

    Larry E. Morris is the author of *The Fate of the Corps: What Became of the Lewis and Clark Explorers After the Expedition* and *The Perilous West: Seven Amazing Explorers and the Founding of the Oregon Trail*. He is a curator with the Historic Sites Division of The Church of Jesus Christ of Latter-day Saints. He was born and raised in Idaho Falls, Idaho, in the Snake River country roamed by the likes of Jedediah Smith, Jim Bridger, and Kit Carson in the 1820s and 1830s. Larry and his wife, Deborah, are the parents of four children and have six grandchildren.